Christopher Martin-Jenkins was the *Daily Telegraph* cricket correspondent from 1991 until his move to *The Times* in 1999. The author of *The Complete Who's Who of Test Cricketers* and a former editor of *The Cricketer*, he edited *The Spirit of Cricket: A Personal Anthology* for Faber and commentates for *Test Match Special*.

Charles de Lisle is a former *Daily Telegraph* journalist, who reported regularly on cricket and politics as well as being deputy editor of the 'Peterborough' column. From 1982–7 he lived in Australia, working for newspapers in Adelaide and Sydney. He now writes for a number of newspapers and magazines in the UK.

by Christopher Martin-Jenkins

The Complete Who's Who of Test Cricketers
The Spirit of Cricket: A Personal Anthology
Summers Will Never Be the Same
World Cricketers

AN AUSTRALIAN SUMMER
The Story of the 1998–9 Ashes Series

CHRISTOPHER MARTIN-JENKINS
AND
CHARLES DE LISLE

faber and faber

First published in 1999
by Faber and Faber Limited
3 Queen Square London WC1N 3AU

Typeset by Faber and Faber Ltd/Parker Typesetting
Printed in England by Clays Ltd, St Ives plc

A CIP record for this book
is available from the British Library

ISBN 0-571-20145-8

2 4 6 8 10 9 7 5 3 1

Contents

Acknowledgements vii

1 More Than Ashes, CMJ 1
2 A Truly Special Relationship, CdL 12
3 Cricket and Society, CdL 19
4 England Prepare, CMJ 32
5 Stormclouds Over England: The First Test, CMJ 51
6 The Broadcasters' View, CdL 70
7 No Respite: The Second Test, CMJ 80
8 The Groundsman's Story, CdL 95
9 Backs, Bets and Bribery, CMJ 103
10 In the Heat Consuming: The Third Test, CMJ 120
11 The Crowd, CdL 132
12 The Prime Minister's XI, CdL 143
13 Nadir and Zenith: The Fourth Test, CMJ 153
14 Tour Groups, CdL 170
15 Cricket in Excelsis: The Fifth Test, CMJ 178
16 The Umpires and Referee, CdL 192
17 Colour and Controversy: The One-Day Series, CMJ 204
18 The Winning Culture, CdL 213
19 Emerald City, CdL 221
20 Whither the Lucky Country?, CdL 232
21 The Pursuit of Excellence, CMJ 239

Appendix
  *England Test Squad, Tour Match Details, First Test Match, Second
  Test, Third Test, Fourth Test, Fifth Test, Test Match Milestones,
  Averages, Carlton & United One-Day Series,* 255

Index, 289

Acknowledgements

I should like to offer my heartfelt thanks to the *Daily Telegraph* not just for the support of many colleagues throughout another tour of Australia but also for the privilege of writing for the last eight years for a newspaper with an exalted reputation for the depth and breadth of its sports coverage.

Thank you, too, to Brian Murgatroyd, Patrick Keane, Graham Gooch, David Lloyd, Bob Cottam, Wayne Morton, Malcolm Ashton, Alec Stewart, Geoff Marsh, Mark Taylor and all the other players and officials in both the English and Australian camps for their assistance throughout an enjoyable series. Also to Terry Blake and Peter Wynne-Thomas for details of their research into social and cricketing trends in England, the latter's Nottinghamshire survey being a typical and remarkable labour of love.

Finally, special thanks to my intelligent and persevering co-author for talking me into working on another tour book after vowing long ago that, for reasons of diminished energy, I had written my last one. His are the contributions that have made what follows a rounded and worthwhile account of the latest chapter in the long saga of Anglo-Australian cricketing relations.

Christopher Martin-Jenkins
March 1999

I should like, first, to thank all those who kindly allowed me to perch on their shoulders during the England tour. To be able to experience an Ashes series such as this through the eyes of the broadcasters, a groundsman, the crowds, the England supporters' tour groups and the match officials was a privilege. Without the unconditional access these parties granted me, and the time and trouble many individuals took – often when under considerable pressure – to discuss the finer points, as well as the joys, stresses and strains, of their lives, these chapters could not have been written.

Warm thanks are also due to the many others in Australia, outside the game as well as within, who agreed to be interviewed, or who provided other illuminating insights or useful information. They include several people who preferred to speak on an unattributable basis.

Many thanks also to officials of the ECB, the ACB, the state associations and other organisations, all of whom were unfailingly helpful. The staff of *Wisden Cricket Monthly* (WCM) gave much appreciated help. I am grateful to the *Daily Telegraph* for the use of its excellent library, and to News Limited newspapers in Sydney for access to its equally good research facilities. The staff at both were invariably patient and cheerful as they educated me in the ways of their systems.

For their valuable assistance and good humour, I should like to thank the following: in Australia, Jamie Barnes, Don and Christine Bennetts, Dr Neal Blewett, Greg Chappell, Philip Derriman, Sarah Farley, Anne Fulwood, John McDonald, John MacKinnon, Ashley Mallett, Mark Ray, Jill Saunders, Peta Seaton, MLA, and her husband Lachlan Paterson, and Jenny Tabakoff; in Britain, Tanya Aldred, Charlotte Blofeld, Sarah Edworthy, Murray Hedgcock, David Karmel, Caroline MacMillan, Carmen Pereira, Stuart Proffitt and David Twiston Davies. My parents, Everard and Mary Rose de Lisle, and sister-in-law, Amanda de Lisle, were especially helpful.

There are four people who deserve a special mention. Araminta Whitley, my agent, provided invaluable advice, encouragement and support. My brother Tim de Lisle, who is occasionally my editor at *WCM*, was a constant source of good advice and encouragement. My sister Rosanna de Lisle, who is also a journalist (though not a cricketing one), gave me unstinting practical and moral support; she also entertained me generously in Sydney. Finally, a big thank you to my co-author for responding so enthusiastically to my idea. As the following pages show, he brings characteristic enterprise, thoughtfulness, wit and devotion to the task. It has been a pleasure to work with him.

Charles de Lisle
March 1999

I

More Than Ashes

CHRISTOPHER MARTIN-JENKINS

It is a quarter of a century, although it truly does not feel it, since I first reported on an England cricket tour of Australia. I loved it and imagined that Australia's commanding victory – Lillee, Thomson, the Chappell brothers and all – was simply part of the ebb and flow of the great drama of the Ashes. England would have their day. Well, they have won the Ashes in Australia twice in my time, but when the 1998–9 tour began they had gone five successive series, home and away, without looking like a repeat and when the dust had settled on Alec Stewart's tour the sequence had been extended to six.

Is it a terminal, or at least a permanent, decline? In the twenty-five years separating Stewart's flawed campaign from Mike Denness's, England's influence on cricket throughout the world has diminished from that of leader to follower. Her status amongst cricketing nations has slipped from an unquestioned place in the top five, even in the worst days, to one which over the last ten years at least has been consistently amongst the bottom four.

Commercialism, having its origins in the Kerry Packer-driven revolution which engulfed Australian cricket within three years of that spectacular series in 1974–5, has driven the game in directions which most who remember the pre-floodlit days would prefer it not to have gone. The essential questions now are where the lines should be drawn; whether England and Australia – for Australia too has lost some of her once unquestioned grip – can influence the march of a progress which in some respects is actually a retrogression; and in England's case whether the recent attempts to make the game more commercial and more Australian in character are a betrayal of her own great traditions or the only route to salvation for the game she invented.

The tour in question and the events surrounding it provided much evidence towards the reaching of rational answers to these questions, but it is as well to remember that cricket has always proved a sport which can adapt itself to changing times and trends. Many a pessimist about the game's future, not least in England, has been confounded in the past.

Talking before the team left for Australia in October 1998, the England coach, David Lloyd, followed an opinion on how events might unfold with a comment that all who pontificate about contemporary sport would do well to bear in mind: 'It's their time now, not mine. It's their opportunity.'

It is a strange thing about the process of ageing that, one or two aches apart, someone in his mid-fifties still feels spiritually on a wavelength with someone in his twenties. Sadly, of course, the feeling is not mutual. The older person sees the younger as a soulmate; the younger tends to see the other as simply a middle-aged man. But the wise ones from both generations will learn from one another.

Because of its context, the last Anglo-Australian series of the second millennium was more than just another struggle for the Ashes. It was played at a period of turmoil in international cricket, the result largely of investigations into alleged corruption and an apparent threat in some parts of the world to the viability of Test cricket. In both England and Australia the five-day game was actually extremely buoyant but the series came at a time when English cricket seemed to be at a crossroads, one route leading towards a continuing relative decline in interest and standards, the other to a brave new world of floodlit county grounds and, according to the optimists, a revived national team.

For Australians, despite the recent economic collapse in Asia, it began during what was, apparently at least, a period of rare stability and maturity in affairs on and off the cricket field and less than a year before a national referendum to decide whether the former colonies should break the final constitutional ties with the Mother Country and become a republic. Before long, another Ashes series would be safely in the bag and triumphant supporters would be celebrating the impressive sweep towards further success in the triangular one-day series. But Mark Taylor's retirement demanded at least a pause for reflection.

For England, the tour arrived at a time of uncertainty and reform both in cricketing affairs and in society generally. Politically, institutions were, if anything, overripe. Major constitutional reform was already in full swing as part of the manifesto which had swept New Labour to power in 1997 to govern a multiracial, multicultural society of the kind which was both less diverse and not so far advanced at the other end of the world. Cricket's relative, if often exaggerated, decline in Britain could not be divorced from all this because it had partly been caused by it.

Football apart, sport no longer exerted the formative influence on British youth it once had, and for cricket, the 1998–9 tour arrived after years of failure at the highest level and at a time of immense upheaval in the game from school playgrounds to Test arenas. At the professional level the catchphrase 'no change is no option' had come increasingly frequently and glibly from the lips of marketing men at Lord's during the preceding twelve months.

Outwardly they were bullish. County cricket was reorganising itself with uncharacteristic and almost unseemly haste; television rights had just been sold for £103 million; youth cricket was stated to be healthy again; and a World Cup was about to be staged with the potential to galvanise that youth and thereby to insure the future in a way that money alone could not. In fact, the sudden rush of unusually radical decisions made in and around Lord's in the autumn of 1998 had much to do with some alarming sociological research.

Half-way through the 1998 season, executives of the England and Wales Cricket Board had blocked off their diaries for a day and met for a brainstorming session at the Marriott Hotel near Regent's Park, half a mile from their headquarters at Lord's. Their marketing chief, Terry Blake, once head boy at Radley, now quite used to offending traditionalists in his search for the sponsorship without which professional cricket would have died in the second half of the twentieth century, solemnly told his listeners the worrying results of intensive research carried out the previous year by Target Group Index Research, well known in marketing circles.

Once – shall we say with certainty, from 1880 to 1950? – cricket would have been first, second or third on the list of sports which every English child liked to play. TGIR's results showed cricket as only fifth on the list of 'sports liked best' for boys from seven to ten years of age in 1996 and it had dropped to seventh a year later: below football, cycling, basketball, roller-skating, ten-pin bowling and rounders. Only 12.9 per cent made it their favourite sport.

In the eleven to fourteen age bracket, cricket dropped to eighth. It was the favourite sport for 23.9 per cent of boys surveyed, but if that sounds an improvement, it was a smaller percentage than football (68.8 per cent), swimming, basketball, running, snooker, tennis and rugby. Worse, in the 15–19 age-group, cricket came 16th. Maturing adolescents in late-twentieth-century England apparently preferred weight-training and mountain biking to the national sport of summer, as cricket was once invariably described.

Relayed to county executives by Blake at the First Class Forum meeting at Lord's on 13 and 14 October and salted further by the revelation that division-one basketball crowds were now larger than those for Sunday League cricket, these findings had a salutory effect. Having procrastinated and prevaricated about fundamental change for many years, the chairmen and chief executives of the eighteen first-class counties suddenly approved a vastly inflated home international programme from 2000 onwards of seven Tests and ten one-day internationals. They also agreed in principle that England players should be contracted centrally by the ECB rather than in the traditional way by their counties; opted for a 45-over national league of one-day matches to replace the old 40-over Sunday League, split into two divisions with promotion and relegation for three counties each season; and approved the further exploration of a two-division County Championship and early season regional cricket.

Two months later, as Australia were on their way to winning the Ashes again, the two-division Championship was duly given a green light to proceed and regional cricket was rejected, even as a means of giving touring sides stronger opposition than they now received from individual counties. Two divisions was a more commercial course to take and it was likely to give county cricket at least a temporary boost as a viable business in its own right; but regional cricket would have been far more likely to lift standards and to prepare county players for the additional rigours of the international game.

Like it or not, and more than one of these decisions was mistaken, cricket administrators in England and Wales were at least doing something about their predicament. If it did nothing else, this had the effect of saving them from the more hysterical condemnations customarily thrown at them by broadsheet columnists and tabloid journalists when the Ashes were lost once more. They remained, however, hopelessly confused about their desire for a more attractive county game and their common need for a stronger and more consistent England team.

Australia had had their own commercial revolution after the intervention of Kerry Packer in 1977 and they had also grasped their own rather less stinging nettles on the field of play itself when Bobby Simpson became national coach in the mid-1980s and set strict standards, one of many reasons for their decade of domination over England. Yet history may show that the Test series in which they were about to prevail once more was at least the beginning of the end of their period of supremacy not just over England, but in world cricket generally.

Having overcome England, they were overwhelming favourites to defeat the West Indies in advance of the 1999 World Cup. The disarray of West Indian cricket, despite their victory over England in the Caribbean at the start of 1998, seemed to go deeper than England's, but Brian Lara's epic innings at Sabina Park and Bridgetown put at least a temporary stop to the decline evident from a 5–nil defeat in South Africa. For Australia, it was only a matter of a short time before the breaking-up of the powerful nucleus of the side. At the start of the series against England, they still possessed the best captain in the world in Mark Taylor; the most consistent batsman in the world in Steve Waugh and one of the most brilliant in his twin brother, Mark; the best slow bowler in Shane Warne; one of the three best fast bowlers in Glenn McGrath; and the best wicket-keeper in Ian Healy.

Taylor's retirement, at the relatively young age of thirty-four, was announced after a period of careful consideration once the Ashes series had finished. It deprived Australia of a captain who was outstanding in every way, never more so than during the ups and downs of his final series.

Warne was twenty-nine when the Ashes series started without him, McGrath only five months younger, so, given reasonable luck with injuries, both could hope for five more years of international cricket, but the other three had left their thirtieth birthdays well behind them and the frantic and exponential growth of international cricket suggested that none of them was so likely to be a matchwinning force by the time of England's next tour to Australia in 2002–3.

Nor, as events immediately before and during the England tour proved, was the surface of Australian cricket quite so smooth as it usually seemed. An often bitter dispute over the pay of professional cricketers had only been resolved by the Australian Cricket Board and the Australian Cricketers' Association shortly before the arrival of the England team in October. Then, just before the Adelaide Test in December, came revelations of a skeleton in the cupboard. Having taken the moral high ground on the allegations of bribery and match-fixing in international cricket amongst the countries of the Indian subcontinent, two of the most brilliant and prominent of Australia's Test players were revealed to have taken money themselves from an Indian bookmaker in return for routine information about the weather, the pitch and team selection.

5

Shane Warne and Mark Waugh, well known to be fond of a gamble, had been targeted, it seemed, in order that they might be sucked into deeper corruption. They were not, because when, as they alleged, Salim Malik, the sometime Pakistan captain, offered them vastly more money to bowl badly, they declined in horror. But they were fined in secret by the Australian Board for taking money from the bookmaker, and the affair was hushed up by all concerned until, as was inevitable, assiduous journalists, led initially by Malcolm Conn of *The Australian,* turned rumour into proven fact.

In both the matter of the pay dispute and the moral weakness, up to a point, of two leading players, Australia were seen to be no more than typical of professional cricket as it had developed, more or less out of the control of an International Cricket Council struggling in vain to keep up, over the last ten years of the century. The problems faced by ICC officials, striving from their office on the edge of the playing field at Lord's to bring some planning and coherence to a world game which was once run more or less by a league of gentlemen needing little expertise in commerce and law, were considerable but in many cases hardly new. Financial disputes between countries, and between administrators, or entrepreneurs, and the talented players without whom no one makes any money from cricket, were as old as the game. Betting on cricket was rife in England in the eighteenth century; and strikes of the kind which the Australian players threatened in 1997–8 had a long history dating back to Victorian times.

Just as England's tour started, another dispute was erupting in the West Indian camp. Its catalyst, it seemed, was the fact that of all the countries taking part in an ICC tournament in Bangladesh in late October, ironically to raise money for the development of the game in parts of the world where it was still a minority sport, the West Indians, several of them long-legged fast bowlers, were alone in travelling to the former East Pakistan in economy-class aircraft seats. On the eve of the first ever West Indies tour of South Africa, a sporting event of immense potential significance for the politically liberated black masses of the Republic, Brian Lara and Carl Hooper, captain and vice-captain of the West Indies and two of the greatest natural talents in the world game, withdrew their labour and refused to travel to South Africa from London, where they had stopped *en route* from the Bangladesh capital, Dhakar.

Lara and Hooper were stripped of their office by the West Indies

Cricket Board and for a day or two it seemed that they, not the board, might be the victims of the dispute. But the former captain, Courtney Walsh, widely respected, put his weight behind his successor and the players already gathered in Johannesburg flew back to London with their manager, Clive Lloyd, a veteran of the last great players' revolt, the one inspired by Packer in the late 1970s. Then it was still possible for administrators to stick to their guns and send second-best teams hither and thither. Australia did so and so, to India in 1978–9, did the West Indies. Now the president of the West Indies Board, the Jamaican Pat Rousseau, was obliged to fly to London himself and, predictably from that point, Lara and Hooper were reinstated and the players' various financial demands were conceded.

In Australia the administrators had lost with greater dignity and less world-wide exposure to embarrassment – not to say ridicule – but the compromise eventually favoured the players there too. The ACB had sought to portray them as greedy by releasing information that Australia's top ten players had received direct income from cricket in 1996–7 of between A$275,000 and A$485,000 each (between £110,000 and £194,000). It was, indeed, big money, but they were very successful players and the board's own income was substantial. Eventually it was agreed by the board and Tim May, the former off-spinning partner to Shane Warne, now the first executive officer of the Australian Cricketers' Association, that first-class players in Australia would receive a 20 per cent share of total cricket revenue each year up to A$60 million, and 25 per cent thereafter. For some Sheffield Shield players it represented a rise of 100 per cent. For one or two of the top players, like Warne, it meant a slight drop in salary, despite the additional rewards to those directly employed by the ACB on annual contracts as current or future Australian players.

The wrangle which preceded this compromise had included a threat of strike action by the players and their recruitment of a negotiator, James Erskine, who was a skilful operator in the nexus between sport, media and the business world. He was himself a successful businessman and at a crucial stage of the negotiations he loaned half a million dollars to the ACA (they already had a small income from the ACB itself) and a further A$280,000 to the players – Steve Waugh amongst them – who had withheld their signatures on ACB contracts. The ACA had some 120 members. The average earnings of the Sheffield Shield players were under A$35,000 a year (£14,000).

Arguments about pay were nothing new for Australia. In 1912 six senior players had refused to tour England for the 'triangular tournament', played between England, Australia and South Africa; an idea, incidentally, borrowed by the Australians some seventy years later. In 1977 no fewer than twenty of the Australian players had parted from the official board and taken far bigger rewards from playing in World Series Cricket. In 1985 fourteen Australians went the way of several of their English professional rivals and undertook an officially disapproved tour to the then politically ostracised South Africa.

The 1997–8 dispute reflected arguments going on in the English game about how much of the centrally gathered profit from international matches and Tests should filter down to county cricketers; and a growing concern amongst county committees about an escalation in salaries. Allied to this was an increasing tendency for clubs with Test grounds to wave ever bigger cheques in front of attractive players. Less well-endowed clubs felt that those with Test grounds had an unfair advantage. The Test clubs themselves felt that the smaller counties often lacked marketing enterprise and also that the central body was swallowing up too much of the profit from the big matches they staged. At the end of the 1998 season they got together as a consortium, with MCC very much involved, under the chairmanship of Robert Griffiths, QC. One way and another, money has always made the cricket world go round, at least where the game is a public spectacle rather than a private recreation.

Much more than honour was at stake, therefore, over the four intensive weeks of cricket during which Australia won the Ashes for the sixth time in succession, only to be surprised by the quality and spirit of the England counter-attack after Christmas. It turned out to be a series of vivid, passionate and enjoyable cricket.

This was the sixty-fourth meeting in one or other of the countries (not always with the Ashes at stake) since a mock obituary of English cricket was published in the *Sporting Times* after Australia had brought England down from her ivory tower by winning by seven runs at The Oval in 1882; and the sixty-third since England's revenge at Sydney the following January had persuaded an ardent and youthful maiden from Melbourne named Florence Rose Murphy to burn something – it was probably a bail, it might have been her veil – and to present it in a little terracotta urn to her future husband, the England captain Ivo Bligh.

More than a century later, Australians have not lost their burning urge to beat the Poms. Theirs is a younger nation than Britain, with a stronger national identity but a population less than a third the size. With correspondingly less political and economic clout, Australians still see sport as a way of influencing the world, one reason why they were not averse to offering a few inducements to greedy officials of the International Olympic Committee when it came to Sydney's successful bid for the 2000 Olympic Games.

From tramps to captains of industry, it is almost a part of the charter of every citizen, whatever his or her origin, to have an interest in 'how A'straya are going in the cricket'. People may not fully understand the game, especially the increasing number of immigrants from the Far East, but they cannot ignore it because it is on the front page every day, especially when Australia are winning and England are losing.

Since the 'White Australia' policy was abandoned in the late 1960s, Asian migration has gradually overtaken the number of settlers from Britain and Europe. What is more, a greater number of Asians are now settling for good. The latest figures from the Australian Bureau of Statistics show that 22,167 people arrived from Britain and Europe between 1996 and 1997 with a view to becoming Australian citizens, whilst 6,303 people who had come with the same intention departed. In the same year 32,084 permanent settlers arrived from Asia whilst only 3,587 from the same region departed. If they did not all know their Gabbas from their WACAs, it was certain that their sons and daughters soon would. The challenge facing England once the dust had settled was somehow to rekindle that sort of national passion for the game.

Close to the action, it was hard not to judge England's failure on their main mission in Australia in isolation. Those trying to plan some sort of strategy for the wider English game, however, were obliged to be positive. The vision of the revivalists at Lord's was that England would be back on top of that cricket world, for the first time since they went twenty-six games without defeat between 1968 and 1971, by the time that they next visited Australia four years later.

The consequences of continued mediocrity would not be pleasant for the optimists beavering away in the open-plan offices in the England and Wales Cricket Board's striking glass building beside the Nursery ground at Lord's. They know that the next television negotiations in 2002, in a broadcasting scene which is about to be transformed by the possibilities of digital radio and television, might be more an embarrassment than a triumph four years on from the much-trumpeted deal with Channel Four and Sky unless England start winning regularly again. A week before the team left, as Lord MacLaurin, the ECB chairman, announced the £103 million television contracts which outlawed the BBC, an almost ethereal glow seemed to be shining from the ground-floor conference room.

The entrepreneurial spirit was its cause: the 'national summer sport' had taken another bold step, claimed administrators, down the path of progress. But if the cricketers do not deliver what the marketing men envisage, the glow will be evanescent. In effect the public is being asked to buy much more – seven Tests and ten one-day internationals a season compared with six and three when the last television deal was done – of a product which has so far sold well more because of its scarcity value than its quality.

The extent of the improvement required had been made embarrassingly clear by the extraordinary victory by Sri Lanka against England at The Oval in August. England scored 445 in their first innings after Arjuna Ranatunga had won the toss and, on a dry pitch sure to turn increasingly, taken the apparently extraordinary decision to field first. 'We think it might do a bit this morning,' said Sri Lanka's Machiavellian little captain at the time. Later he claimed that he had batted second in order to give his unique and controversial off-spinner Muttiah Muralitharan a rest between innings. The alternative, apparently, was that England would have been obliged to follow-on after a huge Sri Lankan first innings and that 'Murali' would have been bowled to exhaustion.

Instead, after an incredible blitz from Sanath Jayasuriya, who scored 213 off 278 balls (Aravinda de Silva had to be satisfied with a relatively modest 156 from 249 balls), Murali followed his seven for 155 in the first innings with nine for 65 in the second and England were beaten after tea on the last day by ten wickets. Only three weeks before, England had been celebrating their most important victory for more than a decade. For Sri Lanka, therefore, this was an amazing triumph; for England an untimely humiliation. It was as if they had put their lips to a glass of champagne and tasted only vinegar.

It meant, too, that the narrow victory over South Africa in Alec Stewart's first series as captain was immediately exposed as another of the false dawns which had punctuated the years of Mike Atherton's captaincy. There was much to enjoy and to admire, as well as much to condemn, during that era; and occasional striking victories to celebrate, not least against Australia at The Oval (twice), at Adelaide and at Edgbaston. Consistent success, however, was lacking and no one could have been unaware of the fact, because it had been repeated so often, that England's rise from the canvas to beat South Africa on a marginal points decision was the first win in a five-Test series for twelve years.

Ashley Mallett, Australia's off-spinner in Ian Chappell's outstanding side of the mid-1970s, wrote in *The Cricketer* that his countrymen were grateful that England were 'starting to get their act together'. He added: 'Thank goodness we don't have to welcome another bunch of English losers for an Ashes series.'

2

A Truly Special Relationship

CHARLES DE LISLE

The Ashes series of 1998–9 was played at an intriguing time in the relationship between Britain and Australia. For nearly three decades, as each country involved herself more deeply in her own region, traditional ties had suffered. The Mother Country and her progeny had drifted apart, politically and culturally, if not so much economically. Then came the Asian meltdown of late 1997. Suddenly the region in which Australia had – to use the phrase beloved of her Labor governments of 1983–96 – become 'enmeshed' was one of collapsing currencies, disappearing markets and half-empty aeroplanes. It was time, as the conservative Government of John Howard (as devoted a cricket fan as any Prime Minister has ever been) had begun to recognise even before the crisis, to reduce Australia's dependence on Asia and put new spark into the relationships with the United Kingdom, the European Union and America.

Nowhere was this more necessary than in tourism. Now the largest single export industry, it had been growing at an astonishing rate since the mid-1980s, partly on the back of a vast increase in the number of visitors from the Pacific region. Now, in the new landscape, Australia urgently needed to fill hotels and aeroplanes with people from older markets. That meant persuading more people from further afield that the beauty, space, colours, sharp light and climate were worth the rigours of a fifteen- or twenty-four-hour flight. She was remarkably successful. In the year ending October 1998, the number of visitors from Europe totalled 931,000, a rise of 8.3 per cent over the previous twelve months.

Of that total, the oldest market of all, Britain, comprised almost half – 449,000, a rise of 11.6 per cent. Arrivals from the Americas climbed 11 per cent to 464,000, while those from Japan dropped 6.2 per cent to 765,000, and from the rest of Asia 21 per cent to 1.07 million. As a result of extra business from expanding economies, therefore, Australia suffered an overall decline of just 3.7 per cent over the year, to 4.17 million visitors.

A number of other Australian industries were equally successful in speedily redirecting their efforts and replacing lost markets. During the first half of 1998, Australian exports to the UK grew by 55 per cent over the corresponding half of the previous year. Britain imported more Australian electrical appliances, transport equipment and aircraft parts, as well as more wine, beer, iron ore, coal and gold. Add in the little-noticed announcement of August 1998 that Britain had become the largest foreign investor in Australia, overtaking the United States, and it is clear that the business relationship between the Ashes rivals was in its best shape for years. 'The substance of the relationship is rock solid,' declared a Foreign Office source. 'The UK makes a lot of money out of Australia.'

The second reason for this being a fascinating passage of play in Anglo-Australian relations, of course, is the question of Australia's constitutional future. It was perfectly possible that this would be the last Ashes series played with the Australian captain spinning a coin bearing the Queen's head. In November, a national referendum will offer Australians their first chance to sever their last constitutional link with Britain, and to replace the Queen as head of state with an Australian. Should the republicans prevail, the country will become, like India, a republic within the Commonwealth.

The imminence of the referendum, the millennium, the 2000 Olympic Games in Sydney and the nation's 100th birthday – the centenary of Federation of the six Australian colonies falls in 2001 – was forcing Australians to think hard about what sort of country, and what sort of people, they really are. Are they a people proud of their British heritage, happy to have a Queen on the other side of the world – albeit one separately designated 'Queen of Australia' – and a flag with a Union Jack in the corner? Or is Australia now so multicultural, mature and, for all the current economic troubles of the Pacific, so involved and relatively at ease in her own region that she should finally take a deep breath and make this powerful symbolic break with Britain? As England's four-month tour began, and the republican debate livened up, there was an almost tangible feeling of desperation, a sense that the host country must take the opportunity provided by these looming events and anniversaries to make a definitive statement, to herself and a watching world, one way or the other, about her national identity and place in the world. As one senior official in Canberra put it, 'There's a desperate feeling that Australia has got to do something before 2001.' For many

Australians, including a majority of politicians and a majority of the arts community, that meant taking a bold step into the next millennium, and 'coming of age' as a republic.

The task of those campaigning for a republic was in some ways made a little easier by the outcome of the Federal election of 3 October 1998, in which John Howard's Liberal–National coalition government was returned with a much reduced majority. Although Howard himself is a monarchist, the true significance of the result lay in the fact that the challenge posed by Pauline Hanson's right-wing One Nation Party was roundly defeated.

Most of the credit for this went to the stubborn, unexciting but decent Howard. 'Honest John', as he is known, campaigned unambiguously in favour of tolerance, diversity and economic liberalism, and against the racism and economic nationalism of Mrs Hanson, a maverick former fish-and-chip shop owner who had aimed to win fifteen seats and the balance of power in the 148-seat lower house, the House of Representatives. In the event, One Nation polled an impressive 900,000 votes, attracting support from the poor, elderly and rural voters in particular, but had not one seat in the House to show for its efforts. Mrs Hanson's defeat – and the subsequent self-combustion of her once spectacularly successful new party – were vitally important not just to race relations and social harmony but also to Australia's image abroad, especially with her Asian trading partners.

An Ashes series is one of the most prominent, enduring and popular aspects of what might be called the 'symbolic' relationship with the United Kingdom. However, Britain and Australia had both recently been working hard to update and refresh their perceptions of each other. There had been a mutual recognition that, like an uncle and nephew whose lives have long since diverged, but who realise – if either stops to think about it – that they are rather fond of each other, the two nations had been taking each other for granted. At the beginning of 1997, therefore, the two Governments launched 'New Images', a year-long programme of trade, cultural, scientific, educational and sporting events designed to enhance and modernise links between the two countries. Britain's aim was to present herself Down Under not merely, as one diplomat put it, 'as a country of the National Trust and cream teas – although these have an honoured place in our social fabric – but also as a creative, dynamic, European, multicultural nation, at the leading edge in important areas such as design'. While Britain wished to banish the old-fashioned, class-ridden and not very interesting image which, research had found, was the principal one she had in the minds of many young Australians, Australia wanted the Poms to realise that she was more than a country of 'ockers', 'tinnies' of XXXX lager, kangaroos, wombats, sporting heroes, soap operas and Sir Les Patterson. The intention, according to Alexander Downer, the Foreign Minister, was to 'increase British awareness of Australia as a vibrant, multicultural society, a country which is well developed economically and a leading producer of sophisticated goods and services'. The exports he had in mind included Australian chardonnay and shiraz, which were already attracting a sizeable share of the UK market, as well as films, stage productions and high-technology products.

The British campaign in Australia, which was much more ambitious and better funded than the Aussie effort in Britain, received a major boost with the election of New Labour in May 1997. For although 'New Images' was a Tory initiative – it was an idea of Douglas Hurd's when he was Foreign Secretary – it was presenting Britain in rather the sort of modern light that Tony Blair and Peter Mandelson wished to shine across the whole range of Government presentation, at home and abroad. And the mere fact of a powerful, lively new administration in London, after eighteen years of Conservative rule, attracted favourable attention in Australia, reinforcing the 'New Images' message.

Sadly, cricket had no place in Labour's vision of the new Britain, or 'Cool Britannia' as it quickly became known. Cricket, in their eyes, was tainted by association with the previous regime. Hadn't John Major, at a low point, both in his own fortunes and those of the England side (1993), been ridiculed for trying to rally political support by invoking 'the long shadows falling across the county ground, the warm beer, the invincible green suburbs . . . old maids bicycling to Holy Communion through the morning mist'? And hadn't he then, the moment he was ejected from 10 Downing Street, showed a nice, but old-fashioned, sense of perspective about the ups and downs of politics by heading straight off to The Oval?

There has long been a gently growing appreciation in Britain of Australia's sophisticated, urban culture, excellent cuisine, natural splendours, friendly people and regional clout in Asia; besides, Australia is the fifth largest investor in the United Kingdom, ahead of Japan, and some 700,000 Australians travel to the Old Dart each year (but then, perhaps of necessity, Aussies are great travellers). What effect has 'New

Images' had? Officials at both ends of the 'Kangaroo Route' from London to Sydney concede that it will never be possible to measure its precise impact, either in terms of changes in public attitudes, or in pounds and dollars. But there is a strong feeling in both governments that the programme has had a positive effect, contributing to somewhat less hostile press coverage of each country in the other; and that relations between the two nations and peoples have not been so warm in a long time. The value of old trading relationships is being recognised – especially in the southern hemisphere – more than even two years ago, and new business, cultural, educational and scientific links are constantly being forged. Philip Flood, Australia's newish High Commissioner in London – a posting, incidentally, which remains the most attractive in the diplomatic service – says simply: 'The relationship is flourishing.'

This is partly because Australia, which seemed three years ago to have thrown its lot in with Asia for good, has been having serious second thoughts. This is not just due to the economic realities of the regional economic crisis, or the fact that Liberal–National governments in Australia have traditionally inclined more to the US, UK and Europe than Labor ones. As the Hanson phenomenon showed, the past few years have seen a major public backlash against multiculturalism, and against what was (and is) perceived by sections of society as the arrogant insistence by the previous Labor government of the republican Paul Keating (1991–6) that Australia had a solely Asian destiny. Despite Mrs Hanson's failure, there remains considerable unease about the degree to which Australia is immersed in the region – witness the enormous sales of the 1998 book *Among the Barbarians*, by the journalist Paul Sheehan. This is an attack on multiculturalism which argues, among other things, that the country has been damaged by the politically motivated mishandling of immigration by Keating and his predecessor Bob Hawke. A senior figure in Canberra summed up the latest position thus: 'Most Australians are not racist. They just feel rather isolated, and they still feel rather threatened by Asia.' This feeling persists despite the fact that the Howard Government did respond to public concern by cutting immigration in 1996, arguing that a sluggish economy could no longer sustain even the dramatically reduced intakes of the later Labor years.

On the trade and investment front, meanwhile, it is safe to assume that the 'Great South Land' will continue, as she was starting to do even before the crash, to put more eggs in old baskets. 'Australia is reclaiming old markets,' said one Government source, 'and now has a better balanced commercial and trading portfolio, from a longer-term point of view. Exporters are also well placed to take advantage of significant growth in east Asia as that occurs, but, psychologically, business has adjusted to the new balance. Australians are more comfortable with that.'

There is no doubt that, starting at the top, personal links between Britain and Australia also remain strong. The Prime Minister, Tony Blair, lived in Australia for nearly four years as a small child when his father was a university lecturer in Adelaide, knows the country quite well, having returned several times as a politician, and has several close Australian friends, Keating among them. Kim Beazley, Leader of the Labor Opposition, is also a good friend. In a glowing foreword to a recent biography of Beazley, by Peter FitzSimons, Blair saluted an essentially 'principled and straight man' with 'no side, no love of status or position' who had made huge efforts to help him with 'advice, friendship and encouragement' when he was struggling to move up in the old Labour Party. On one level this was a heartfelt tribute to a political colleague – a 'mate' – on the other side of the world, highlighting some very Australian qualities. But Blair was also publicly acknowledging his own, and New Labour's, debt to the Australian Labor Party (ALP) of the 1980s, which had showed the world that responsible pro-market policies tempered by a social conscience could be electoral winners: the party won five successive elections and brought a previously protectionist economy into the late twentieth century.

Meanwhile, the present Australian Government was hopeful that Blair might find time, perhaps during the centenary celebrations, to underline the new warmth in relations by making what would be the first visit by a British Prime Minister since Margaret Thatcher's in 1988; John Prescott, Blair's deputy, has already been twice. He will have noticed that the ALP now looks comparatively Old Labour, and that, in terms of policies, the Blair Government has more in common with Howard than Beazley.

As the Australian Summer opened, most of the 18.5 million inhabitants of the 'Lucky Country' – originally the title of an influential 1960s book by the academic Donald Horne, who intended the reference to be ironical – had some reason to smile. Despite the earthquake which had rocked Australia's major export region, the economy was booming, unemployment was about to hit its lowest levels in eight years, the stock market was approaching the end of its fourth successive year of double-figure growth, and, in keeping with the country's reputation for rapidly embracing new technology, Internet usage was the second highest (per capita) in the world, after the United States. Australians, being Australians, had found some characteristic uses for it. First in their beloved Rules football, and now, for the first time, in cricket, fans wired up to the Net could indulge in the national blood sport of 'barracking' the opposition, without leaving their homes or work-places. At the press of a button, at any hour of day or night, the Poms could be baited by the despatch of a sharp comment to the Melbourne *Age*'s 'e-mail barracking' web site. The only drawback, for the barracker if not the audience, was that his message could only be seen, not heard.

3
Cricket and Society

CHARLES DE LISLE

Ask any Australian to account for his country's magnificent record on the cricket field – and in many other sporting arenas – and the first explanation he will reach for is the climate. The second is geography. The twin blessings of superb weather and plenty of space mean that the majority of Australia's population of 18.5 million people, spread across a land mass thirty-two times the size of the United Kingdom, has opportunities for sport, recreation and leisure that are the envy of much of the rest of the world.

Fly over any of Australia's major cities and you will be struck by the huge number of playing fields – 'ovals' to the locals – and parks threaded through the blocks of suburbia; drive into even the smallest and most remote country town and you will soon find a well-maintained cricket ground (though the wicket may be concrete rather than turf, and the visiting side may have had to travel 200 miles to the game). Partly as a result of the climate and geography, there is a rich sporting culture which encourages large numbers of people to involve themselves in sport, as well as to watch it. This produces a depth of involvement, spread widely through the social spectrum, and an intensity of competition whose consequences are so often evident when Australians take on international competition in any sporting theatre.

Official figures show that almost a third (30.7 per cent) of all Australians aged fifteen and over – a total of 4.25 million people – participated in organised sport and physical activities in the year ending June 1996. Another survey simply covering teenagers provided further grounds for optimism. The 1996 survey of 25,525 people in New South Wales aged between eleven and nineteen showed that a healthy 92 per cent had participated in at least one sport over the previous twelve months. Basketball came first with 30 per cent, followed by soccer (24 per cent), swimming (23 per cent), tennis (20 per cent), netball and cricket (each on 15 per cent) and rugby league (13 per cent). Such is the pre-eminence of sport that it is said that some less athletic job applicants habitually exaggerate or even invent club memberships when approaching prospective employers.

The number of Australians playing organised cricket has been rising – genuinely – for several years. In 1997–8 New South Wales, for example, had 104,500 players registered with clubs, including women but excluding schools, a figure which represents a 38 per cent rise over three seasons. Of these, an impressive 54,000 were junior players; in other words, Under-16s. Of those, some 30,000 belonged to clubs in the NSW Country Cricket Association, underlining the game's strength in the bush. Across the continent there are 500,000 registered club players in all. The World Cup, like the 1997 Ashes series in England, is expected to boost recruitment still further. Cricket now employs eighty development officers to promote the game among juniors, about four times more than a decade ago. Set against the alarming evidence of the decline of cricket among young people in Britain, it is clear that Australian cricket authorities have been doing better in defending and promoting their sport against the rise of others, particularly the American ones.

Confirmation that Australians are still among the world's most dedicated spectators came with a survey by the Australian Bureau of Statistics, in March 1995, which found that 6.2 million people aged fifteen years and over – 3.5 million men and 2.7 million women – had been to at least one sporting event in the previous year. Cricket, with 1.2 million people having attended at least one match, ranked as the fourth-best attended sport after Australian Rules football (1.9 million), racing (1.7 million) and rugby league (1.5 million). During the 1998–9 cricket season, combined attendances at the Tests and one-dayers were some 940,000, the highest since the Ashes summer of 1982–3, the heyday of Dennis Lillee, Rod Marsh and Greg Chappell.

The very high level of public interest and support is also evident from the latest annual tracking study undertaken on behalf of the Australian Cricket Board (ACB). It shows that just under half the population over eighteen years of age has an interest in cricket. Among this group, 69 per cent expressed a high interest in Test cricket, up from 66 per cent a year earlier, while 63 per cent claimed a high interest in the Carlton & United one-day series. Forty-two per cent of all respondents nominated cricket as their favourite summer sport, a figure well ahead of tennis (16 per cent) and golf (8 per cent). Unsurprisingly, therefore, televised international cricket continues to out-rate all other summer sports.

Meanwhile the most recent annual 'Australians and Sport' survey conducted by Brian Sweeney & Associates confirmed that cricket enjoys the largest following of all team sports in the country. Of those questioned, 54 per cent stated an interest in cricket. Australian Rules was second with 50 per cent, followed by soccer (41 per cent), rugby league (38 per cent), basketball (35 per cent) and rugby union (30 per cent). The survey also found that cricket has the equal largest team sport participation base with 11 per cent of all respondents saying they play the game. 'I think that cricket is perceived as something that Australians own,' says David Fouvy, the ACB's general manager, marketing. 'It's something they have a huge emotional commitment to. At times Australians look to the Australian team, and particularly the captain, for leadership and inspiration. Success on the field gives all Australian citizens a kick. They say: "Yeah, that's good. That's *our* team."'

Australia's climate and space lend themselves to four varieties of the game – 'backyard cricket', 'beach cricket', 'street cricket' and 'paddock cricket' – which are deeply embedded in the culture. Many young Aussies, male or female, are still likely to pick up a bat for the first time in the family's spacious back garden, though with the rise of the private swimming-pool fast bowlers cannot fit in quite such long runs. For many leading players, the backyard, the beach, the street or the paddock really are the places where it all began. On the day his appointment as Australian captain was announced, Steve Waugh spoke of how he developed a childhood obsession with the ambition of representing Australia during backyard games with his brothers Mark, Dean and Danny at their home in the Sydney suburb of Bankstown. Weeks earlier, to mark his selection by the national broadsheet *The Australian* as its Australian of the Year, Mark Taylor posed while playing a street game with his wife Judi and two young sons, a dustbin for a wicket. Judi was the one bowling the tennis ball, 'Tubby' was the 'keeper. It was a striking photograph.

The importance of these unorganised games is particularly noticeable at Christmas. Acres of newsprint are devoted to the joys of a peculiarly Australian festive tradition. On the first morning of the Boxing Day Test in Melbourne, the city's best newspaper, *The Age*, filled its front page with an evocative photograph of a young boy swatting the ball to leg in a game of beach cricket. 'Cricket will be played on beaches and in backyards, in parks and on strips of pavement,' wrote Alan Attwood in the accompanying copy. 'Stumps . . . will be improvised with rubbish bins, folded umbrellas in the sand, or lines scratched on a wall.' Attwood went on: 'Today, as happened yesterday, Christmas lunches will have as their last and longest courses games of social cricket, with rules adapted to suit conditions: no ducks for batsmen (and women); no grandparent can be run out; LBW dismissals are unlikely, no matter how palpable; all fielders must check the depth of water at the beach before attempting a classic catch in the shallows.' An article in the same newspaper on Christmas Day, headed 'My ton at mum's on Christmas Day', covered similar territory. According to this writer, Greg Champion, 'hitting into the apricot tree, the peach tree or the nectarine tree on the full is out'. A fortnight later, Stuart MacGill, fresh from his twelve-wicket triumph in the fifth Test, was interviewed on an ABC radio phone-in programme. Here, too, there was animated discussion of the optimum rules for backyard cricket, MacGill dealing with skill and humour with questions such as: 'Can the family dog field for both sides?' Such is the drawing power of this format that in recent seasons a Melbourne radio station has run a 'Battle for the Backyard Ashes'. The winner of the competition, which is designed to promote the Boxing Day Test, is invited to lead half-a-dozen 'mates' against six members of the Victoria State XI – in his own backyard.

Anecdotal evidence suggests that some non-British migrants also play cricket socially. In Melbourne on Christmas Day a charming Kuwaiti-Lebanese taxi driver told me he did not follow the professional game, but loved beach cricket. 'I discovered the game through Indian friends who played in Kuwait,' he said. 'I play here with my cousins. I love it. You work up a sweat and then you jump in the sea.' And with that he took both hands rather alarmingly off the steering wheel, as we turned a corner, and demonstrated his favourite cut stroke.

This season, for the first time, the ACB used images of backyard, beach, street and school cricket in its marketing of the international programme. The advertisements in the nationalistic 'Go Aussie Go' campaign, screened on television and in cinemas, intercut scenes from games played by young Aussies with action footage of Sir Donald Bradman, Lillee, Allan Border and the current stars. So you saw a batsman being bowled on the beach, then the ball disappearing over the washing line on a suburban back lawn, then a replay of Shane Warne's 'magic' ball to Mike Gatting. The cultural connection between the greatest arenas and the humblest was underlined by the way the 'ordinary' young players – girls as well as boys – celebrated their feats with all the gusto and triumphalism of a Warne. Although the commercial opened and closed with the same typically Anglo-Saxon Australian small boy, wearing a baggy green cap (minus badge, of course) in a school playground game, Europeans and Asians also featured. David Fouvy admits this stretches the truth about the breadth of participation. 'The only thing that might not be 100 per cent accurate', he says, 'is that the ad tries to reflect where we *want* to be in terms of ethnic participation, not where we are. What we want to get across is that cricket is a game for all people in Australia, regardless of race, creed, birthplace or whatever.' He adds: 'Our advertising aims to capture a whole, if you like, kaleidoscope of cricket, to capture the spirit that underlies the game. That way, we hope to motivate people to attend games.'

International cricket in Australia is currently enjoying its highest profile since the Bradman era. More than anyone, Mark Taylor personifies this. Early in the season, Taylor joined the select group of cricketers to have been photographed for the cover of *Time* magazine, which explored how 'the world's brilliant young stars are breathing new life into Test cricket'; on Australia Day, 26 January, he became the eleventh sports person, but only the second cricketer (after Border in 1989), to be chosen as 'Australian of the Year' in the thirty-nine years of the government-backed award; when he announced his retirement from Test cricket, all four television networks interrupted normal programming and crossed live to his press conference in Sydney; and the following day, the only national newspaper, *The Australian*, carried a four-page pull-out celebrating his achievements.

It is hardly surprising, therefore, that the leading Aussies reap rewards of an order which no England cricketer since Ian Botham has managed. According to *Business Review Weekly*'s annual survey of the fifty highest-earning sports people in Australia, Shane Warne is the highest-paid cricketer, with earnings from all sources of an estimated A$1.1 million (some £440,000) in 1998 (despite his seven-month lay-off), followed by Taylor (A$710,000, £285,000) and Steve Waugh (A$690,000, £277,000). However, the trio only ranked, respectively, in twenty-sixth, forty-fourth and fiftieth places in a list headed by the golfer Greg Norman, with an estimated A$37.3 million (£14.9 million). Although Warne lost writing contracts with two newspapers as a result of the 'bookie affair', his A$200,000 (£80,000) deal to promote the smoking cessation aid Nicorette – he gave up smoking on New Year's Day, twenty-four hours before his Test comeback – should help keep his earnings above the million-dollar mark in 1999.

The huge corporate investment in sport was underlined a few days in to the New Year with the release of figures from the Bureau of Statistics showing that sport attracts nearly ten times more business sponsorship than the arts and cultural activities. Despite the flourishing arts scene, Australian business put A$282 million (£113 million) into sponsorship of sport in the financial year 1996–7, but a mere A$29 million (£11.6 million) into the arts. No wonder sport, as an industry, accounts for about 8 per cent of Australian gross domestic product.

Another factor in Australian sporting success is the high level of government expenditure on the sector – and the willingness of voters of most political persuasions to pay such bills. In 1994–5, the latest year for which I have figures, Federal, state and local government spent a total of A$1,661 million (£665 million) of taxpayers' money on sport. Some A$20 million (£8 million) went to the Olympic Athlete Program to assist in the preparation of athletes for the 2000 Sydney Olympic Games and Paralympic Games – a programme which has as an explicit aim an Olympic medal tally of sixty, of which twenty must be gold (the rest can be in lesser currency). Even allowing for home advantage, it is an ambitious target considering that Australia was one of only five nations at Atlanta in 1996 to reach the forty-medal mark, her haul being forty-one – nine gold, nine silver and twenty-three bronze – compared with Britain's fifteen (one, eight and six). But then Australia is also the country which attaches more importance than any other to Commonwealth Games performances.

Of course, there would be nothing like this level of expenditure on sport were it not for the central place which it occupies in Australian society, the fierce national pride which motivates sportsmen and sportswomen, the public's love of winners, and the country's proud and aggressive sporting traditions. 'You don't produce top cricketers without a huge amount of social support,' says Richard Cashman, a cricket historian who is now Director of the Centre for Olympic Studies at the University of New South Wales. 'By social support I mean that good cricketers are admired by their family, by their school, by their community.' He adds: 'We Australians are very satirical and very critical of politicians and business people, and we even tend to be a bit hard on the artists, anyone with pretensions. But we put sports people on a pedestal. They're the sacred cow. I think the community support, the community's yearning for their sports stars to succeed, is a sort of self-fulfilling prophecy. It creates a climate in which people want to get up at four o'clock in the morning and swim for three hours or something ridiculous like that.'

Can Cashman identify other elements peculiar to cricket? 'I think

"The Living Legend" is a factor in cricket's position,' he says. 'In Don Bradman, cricket has the most respected person in the country.' He believes another of cricket's strengths is that from its beginnings in Australia, early in the nineteenth century, it was an egalitarian sport which fitted in well with that key element of the national character. It was also organised well before potential rival games, and was the first sport to benefit from international tours. As Australian nationalism developed, contests against the Motherland assumed an extra significance because of the fervent desire to 'whip the Poms'. That desire may have diminished, but in 1998–9 it was still a powerful motivator for players and followers alike. 'I don't think my audience has yet got tired of whipping the Poms,' says the ACB's David Fouvy. 'Australians love nothing better than grinding the Poms into the dirt again. We don't like receiving it, mind you!'

There is also a belief at the ACB that the excellent crowds for the Ashes Tests – 472,000 in total – reflected an upsurge in national feeling as the country approached the millennium, the Sydney Olympics and the Centenary of Federation in 2001. Says a figure close to the board: 'There's an idea around that cricket is a ready-made national symbol for this heightened feeling. But of course it's impossible to quantify.' A more concrete factor in Australian success in 1998–9, I am sure, was the self-belief and sense of history evident in Steve Waugh's remark, when asked his reasons for wanting the captaincy, that Australia has the 'greatest tradition' of any cricketing country. It is a tradition of which no senior player can lack detailed knowledge, since the game's history is taught at the Cricket Academy in Adelaide and to the most talented players at some lower levels too – for example, those in Victoria's Under-13 and Under-15 squads.

Cashman also argues that from the outset Australian cricket had a wider social base than the English game. This was partly because Australian administrators were 'a bit more entrepreneurial' than their English counterparts, consciously setting out to create a working-class base for the sport in the late Victorian era, when large grounds were built to accommodate 'the shilling patron'.

Over the past thirty years Australian cricket has had to face the challenges posed by a rapidly changing society. The overwhelmingly white Anglo-Celtic Australia of the first half of the century has developed into a sophisticated, multicultural, pluralist nation. Large intakes of settlers from southern Europe and elsewhere in the decades after the Second

World War were followed by the first substantial waves of twentieth-century Asian migration, following the abandonment of the 'White Australia' policy in the late 1960s; migration from the United Kingdom is still quite substantial. Almost one in four (23 per cent) of the Australian population was born abroad. In 1995 the population included 1.2 million people born in the United Kingdom or Ireland, 790,000 in Asia, 290,000 in New Zealand, 261,000 in Italy, 180,000 in the former Yugoslavia and 145,000 in Greece. As for languages, Italian remains the second most widely spoken language, although since 1990 more university students have studied Japanese than any other language. However, having embarked on the multicultural journey more than twenty years later than the Mother Country, Australia is, hardly surprisingly, fifteen or twenty years behind on that road; but the gap is closing.

The majority of Australia's leading cricketers still come from Anglo-Saxon or Irish stock but since 1945 there has been a small but growing immigrant presence in the first-class game. Current internationals born outside Australia include the all-rounder Brendon Julian (New Zealand), whose ancestry is part Tongan, and Andrew Symonds, another excellent fielder (England, believe it or not!). More numerous are Australian players who are the sons of immigrants: Michael Slater's parents were born in England, so he could have opted to play for a team which could have guaranteed him a place for life; Shane Warne's mother was born in Germany, moving with her parents to Australia in 1949, aged three; Michael Di Venuto's ancestry is Italian, Michael Kasprowicz has Polish blood. Going back to the 1980s, Mike Veletta was the first player of Italian ancestry to represent Australia, playing eight Tests, and Carl Rackemann, the big fast bowler from Queensland (twelve Tests), had a German-born grandfather. Fellow fast bowler Lennie Pascoe – Lennie Durtanovich until he anglicised his name, some time before his first-class début – was the son of immigrants from the former Yugoslavia, and played fourteen Tests between 1977 and 1981, taking 64 wickets at 26.06. In recent years Richard Chee Quee, New South Wales's first player of Chinese descent, has enjoyed some success as a hard-hitting batsman, though he left the staff in 1998. 'Cricket is a game of patience,' he has said, 'and patience, I've always thought, is a virtue of the Chinese especially.'

Although some of the above have carved out positions as minor role models, penetration of high-level cricket by ethnic minorities is proving a painfully slow process. A survey of eighty Under-19 cricketers – the cream of the crop – conducted by Richard Cashman in 1995 under-scored this. It revealed that only one player was not born in Australia (he hailed from South Africa). For 97.5 per cent of the sample English was the only language spoken at home, a striking contrast to the Australian population at large, 14 per cent of whom speak a language other than English at home.

Bobby Simpson, now a coaching consultant to the ACB, is among those disappointed by progress in broadening the base of the game. 'For thirty years I've had a great dream – that our national team be made up of mainly unpronounceable names. It's a great shame that all this talent isn't being utilised in cricket. We're not getting the Asians yet, but we will. But if you look at the top fifteen- to twenty-year-olds, we are getting Greeks, Yugoslavs, Italians are very big. You see them in every state.' Simpson, himself a second-generation Australian, says he was 'really upset' that Pascoe changed his name. 'It would have been a huge breakthrough, twenty years ago, to have had an international called Durtanovich. And if Shane Warne had been Italian, that would have been fantastic.' Yes, it would – at least until the 'bookie affair', when Warne would have been endlessly reminded of his origins!

Simpson, a former Australian captain, concedes that 'as a young man' in grade cricket Pascoe had to endure 'being called a "wog" and things like that, but that's part of our culture'. Even at Test level, Pascoe – once described by Ted Dexter as 'the first white Russian to open the bowling at Lord's' – was, according to Geoff Lawson, regularly teased by the Chappell brothers because of his ethnic background. But that would be much less likely to occur in today's more sophisticated and tolerant Australia. And judging by a few comments I overheard in the Ashes crowds, some fans would welcome a more multicultural side. As one white Anglo-Saxon man put it to his equally white Anglo-Saxon girlfriend at Sydney: 'The day our batting's opened by Djurkovic and Patel is the day Australia really comes of age.'

Although cricket has lagged well behind most other sports in reaching out beyond its traditional base, it is finally making positive efforts to become more multicultural – more like the England team, in fact. Late in the 1998–9 season, the ACB unveiled a three-year strategic plan for 1999–2001 in which, for the first time, it adopted as official policy the objective of recruiting more players from Aboriginal and non-English-speaking backgrounds. The plan, which took effect immediately, involves the appointment of additional development officers to work with Aboriginal communities to develop the considerable sporting talent there (it was, after all, the indigenous people who comprised the first team to represent Australia abroad, on the 1868 tour of England). The board, which conceded that the game was still a largely Anglo-Saxon one, is also commissioning two studies of children's attitudes to cricket, one in a predominantly Aboriginal rural community, the other in a non-English-speaking metropolitan area.

However, in New South Wales and Victoria, the states with the most diverse populations, efforts to broaden the base have been going on for some time. In 1997–8, for example, the Victorian Cricket Association (VCA) ran a pilot programme in the predominantly Asian Melbourne suburb of Springvale. 'The Asian kids were very keen to play,' says Mark McAllion, coaching and development manager. 'But they were intimidated about going along to a principally white club, especially by themselves. So we ran clinics in schools and linked up schools and clubs. A couple of clubs picked up four or five Asian kids each.' He adds: 'Asians who've just arrived here can hit and throw as well as any other child, it's the bowling that's a problem – it's an unnatural action. But we might just have an Asian opening the batting for Australia in fifteen or twenty years' time.' Meanwhile, also in the 1997–8 season, Cricket NSW succeeded in persuading thirty-seven children from Turkish, Arabic and other ethnic backgrounds in the Sydney suburb of Auburn to register with two struggling local clubs. In the two seasons before that, Richard Chee Quee, a fiercely proud Australian, led attempts to involve the Vietnamese and other communities, but with mixed results. 'Ethnic participation is increasing,' says David Eland, Cricket NSW's development manager, who spent a season with Northamptonshire in 1998. 'Not many Asians play. Our challenge is to make it part of their culture. I think we can.'

If cricket's leading personnel are not yet representative of society, crowds at one-day internationals – though not Tests – are becoming more so. The ACB estimates that between 15 and 25 per cent of spectators at one-dayers – 25 to 30 per cent at Sri Lanka's matches – come from outside the traditional white Anglo-Saxon base of the Australian game, and believes that the proportion is on the way up. Certainly there are now quite a few Asian faces in all one-day crowds. One-day cricket is, without doubt, far more accessible and appealing to people who have not been brought up with the game, and consequently televised day/night matches attract a more multicultural audience. And most metropolitan taxi drivers, whatever their roots, tune in to the one-dayers, less so the Tests.

The television commentator and former England captain Tony Greig, himself a naturalised Australian, believes that many migrants are quickly absorbed into mainstream activities such as cricket. 'Second-generation Aussies are bloody Aussies, Aussies, Aussies,' he says with characteristic gusto. 'The minute the kids go to school here, they become Aussies straight away, and do Aussie things like play cricket. Market gardeners from Italy know all about cricket – they almost feel compelled to get into the important things in the society.'

Of course many Italian market gardeners and other 'new' Australians come from cultures where soccer is the number one sport. Soccer – or 'wogball', as a few unreconstructed Australians call it – is in fact the most popular winter game in Aussie primary schools, and while most pupils later concentrate on other forms of football, interest in soccer remains high, particularly among migrants: the newspapers provide astonishingly full coverage of British league football, and it certainly does not just focus on the Aussies involved.

The diversification of society has also increased competition from other sports, not just the long-established football codes. You only have to talk to a few parents of talented children aged eleven to fifteen to grasp the intensity of competition for their offspring's sporting skills. Cricket is fighting its way successfully through this jungle. It began the 1990s under threat from baseball and basketball but has withstood both challenges remarkably well. The ACB regarded baseball as the greater worry, partly because it did not think an indoor sport could ever really take off in an outdoor country. It may have been right: the basketball bubble burst two or three years ago, and its move to a summer season in 1998–9 (after making little headway against the big winter sports) is not expected to do the trick. Baseball, which switched to summer in the 1980s, is doing well but, again, without inflicting serious damage on cricket, either in terms of public support, or recruitment of talent.

There is no doubt that Australian cricket is extremely well served by its coaching and development network. The development officer's role, says the VCA's McAllion, is 'not to find the next Dennis Lillee or Shane Warne but to develop structures that will ensure the star will come through the system. We aim for strong local competitions, with lots of people playing, positive experiences for kids all the way through – and kids dreaming of playing for Australia. While the national team is doing well and we have promotable stars, the desire is there.' Some recruit-ment literature from Cricket NSW underlines the value of role models. A photograph of Michael Slater kissing his helmet is shown next to a striking shot of a teenage girl, bowling quick. In between them is the Australian cap. 'It's not out of your reach!' reads the headline. 'Take your first step to The Baggy Green Cap!'

A Sydney Under-14 team which recently toured New Zealand may not be typical in ethnic terms, but it does emphasise the healthy state of the grassroots. The Canterbury–Western Suburbs Under-14s were led by Luke Reynolds, whose mother's family fled Russia, and included boys with forebears from India, Sri Lanka, China, Iran, Greece, Ireland, Ger-many, France, Switzerland and Italy. Luke, an all-rounder who bats at three and bowls fast, is regarded by many as the best cricketer of his age in NSW. 'We don't think of multiculturalism,' he says. 'We're Australian friends who like playing cricket together.'

His mother, Nadia Reynolds, adds: 'The passion the boys have for the sport brings them together.' Anurag Verma, a medium-fast bowler who arrived from India aged five, speaks for several team-mates when he declares that it is his ambition to emulate his heroes in today's national side and play for Australia. He will, he adds a mite superfluously, be barracking for the home team in next summer's Tests against India.

Verma's loyalties are typical of the majority of migrant families. Most 'new' Australians, certainly from the second generation onwards, would pass the former Tory minister Norman Tebbit's infamous 'cricket test' – his idiosyncratic measure of a model British immigrant – with flying colours. With notable exceptions, such as the lively Sri Lankan commu-nity and most (but by no means all) of the British, they generally sup-port their adopted country, rather than the land of their roots, in international competitions. 'Their first level of loyalty is to Australia', is how one ambassador in Canberra put it.

Encouraging as all this is, some of those involved in nurturing future generations are concerned about the potential impact of other changes in society. 'City kids aren't playing as much backyard cricket or street cricket as previous generations,' says Mark McAllion. 'They're busy with computer games, and extra school pressures. Out in the country, though, primary school kids are still developing the basic skills infor-mally, in their own time, after school. Catching, throwing and hitting skills are much more developed in those areas.'

On the other hand, facilities and coaching for up-and-coming players, in country or city, are generally the best in the world and, as Simpson points out, 'for the first time in years, councils are building new cricket grounds. There are five new grounds planned [for free use by the public] in the Blue Mountains area [near Sydney] alone.'

And what of top-level cricket, or 'élite cricket' as the Aussies, forgetting their egalitarianism for a moment, prefer to call it? Craig McGregor, a leading author and cultural commentator, believes that it has adapted well to changes in society. 'Cricket has become a spectacular pop entertainment,' says McGregor, brother of the cricket writer Adrian. 'At one-day internationals you now have a very prominent 'yobbo' audience which goes with a lot of shouting and barracking and drinking and good humour and bad humour and insults and Mexican waves and the whole damn panoply of pop culture.' He adds: 'One might regret some of the changes in terms of the game itself but those changes have certainly enabled cricket here to survive this incredibly different, competitive, highly commercial, globalised world.'

4
England Prepare

CHRISTOPHER MARTIN-JENKINS

The England team had barely four weeks to prepare for the first Test in Brisbane in mid-November and only three first-class matches. When they subsequently and belatedly won the Melbourne Test against the head immediately after Christmas, Alec Bedser, one of the greatest of English bowlers, expressed the view that it was because they were finally properly acclimatised. But to expect a different itinerary these days is to dream. The commercial realities mean that as many matches as possible have to be 'big' games: money-spinners.

This was to be the most intensive, contracted series in Ashes history. The first Test ended on 24 November, the fifth and last started in Sydney on 2 January, fewer than six weeks later. Such a rushed itinerary, at least by the standards of all previous Ashes series, gave a theoretical advantage to the home side, because they had limitless reserves on hand in the event of tiredness or injury to key players, and it certainly suggested that whoever got the better start would probably win.

So it proved, but England were to have their chances and fail to take them until it was too late. More to the point, perhaps, the Australians were again about to show themselves to be that much tougher and more resilient in tight corners. Because the one-day matches on the tour of Pakistan had lingered on into the start of the Australian first-class season, most of the home players were actually less well prepared for the first Test than England's were. Before a ball was bowled, however, the form book suggested that they would win again, for the sixth time in succession. Since 1989 they had won seventeen Tests to England's four and only one of England's successes had been achieved before the main issue, the Ashes, had been decided.

Only if virtually everything went right in the eleven weeks before the programme switched to the one-day game (at which England's status was higher) was there a chance that the ratings, which put Australia top by a distance and England seventh out of the nine Test-playing countries, would be proved wrong. England had to win tosses, catch half chances, make big first-innings scores, keep their bowlers fit and bowl tightly to upset the best team in the world.

As in most rugby internationals, it seemed in advance that the battle was likely to be won or lost up front. England eventually beat South Africa both because their luck changed at last, with a vengeance as far as marginal umpiring decisions were concerned, and because Mike Atherton and Mark Butcher managed to score just sufficient runs against Allan Donald and Shaun Pollock. In Australia, England would have no hope unless they could see off the new ball more often than not; every chance if they could.

By the same token Darren Gough and his prescribed partner Angus Fraser would have to have success with the new ball, not least against Mark Taylor, whose 426 runs in one Test in Peshawar in October had consummated his love affair with the Australian public. Under the cosh from the press at the start of the 1997 tour of England, when he had lost all confidence as a batsman, though not his sure touch as captain, Taylor had become almost as great a national sporting hero in Australia as his predecessor, Allan Border. Around him and the redoubtable Waugh brothers – all three of them in the top fifteen of the world ratings – Australia's selectors had to choose between Michael Slater, Justin Langer, Darren Lehmann, Ricky Ponting and Greg Blewett. Such players as Matthew Elliott, Michael Bevan, Stuart Law and Matthew Hayden, all of whom had enjoyed much success in England, could only wait and hope.

Whether Ian Healy batted at six or seven, however, Australia clearly had a tail to be exploited. So did England, but this time they knew they had to make runs between seven and eleven, one reason why Peter Philpott, the Australian leg-spin expert, had been recruited by Stewart to help them during the tour. Bob Cottam's job as bowling coach would be to fine-tune the actions of Gough, Fraser, Mullally and Cork, who were pencilled in for the first Test with Croft as the preferred spinner, but one of David Lloyd's duties, as chief coach, was to help his tail-enders contribute with the bat as well.

'It needs a fully collective effort,' he said before the team left. 'From seven to eleven we have to eke out as many runs as we can – 125 at least.'

'Eking out' would be necessary sometimes, no doubt, but so would putting bat to ball at the right time. The danger of a combination of England tour selectors comprising Lloyd, Alec Stewart and the manager, Graham Gooch, was that they would be too inflexible and, if things started to go wrong, too inclined to make excuses. Things did go wrong, soon enough, not least because the tail consistently failed, but at least these pitfalls were avoided. Selection policy turned out to be adaptable, and whingeing was conspicuous by its absence.

Hussain, restored as vice-captain, was not allowed an official vote in selection matters, but, as a free thinker, he had his say, and sometimes his way. Speaking at the MCC indoor school a few days before the team left, his formula for success was straightforward. 'We've got to stay with them all the way. Start well and compete throughout the series. The first innings is the key to all we do. If we get 400 it gives our bowlers a chance to put pressure on them. Our fitness and fielding got shown up in Australia last time but we've progressed a lot in those areas in the last couple of years. We still have a problem in that some of our quickest fielders are needed in the slips but we'll work on total cricket.'

Hussain was the only one of England's seven specialist batsmen not to have been on a tour of Australia, although Mark Ramprakash joined the last one late and Butcher's previous trip was the 'A' tour which confirmed him as a serious Test candidate. Butcher and Atherton finished first and second in the averages against South Africa, which seemed to augur well, especially as Donald and Pollock were first and second in the bowling averages. Although he failed in England's subsequent capitulation to Sri Lanka, Butcher could point proudly to the fact that England had won two of the three Tests in which he played against South Africa and had had much the better of the other one, at Edgbaston.

Graham Thorpe, provided he was truly fit after his back operation, would provide a second left-hander in the top five, which could only be a help if Shane Warne returned after surgery to his right shoulder and Stuart MacGill maintained the promise he had already shown in taking 14 wickets in his first two Tests against South Africa and Pakistan. Thorpe averaged 49 against Australia, three of his six hundreds had been scored against them and it was my view that he should have returned to four so that Stewart, whose prodigious energy would inevitably be sapped by captaining and keeping wicket in hot weather, could drop to five or six.

This was one preconception which proved wide of the mark, for various reasons. Another was that Glenn McGrath and Jason Gillespie would immediately be able to resume their new-ball partnership after serious injuries, McGrath to his groin, Gillespie to his back.

Damien Fleming, Paul Reiffel and Mark Kasprowicz were all vying to support them. Two might miss selection, it seemed, when Warne was deemed fit to resume alongside MacGill, because England's continuing weakness against top-class spin, cruelly exposed again by Muralitharan, had not gone unnoticed by the Australian selectors.

MacGill had played some cricket in Devon, so he was a bit more familiar, if only a bit, than Colin Miller, who had also done well in tough circumstances in Pakistan and was likely to remain close to the team until the champion's return. Miller had risen from the ranks of the journeymen of the Sheffield Shield at the age of thirty-four, having played first-class cricket for thirteen seasons. Truly a jack-of-all-trades, he took the new ball for Tasmania as a right-arm swing bowler but he owed his advance to the fact that he had made himself into a useful off-spinner rather in the mould of the former West Australian Test bowler Bruce Yardley.

Originally from the same unpretentious Melbourne club, Footscray, which produced Merv Hughes, and now living in a pub in Hobart, 'Funky' loves a party but he is a serious professional for all the blond rinsed hair and ear-rings he was sporting in Pakistan. He had never done anything for a living but play cricket, in England and Holland as well as for three State sides in Australia.

There was much speculation in the early weeks of the tour about when Warne would make his bow in the series but the instant success enjoyed by MacGill enabled him to take his time. In the past three years Warne had undergone two operations for wear and tear. The spinning finger went first, needing tendon surgery; the bowling shoulder second. In theory Australia's chances were reduced by his absence: he had taken 85 wickets at a cost of 23 runs each in seventeen Tests against England; 313 in all from his sixty-seven Tests for Australia.

To take advantage of Warne's delayed return, England needed their seasoned batsmen to succeed against bowlers of relatively little experience like MacGill and Miller. This was especially true of Atherton, undone by McGrath nine times in eight Tests but still the man Australia were keenest to conquer, and Stewart, who needed to improve on a poor personal batting record against Australia if his confidence as a captain was not to be crucially undermined.

In Warne's absence, McGrath (42 wickets at 22 against England) was the key bowler for Australia and like everyone he was keen to make an early impact at the Gabba, the gateway to the series. England wanted to play the first Test of the series at Perth instead, leaving two Tests until the new year, but Simon Pack, who handled the tour negotiations for the

ECB, thought that the compromise which emerged was a big improvement on recent tours. In particular, the separation between Tests and one-day internationals made sense for both countries: 'We tried to minimise the amount of travel. We would have preferred not to have two blocks of back-to-back Tests but it wasn't an issue to die in a ditch over.'

Perhaps not, but the lack of a first-class match between the first two and the last two Tests was always likely to work to the advantage of Australia. The contraction of the Test series at least gave a potential chance to England's reserve fast bowlers, Dean Headley and the two who had their twenty-first birthdays early on the tour, Ben Hollioake and Alex Tudor. Both of them were carefully watched in the first week of net practice in the bright light and on the hard pitches of the nets at the WACA ground in Perth. Tudor, seriously quick and fully recovered from a stress fracture of his left shin, rapidly made an impact both with the quality of his bowling and with his strength of character. This was one young Englishman of West Indian extraction who was really eager to develop his talent and not to be deflected by the bright lights of fame.

Hollioake, with two Test caps in his cupboard already, had more to prove. It was hardly his fault that so much publicity and material reward followed his two dazzling one-day innings at Lord's in 1997 and his apparently casual approach to life hid a determined personality, but his cricket in 1998 betrayed a lack of patience and for all his evident natural ability he was fortunate to be picked for the tour. Between them, Hollioake, Mark Ealham and Andrew Flintoff, all playing as all-rounders, managed five wickets and 55 runs in five Tests against South Africa, which was the best evidence yet of the futility of trying to field all-rounders who were not quite good enough either as batsmen or as bowlers.

The England team which left for Australia on 21 October (the one-day team was engaged, meanwhile, in an ICC tournament in Bangladesh where they fell at the first hurdle against South Africa) was operating in an environment altogether more conducive to success than the one which had surrounded Mike Atherton's side four years before. The decision to employ Philpott as an adviser during the tour was just one example of the support the national side now received.

The changes had been watched with perhaps a tinge of regret by Patrick Whittingdale, the city financial services expert who invested £3 million of his company's money in the early 1990s in just the sort of back-up support – more expert coaching, better medical and fitness advice, pre-tour get-togethers, help with lifestyle, etc. – which the ECB was now providing at David Lloyd's behest.

Looking back to the contract which ended in 1995 when he finally lost patience with the old order, Whittingdale says: 'A lot of things are better now but too much was left undone for too long. I believe there is still too little man management. To get the best out of young men you need regular personal reviews, advice and support. People like Ray Illingworth and Keith Fletcher honestly believed that an occasional chat on the edge of the boundary was sufficient. Ian MacLaurin built Tesco up by strong management and team building so he understood what was needed.'

Pack, the former NATO commander who is gaining gradual acceptance amongst those who thought his role superfluous at first, organised a week with the Impact Development Group in the Lake District in the autumn for the England 'A' and Under-19 teams, designed to build their confidence and team skills. Alas, this was to some extent negated by the sheer foolishness of organising a tour for the 'A' team to Zimbabwe at a time of year when rain all too often ruins attempts to play cricket.

It did not diminish the value of the attempt to expand the horizons of English professional cricketers and to encourage them to play for their team-mates as well as for themselves. Australians have always believed that the selfishness of the average English professional reduces his chances of metaphorically dying for his country in battle. The senior side would have had the same treatment if there had been more time between the end of the English season and the start of the tour. Similar to the training given to the British Lions before their successful tour of South Africa, the programme was carefully designed to enable individuals on both teams to identify their personal strengths and weaknesses, to give them a shared sense of values and to equip them better for the life of a professional sportsman.

One of the eventual benefits should be a more enlightened attitude from future England teams to public and media relations. It was an area which never interested Atherton and in which the articulate but dangerously passionate Lloyd had twice got himself into very hot water with the ECB. Officials like the chairman, Lord MacLaurin, and his chief executive, Tim Lamb, were rather too concerned, however, about what their coach said in public and rather too slow to recognise the improvements he had made to the purpose, organisation and morale of the England team since taking the tracksuit from Ray Illingworth (the latter having become involved at least ten years too late) in April 1996.

To the objective observer, there was something thoroughly demeaning about the sacking of the England football coach early in 1999 because of a comment made to a journalist about his spiritual views. After the disastrous publicity they had received the previous year following the unfair dismissal of a female employee made pregnant by a young executive at Lord's, the ECB had appointed an experienced spin doctor to try to improve its public relations and they were image-conscious to the point of paranoia.

Under pressure from speculation about his future later in the tour, Lloyd pointed out that England were now setting some trends rather than following them: 'Other countries follow some of the things we do, including Australia, who have appointed a sports psychologist, set up a digital computer and video system like ours and pinched two or three of our practice drills, like using tennis rackets and balls for reflex catching.'

Lloyd started the tour on a final warning after his comments on Muralitharan's action during the Oval Test and his grip on the team was loosened by the appointment of Graham Gooch as a manager of a different kind from the traditional suited figure whose main duties were administrative and diplomatic. Gooch's first instinct was to be with his players at all times, talking tactics and techniques. He was happiest in the England training gear, once he had gone for his obligatory morning run – at forty-five when the tour started, he was still keeping himself remorselessly fit – and he was seldom out of the nets or off the field in the days when the players were working off their jet lag in assiduous practice and training to acclimatise to Australian conditions.

What is more, Gooch was in sole charge until Lloyd arrived from Bangladesh, disappointed that England's one-day team, led by Adam Hollioake, had lost to South Africa but perhaps also glad to get to Australia as quickly as possible to take overall control of the practices.

The team was staying at the Hyatt hotel in Perth, only a relatively short jog across the vivid gardens of Victoria Park from the 'Wacca', as the Western Australian Cricket Association ground is universally known. Even my Korean taxi-driver, newly arrived in Perth and barely able to speak a word of Strine, knew that destination.

Like all the hotels in which the players were housed throughout the tour, the Hyatt was luxurious as opposed to merely comfortable. When I first started reporting tours, team hotels, even in Australia, were far less sophisticated and the pennies spent by the Test and

County Cricket Board on board and lodging for their players abroad were carefully watched. Accommodation in certain parts of the West Indies, country areas of Australia and, notoriously, in India and Pakistan, was often basic. Standards have risen everywhere, however, and so have expectations.

Lord MacLaurin saw that England players were still sharing rooms in a soulless hotel when he visited the team in Bulawayo in Zimbabwe on the unhappy little tour of 1996–7 and resolved that they would be treated as VIPs in future.

It is always the case at the start of a tour that team spirit is good, the mood optimistic and the players all eager to get out of the nets and away from the most rigorous of the fitness exercises and into a proper match. England's first game was at Lilac Hill, the home of the Midland Guildford Cricket Club. This has become Australia's answer to Arundel; a one-day game in sylvan surroundings against a scratch side.

Being Australia, however, the match against the ACB Chairman's XI was no gentle introduction. The facilities at the ground by the bank of the River Swan were sensationally good compared with those of the average English club. There are three grounds, each with excellent pitches and net facilities and, because it was easiest to put up marquees on the third-best ground, that was what the club members did.

They have built this game into a regular feature at the start of overseas tours and the administration of a crowd of 11,000 was admirable on a hot day in which the harsh glare of Australian sunlight bore down like a laser beam on the heads of those, like me, newly arrived from the soft grey light of an English October. One had forgotten the flies, too. When the former Test bowler Keith Slater took the public address microphone to welcome the crowd shortly before the captains tossed, he got only a word or two out before gasping as if someone had grasped him by the throat with both hands. He had swallowed a fly. Welcome to Western Australia, ladies and gentlemen!

It was a long and exciting day for the crowd and however serious the cricket, the mood was one of pure merriment: unsophisticated folk having a good time. Even the so-called VIP tent in front of our cordoned-off media area was full of inebriated, shouting men well before the game reached a thrilling climax. Good-humoured they were, but they all wanted to see the Poms beaten and they very nearly were.

Six of an Australian Board Chairman's XI which took the game until the final ball in splendid pursuit of England's own testing total of 297 for five were in the State side for the four-day match at the WACA. It was just as well, perhaps, that of this extremely proud cricketing state's strongest available side Tom Moody and Jo Angel were not match fit and that three more international players, Brendon Julian, Adam Gilchrist and Damien Martyn, were still on tour with Australia in Pakistan, playing in the one-day internationals with which the tour finished.

Talented and ambitious young cricketers are never far behind the established ones in Australia, however, and apart from the six who all made some kind of mark at Lilac Hill, Western Australia gave a first opportunity to a young left-hander named Chris Rogers whom Peter Loader compared to the young David Gower. Loader, once a mean fast bowler for Surrey and England, had taken up umpiring in his late sixties and was relishing the challenge.

Returning to the scene of several happy seasons of winter cricket in Perth, Stewart made an impressive start to his tour, hitting 74 off 68 balls with strokeplay of considerable relish. John Crawley, another former member of the Midland Guildford club, also played with immense panache and confidence for 74 off 50 balls on a true, firm pitch ideal for the purposes of entertaining so many spectators. The majority of them were seated from an early hour in one or other of the seventy-seven open marquees crammed in amongst the gum trees.

Before their picnics beside the Swan River they had seen a third England batsman, Atherton, making an ideal start to his tour. He and Mark Butcher, later presented with an unusual award, a Corby trouser press for being judged the best-dressed man of the match, negotiated some awkward balls in the opening overs from the veteran maestros Dennis Lillee and Bruce Reid. Butcher played on to Reid and Ben Hollioake, having hit four majestic fours off successive balls, top-edged a pull.

Atherton showed himself to be in ripe form. No fewer than thirteen fours across a slow outfield emphasised as much, before he drove fiercely to extra cover and was quite wonderfully caught, left-handed and off the ground, by Simon Katich, one of the Australian Institute of Sport's outstanding recent Test candidates and potentially a future Test player. But England were now flowing: Stewart hit ten fours, Crawley five and two sixes, one of them straight back over Angel's head.

The eventual victory by one run was Pyrrhic. Stewart and Atherton both aggravated their suspect backs and Hollioake pulled a groin muscle, an untimely and unlucky setback. By the time he had recovered, his chance of playing in the Test series had already almost gone.

There was a nastier, if less far-reaching, injury in store for Butcher when the first first-class match got under way at the WACA. England started the game reasonably satisfactorily in the field, Gough and Mullally taking seven of the eight Western Australian wickets, worthy reward for purposeful and well-controlled bowling by them both, in Gough's case at full pace.

Each of them took an additional wicket in his first over on a cooler, cloudier second morning after hot labour in 90 degrees plus on the first day, but Matthew Nicholson, twenty-four, played many a bold, robust stroke on the way to a maiden first-class fifty. Once the best schoolboy cricketer in New South Wales – unusually for outstanding fast bowlers in that particular state, he was the product of a fee-paying grammar school – he was frustrated by the bias towards spinners on Sydney Cricket Ground pitches and so went west in search of a Sheffield Shield place. Before his first full season, however, he succumbed for several months to Chronic Fatigue Syndrome, brought on by a fearsome cocktail of illnesses: glandular fever and Ross River fever the most serious of them.

The pace and hostility of his bowling against England in this game, on the quickest pitch in the world, made up for lost time after a full season wasted the previous year, when getting out of bed was sometimes more than he could manage. Six foot six and fully restored to fitness with the help of a diet which eschewed meat and dairy products, he finished the innings with eye-catching, but thoroughly deserved, figures of seven for 77.

I remember seeing Jeff Thomson bowling against England for Queensland at the start of the 1974–5 tour, when no one expected him to be picked for Australia. Within weeks he was teaming up with Dennis Lillee and paving the way to the regaining of the Ashes. The Australian selectors have almost always been acutely attuned to the Sheffield Shield network, and quick to spot the discomfort of visiting batsmen, especially English ones, when a bowler has them hopping about. In Nicholson's case on this occasion, there was no doubt that he was flattered a little by England's lack of acclimatisation and the adamantine hardness of the pitch, but there was something about this young man with his long run, open-chested action, short delivery stride and controlled aggression which made one think his performance was not a flash in the pan.

41

Butcher had ducked into the second ball that he bowled and the consequent cut above a badly bruised left eye required ten stitches. He spent the next few days nursing a fierce headache and an eye more swollen and sore than that of any defeated heavyweight boxer. Hussain, leading the side for the only time until Stewart finally gave himself a rest towards the end of the one-day series (he was also to miss the Hobart game, but so did Hussain), came to the rescue with a determined and patient hundred. Equally true to the formula of England's batting in the first few weeks of the tour, only Thorpe and Ramprakash gave him much support.

The worst aspect of the opening match was the lack of sharpness in England's fielding. Some 50 per cent of the chances offered were not taken and Justin Langer, who captained the State side for the first time with some flair, was blunt about the lack of urgency evident in England's performance when he spoke to the press after the game.

His own youthful side had done particularly well. Nicholson with the ball was only marginally more impressive than two of the batsmen, Katich and Ryan Campbell. Compact and aggressive, Campbell gave Angus Fraser a horrible mauling in the second innings, which led directly to his eventual omission from the Perth Test. Katich, a left-hander, is a less destructive player but a patient and well-organised one.

Altogether, England had much to think about as they took the long journey across the 'wide, brown land', swapping the pristine modernity, strong breezes and wide streets of Perth for the stately Victorian splendour of central Adelaide. Social life in Perth had reached a modest peak with a Mardi Gras parade on the Saturday night of the Western Australia match, a rather less *risqué* and avant-garde event than it threatened to be. There was more genuine temptation for some waiting in the plush, air-conditioned casino beside the Festival centre at Adelaide, and Mullally came away one night several hundred dollars richer.

This was nothing compared to the A$10 million (£4 million) which Kerry Packer and his gambling partner Lloyd Williams, chairman of the Crown Casino in Melbourne, had reportedly won from bookmakers by backing Jezabeel, the New Zealand-trained winner of the Melbourne Cup, during the match at the WACA. It was a bizarre sight on the morning of the race to see Perth's high society gathering in the Hyatt and other smart hotels to watch the big race on television, the men suavely dressed in dark suits, some in tails; the women in silks and elaborate hats. It rather stressed the isolation of Perth from the rest of Australia.

After all, Singapore is nearer to the Swan River than the Flemington racecourse at Melbourne is.

Mike Atherton had won the team sweepstake on the big race and young Ben Hollioake was also spotted in the TAB office on the edge of the ground, picking up a handsome reward for a shrewd investment. Sadly, neither of them was due to have similar good fortune on the field of play.

Atherton, indeed, was just starting another painful period in his increasingly mercurial career. Stewart had soon recovered from his back stiffness but there was a worrying vagueness about the nature of his predecessor's injury, officially described as a bruised hip. In fact he was suffering from one of the recurring bouts of back soreness and immobility caused by his chronic illness, ankylosing spondylitis.

One had sensed he was not happy despite the fact that he had batted with typical determination in a potentially very embarrassing England second innings against South Australia at Adelaide. They had made a mess of their first innings, slipping to 22 for four on the first morning against a new ball purposefully used by Jason Gillespie and the fast, left-arm Mark Harrity, and despite some steady bowling in reply, not least by Peter Such, they began batting a second time before tea on the third day with a deficit of 138. On a slow pitch, Greg Blewett had scored a stylish and confident century.

Now England lost Butcher cheaply for the second time in the match and when Hussain, top scorer once more in the first innings, went leg before after ninety minutes' batting and Stewart was also lbw to complete his first pair in any game for England, a big innings from Atherton seemed imperative. He had played well, hitting six crisp fours, but had also bent over in pain from a back spasm at one point, despite doing his best to hide it from both his opponents and the watching press.

His innings was ended by sheer bad luck. Harrity deflected a firm drive by Graham Thorpe on to the bowler's stumps an instant before Atherton, backing up, had replaced his bat. He was given out by the third umpire, apparently, not because the replay was conclusive (it was not) but because he walked towards the pavilion once the umpire on the field, Steve Davis, confirmed that Harrity's hand had touched the ball. It was a little freakish, but these things happen, especially to England, and as it transpired this was not to be the last time on the tour that a third umpire would condemn Atherton at Adelaide in controversial circumstances.

For now, it was his back which concerned him. Towards the end of play on the following afternoon, I happened to be beside the England scorer and tour administrator, the genial, efficient and devoted Malcolm Ashton, just as a courier from the local hospital arrived with a bill for a scan and an injection into Atherton's back. Incredibly, none of the other newshounds in the press box registered the man's arrival or the nature of his business. I was therefore sitting on a potential scoop, but these things have to be checked and, having been on friendly terms with Atherton for many years, I had a quiet word with him at the end of the day.

He confirmed that he had received the medical treatment and that he was struggling but asked me not to write about it, which had to be respected. Many a journalist would have been duty-bound to ignore the request, or at least justified in doing so, but sensational news stories are here today, gone tomorrow, and the respect of a distinguished cricketer and likeable man was not something to throw away, a truth which my own sportsdesk at the *Telegraph* would appreciate much better than most. In any case, I was a little better informed than some when the seriousness of his back pain became public knowledge in Cairns a week later.

Meanwhile, there were consolations in adversity in Adelaide, starting with another steady performance by the bowlers in a third-morning session which saw South Australia losing their last five wickets for 63. Alex Tudor was ill-suited by the pitch but he got a few balls past the outside edge in all his spells and had not done badly in his first game. In the field he showed himself to be quick to the ball and an accurate, strong thrower.

It was certainly not a pitch on which ten wickets should have fallen in a day of clear, warm weather and Thorpe and Ramprakash put things into a slightly truer perspective with an untroubled partnership of 69 for the fifth wicket over the last 25 overs of the day. It still left England with a perilously slender lead of 11 runs as the fourth day began.

Daily Telegraph, Wednesday, 11 November
It would be unwise to read too much into what turned out to be an epic partnership between Graham Thorpe and Mark Ramprakash. The fact remains that they compiled the highest partnership ever scored by any pair of batsmen on any tour of Australia by any national team.

They batted all of the final day together until rain intervened and extended their stand for the fifth wicket, worth 69 overnight, to 377. Thorpe, eventually assisted by some fielding lapses as he raced to his second hundred in 89 balls with four sixes and 21 fours, made his third double hundred and his first for an England team, despite being under the weather with a tummy upset. Ramprakash, only too well aware, he said, that he was not yet an automatic selection in the Test team, made his first hundred against Australian opposition.

When these two last played a substantial partnership together it was in the pressure-cooker atmosphere of a Barbados Test, last March, when they came together at 56 for four and eventually added 205. Yesterday there were fewer than 1,000 in the ground (although 9,500 watched the four days) as Thorpe, pale, unshaven and fortified by Imodium, resumed the struggle on a pitch now completely dead and with never a sign of the one ball of very low bounce which had done for Nasser Hussain on Monday.

The first objective was to bat the 16 overs with the new ball; the second to get through the period which was obviously going to decide whether South Australia could force a victory. Greg Blewett took it as soon as it was available after 80 overs, when England, at 190 for four, were 52 ahead. Jason Gillespie, long-limbed, menacing and eccentric, again bowled with pace to a full length on a remorseless off stump line which not only allowed no liberties but demanded that virtually every ball must be played, whether to left-hander or right. His first four overs with the new ball were maidens before Thorpe was at last able to chop down on a shorter ball and cut it to the third-man boundary.

The cricket was played throughout in sultry weather with rain threatening but it would have been a shame indeed for the two stern-faced heroes, both men to whom the art of understatement comes naturally, had they been robbed of the chance to capitalise on their earnest groundwork. England's 200 took 89 overs, but once lunch was reached at 229 for four, Thorpe 76, Ramprakash 61, it was as if shackles had been cast away.

Thorpe, especially, played like a butterfly emerging from his chrysalis. As always playing the ball from under his nose, he reeled off four quick boundaries to reach his first hundred in 252 minutes, with only nine fours. Under the weather or not, both men continued to run their singles busily and by the time they had finished they had made full use too of the longest straight boundaries in the world, taking the overall count of all-run fours to eleven in the match.

Once the two inexperienced spinners came on for long spells, however, it was the boundaries which began to multiply. Andrew Crook remained tidy enough for an 18 year old off-spinner playing his first senior match but Thorpe took a particular fancy to the unsubtle, flighted leg-breaks of Evan Arnold and four times thumped him with pull-drives into the new seats in front of the Victor Richardson gates. He was dropped at mid-on when 146, off Arnold, and again when 193 off Blewett, who, much earlier in the day, had come closest to dismissing the immaculate Ramprakash when a fierce cut flew through the upstretched fingers of the only slip fielder.

Ramprakash's 100 arrived ten overs after Thorpe's with a beautiful straight drive along the ground played from well down the pitch to Arnold for his 14th four. He, too, was able to relax now but, like Ken Barrington in the late 1950s, he has turned from being a batsman notable for his flair into a methodical one who is extremely difficult to dislodge.

At tea-time Stewart was intending to declare but not until Thorpe had passed by one his previous highest first-class score against Glamorgan in 1997 did the umpires decide that the drizzle had become strong enough to call a halt. Shortly before, Gillespie, who had resorted to occasional contortions of his face or body as he ran in to try to put the batsman off, dropped Thorpe off his own bowling. Oh yes, Australians can also make mistakes under pressure.

Apart from Gillespie and Harrity (still fast but without an inswinger) the record stand was achieved against a modest attack but it has boosted the morale of the touring team at an important time, with only the match against Queensland in Cairns this weekend before the first Test in Brisbane begins on Friday week.

Thorpe said later that his back is still inclined to stiffen after the surgery to correct disc trouble last season. 'This was my first really long innings since the operation and I'm not looking too far ahead at the moment. It was difficult coming from a fast wicket in Perth to a slow one here but it's been good getting used to the conditions and we'll try to progress our performances now through-out the series.'

Ramprakash said that there had been no thought of records until late in the day. 'The first session was quite hard work but we got more relaxed as we went on. We've not played well in this game but we've shown now that we'll be hard to beat. I've played nine Tests in a row now but on this tour I've felt pressure that places are all open again. It's healthy that there is competition. You have to make the most of every opportunity which comes along.'

South Australian attacks better than this one have been plundered in the past, not least when Colin Cowdrey (on his way to his highest score of 307) and Tom Graveney put on more than 300 here in 1962–63 or when A. C. 'Jack' Russell shared a stand of 368 with Wilfred Rhodes in 1920–21. But this was an effort the worthier for the tense circumstances in which it began and England made the long journey north to Cairns today in good spirits.

Cairns was quite a contrast. Few of us had been so far north in Australia before. Suddenly we were in the tropics, beside the Coral Sea, with the Barrier Reef not far off shore, exotic shrubs in flower everywhere, and abundant rainforests leading to the Great Dividing Range inland. There is not much time for such indulgences on contemporary cricket tours but I managed a game of golf on a magnificent new course called Paradise Palms where the consolation for hitting your ball into the trees was a liberal supply of ripe Bowen mangoes blown to the ground by the wind.

The day before the Cairns game was showery, however, and this plus general exhaustion dissuaded any of the players except the enterprising Dean Headley from taking the chance to go snorkelling on the reef. Accompanied by David Lloyd and Malcolm Ashton, Headley enjoyed himself with that gusto for life which makes him such a good companion. He does not, however, have a reputation for being overburdened with grey matter (some of his colleagues irreverently call him 'Headless') and I still do not know if he was joking when, during a plane journey in the Caribbean earlier in the year, he looked up from a newspaper quiz and said: 'Here, C. M-J; you'd know this: one of the Seven Wonders of the World; would it be The Hanging Baskets of Babylon?'

The showers which kept less adventurous players near their hotel were no surprise. The monsoon season was not quite finished and heavy recent rains were said to be threatening the game at the capacious Cazaly's Oval, which is primarily an Australian Rules football ground but an attractive one, fringed by palm trees with hills and rainforests in the distance. The intense heat and large, cheerful, disrespectful, more or less inebriated crowds on the first two days were a good preparation for the imminent Brisbane Test. One leathery-skinned spectator spent much of the time when Queensland were in the field advising the captain in a loud and gravelly voice to 'Put Jimmy Maher on' (Maher being a locally bred hero) but he found time to peer into the press tent, recognise the correspondent of the *Independent* and to delight him with the verdict: 'Derek Pringle. One of the best cricketers the Poms ever had.'

Heat and atmosphere might have been suitable for a dress rehearsal. The spongy, awkward pitch was not.

Daily Telegraph, Monday, 16 November

England's final preparatory game before the Test series which starts on Friday developed by slow degrees towards a surprisingly thrilling climax on the third evening yesterday. Win or lose against Queensland this morning on a pitch on which the ball had begun to keep impossibly low at times, Michael Atherton was bound to be the centre of attraction following last night's decision to call up Graeme Hick in case the former England captain does not recover from his latest back injury.

Atherton was out to his first ball on Saturday, flicking down the leg-side at a ball from Queensland's sturdy, steady but unexceptional medium-paced swing bowler, Adam Dale, whose first innings figures of seven for 33 were a career best. He was unfit to field yesterday and therefore not allowed by tour regulations to bat higher than number seven when England began their chase for 142 to win on a pitch keeping low.

John Crawley, Atherton's probable replacement as Mark Butcher's opening partner in the first Test on Friday – England will certainly be put in if they lose the toss – was bowled for three, making the same mistake as the first three batsmen: playing back instead of forward on a pitch keeping low.

For both Brisbane and Perth this match in Cairns has been a hopelessly inappropriate preparation, other than getting the players used to the heat. It has turned out to be a very tight game on a ground immensely pleasing to the eye but displeasing to players of both sides who have struggled on a slow pitch and a spongy outfield.

After a second day of attritional cricket, 18 wickets fell yesterday, including England's last three in the morning for a further ten runs. Queensland gained a precious first innings lead of 17, despite Matthew Hayden's broken finger. Dale took two more wickets under the gaze of Allan Border to put himself in the running for the first Test team which is named today.

Darren Gough, who again bowled splendidly in the heat, took two wickets before lunch, the first thanks to the low bounce but the second a beauty which knocked out Stuart Law's off stump. Jimmy Maher, the left-hander from Cairns, now played with the utmost resolution and exemplary technique, despite getting a ball on the glove from Gough very early in his innings. Skilfully using the pace of the ball to steer to third-man or leg-glance, he had made 56 out of 99 when he was sixth out, caught in the gully off the splice to demonstrate how increasingly unpredictable the pitch had become.

Robert Croft again gave Stewart valuable variety in the heat but he twisted his right knee when long studs in his new boots stuck in the turf as he pivoted in his action in the last over before lunch. To his credit he continued to bowl, picking up Andrew Symonds at short-leg and Geoff Foley, yet another lbw victim. But as the quicker bowlers finished the job it was clear that 142 runs would not easily be made.

An increasingly excited crowd sensed a humbling of the Poms from the moment that the unfortunate Butcher went back to his second ball from the pacey, uncomplicated Andy Bichel and was defeated by low bounce. Dominic Cork, opening in Atherton's place, now played an enterprising innings in which he wisely got well forward and for a time Hussain played superbly, with every ball ringing out of the middle of his bat. But Michael Kasprowicz removed Hussain, Stewart and Crawley in the space of two overs and when Cork was given out lbw, unlike the others hit on the front leg, the game had veered towards the home side.

Atherton was padded up to come in at the fall of the fifth wicket but with only an over to go his appearance was delayed in order to give him a chance of batting in less discomfort today after a night's sleep.

He duly batted on a tense final morning but he was soon stumped, and in the face of some marvellously well-sustained and accurate fast-medium bowling by Kasprowicz England won in the end only through a spirited and unlikely last-wicket partnership of 36 between Croft and Mullally. Both of them played very well, Mullally indeed well enough to make his subsequent failures in the Test series almost inexplicable.

This was just the sort of game England sides of recent vintage would have lost on tour, especially in Australia. They had been up against a powerful Queensland side on an awkward pitch and in extreme heat. But they got on with it and squeezed home in circumstances which gave everyone's morale a boost at what seemed like the perfect time.

Almost everyone. In the excitement of the finish, watched under open-fronted marquees by a small, enthralled Monday crowd, no one noticed that John Crawley was not on the ground. The previous evening he had been out for a few drinks some half a mile from the team's water-front hotel with various members of the Queensland and England teams. He left with Dominic Cork for the hotel at around eleven and on the corner of a street was accosted by a drunk who apparently asked him if he was Irish and called him a wanker. What seems to have happened then is that Cork, quickly sensing danger, sensibly ran for safety rather than get involved. Crawley is not the sort of person to get sucked into an argument with a stranger but as he moved to escape, the man, who had his back to him, turned and punched him hard enough to knock him to the ground, momentarily semi-conscious. He was badly cut and bruised about the face.

The manner in which England's management dealt with the incident was curious, but had much to do with the fact that Crawley's unknown assailant was an Aboriginal. Crawley left with the rest of the team for Brisbane and it was not until late that night, twenty-four hours after a man with a fair chance of playing in the first Test had been brutally mugged, that the tireless press officer, Brian Murgatroyd, released a statement: '. . . John was verbally abused and then punched by an unknown man, causing him to fall to the ground. He sustained cuts and bruises above the eyes, a cut above his lip, and bruising to the face.'

The mayor of Cairns, Tom Pyne, understandably concerned for the reputation of a town with a big stake in tourism but also something of a reputation for violence, was apparently furious that Graham Gooch, as manager, and Crawley himself had decided to try to forget the matter as soon as possible and not to press any charges. Gooch asked the local

CID, led by the delightfully named Inspector Wardrobe, not to pursue the matter. The snag was, of course, that questions began to be asked and rumours spread. Was Crawley himself inebriated? Had there been any women involved?

It leaked out that Cork had been close to the scene. Inevitably perhaps, in view of the delayed explanation and the absence of a more complete statement, people began to wonder whether the story might have been invented to cover up what had actually been a fight between the two English cricketers. Such conspiracy theories were actually hatched in the UK, not Australia. This very query, in fact, was put to me by a columnist in England, who also reported that there was even a parallel being drawn with the recent disgrace of a member of the Cabinet after a 'gay' encounter with a stranger in a public park.

The truth was simply that Crawley, not, it seems, one of cricket's lucky men, had been in the wrong place at the wrong time. Being, by nature and from past experience, shy of media attention, his reaction was to avoid the cameras and journalists and get on with his preparation for possible participation in the Test in case Atherton did not recover in time and England decided to play seven batsmen. The fact that it was a black man who had inflicted the damage was apparently the main reason for a certain lack of detail in the official descriptions.

Whether this attempt to avoid wider repercussions did Crawley himself any favours is questionable. He had started the tour so promisingly after a brilliant season for Lancashire and the hundred for England against Sri Lanka at The Oval which had earned him the last batting place ahead of Graeme Hick. He was to end it, as he had the previous tour of the West Indies, back in the wilderness of county cricket. Some critics, notably Ian Chappell, were bluntly disparaging of both his technique and his temperament. This was the man Bobby Simpson said had played by far the best innings by any English batsman against the 1993 Australians and whom Majid Khan had recommended for immediate promotion to the Test team when he was only nineteen. Was it Crawley who had failed, or the English system and the intense media focus on the national team which had failed him?

5

Stormclouds Over England: The First Test

CHRISTOPHER MARTIN-JENKINS

Mark Taylor, playing his 100th Test, batting as well as he ever had and in command of a side which had frequently passed the acid test by winning overseas against all their opponents except India in the last three years, had every reason for the honest, cheery confidence he was expressing on the eve of the Brisbane Test.

Taylor was already what the Australians call a champion. That is one step removed from their absolute heroes, who are known as legends, but if Australia were to win the Ashes for the sixth time in a row, and they were four to one on to do so even with the most generous bookies, the apotheosis would be complete. As player and captain Taylor was never to know what it is like to lose a series to England. Since his first blaze of glory in 1989 – 839 runs in eleven Test innings – his batting, with the exception of one almost disastrous slump in 1996–7, had been a major factor in the team's success.

When a fast bowler had to be blunted – Curtly Ambrose, Allan Donald, Wasim Akram, Devon Malcolm – as often as not it was Taylor who did the job, frequently in the first innings of the first Test of a series, when early initiatives are so significant. The battle between himself, Slater and Darren Gough was no less important to the outcome of the series than that between Mike Atherton, Mark Butcher and Glenn McGrath. Atherton had to be tough for all sorts of reasons in his years as England's captain but if 'Iron' Mike was a fitting epithet for the Pom, 'Iron Mark' was no less apposite for the Aussie. Ask anyone who has played with him.

The fifth Australian to play a hundred Tests is as down-to-earth and unaffected a bloke – and bloke is the word – as you could meet. Until recently he lived in an unpretentious house in Sydney's respectable northern suburbs. He could have afforded to move with his wife and two young children, but Mark and Judi liked the neighbours.

Already when the series began he had scored more Test runs, 7,297 at 44, than anyone still playing, but not many people knew it and he was not likely to remind them. He did not look like a great player. Essentially, he limited himself to a solid defence, skilful leaving of the ball early in an innings, and a few bread-and-butter scoring strokes: the pull, the glance off his legs and a drive past mid-off. Nor, largely because he was so undemonstrative, would one have thought of him as one of the great fielders, with his waddle from one end of the pitch to the other and his nickname of 'Tubby'. But by the end of this series he would have taken more catches than any other man in Test history, passing Allan Border's record of 156 catches from fifty-two fewer matches. There may not have been a safer slip catcher in any era.

This determined, shrewd, honest, frequently underestimated cricketer likes golf, fishing, Aussie Rules football and a few days away at a farm in the country. He doesn't use long words, yet I have never known a more articulate or interesting captain in press conferences. He himself seemed to be interested in every question asked and he would answer without hesitation with bright eyes fixed on the questioner with such intensity that it felt rude to make a note whilst he was speaking.

Speaking at the Gabba two days before the Test, he reflected on changes in the game during his four years as captain and ten as an international cricketer: 'I don't go out with the boys as often as I did. As captain you've got to get involved in a lot of the off-the-field activities. I hadn't thought much about becoming captain but when they made me vice-captain I thought I'd like to give it a go. All the players have taken off some rough edges in recent years to become a successful cricket team. Every series is important these days. We talk much more openly than we ever did. We try to win every series we play.'

Australia had not only won but made friends doing it since Taylor took over from Border. The accusations about Aussie sledging were always an exaggeration, he said, and he was happy as long as none of his players lost control. His aim was truly to try to win every game and to entertain crowds in the process. He saw no need for the World Championship of Test cricket which the ICC were considering at the time, with a running league table leading to occasional play-offs for the top four. The need to increase Test crowds was perceived to be greatest on the sub-continent, but Taylor pointed out that Australia played to full houses in India and fullish ones in Pakistan; and he added shrewdly that league tables would often oblige teams to play for a draw.

Common sense is not the least of the attributes of a man who moved from Wagga Wagga to Sydney in the interests of his cricket as a teenager.

and not long after played in a grade semi-final on a pitch which was wet and dangerous at one end. He stood there and made 10 in ninety minutes, refusing ones and threes to protect his mates. He remained firmly in the front line throughout his Test career when the flak was flying.

Asked if the series about to start would be his last, he said that it would depend on results. He could walk away from cricket at any time, he said, because it is just a game and he has never treated it as anything else. He could have gone back to his other profession as an agricultural surveyor but he had made himself too valuable for cricket to let him go. Channel Nine had been paying him for three years when he finally decided to make the switch from pitch to commentary box.

He might have made it after the tour to England in 1997 had he not scored his recuperative hundred in the second innings at Edgbaston after going twenty Test innings without a fifty.

'That was a tough time for me personally but it was a strange time too because the team was doing so well. The captaincy was a bonus then because you could get some enjoyment from the fact that you were leading a side that was being successful. But if I'd missed out at Edgbaston I'd have had to have a very honest appraisal: is the side being affected by the fact that the captain's out of form and if I'm not in the side would the side play better?

'The 129 at Edgbaston wasn't a great innings by any means but I realised that over the six to eight months I'd been batting badly I'd started to look for the perfect innings to get myself out of trouble. I wanted to play the lovely cover drive and the nice square-cut, play the pull well and then hit a nice straight drive straight after that and score this beautiful hundred to say to everyone "hey, I'm back in form". But if I look through my career I haven't played too many innings like that and I don't think many players have. In every innings they've squirted one here, inside edged one there. Since then I've relaxed a lot more and realised that some days you get dropped and make a hundred; other days you hit 'em really well, someone takes a screamer at point and you're out for 35.'

The real test of his priorities had occurred only a month before in Peshawar when he walked off after the second day with 334 not out to his name, equal to Australia's highest score, made, naturally, by Sir Donald Bradman. Taylor was within perhaps an hour's batting on the third morning of passing Brian Lara's world Test record, but with a fine disregard for commercialism he barely even considered putting his own possible immortality above Australia's best chance of winning that game.

'I thought it might mess up their openers, Aamir Sohail and Saeed Anwar, if I carried on a bit to keep them guessing rather than know they'd be batting at the start of the day but then I thought we usually aim to get 600 and we'd got four for 599 so why not declare and get on with the game?'

That was typical of Taylor and the general feeling of 'all for one and one for all' which he had developed in his Australian side was as big a reason as any for his confidence that they would rise to the challenge again. Recently two of his right-hand men, Steve Waugh and Ian Healy, had publicly predicted that Australia would win the series three–one. But without one of their two great match-winning bowlers, Shane Warne, for at least the first two Tests and as inappropriately prepared for the start of this Ashes series as they were for the last, they were vulnerable, or so I believed:

Daily Telegraph, Thursday, 19 November
To achieve parity, or the still greater prize of being the first England team for 28 years and only the fifth this century to regain the Ashes in Australia, Stewart and his fellow selectors have to be positive when they choose their final eleven tomorrow to play on a hard, true-looking pitch which is covered with such a perfectly even spread of dry grass that it might be made not of turf but of light green plastic.

That suggests two things to me, assuming showers and clouds are not to be the dominant weather pattern over this weekend: that bowling will be hard work once the new ball has lost its shine; and that variety will help. Following his much improved all-round effort in Cairns, Robert Croft, who was named yesterday along with all seven batsmen and the four expected fast bowlers, deserves to be given the chance to resurrect a Test career which has been far more successful overseas than it has at home.

True pitch or not there will probably be a result here one way or the other – I expect Adelaide to produce the only draw of the series – and England have to try to win rather than setting out not to lose. The Australian Cricket Board allowed the tour of England last year to be immediately preceded by a demanding tour of South Africa and England duly swept to victory in the first Test at Edgbaston. The board have again done Taylor and his team no favours by agreeing to a tour of Pakistan which, for the Test players also included in the one-day team, lingered on into last week.

Those returning from a succession of high-scoring one-day matches on slow, grassless wickets, include Glenn McGrath, a fast bowler to be mentioned in the same breath as Allan Donald and Curtly Ambrose. He may not have his open-ing partner from 1997 to help him until next week's second Test in Perth because Jason Gillespie is expected to be 12th man here.

McGrath is a high-class bowler with a simple, repetitive action but he only has to get his length wrong here as he did at Edgbaston (2–149 in the match) to squander Australia's best chance of exploiting England's current uncertainty against the new ball. Michael Atherton's back inflammation seems to have responded to treatment this time and he is expected to play but Mark Butcher has recovered only his unblemished features, not his confidence, since he was badly cut above the eye in Perth, whilst being set upon and punched to the ground by a thug has not helped the preparation of the reserve opener and poss-ible seventh batsman, John Crawley.

Crawley could yet play anyway in preference either to Mark Ramprakash or to Butcher, who was hitting the ball freely in the nets at the Gabba yesterday before a prolonged thunderstorm swept in dramatically in the afternoon. Butcher, however, deserves to retain his place given the enterprise with which he dealt with Donald and Shaun Pollock last season and although Ramprakash's best score against South Africa in nine innings was only 67 not out, he has been a stabilising influence at number six in England's last nine Tests.

All the batsmen will have to produce if England are to give their steady but ordinary bowling attack a fair chance. Atherton averages a relatively modest 34 from 24 Tests against Australia, Stewart an unworthy 26 from 19 games. Ather-ton has been defeated by McGrath nine times in eight games but he has to win that battle this time, as well as the one against his back pain, if England are to prosper. Graham Thorpe, by contrast, has relished Australian competition so far – he averages 49 – and Nasser Hussain is playing better than anyone.

At the other end of the team England's hopes rest mainly on Angus Fraser's continuing reliability, on Dominic Cork's contributions with both ball and bat and, above all, on the partnership of Darren Gough and Alan Mullally. The laconic Mullally is suddenly a key man in the England team. Ian Chappell wrote recently that he failed in Sheffield Shield cricket but although there has been some rubbish talked about his 'sudden' discovery of a lethal inswinger, he is a far better bowler since he shortened his run, got closer to the stumps in his delivery stride and strengthened his upper body. He is about to surprise not a few Australians.

Even to arrive at this first and crucial Test match with an undefeated record has required an extremely fallible England team to scrap and scramble. They have not, generally, played very good cricket and especially they have struggled to make runs against the new ball, the period in which most matches in Aus-tralia are won or lost. But they are still looking the hardest and best organised England side of the last decade and the law of averages suggests that they will at last have more than their share of good fortune this time.

The Gabba is a mess at present with the famous Cricketers' Club swept away as the builders turn a ground which still had some character into a concrete bowl. It will hold 50,000 for the Olympic soccer matches in 2000 but for this game its capacity has been reduced by construction work to a mere 15,000. Still, it is the pitch which matters and the groundsman, Kevin Mitchell, who, like Paul Brind at The Oval, took over from his father, thinks it is the best he has produced in six years.

In that time Australia's lowest first innings score here is 379. If England are to win they must reduce that figure and produce a similar or higher total themselves: in the first innings, not the second.

To those with affiliations to either side, there is nothing quite like the feeling of anticipation which precedes an Ashes series. Two evenings before the game both teams attended the only joint official function of the tour (twenty years previously they would have been almost weekly events) in the ornate splendour of the Brisbane City Hall, where the central chamber is shaped like a mini Albert Hall. The England party were subjected to a full dose of Australian chauvinism and the public launch of the marketing theme song for the series, 'Go Aussie Go', sung on stage at the end of the meal by an Englebert Humperdink-type male singer and a massed choir of Brisbane schoolgirls.

The song itself was the latest in a long line of musical aids to the marketing of Australian cricket, stretching back to 'Come on, Aussie, Come on' at the time of the Packer revolution in the late 1970s. Had it been balanced by some appreciation of the tradition of English cricket the jingoism might have been acceptable to their chief guests. But this was probably not the most tactful moment to introduce the theme song for the series, highly effective motivator though it no doubt was as it was played over the public address in the intervals of every match to come, accompanied by replays on the giant screens of moments of Australian triumph like the ball with which Shane Warne dumbfounded Mike Gatting at Old Trafford in 1993.

'Go you gold and greens / Keep the spirit going / Fire all our dreams / The legend keeps on growing' warbled the macho singer and his enthusiastic choir in strains which were to become very familiar. The circumstances of this first outing for the song of the summer put me in mind of the Hitler Youth song which suddenly bursts forth in the classic film *Cabaret* but, happily, there is nothing sinister about Australian patriotism. On the contrary, it is simple and unashamed, and a big part of Australia's sporting success. Men and women brought up in the sports culture would move mountains for their country, whenever they put on the green and gold. Such passion comes less naturally to their English opponents.

Much of the evening had a mildly embarrassing air about it. As they arrived on a humid sub-tropical evening, all the guests were presented with bow ties in the same green and gold, as if it were some hallowed privilege, even for the English. This was naïve rather than calculating. Later, in a generous gesture to which no one could object, they were each given a photograph of the two teams on stage, England in their evening dress, Australia in their – you have guessed it – green and gold blazers.

Those who spoke on stage, including the comedian Campbell Mac-Gregor, with a clever act as the fictional Alf Durand, retired scorer of the 1948 side in England, went down more or less like lead balloons because of a faulty public address system. My own evening, however, was enlivened by the presence in the seat next to me of the New South Wales off-spinner, Gavin Robertson, who had just been brought back into the international fold and had been invited along with the other players newly returned from Pakistan, even though several of them had not been selected for the first Test.

Balanced, intelligent, amusing and observant in his views on both cricket and life, Robertson would have made an ideal successor to Taylor as captain if only he had been able to find a regular place in the Test side. As it was, his only Test experiences had come on tours to the sub-continent where the most important rule in his book for any touring team was never to whinge. Alas, he was to injure himself and take no part when his only chance came to make a mark on the 1998–9 season, in the Australian 'A' team's match against England at Hobart, shortly before Christmas.

The tension around Brisbane seemed to rise between the showers of another warm and humid day before the series started. In the elegant foyer of the Heritage hotel, one of the gems of a riverside development which has helped to transform Brisbane from the hick country town it once was into a thriving modern city, I came across Alan Mullally, pacing up and down like a caged tiger. Was it apprehension, or anxiety for the show to begin? Perhaps it was merely that his dinner companion was late on parade.

Daily Telegraph, Saturday, 21 December

Mark Taylor at the start of the day and Steve Waugh and Ian Healy in an extended final session stood between England and a very good start to the 64th Ashes series. So, too, sad to relate, did the same old English tendency to miss important chances in the field.

Well as Waugh played, he should have been both run out and caught on the way to 69 not out, the top score of an intriguing first day. Healy, too, was missed off a luckless Darren Gough when he was 36. Like Waugh, however, he rose to the big occasion with customary relish and the 68 they added for the sixth wicket in the last 22 overs sliced the gilt from England's gingerbread.

Having lost the toss and been asked to field on a true and not yet very fast pitch, Alec Stewart could feel reasonably happy with a close of play score of 246 for five and a good performance all round by his bowlers. But half-way through the afternoon Australia had been 106 for four and if the chances had all been taken England would have been in amongst a vulnerable looking tail with a hard new ball in their hands.

It was Australia's oldest hands and sagest heads who kept them in the game. Taylor's innings in his 100th Test was typically staunch and Waugh and Healy, with 212 Tests already behind them, demonstrated again what durable, cussed, talented cricketers they both are. But England's effort was a vast improvement on the events of the corresponding day four years ago and further evidence, surely, that it is going to be a series to savour.

One or two close lbw decisions did not go England's way, although a marginal one against Justin Langer did, and there were expert catches by Stewart and Mark Butcher to weigh against the lapses which followed. Stewart, watched by his parents, switched his bowling resources shrewdly and there was encouraging evidence of forward planning in the field placings. For a while there were two short mid-wickets to plug Taylor's tendency to clip in the air and the one-savers made sure they were close enough to prevent most of the stolen singles which all the Australians enjoy.

Taylor bore the brunt of some fierce opening overs from Darren Gough, leaving everything which did not have to be played. In his six-over spell Gough was allowed only five balls at Michael Slater but the ball swung encouragingly in relatively cool weather by the standards of a Brisbane summer: the highest temperature was only 78 degrees.

Slater made 176 in this match four years ago. This time he managed only one back-foot four and another edged at catchable height just to the right of a diving Nasser Hussain at second slip, before, in the 17th over, he drove at the bounce of an off-side ball from Mullally and was deftly caught at head height by Butcher at third slip.

Langer and Mullally, who are both, like Cork and Stuart MacGill, playing their first Anglo-Australian Test, had a close duel, Mullally twice getting past the outside edge, but Langer was still there at lunch and Taylor with him, impassable as a red traffic light.

Langer went two overs after, to a ball which might have missed the leg stump, recompense for Gough for a close call against Taylor in the very first over. He soon troubled Mark Waugh too, with bowling of pace and purpose. Playing too often with his bat divorced from his feet, Waugh still managed to hustle things along to the satisfaction of a crowd filling every available space in a Gabba which has been transformed from a rough-hewn, homespun cricket ground into just another concrete stadium. You can still see a few blooms on the jacarandas and the poncianas, but only just.

By mid-afternoon the Australian-made Kookaburra ball had softened and the occasional edges were starting to drop short, but in the 44th and 45th overs, England struck twice. Flailing at a ball outside his off stump, Mark Waugh was taken by Stewart, low but in both hands, off the inside edge. It needed a few replays to confirm as much.

Taylor had been batting for three hours and ten minutes when, two balls later, he was surprised by a ball of extra pace and bounce from Cork. Hussain clutched the edge to his midriff at second slip. England now had Steve Waugh and Ricky Ponting together without a run to their names and only Healy separating them from the tail. But each unfurled a perfect off-drive for four, Waugh followed up with consecutive fours from Cork off balls too short and wide and Australia, typically, had counter-attacked with 29 runs in four overs.

Only eight balls were bowled after tea before the umpires quite unnecessarily offered Waugh and Ponting the chance to come off again for what was deemed to be bad light. There was a 35-minute delay but all but one of the lost overs were retrieved at the end of the day. England officials have rather wetly refused the idea of using floodlights in bad light during this series, despite a successful precedent last year in Australia.

When the sun came out again Waugh would have been run out for 29 if Mullally's hand had not broken the bails before Stewart's quick and accurate throw to the bowler's end. It was the start of a battle between Waugh and Mullally which became heated when Mullally was twice denied lbws by thin edges onto the pads.

Waugh, his defence as usual completely watertight, loved every moment, of course. He lost Ponting at 178 when he drove on the up low to Butcher at close cover, a brilliant catch because Butcher was moving in quickly, but this was England's high point.

Healy almost immediately regained the initiative with unorthodox, shrewd batting of the kind with which Alan Knott used to irritate his opponents. He had cut and driven his way to 36 when he tried to pull Gough and could only scoop the new ball high towards Fraser at third-man. He dropped it. Soon after, Waugh, now 68, edged Gough low to second slip: Hussain dived forward but could not cling on. Much more of this and England would lose the disciplined bowling and team cohesion which have to be sustained for seven weeks if they are to knock Australia from their perch.

England continued to pay dearly for their failures in the field on the second morning as Waugh and Healy raced each other to their first hundreds against England in Australia. Waugh got there first, but only just, twenty minutes before lunch with the sharpest of singles against Gough, who alone looked likely to break what had become the highest sixth-wicket partnership for Australia against England at Brisbane.

Healy followed him two overs later, having given Waugh a 48-run start when he joined him at 178 for five with the game in the balance. It was Waugh's sixth hundred against England, his sixteenth in all and it pushed his Test average above 50, the benchmark for a great batsman. It says a great deal about Healy that his fourth Test hundred was also his fourth in first-class cricket. The bigger the occasion, the tougher the challenge, the more these two titans of Australian cricket love it.

England were short of luck, tactically awry and increasingly impotent as the dashing Queenslander and his obdurate colleague rubbed more and more salt into the self-inflicted wounds of the previous evening. By lunch-time Australia were 348 for five, their recovery complete and a platform for victory built.

The second new ball was only eight overs old when play started but Alec Stewart gave Gough only two slips and no other close fielders. If this was intended to stifle two aggressive batsmen into making their own mistakes, it failed miserably because 24 runs came from the first four overs as Dominic Cork drifted to the leg stump and Gough was twice edged fine to the third-man boundary through the gap where a third slip should have been.

In his third over, Gough's ill fortune reached outrageous proportions as Healy jabbed the ball quite firmly on to the leg stump via a pad without dislodging the bail. There was no doubt now which way the wind was blowing and after a brief spell from Mullally only the steadiness of Fraser and Croft stemmed the flow.

After a merry afternoon romp from Fleming, Australia finished with 485 and although England's reply was positive there was a portent of things to come when McGrath claimed Atherton in only the fifth over.

McGrath is a friendly country boy off the field but on it, straight-backed as a Hereford bull, he oozes malice to opposition batsmen from every pore. He had an unusual supporter in the crowd that evening, an attractive blonde English girl named Jane Steele, who was soon to become his fiancée. They met when he was playing cricket in Hong Kong in 1995 and she was a flight attendant in her sixth year with Virgin Atlantic. A year later she ditched her job, rented out her house in the Cotswolds and flew to Sydney. McGrath was not there: he was away playing cricket, as he has been often since. But he helped her through a harrowing period when she developed breast cancer and had to face the trauma of a mastectomy and six months of radio- and chemotherapy. Such experiences bring cricket into perspective, even for so furious and dedicated a performer as McGrath.

Later, Jane Steele would tell Louise Evans of the *Sydney Morning Herald* how her cricket-loving father had started to support Australia after years of following England and of her own fierce support for her new country. But it was not always easy: 'Glenn and I can't go anywhere without people coming up and saying, "Shove it up those Poms, make sure you give it to them." I think, "Hold on a minute, don't mind me." And they don't. They never say, "Shove it up the West Indies," only the English.'

It is a graphic enough example of the strange passions aroused by the Ashes contests. Long gone are the days of rest in the middle of a Test match, so Sunday brought no respite:

Daily Telegraph, Monday, 23 November
Test cricket in Australia is always front page news when the home side are on top and England woke to a blaring headline in Brisbane's main Sunday paper yesterday: Poms Get The Shakes. Quite soon, however, the local press will get the message which the Australian players have already absorbed. This is not going to be another easy series. Just to rub it in, Mark Butcher played what in all the circumstances was a great innings.

Only the fifth Test hundred by an England batsman in a Brisbane Test and the fourth at the Gabba, it saw his side most of the way towards avoiding any possibility of following on and firmly reasserted his right to be Michael Atherton's opening partner.

Graham Thorpe, the other Surrey left-hander, was in no less authoritative form and England had duly sailed past the 285 needed to make Australia bat again by the time that a thunderstorm of typical Brisbane intensity had burst around the Gabba from a granite-coloured sky. With two days left it seemed that the only thing which could prevent a draw was one of the sticky dogs which preceded the days of efficient pitch covers.

The tarpaulins were safely in place, however, by the time that it really started raining and this will remain a beautiful pitch for batting. It was beginning to take just a little turn out of the rough by the time that Butcher succumbed to a brilliant caught and bowled by Mark Waugh, the seventh bowler tried by Mark Taylor, but by then Butcher had played the leading part in a team performance of spirit and substance all round.

It exposed Australia, at least in conditions as comfortable for batting as these, as largely a one bowler team. In the absence of Shane Warne only Glenn McGrath was a consistent threat, although Michael Kasprowicz in particular gave him steady support. Jason Gillespie was conspicuous by his absence and Stuart MacGill, with no significant rough to exploit, was not only innocuous but inaccurate.

He offered a liberal supply of full tosses and although one of them accounted for a suitably appalled England captain, who helped it down the throat of deep backward square-leg with the accuracy of a Tomahawk missile, Australia's selectors will be all the keener now to have Warne back in the side for the third Test in Adelaide. Already, therefore, next week's Perth Test is looming as a critical fixture.

With Gillespie back as his partner McGrath will have more support there, so Butcher has done well to rebuild his confidence and self-esteem after his nine runs in five previous first-class innings on tour on a pitch he described as 'very pleasant indeed'. He added, during an engagingly honest and matter-of-fact press interview after his innings: 'the best policy seemed to be to play a few shots'. He certainly did that, hitting 16 boundaries in his second Test hundred in three matches and one which he will especially treasure when he looks back on a career which is blossoming.

McGrath accounted for Atherton once again on Saturday evening, for the tenth time in nine Tests, when a good-length ball left him enough to take a thickish outside edge and fly to second slip. Alec Stewart, too, was out in a manner which might have given him nightmares for the rest of his days had the other batsmen not rallied round his brother-in-law so well. But Nasser Hussain confirmed his good form with a commanding innings; Thorpe, playing at his best and most responsible, was two thirds of the way towards a fourth hundred against Australia by the close yesterday; and Mark Ramprakash played in the same positive vein as the others despite another painful blow to a bruised right elbow.

When Atherton fell in McGrath's third over, a substantial innings by Butcher became almost imperative to England's chances of leaving Brisbane with the series all-square. Helped by Hussain's equally confident and positive batting at the other end, he did himself and his country proud. Playing beautifully straight, moving his feet decisively, never taking his eyes off the short balls which inevitably came his way after his painful experience in Perth three weeks ago, he proved himself again to be not only a top-class opening batsman but also a man of exceptional character and the soundest temperament.

He could not have asked for a truer pitch or a better light in which to bat when the England reply to Australia's 485 began 19 overs from the close of the second day. Alan Mullally had thoroughly earned his first five-wicket analysis in a Test by his control and persistence, but all the England team had had a long grilling in the sun and Butcher and Hussain did well to get to 53 by the close without further mishap.

From the outset yesterday runs came as regularly as the ferries which hurry hither and thither across the nearby Brisbane River. There were 18 fours in a morning session producing 126 runs and two wickets in 28 overs of scintillating cricket. Taylor, ever the attacking captain, helped by leaving the third-man boundary unprotected throughout Butcher's four hours and 40 minutes at the crease and by lunch-time 32 of his 93 runs, and six of his ten fours, had been scored through or just wide of the slips.

This was either bold, or unwisely generous captaincy, according to taste. The fact is that Butcher never gave a chance and that even his edges went along the ground. So sweetly did he time the ball that Thorpe might actually have done him no favours by reminding him, as he raised his arms in restrained triumph after getting to three figures with a classical cover drive off MacGill, to calm down and savour the moment. He hit only one more four afterwards before driving without quite getting to the pitch of an off-break from Waugh and falling to a leaping, right-handed catch.

At 92 Butcher had actually been bowled by Kasprowicz off his pad from round the wicket, but the strapping Queenslander had overstepped the crease with his front foot. Since October, by ICC decree, runs scored off no-balls have been added to the penalty of an extra run, a fact which underlines how wise Bob Cottam has been to insist that his bowlers do not overstep in practice or under match conditions. England bowled only six in 158 overs in Australia's innings.

Waugh's catch and Stewart's aberration apart, Australia took only one legitimate wicket yesterday when Kasprowicz produced two fine balls in succession to end Hussain's fluent 98-ball innings. Surprised by one which cut back off the seam into his thigh pad, Hussain got a thin outside edge to the next, which held its line.

After three days only one wicket had fallen other than to catches: it is that good a pitch. Play was due to resume half an hour earlier today, with another half an hour extra at the end of the day and six minutes at the start of Tuesday's play to make up for the time lost to the storm.

The opening paragraph of this dispatch was not entirely objective, and I was definitely unwise not to temper my observations on MacGill's disappointing start for Australia. The truth was that he bowled far too many bad balls, as most wrist spinners will, but also that England's batsmen failed to take the opportunity to pulverise him as, on this occasion, he deserved. That had far-reaching consequences, because the fact that he had got away with it, and his fortunate dismissal of Stewart, helped him towards an inspired second-innings performance from which he never looked back.

Perhaps I was also guilty, in underlining England's promising batting performance on the third day of the series, of over-reacting to some extremely subjective reporting in certain sections of the Australian press. In the case of one very experienced and respected journalist it was apparently based on his firmly held opinion that England were hopelessly old-fashioned in all things cricketing (perhaps in all things generally) and in particular that arrogant administrators at Lord's had an agenda to avoid contact with the Indians, Pakistanis and Sri Lankans whenever possible. There might have been an element of truth in both opinions – especially the disgraceful failure to offer Sri Lanka more Test cricket in England for blatantly commercial reasons – but my old colleague Mike Coward was protesting too strongly, as I told him a few weeks later after we had been somewhat unlikely members of the same list of lesson readers at the Advent Carol Service in Perth Cathedral.

His unqualified reservations about the quality of this England team were, in any case, about to be triumphantly vindicated for the first, and not the last, time:

Daily Telegraph, Tuesday, 24 November
The Australian team got what one former Test player referred to as a 'spraying' from their captain when they came off the field on Sunday evening. The consequence was a first Test match which advanced in dramatic leaps and bounds towards a potentially quite extraordinary climax today. During a seven-and-a-half-hour fourth day the outcome of the game was amazingly transformed from a probable draw into an improbable victory for either side.

It was Glenn McGrath who made it possible, aided by some heedless English batting. If their opponents got a spraying, all but Ramprakash deserved a positive hosing when England went into lunch yesterday after losing their last six wickets for 60. The old tendency not to sell their wickets dearly enough had got them into trouble quite unnecessarily, albeit against fast bowling of the highest quality.

McGrath was bowling again by the end of the day after a dazzling ninth Test hundred by Slater had given Taylor the chance to throw down the gauntlet with a flourish. Dashing to 113 off 139 balls with 13 fours and a six, Slater knocked the stuffing out of England's fastest bowler, Gough, whose match figures of one for 185 are a salutory warning to him with the fast pitch at Perth beckoning next week. Height is a valuable asset for any bowler on Australian pitches and on this slow surface, with no sideways movement off the seam, Gough's deliveries merely skidded invitingly on to Slater's punishing bat.

Declaring when Australia had extended their first-innings lead of 110 at a rate of four an over, Taylor was able to set England 348 to win in a minimum of 99 overs. It left them plenty of time in fast-scoring conditions if they are good enough but history, of course, was against them.

England would need to score more than any side has ever managed in the fourth innings to win a game in Australia. In the absence of Shane Warne, they might not get a better chance to improve on the 332 they scored at Melbourne in 1928–9 and Atherton and Butcher made an encouraging start in the final seven overs last night, reducing the target to 322.

If by some minor miracle Australia were actually to lose today, Taylor will have achieved the remarkable feat of being mentioned in the same breath as Sir Donald Bradman and Sir Garfield Sobers within the space of a few weeks. The great Sobers has still not been entirely forgiven by some for setting England an achievable fourth-innings target in Port of Spain in 1968.

Now, as then, however, the proper reaction to Taylor's declaration is to praise him for his adventurous approach to Test cricket. He hates draws but he could easily have waited for his declaration until this morning, giving Australia perhaps 30 runs' greater insurance. He has been happy in the past to give his bowlers no more than a day to bowl England out but having seen how feebly their tail succumbed yesterday to McGrath, his confidence was understandably high. He must, also, have weighed the huge advantage of getting either Atherton or Butcher out in the brief twilight session.

Instead the England openers took the scoring opportunities offered by attacking fields and the occasional short or overpitched ball, Atherton removing the spectre of a pair with a decisive cut for four against Kasprowicz and then answering McGrath's first bouncer with a hook which ran quickly to the boundary at backward square-leg and brought the first wave of England's ever optimistic winter supporters to their feet.

The more experienced of the travellers must have known that the odds were on Australia, especially if McGrath could repeat on the fifth morning his dominating performance on the fourth. Running in with ramrod straight back, bowling flat out with his high action yet with a plan behind the line and length of every ball, he began by giving Thorpe every chance to hook. For a while he was resisted but, having missed with his first attempt, Thorpe hit the second, played at head height from just outside the off-stump, straight to square-leg.

McGrath now dealt with Cork with summary efficiency. Cork has the ability to be a Test number seven but whether he has the nous is questionable. For an over he evaded the short stuff competently enough but, needled by a few well-chosen words from McGrath and unable to resist the temptation to turn this into a trial of strength when he would have been better defending until the bowler had shot his bolt, he tried to pull a short ball, only the eleventh he had faced, and spliced it weakly to mid-on.

Croft showed that he has learned to handle the short stuff better in a stout 51-minute innings and Ramprakash continued to play everything on its merits, only once in trouble when Kasprowicz surprised him with a quicker bouncer. He responded with two hooks for four but Kasprowicz brought one back through Croft's gate before McGrath returned to finish the innings with clinical efficiency.

As at Trent Bridge last season, Ramprakash was left unbeaten but McGrath still took his last five wickets for nine runs off 35 balls. Darren Gough alone was unfortunate, given out by Darrell Hair despite being at full forward stretch. There is no justice sometimes for tailenders.

Much worse awaited Gough against the rapier blade of Slater's bat. The early start provided for in the regulations as a result of the previous evening's storm meant that 71 overs still remained of a day of steamy heat and in circumstances made for his buccaneering style Slater enjoyed himself memorably.

He started with a blazing array of cuts, drives and whips to leg, taking 27 off Gough's second and third overs. So well did he play on a pitch still blameless that it made little difference when Taylor played an inswinger on to his stumps in Cork's second over. Justin Langer settled neatly into the role of left-handed assistant whilst Slater, his footwork nimble as a dancer's, raced to 71 of the first 100 in 26 overs, constrained only by Alan Mullally's thoughtful and steady bowling and, for a time, by Angus Fraser's length.

Croft bowled steadily for 20 overs against a light breeze from the Stanley Street End, but such turn as he managed from the rough was slow and Slater and Langer worked him around easily enough. The Gabba is a big enough ground to give spinners a chance but Slater hit him straight into the second tier of the Clem Jones Stand before reaching his hundred off 129 balls and celebrating with a trademark kiss of his helmet and another blown to his wife on the terraces. He hit three more fours before giving Fraser a knee-high caught and bowled.

Croft's only reward was a skier from Langer, caught on the run by Mullally at mid-on. Mullally also managed to frustrate the Waughs with shrewd defensive bowling, sufficiently at any rate for Taylor to decide that the time had come.

Of course, England had no realistic chance on the last day, but English optimists could not help hoping. By mid-afternoon, hope had turned to prayer.

Daily Telegraph, Wednesday, 25 November

Armageddon arrived twenty minutes before tea at Woolloongabba yesterday, not a moment too soon for an England side struggling desperately for survival. The long expected storm saved them at 179 for six, their barely credible pursuit of 348 long since forgotten. England thus take their unbeaten record with them to Perth today, according to Alec Stewart rescued by rain for the first time in his 82 Tests.

They were overdue some help from the weather, although they scarcely deserved it. Not since The Oval in 1989 have England enjoyed such assistance when in mortal danger, although at Lord's last year Australia would probably have won had there not been only an hour and a half's cricket on the first two days. By contrast, England would have had a great chance of beating the West Indies at Bridgetown and South Africa at Edgbaston had it not rained on the last day.

Yesterday, with a minimum of 30 overs remaining and the last two batsmen of any serious pretensions together, Australia would surely have won this first Test if the game had gone the distance. They gave their opponents a severe mauling in the later stages of an excellent game played on an ideal Test pitch, which began yesterday to take some sharp spin. Once Glenn McGrath had extended his domination of Mike Atherton, it was the combination of the inexperienced leg-spinner Stuart MacGill and the off-breaks of Mark Waugh which looked like putting the gloss on two days of irresistible Australian cricket.

As the light faded before the storm, obliging Mark Taylor to keep McGrath out of the attack, MacGill emerged as the likely match winner, spinning his leg-break sharply and defeating Nasser Hussain with a classical googly. Instead of playing in the second Test at Perth on Saturday, however, he will be bowling for New South Wales against Western Australia at Sydney. Because of Perth's uniquely fast pitch, Colin Miller of Tasmania, the utility bowler who switches from seam-up to briskish off-breaks, has been called into an otherwise unchanged Australian 12. Jason Gillespie is equally certain to play in place of either Michael Kasprowicz or Damien Fleming.

England set out yesterday merely to 'be positive' and see what transpired. Fleming was given the first chance as McGrath's opening partner and he swung balls past the edge of both Atherton and Mark Butcher but it was at the other end that the battle was really tense. Determined not to be bullied by his tormentor, Atherton took the short ball on three times in McGrath's first over, hooking him twice for four, but when the bouncer was offered again in the tenth over of the morning, he was unable to roll the wrists and lifted the ball high to Fleming, five yards in from the long-leg boundary.

Incredibly McGrath has now dismissed Atherton 11 times in his last 15 innings against Australia. He got Brian Lara five times in nine innings here two years ago but it is doubtful if one bowler has exercised quite such control over another top-class batsman over so short a time span. Alec Bedser famously got the wicket of Arthur Morris 18 times in his 21 Tests, which is probably the nearest parallel.

It was a different game now, for all the brilliance of the hook with which Nasser Hussain despatched McGrath's next bouncer, well in front of square-leg. From the moment that MacGill took over, Hussain's command was less obvious and Butcher, having played beautifully straight against the quick bowling, was not quite so convincing with the spin biting. After 28 overs of sensible accumulation he was given out lbw when what to him was an off-break hit him on the back leg. Three overs later Stewart's rotten run with the bat continued when he thrust forward at Waugh and was caught off pad and bat at silly point.

Graham Thorpe battled for 11 overs after lunch as Hussain's partner but in the 11 which followed both these two and Mark Ramprakash were defeated. Thorpe was caught off the face of the bat at short-leg, Hussain failed to spot the googly out of a now murky background and cut onto his stumps and Ramprakash tried to move his feet to the pitch of a leg-break, only for sharp spin to pass him.

Had England agreed to use the floodlights – a development which both Taylor and Stewart supported in principle – Taylor could now have called back McGrath and 20 minutes would not have been lost to bad light before tea. Cork and Croft did well in this uncertain twilight period, however, and not long after the umpires decided that it had become too dark. It was quickly obvious that there could be no further play. Within minutes of the rain's arrival the Gabba was under water.

It was the luckiest of escapes for England, not just because of yesterday's events but because they fell into so many of the traps which have swallowed them up in the recent past. They dropped catches – by far the biggest reason for the plight they later found themselves in – batted on the fourth morning as though the game was safe when it was not and proved vulnerable once more to the two types of bowler they do not themselves possess: a leg-spinner and a match-winning fast bowler.

The selectors will surely now be right to take a chance with Alex Tudor. If so, they must decide whether to risk him in a fortified batting order. There are precious few laurels on which to rest and something has to be done to shake Australia from their familiar, confident stride. It is possible that if Tudor is nervous he might prove a costly mistake but he bowled with encouraging control on the flat, slow pitch at Adelaide, his pace is unusually fast and both his bowling and his demeanour in practice have impressed everyone around him.

The bold eleven for Perth would therefore include John Crawley instead of Croft at seven and, more debatably, Tudor in Angus Fraser's place, leaving Cork to bowl into the breeze. The WACA is a ground where, in the words of Justin Langer, bowlers either have to pitch the ball up or bounce it at head height. In his last Test there four years ago, Fraser's match figures were 53–14–158–3.

His reappearance against Western Australia three weeks ago was not a happy one – none for 128 – and although he is a far more consistent bowler than Cork there is clearly a case for leaving Fraser out just for this one game. Horses for courses, as the Australians say. Tudor and Crawley for Fraser and Croft would sharpen the fielding, too.

6

The Broadcasters' View

CHARLES DE LISLE

'There's no more exciting time in cricket than the start of an Ashes series,' says the television reporter, 'and the Australian captain has managed to coincide it with his 100th Test.' So begins a first Test preview presented by the most surprising member of the media corps, Ian Healy, Australia's superb wicket-keeper/batsman. Viewers of Channel Nine's *National Nine News*, broadcast at six o'clock on the eve of the match, then see Healy interview his captain, Mark Taylor, beside the swimming-pool at the team's hotel in Brisbane. The questions are, understandably, friendly enough, but the report is punchy and highly professional; his use of the verb 'coincide' would offend the purists, but would barely raise an eyebrow in many Australian newsrooms.

After asking Taylor how he had survived his 'career-threatening slump' with the bat (in 1996–7), Healy, wearing a crisp light blue shirt, says confidently to camera: 'There's plenty of mutual respect between the two skippers, and Alec Stewart is looking for some Taylor-like grit from his own out-of-form opening batsman Mark Butcher.' There follows a clip of Stewart – not, presumably, interviewed by Healy – saying, presciently in the case of his brother-in-law, that 'mentally strong people always come through bad patches' before Healy signs off, like any other reporter, 'Ian Healy, *National Nine News*.'

While Healy cannot be an objective reporter, his piece is more balanced than much of the press coverage. And it is not a one-off: during the season he previewed all five Tests, and commentated on one-day internationals, as part of his contract with Kerry Packer's Channel Nine. His colleagues Taylor, Steve Waugh, Shane Warne and Michael Slater have also had contracts with Nine for the past few years: it is the station's way of stimulating extra interest in its cricket coverage, and of developing a new generation of talent. On his performances so far, Healy must be comfortably the favourite to slide into Richie Benaud's shoes whenever he decides to retire.

Within half an hour Channel Nine is again underlining the high profile which cricket enjoys in Australia – and the gift for promotion and, frankly, gimmickry which the station regularly employs in its ratings struggle with two very similar commercial networks. In another scene unimaginable in Britain, the country's leading daily current affairs show, *A Current Affair*, is presented direct from a floodlit Gabba. About a third of the half-hour programme is devoted to the Test. Urbane presenter Ray Martin, a television personality so widely admired that he is known (to his irritation) as 'Mr Australia', is unashamedly partisan. 'They'll try anything, these Poms,' he says, 'even employing Australian spinner Peter Philpott to teach English batsmen how to play Shane Warne – just in case.'

However, the centrepiece of the feature is an interview with two old sparring partners about to be reunited in Nine's commentary team. Ian Botham and Ian Chappell had a celebrated row in a Melbourne bar at the time of the Centenary Test of 1977. Versions of the contretemps still vary, but Botham has said that he warned Chappell to cool his 'Pommie-bashing', then, when it did not stop, he threw a punch at him and, finally, under further provocation, he 'exploded' and chased the former Australian captain into the street. Things only calmed down when a police car drew up. 'I haven't had many words with him since,' Chappell said when Nine announced their pairing. 'It would suit me if I never spoke to the guy again.'

The joint interview is faintly embarrassing, each Ian looking uncomfortable, arms folded, and slightly bored as the other answers a question from Martin. Botham is the more conciliatory, saying: 'Well, I think we probably know a fair bit about the game between us, so, yeah, you'll have an English opinion and an Australian opinion.' Asked if they would be 'having a beer together after play', Chappell says firmly: 'I won't be.' Botham neatly sidesteps the question, replying diplomatically: 'I'll have a glass of wine.'

In the event, Botham and Chappell's much-hyped 'own Ashes battle' is a damp squib. As the two take their seats for their first session together, Channel Nine's commentary box fills up with staff from BSkyB eager to see the action off the field for themselves. But if there is no warmth, there are no fireworks either. Late on the first day, as Healy and Steve Waugh put down the foundations of their big partnership, there is even a hint of an easing of tension. 'I agree, Ian,' says Botham, telling viewers that Alec Stewart should indeed be a 'little bit more aggressive' in his field placings. By day three, Graeme Koos, Nine's executive producer, seems to have decided the stunt is scarcely worth persisting with.

Channel Nine is one of four broadcasters covering every ball of the Test live, the others being BSkyB, Australia's ABC Radio, and of course the BBC's *Test Match Special*. Nine, which provides the BBC with its thirty-minute highlights package, is relying heavily on what it calls its 'core four' commentators: Richie Benaud, its 'host', Tony Greig, Bill Lawry and Ian Chappell. However, mindful that it is nearly twenty years since the last of these – Chappell – left the Test arena, Nine also fields Simon O'Donnell, the former Test all-rounder, and the player more talked-about than any actually on the field in Brisbane, Shane Warne (though he is unable to commentate on days two and three owing to his participation in a club match in Melbourne).

Like their counterparts from Sky and the ABC, the Nine team is operating from a well-positioned commentary box on the main deck of the new Northern Stand. These boxes are not too high, have excellent views of the ground, are right in line with the wicket, and have ready access to the press box, players and officials. They are generally reckoned the best on an Australian Test ground. Not so fortunate is *Test Match Special*, which finds itself allocated a distant, slightly cramped box at the very top of the stand. Not only is this too high a position for the taste of most of the BBC team, it is also a climb of several minutes away from any fellow broadcaster. This is a particular nuisance for the BBC's cricket correspondent, Jonathan Agnew, who is also commentating for the ABC, and for the ABC's Jim Maxwell, also a member of the BBC team. It also means that, when thunderstorms stop play on the third and final days, reaching the BBC's eyrie involves a drenching. 'I think we're up here because Sky have got a radio box,' says Peter Baxter, the BBC producer. 'These are minor irritations but the authorities want shooting for not making more provision for the media in a spanking new facility like this stand!'

There is also an overlap between the voices heard on Channel Nine and Sky. Botham and Chappell also appear on Sky, though to his credit John Gayleard, the executive producer, does not put them on air in tandem. 'I think we probably get more out of them by not having them on together,' he explains, adding: 'Nine have just done it as a promotion, as a bit of a gimmick.' The incisive and urbane Mark Nicholas, covering his last Test series for Sky before moving to Channel 4, presents the coverage, his fellow commentators including Allan Border, Paul Allott and Bob Willis. Meanwhile, Charles Colvile is busy conducting interviews with players and management, and reporting for Sky's news programmes.

Despite the remoteness of its position, its only immediate neighbours a room occupied by the TV replay umpire and the match referee, and a police post, *Test Match Special* begins the match in cheerful mood. There is an atmosphere of 'first day back at school' as Agnew, Henry Blofeld and my co-author are reunited with their regular summarisers Mike Selvey and Vic Marks, Baxter and scorer Bill Frindall. The third summariser is Jeff Thomson, whose laid-back style was such a success with listeners during the Ashes series of 1997 and whose knowledge of Brisbane's sub-tropical conditions is second to none. Although Blofeld is later to mention that it has taken him a day to get properly into his stride, he sounds as perky as ever as he takes listeners into the lunch interval – 2 a.m. in the UK – describing how, 'with the soup almost being put on the luncheon table', Taylor, on 30, is 'not to be tempted' by an offering from Angus Fraser.

Away from the microphone, Thomson makes it clear that while he enjoys commentating, he is only watching the match because he is being paid to do so. 'If I wasn't doing this,' he says, 'I wouldn't be watching, I'd be getting on with my life, doing the things that I do. I don't just sit down, turn on the TV and get enthralled in the Test. For me to watch somebody play out there they've got to be – as far as I'm concerned – up to the standard I like. If I don't rate what's going on out in the middle, and I'm not commentating, I don't bother watching.'

Warming to his theme, Thomson, now silver-haired, goes on: 'It's like when I retired. I used to watch Viv Richards bat, but when he got out I turned the set off and walked out. I wasn't interested in watching anybody else.' Which present-day batsmen does he consider worth watching? 'Occasionally I might watch Mark Waugh or Tendulkar go mad, because they're entertaining, but generally unless people come up to my standards, I'm not really interested. At the moment there are a handful of players that are really world class. The others do a fine job, but I think the standard's generally slipped, unfortunately, since the era I played in.'

A few minutes after lunch Tim Lane, on the ABC, articulates to his listeners every broadcaster's overriding priority – an exciting match. 'I'm not parochial,' he says. 'I like the broadcast to go well and if the game's good, the broadcast goes well.' Meanwhile, summariser Peter Roebuck, the former Somerset captain who has recently become an Australian citizen, is getting some stick about his new allegiance from Jonathan Agnew. With commentary from the lively, authoritative Jim

Maxwell, and equally pertinent summaries from Dean Jones and Bob Massie, the ABC's line-up is a strong one. The organization, which has been covering cricket since the early Bradman era, is proud of its tradition of ball-by-ball coverage 'untainted' by the commercials which interrupt Channel Nine's broadcasts after almost every over.

The ABC is, however, dependent on Nine for a 'feed' from the pitch microphones. It receives a sanitised version of what is going on out in the middle – a version edited by Nine. The editing ensures that almost no 'sledging' or swearing can be heard by ABC broadcasters, let alone listeners (or Nine viewers). With the sound on the microphones turned down until the moment the bowler delivers the ball, most of what is broadcast consists of the sound of the bat striking the ball, the ball thudding into the wicket-keeper's gloves, the 'keeper shouting encouragement to the bowler, or the fielding team appealing.

The nerve centre of Sky's operation is a truck parked near the nets at the Gabba. It is from this vehicle that John Gayleard directs and produces their coverage. Gayleard's loyalties are divided. Born and bred in Sydney, he worked on Channel Nine's cricket for years, starting in the World Series Cricket period, before moving to Sky five years ago. Ginger-haired and ginger-bearded, Gayleard, forty-four, is a forceful personality from a different professional culture from most of those involved in the BBC and ABC productions.

As England and Australia limber up on the field, an hour before the start of the second day's play, I make my way to the Sky truck. I am to spend a morning watching the production team in action. Gayleard, in shorts and a T-shirt, and his 'vision mixer', Lisa Collette, are already seated in front of a bank of some twenty-five monitor screens. The pictures Sky will be sending home will be essentially those provided by Nine, enhanced by special footage from Sky's own three cameras. 'We personalise Channel Nine's coverage for our own market,' says Gayleard. 'They're very parochial, and that's fair enough. We use our cameras to illustrate things that our commentators specifically want to talk about, and for interviews.'

The first event of the morning, Ian Botham's pitch report, is successfully recorded, although it takes three takes to get it right. Gayleard drives the operation forward relentlessly, issuing instructions to the commentary team, his two cameramen and one camerawoman, Nicholas, Colvile, and Sky's headquarters in west London. He also tells Collette which camera angle or replay he would like her to switch to next. Both jobs require fierce concentration and rapid reactions, since the average ball involves six 'camera cuts' – more if something happens – and there is only a commercial break every twenty minutes or so, and when a wicket falls.

After some forty minutes, with the Waugh–Healy partnership already past the 100 mark, Gayleard is becoming restless. 'Give me some crowd!' he shouts into his microphone. Camera one responds with a shot of a suitably striking female spectator. 'Oh, look at that, spunky!' cries Gayleard, and one can almost hear brighter-eyed viewers on the other side of the world echoing his laddish excitement (it is only 12.40 a.m. in the UK, and it is Friday night).

Gayleard describes his task as being '80 per cent entertainment and 20 per cent information'. He adds: 'The kids and the female audience are a very important part of what we do. But I think all viewers like having the intricacies of the game explained.' To this end Gayleard makes good use of his own three cameras, one high at each end of the Gabba, and one down on the boundary. One can only admire the skill with which those operating the cameras follow the ball all round the ground – and Australian grounds are big. You also have to remember that the camerapeople are doing this with black-and-white viewfinders. At this Test, Gayleard's only complaint about the 'feed' from Nine is that the latter has chosen to position both its stump cameras at one end of the wicket, rather than one at either end. But then he has the distinction of having been the first person ever to bowl at a stump camera. It was more than a decade ago. Nine was pitch-testing its prototype 'stump-cam' and Ian Chappell was the batsman. 'The stumps weren't hit,' admits Gayleard, a one-time grade cricketer.

Shortly before lunch, Ian Healy becomes surely the first television reporter to score a century in a Test which he has previewed. Gayleard, only too aware that the session has been disheartening for his viewers, wants to liven things up with a pre-lunch interview with Geoff Marsh, Australia's coach, but even with both batsmen in three figures, he is not interested.

In Sky's commentary box, after the interval, the frustration of Messrs Nicholas, Botham, Willis and Allott with aspects of England's performance in the field is evident, at least away from the microphones. As the ball yet again flies off the edge through where a third slip would be, during the Healy–Fleming stand, Allott cries, 'Why, oh why, oh why?' Botham, biting his nails at the back of the box, chimes in: 'Jesus Christ!'

The team agree that Mark Butcher, at fourth slip, must be moved to third. As Nicholas points out on-air, a bowler's main objective is get the batsman out bowled, lbw or caught close to the wicket from a thin edge. It stands to reason that more edges will go to third than fourth slip. It is a simple point made effectively, and leaves one in no doubt that the commentators desperately want England to prosper.

Topics of conversation off-air are probably not very different from those once aired in the dressing room by these stars of yesteryear: who looked 'peaky' this morning, where they should dine this evening – Willis spends part of the afternoon flicking through a restaurant guide, looking for a suitable venue – and plans for those parts of the Australian Summer when they are off duty. There is talk of golf – Botham's great obsession these days – and of the early morning tennis matches Willis and Gayleard play with Graham Gooch, the England tour manager. And there is more cricket talk, including discussion of the possibility of bringing Alex Tudor in for the next Test, though someone is worried that the new boy might go for 'six an over'.

As commentators, Botham and Willis are a slight disappointment. Although highly professional, they are somewhat bland, lacking the out-spokenness of their more stimulating newspaper columns; perhaps, on-air, they are too anxious not to treat their successors with the contempt which Ray Illingworth and Fred Trueman sometimes showed the Botham–Willis generation of England players. All the same, Botham has a nice, humorous turn of phrase – 'buffet ball' is a favourite – and is remarkably unegotistical, rarely referring to his own playing days. Meanwhile, Ian Chappell is sharp, laconic and fiercely patriotic. 'That's the thing about this Australian side,' he will say. 'They've got a lot of ways of beating you.' Border, however, is not a natural behind the microphone. He is inhibited, though maybe with good reason: he is an Australian selector. Whether this role should exclude him from the com-mentary box is a moot point, though one cannot question the impartial-ity of his comment to Sky viewers as Australia sail towards 450: 'The pendulum has stuck.' Not that Border's double duties preclude a little relaxation. Later in the series, in Adelaide, he was 'caught' watching the golf on television in the media hospitality area, his back turned to the action in the Test. When it was suggested that he might be neglecting his work as a selector, he had a ready answer: 'I'm not the selector on duty.' How does he find commentating? 'Playing cricket is bloody hard work,' he says, 'but commentary is a piece of cake.'

That may be, but as in Britain, some cricket lovers prefer to turn off the sound on their television sets and listen to the radio commentary instead. The ABC's ball-by-ball coverage is relayed around the continent through 260 transmitters, and can be heard by 99 per cent of the population. Speaking as England press serenely towards 300 on the third day, Alan Marks, who has produced the programme since 1978, says that compared to *Test Match Special* the ABC places less emphasis on entertainment and more on information. One of the reasons for this is that listeners are spread across five time zones, and a high proportion are tuning in and out all the time. So Marks reminds his commentators that the score must be given at least once every ten minutes. He says he is not sure that Australian audiences particularly want a *TMS*-style approach: 'I think the entertainment value of the coverage, while it's important to us, is perhaps considered more important among the British than it is by Australians, who really just want to know the score, who's in, who's out, and how the game is changing.'

Even so, the ABC's approach is more relaxed, less straight than it was five or ten years ago: it seems that audiences reared on a pretty factual style of sports reporting have responded favourably to the slight loosening-up. As ever, team selection has played its part. 'Very, very deliberately,' says Marks, 'we've chosen commentators with different skills and different styles. Tim Lane is a raconteur, well read, knows the history of the game, and Jim Maxwell is the purist, who just loves the game.' Until 1997 ABC's 'entertainer' was Neville Oliver, who joined *TMS* for that summer's Ashes series, but following his departure it is, perhaps, Agnew who is taking up that baton. He seems to be making an impression on Australia. Within a fortnight he is being identified on a television news bulletin as the 'new cult figure' from Blighty.

Agnew is at the ABC microphone on that third afternoon as flashes of lightning traverse the sky. Marks takes a call from a local Internet site which tracks lightning strikes. In a flash, so to speak, he is on air himself, announcing that 'there have been 103 lightning strikes in the last five minutes to the south and to the west of Brisbane, and in fact there have been over 400 lightning strikes in the last 45 minutes'. 'Good grief, that's terrifying,' exclaims Agnew. 'Where are they landing?' 'Fortunately not at the Gabba, not yet,' replies Marks, drily. As he correctly forecasts, off air, it will be a matter of minutes before the players have to come off for the day. At about 4 p.m. they do so. Half an hour later, the broadcast over, Dean Jones returns from a visit to another box with some major news. 'Botham has ordered two bottles of nice white wine for Sky,' he says. 'Nothing changes!'

The following day, I take a look at things from Channel Nine's angle. Shane Warne is back behind the microphone, and while he is a good, lively talker, his performance lacks the bite of his bowling – as it must, given that he is far from retired from the game. His commentary stint over, he makes clear where his true loyalties lie by joining his team-mates in the 'dug-out' to watch Australia take command of the game. Meanwhile, Messrs Benaud and Lawry are telling viewers that the Test has had just about everything. The phrase used is a rather unBenaud one – 'a standard of excitement'.

Nine's main innovation this season is a disc-based video-recorder which allows instant access to any ball in the match; it used to take up to half an hour to locate a given piece of videotape. The new equipment is used to good effect as Ian Chappell talks viewers through the 'mental errors' which have left England struggling to save the Test. The expressions on the faces of Alec Stewart, after Alan Mullally's fluffed attempt to run out Steve Waugh, and of Angus Fraser, after he dropped Healy at third man, also on the first day, are two of the match's most memorable images. This technology has also enabled Nine to introduce an 'On This Day' feature – though for some reason Australia's bad days are usually left in the archives.

As for the commentators, it is noticeable that Tony Greig and Bill Lawry – celebrated for his cries, 'Got him, yes!' and 'It's all happening' – no longer goad each other the way they have during past Ashes series. 'In the past we tried to push that angle, and they were playing up to it as well,' says Graeme Koos. 'But now they've probably said it all.' Despite their ages – at fifty-two, Greig is the youngest of the 'core four' – Koos retains faith in his ageing team's audience-pulling power. 'Our commentators have become bigger than life in some respects,' he argues. 'Every year Bill Lawry has become more Bill Lawry, and Tony Greig has become more Tony Greig. That's why we're so reluctant to change them. They work as such a good team, such a good balance.'

It can be argued that, unlike their counterparts with public broadcasters, commentators on Nine and Sky are under commercial pressure, at times, to make a game appear more exciting than it is. This is not a problem in Brisbane, where the match does indeed have pretty well everything except a fitting climax, but it is a suspicion which Koos perhaps inadvertently confirms. 'A commentator never wants to be telling the viewer that something is bad, otherwise what you're saying is that the game's ordinary,' he says. 'You never want to be telling people that. You want to tell people that there's better to come . . . you can criticise Glenn McGrath's batting all you like but if somebody's in a bad patch of form, you want to push the fact that the next ball could be something very exciting or very good.'

On the final day, as the risk of an England defeat increases, I return to the *TMS* box. Baxter is aware that between lunch and tea – 2.40 a.m. and 4.40 a.m. at home – his audience is at its lowest, and maybe consists mostly of 'long-distance lorry drivers on the M6'. But, he adds, there are many more people waking, checking the score, then dozing off again. Many cricket fanatics, though, set their alarm clocks for 5 a.m., to hear the last session, and from 6 a.m. the audience swells considerably as people rise 'quite normally'. This morning, with England six wickets down not long after lunch, there is a considerable danger that listeners (on Radio 4 long wave) will wish they had opted for the extra hour's sleep.

As Henry Blofeld says, the big question is whether the forecast storm will reach the Gabba in time to save England. An hour or so after lunch Jeff Thomson, at his elbow, predicts that the players will have to go off in thirty minutes. 'Thommo' is almost spot-on – actually it is thirty-five. The match's second storm provides some spectacular television pictures, though Nine's coverage is briefly interrupted when lightning strikes its control van, blacking out Richie Benaud. The people behind the pictures are left feeling cheated. 'It's a disappointment when you do four and three-quarter days' work, and then it's an anti-climax,' says Gayleard. 'You don't like to see a game of cricket spoilt by rain, but from a Sky point of view I suppose it's mostly good that England got out of it with a draw.' It is also good for the game – if not necessarily the television companies – that there has been so little controversy requiring resort to TV replays.

For Mark Taylor, his 100th Test does have a climax. As his post-match interview with Greig draws to a close, he is ambushed by a team from Australia's *This Is Your Life* (Channel Nine again, inevitably). That evening, instead of the sponsors' dinner he was expecting, Taylor is in a Brisbane television studio talking about how he came to carry out with such distinction what the programme calls 'probably the second most important job in Australia'.

7

No Respite: The Second Test

CHRISTOPHER MARTIN-JENKINS

It would have been possible to fly from London to Bombay, or, if you prefer, to Barbados in quicker time than it took the England and Australian teams, and the media entourage which went with them, to travel from Brisbane to Perth. If the England team had any consolation during a trip lasting twelve hours, it was that the man who had been spinning them to defeat when the storm arrived at the Gabba had been dropped.

Stuart MacGill, who as a promising youngster four years earlier had accepted an English invitation to be a net bowler in Brisbane, to help them prepare for Shane Warne, was on the verge of becoming a regular Test matchwinner. His omission was a case of Australian pragmatism at its shrewdest. Whereas England selectors, with a wide choice of cricketers who are much of a muchness, are seldom absolutely sure what their best eleven for a particular pitch may be, even on home territory, the Australian committee seemed throughout this series to get everything right, not least in sticking by Justin Langer as their number three when there were various apparently more talented alternatives.

Three men did the job, a smaller committee than England had had until recently. Trevor Hohns, in his fourth year as chairman, worked in harmony with the coach, Geoff Marsh, and with Mark Taylor, both of whom had been his team-mates in England in 1989 when Hohns, though his was a brief international career, played in five of the six Tests, took eleven inexpensive wickets with his leg-breaks and averaged 31 with the bat. His colleagues now (apart from Marsh and Taylor, not on the committee but always consulted) were Andrew Hilditch, in his third year, a representative from a less settled period of Australian cricket but, as Bobby Simpson's son-in-law, a man steeped in Australian cricket lore; and Allan Border, the captain who, with Simpson at his elbow, had turned the tide Australia's way with such a vengeance in 1989 and beyond. Border had been allowed to carry on as a television commentator and newspaper columnist, which was useful to the committee when it came to explaining the reasons for a controversial decision like the one involving MacGill.

His omission was really no great mystery, and it was interpreted to MacGill himself, the Paddy Ashdown lookalike who was known to have a fiery temperament (he had been banned from two different leagues after incidents in England), in such a way that he took no umbrage. He duly picked up another handful of wickets in the Sheffield Shield whilst the fast bowlers were cutting swathes at Perth. Jim Higgs, another former selector, was the only leg-spinner from any country to have enjoyed a serious success in a WACA Test, and that only once. The great Warne averaged 35 for his 17 wickets there in six Tests and another renowned matchwinner in suitable conditions, B. S. Chandrasekhar, had the embarrassing analysis of one for 181 from 49 overs in his only match on the ground.

Into MacGill's place, therefore, came the jolly rover, Colin Miller, to bowl his mixture of outswingers and off-breaks and, first, to have some fun with a local journalist. Cornered for his comments on a first home cap on arrival at Perth ahead of the rest of the team, he told the eager young reporter that he not only bowled fast and slow but left-handed as well. He often bamboozled his colleagues in the nets, he said, with various varieties of left-arm spin. Into the paper it went but there was no sign in the nets the next day of a versatility which would have put him in a higher league even than Garfield Sobers.

Australia made one other change: instead of Michael Kasprowicz it was common knowledge that Jason Gillespie would also get his chance to renew a career that had peaked on his last appearance against England in Leeds the previous year. The amiable 'Kasper' had bettered Gillespie's seven for 37 in the England first innings at Headingley with seven for 36 at The Oval but at the WACA when there is grass on top of a surface like polished teak it is a case of the faster the better.

England's logical counter was to give Alex Tudor his first cap, but they kept their hand covered until the last possible moment. Like his Barbadian father Daryll, one-time London bus driver, now a pillar of the backroom staff at The Oval, there is an impressive dignity about young Tudor off the field and the senior members of the touring party were delighted with his attitude – an all-important word in English professional cricket. Ashley Cowan, the Essex bowler in whom similar hope had been invested on the previous tour, had not impressed the senior professionals in the same way. Tudor himself had been pleasantly surprised by the way he had been absorbed at once into the team atmosphere. 'The other bowlers have been helping me from the start and I feel part of the team. I'm surprised how easy it was to settle in.'

There had been no sign, during extensive net practice or in the match against South Australia, of the stress fracture on his left foot which had kept him out of Surrey's side from the end of July. Shortly before he had made his first acquaintance with Bob Cottam in a 'one-to-one session' which left an indelible mark on both parties. The coach was impressed by his speed, his good, natural, orthodox action and his willingness to learn. Tudor immediately accepted the need to stop bowling no-balls, evening out the steps on his run to the wicket and hitting the crease at a spot sufficiently far back to be able to concentrate on the business area.

Graham Dilley had been his first bowling mentor at Surrey, drumming it into him that his pace was natural and that rhythm was the key, 'not running in like a lunatic and trying to bowl with a quick arm', as Tudor expressed it early in the tour. Tricks of the fast bowler's trade, including a slower ball flicked off the back of the middle finger, had been coming his way from England's conscientious new bowling coach from the first nets of the tour in Perth, but Stewart, who had seen Tudor have some wild days at The Oval, was the least convinced of the tour selectors that he should be given his chance, even on the fastest pitch in the world.

His caution was misguided but it was also understandable. Tour after tour here England had sent a bowler whom they hoped might emulate the great West Indians by giving Australian batsman the hurry up, but although each in turn had had his moments, none of them had been able to develop into a major Test bowler. Norman Cowans in 1982–3 had a good match at Melbourne; Philip DeFreitas played an important supporting role on Mike Gatting's tour four years later and, although he was never the tearaway those who selected him had probably hoped he might become, he developed into a fine craftsman, contributing mainly with the bat to the unexpected win in the Adelaide Test in 1994–5 when Chris Lewis and Devon Malcolm, two further examples of the genre, bowled Australia out in the fourth innings.

Malcolm bowled very fast at times on successive tours to Australia, not to mention in other parts of the world, and his inspired nine for 57 against South Africa at The Oval in 1994 ensured his place in history but, as Ray Illingworth for one tried in vain to point out, his was not an action which allowed consistency. Tudor's is, and although he was destined to play in only two of the five Tests, he learned sufficiently fast to encourage the hope that if he can be kept fit and fresh enough he might become the desired role model for the black youth of London, something which none of the others quite managed. His two clubs in Surrey, Spencer and the West Indian community side Old Castletonians, had both left him in no doubt before he left that they would be willing him on.

Not too much, however, could be expected of Tudor on a first Test appearance. It was Darren Gough to whom England looked for an immediate improvement on the Brisbane experience. On the flight west he was still quietly marvelling at the audacity of the man who had been chiefly responsible for his deceptively horrible match analysis of one for 166. Michael Slater had been through a sticky period in his career until his recall as Taylor's partner for the tour of Pakistan which preceded the current series. The plunderer of 623 runs and three hundreds in the previous home series against England had been dropped for impatience and it had hurt. By his own high standards, and the prolific scoring criteria of the Sheffield Shield, he had hardly demanded his recall even now. In England on tour in 1997 and again as an overseas guest for Derbyshire in 1998 he had done only fairly well, averaging only 19 on the tour and a modest 35 the following season to finish sixty-first in the national averages. The other Australian batsmen in county cricket – Langer, Lehmann, Bevan, Moody, Boon and Law – were all in the top forty.

Back on the hard pitches of home, however, this batsman of irresistible charm was scintillating once more. No modern player, with the possible exceptions of Brian Lara or Sachin Tendulkar, is more thrilling to watch. Reflecting before the century at the Gabba which had consolidated his position again, Slater said that he did not think he had changed much during his eighteen months in the wilderness. 'Whenever you go to the crease,' he said, 'shot selection and judgement are the keys. I've learned it's a simple game made complex by the people around it. I got a lot of great advice and a lot of advice which wasn't so good.'

If that was stating the obvious, so was the self-analysis of his approach – his 'attitude' as his opponents would express it: 'I play for Australia with a passion and love every ball. You miss it because there is nothing better. I'd love to play a hundred Test matches. It's what I'm aiming to do.' In the circumstances it was strange that Slater's name was never mentioned as a possible future captain of Australia. Like Taylor, he is a man who seems to have time for everyone and his enthusiasm for cricket is unquenchable.

Although the constant travelling was to get too much for him by the end of the fourth months in Australia, the same applies to Gough. His face on the plane to Perth was already mahogany brown, his ready smile consequently dazzling, as he interrupted attempts to read his first grown-up book, the life story of Arsenal's centre-half, Tony Adams, to voice his thoughts about the prospect of renewing battles with Slater and the rest so quickly. Gough had enjoyed his bowling at Perth against the West Australians, but not the English catching. He knew that every chance would have to stick this time.

Everyone knew that. For all the English relief that they had got away with it at Brisbane, it was hard to be optimistic.

Daily Telegraph, Friday, 27 November
Mike Brearley's first touring team to Australia 20 years ago remains the only English side to have won a Perth Test match and the chances of Alec Stewart's team improving the record in the second Test starting at the WACA tomorrow are small. The WACA pitches lost a little of their pace and quality some years ago but they are uniquely quick again now and the high bounce gives the home side a definite advantage.

Add this to the indisputable evidence from the first Test that Australia continue to be the stronger side in all departments and it is clear why the TAB, the equivalent of the Tote, put a full page colour advertisement in yesterday's *West Australian* newspaper enjoining readers in huge letters to 'Do Something Nobody's Done For Years – Bet On The Poms'.

At no more generous odds than five to one against, however, even the thousand plus who have travelled to Perth to support England might feel that the money is best kept in their pocket. The only dangers to Australia, it seems, are over confidence with the bat on a rock-hard pitch on which even the best players may need some luck early in an innings, and some injury to Glenn McGrath.

There is another way of looking at it, however: namely, that England were saved by the rain in the first match at Brisbane, and are not incapable of repairing their errors here. They certainly played some poor cricket, missing two crucial catches on the first day, batting brainlessly after Graham Thorpe had fallen to McGrath in the first innings, and inadequately against Stuart MacGill's increasingly dangerous leg-spin in the second. The positive approach is certainly the one which will be stressed to his players tonight by Stewart himself, chastened though he is by the way Australia suddenly lifted their game on the fourth day at Brisbane.

Stewart is badly in need of runs himself after the double failure at the Gabba which reduced his average in Tests in Australia to an unworthy 22. If he does not get runs here he will have to take seriously the view that it is asking too much of a captain to keep wicket and bat at number four in the heat of an Australian summer. But as he points out with that dry wit which endears him to

Australians, he has not taken much out of himself while batting on this tour so far. A single fifty in Cairns and a sparkling 74 on his former club ground at Midland Guildford in the one-day game with which the tour started are the only times he has broken sweat.

If he could get in at the WACA, with its pace and even bounce, one would have thought this a pitch ideally suited to Stewart's style. He loves a true surface on which the ball comes quickly on to the bat. Both because of his associations with Perth and the conditions, he will not get a better chance to lead from the front and, having been out cheaply to Craig McDermott in both innings eight years ago and subsequently missed the match because of his broken finger last time, this will be his last opportunity.

Graham Thorpe, though he was worried about a stiff back yesterday after the long journey west in a cramped aircraft seat, scored 123 here in 1995 and Mark Ramprakash made 72, despite which England were bowled out for under 300 in their first innings. To compete this time, England will need to blunt McGrath and the returning Jason Gillespie with the new ball and earn a substantial first-innings lead. Although Miller is an unknown quantity with his swing bowling into the wind and his aggressive and progressive off-spin, he will cause less consternation, surely, than MacGill.

It is time that the latent power of the top six batsmen was released together on a decent attack but, just in case, it is likely that Crawley will be grafted on at seven, leaving Ramprakash to bowl the off-breaks instead of Croft. The indications were that Headley, not Tudor, would be the first choice as replacement for Fraser, but Cork may not have done enough at Brisbane to retain his place as the all-rounder and Gough, Mullally, Headley and Tudor is the quartet favoured by at least one of England's tour selectors.

None of the fast bowlers can be expected to turn the heat back on Australia unless the slip catches are held. Four years ago, when McGrath was a tyro but still took three wickets in each innings, Slater was dropped so many times on his way to his third century of the series that he was embarrassed. Devon Malcolm, although he dropped the easiest of them himself, bowled very fast but without luck and Gough had much the same experience here four weeks ago against Western Australia.

Gough still took four for 73 in the first innings. In a way his confrontation with Slater will be no less important than McGrath's with Atherton and Butcher. Slater simply mugged Gough at the Gabba last Monday and it is the pace at which he scores which makes the dashing little New South Welshman not just so entertaining to watch but also so especially valuable to Australia. He buys the bowlers time to win.

Not only has Slater scored nine Test hundreds in his 41 Tests, but five innings of 90 or more too. An enterprising statistician worked out yesterday that this makes him, judged by the percentage of his innings over 90, the sixth most effective batsman in Test cricket, bettered only by Bradman, Headley, Weekes, Walcott and Sutcliffe.

Woe betide England, therefore, if they do not catch Slater the first time that he edges something towards the slips tomorrow. With no leg-spinner in the Australian side and the tendency of the pitch to get slower and easier as the game goes on, the chances are that they will choose to bowl first if Stewart should win the toss. He is starting to look like a lucky captain, so perhaps the bookies will get some optimistic investors after all.

Pause for hollow laughter! Stewart lost the toss, although time would show that he was only just warming to his task. In this particular game, it was not one of the more significant examples of his misplaced faith in 'heads', but, once again, England were to start the game so badly that they did not give themselves a chance. In another familiar repeat of so many Test build-ups in recent years, they were obliged to start the match without a key batsman.

Atherton's back was more or less behaving itself but Graham Thorpe's developed spasms after the long flight across the continent and Graeme Hick, hopelessly under-prepared to bat against McGrath and company, had been told to stand by. The WACA pitch was both harder and easier than most for a man about to be plunged into a Test match ten days after his arrival. Its pace made it harder to adapt to than most; but its trueness and even bounce was, in fact, not unlike that of the indoor nets on which Hick had been keeping his game in trim, just in case.

The team had swapped the elegant modernity of their first Perth domicile for the rather more garish attractions (to some) of the Burswood Hotel and Casino, a couple of miles from the ground across the glistening blue water of the Swan River. The approach to the Burswood is undeniably impressive, a wide, palm-fringed drive leading to automatic doors past so many brightly coloured bedding plants that it would be possible to open a couple of garden centres with only half of them. The huge, echoing foyer within, lit by high, sloping glass walls, has all the intimacy of an airport check-in hall, but the players approved of their spacious bedrooms.

For those not attracted by the gambling opportunities, the hotel had its own golf course, but the cricketers had no time for either distraction: they were too busy with their preparations for a match likely to prove crucial to the outcome of the Ashes. Journalists, fortunately, can be more flexible, given the time difference which in this part of the world pushes deadlines dangerously far into the small hours of the morning. I managed to fit my writing duties around a memorable game of golf much further afield, at The Vines, in amongst some of the earliest of the Western Australian vineyards which, further south beside the Margaret River, are now producing some exquisite red wines.

The four-ball included Mike Selvey, a sturdy seam bowler for Middlesex and, briefly, England, now a writer of flair for the *Guardian* and an accomplished golfer with a fastidious and intelligent approach to the game's problems. My partner, however, had greater local knowledge. Richard Duldig had run The Vines for a number of years and succeeded in making money out of the combination of hotel, homes and two expensively maintained golf courses which are produced as the composite course on which a major professional tournament is held every January. These sorts of 'resort' project are not by any means always potential gold-mines, whatever the attractions of their location, and in Perth there are problems for any sporting enterprise because of the smallness of the population: just over a million. That is, two thirds of the total number of souls in Western Australia's vast acres.

For all the smallness of the market there are no fewer than sixteen similar courses in and around Perth. The cricketers were to get an unexpected chance to play on one of them, when the Test match ended earlier than scheduled. I took the same opportunity to play, albeit on a much older course, Royal Perth, with my *Test Match Special* colleague, the former England off-spinner Vic Marks. Royal Perth lies to the south of the city, near the club at which Vic had based a very successful season in Shield cricket at the peak of his career, and it is a marvellous test of golf in the wind which always blows at some time of the day here. In particular, it gets to the truth about everybody's ability near the greens. Amongst the well-known royal courses around the globe this one is laid out, I believe, in a smaller area than any. It is a model of design, making the most of its sandy soil, native bush and natural slopes.

I seem, however, to have a penchant for unintended comedy at this place. Years ago, on another tour, I had come to the tricky little par four which, early in the round, leads downhill to a green perilously close to a busy road and had failed to play my second to the wide side of the dog-leg. To put it more truthfully, I had put my ball behind a small gum-tree and left myself a stroke requiring such a draw back into the green that only Seve Ballesteros or someone equipped with a boomerang rather than a wedge could have managed it. The consolation, as I boldly prepared for this impossible shot, was that I was using a hired set of golf clubs. When I broke the shaft of the club in two against the trunk of the eucalyptus, however, it became an expensive and embarrassing mistake. I blamed it on a bad shot, of course, not on imbecilic strategy.

This time the farce was less predictable. Driving off towards a tree-lined fairway early on the second nine (with our match as nail-bitingly close as my occasional friendly head-to-heads with Victor usually are), I made good contact but the ball made equally firm acquaintance with a willowy looking tree on the extreme right of the fairway. (I like to draw my drives back into the middle of the fairway, in my imagination at least.) The ball became invisible after being so discourteously intercepted on its way to the intended target and there were perhaps five seconds of total silence as player and opponent searched for a ball curving back into the fairway. Instead there was a sudden, but barely discernible, plopping sound some ten yards behind the tee from which I had driven.

The ball had been catapulted back so far that I played my second from just behind the tiger tee. Modesty forbids a detailed description of how I subsequently halved the hole. Honesty, however, compels the admission that I eventually lost the match itself, albeit narrowly.

We had enjoyed a similarly close contest at Royal Cape Town on New Year's Eve three years before, another match not to be forgotten, but for quite different reasons. We had started a little late in the afternoon, changing our shoes in the men's dressing-room and eschewing any assistance with the carrying of our clubs from any of the caddies who usually line up in droves in countries where the discrepancy between rich and poor is marked. The sun was close to setting when we finally made our weary way off the eighteenth green almost four hours later. It took some time, however, to dawn on us that everything was strangely quiet around the club house. I tried the door of the dressing-room without luck, whereupon Vic went in search of a drink from the bar. But there was no barman; not even an open bar.

The course had been closed, and in South Africa, with its high crime rate, that means not just locked doors but barbed-wire fences. Bizarrely, with night falling and New Year's Eve celebrations due, we were shut inside a golf course with our clubs, neither a drop to drink nor a bite to eat and not a soul anywhere within sight or sound. The situation was saved only by the fact that we had ordered a taxi in advance and as we were discussing possible means of escape we eventually heard the purring of an engine in the car park outside. We yelled at the driver to wait and I ordered Vic, who is shorter than me, to climb on to my shoulder and thence on to a flat roof above the dressing-room. I passed the two sets of clubs to him, one by one, then clambered up myself, with much leverage from Vic, on the roof. The procedure was then reversed as the driver, rather bemused but mercifully obedient, helped first our clubs and then ourselves into the car park below. It had to be champagne after that.

Modern cricket tours are so intensive and the cricket so all-consuming that one needs an occasional respite like this to keep things in perspective. For players constantly under the microscope of media and public attention, it is not so easy.

Daily Telegraph, Monday, 30 November
Thirteen wickets made the first day of the WACA Test remarkable and exhilarating enough but the pace became white hot yesterday afternoon as Australia collapsed from a virtually impregnable position, reasserted control in the field through Damien Fleming and then in evening light of the purest clarity reeled afresh before a volley of daring strokes by Graeme Hick.

It was cricket to refresh the soul, like a country walk on a flawless spring morning. Australia still held a two-run advantage with only five more wickets to take but there had been a time when it seemed that the ground on which Barry Richards scored 325 in a five-and-a-half-hour day, and Steve and Mark Waugh compiled the highest fifth-wicket partnership ever made, might also be the first to stage a two-day Test since Australia overwhelmed New Zealand at Wellington in the first season after the Second World War.

England managed to take the game into the third day not because Australia bowled any less venomously nor caught any less reliably than they had in blowing the batting away for 112 in the first 39 overs of the game on Saturday, but because they managed to some extent to learn from their mistakes. The bounce off a good length, or just short of it, is so steep and fast that to anything but a straight ball the only absolutely safe stroke is no stroke at all. Mark Ramprakash took that in and despite being cut on the chin in only his second over at the crease on Saturday by a nasty lifter from McGrath he batted longer than anyone in both the England innings.

This may be the fastest pitch in the world, by a distance, and its bounce is reliable, but in this match at least the movement off the seam and the swing through the air make it one on which only the fullest half-volleys or the longest hops can be safely driven or pulled. The bowler who has done best is by no means the fastest. Fleming had taken nine for 62 when he was rested after a new-ball spell of four for 14 in England's second innings yesterday, bowling hit-the-deck swing and seam of the type which Ken Higgs occasionally purveyed for England off a similarly economical run-up and with an equally strong body action.

For England, on the other hand, raw pace was the eventual answer, although Alan Mullally bowled with verve and no luck. The Australian wickets fell in a heap after lunch to bowling of high pace from both ends, a happy vindication of the decision, from which the tour selectors so nearly shrank, to give Alex Tudor his first Test cap at the age of 21. His immensely promising return of four for 89 was reward, too, for the foresight of the national selectors in picking him for the tour in the first place.

150 for three overnight, Australia made only 44 more runs in 30 overs in the morning as they battled against excellent bowling to extend an overnight lead already worth 38. Mark Waugh added a mere 15 to the 19 he had scored with breezy insouciance the previous evening. Never in command yesterday, he still played with great care and patience. But he and his colleagues abandoned their careful approach after lunch with spectacular results. Trying to blast the new ball away but instead getting a potent dose of their own medicine, they lost their last six wickets for 46 in ten overs against the second new ball.

Tudor bowled very fast and very well too and Darren Gough at last had some reward for bowling which has deserved better all tour. The slip catchers have let him down badly and when he himself dropped a straightforward high catch at long-leg off Tudor from Ricky Ponting's top edge, it was the sixth chance of varying degrees of difficulty which England had missed. The most expensive of them reprieved Mark Taylor, dropped by Hick off Gough when 38, and Steve Waugh, who escaped a slash at Mullally when he was 11 which Mark Butcher at third slip could not lay a hand on. Taylor and Mark Waugh made similar chances look easy.

Hick and Butcher both made amends during the afternoon crash which showed that Australia could be just as reckless under pressure as their opponents. Only Ponting, who may not have touched the ball from Tudor which climbed past his chest, was unfortunate. Until the second new ball, Taylor's sturdy innings and England's imperfections in the field had combined, it seemed, to remove any serious chance of an England recovery.

After the two bursts of vivid action in which they excelled yesterday, the new-ball blitz and the late flurry of strokes by Hick, England nevertheless started the third day with hope by no means abandoned. Even if they are easily beaten today, they will be able to draw considerable consolation from these two counter-attacks and especially from the emergence of Tudor.

The innings which set the pattern for the match, England's first, was written in the runes; all the more clearly from the moment that Graham Thorpe withdrew with his stiff back and Taylor won the toss. With two exceptions, John Crawley, who batted like a man in panic, and Hick, who got an outside edge to his second ball to give Ian Healy one of his five catches, the top-order batting was flimsy rather than inept. Australia bowled superbly at or just outside the off stump and the close fielders caught with wonderful facility.

There were only two partnerships of any substance, both involving the stoical Ramprakash, who soon found in Thorpe's absence that batting at number five for England can be much like batting at six: he still played his innings throughout as if perched on the edge of a precipice. Stewart, who for just on an hour drove and pulled splendidly, was threatening a memorable attacking innings when the steely Glenn McGrath bowled him off his pads with a ball which cut back. Only Ramprakash, who needed six stitches in his chin, and Tudor, confirming his all-round ability, batted for long after that.

Fleming dealt even more summarily with the start of the second innings. Butcher was squared up and edged to third slip; Nasser Hussain was, given earlier rejections, unfortunate to be given out playing forward; and Stewart sliced a back foot force off a thickish edge to the redoubtable Taylor at first slip.

Mike Atherton averted the humiliation which threatened at 15 for three, striking some handsome shots after tea before Fleming found his outside edge with movement off the seam on a good length. For 16 overs Crawley also played much more soundly than in the first innings until Colin Miller, turning to his off-breaks, made his first mark on the game with a ball which bounced and turned a fraction to take the inside edge of a defensive bat and carry via the pad to short-leg.

In the 11 overs which remained, Hick made his long journey worthwhile. He square-cut his first ball from Miller for four and, after Ramprakash had survived a confident appeal for a legside catch by a dissenting Healy off Miller, launched a magnificent assault on Jason Gillespie. In successive balls, all short but fast, he pulled over square-leg for six, square cut for four and pulled again for a still more emphatic six, well in front of square and far into the seats on the Swan River side. For a crowd of nearly 18,000, it was a rousing finale.

It had been a hectic weekend as well as an exhilarating one and St George's Cathedral was just the place in which to reflect. The Dean, John Shepherd, an Australian who had previously been chaplain at Christ Church in Oxford, had persuaded David Jenkins, the former Bishop of Durham, to preach on the Test match Sunday four years previously. His sermon was stimulating, but no more intelligent or thought-provoking than several I have heard from Shepherd himself. Without offending the most traditional of Christian thinkers, for example, he managed to explain the second coming of Christ at Advent as being not a literal return to earth but a coming again to each willing individual soul. At once those inclined to be concerned by the problems of a strict literal interpretation of the Bible must have been encouraged to think again.

The scholarly dean's morning sermon this time had been full of cricketing analogies and terminology and the lesson readers at the Advent Carol Service in the evening included Ian Brayshaw, a stalwart of Western Australian cricket, whose son, Jamie, had followed him both into first-class cricket and to the media, John Moody, the gentlemanly father of Tom, the current State captain, and John Inverarity, revered as a leader as both cricketer and headmaster.

The chief pleasure from the service, however, was the music of the St George's Singers whose quality would not, at least to my untutored ears, have disgraced any much larger English cathedral. Pitch and tone under the direction of Simon Lawford were lovely in a church of simple beauty built over eight years in the 1880s.

Next morning, England faced music of a different kind.

Daily Telegraph, Tuesday, 1 December
England batted until the stroke of the scheduled lunch interval yesterday but once the alliance of Graeme Hick and Mark Ramprakash had been broken by Jason Gillespie, Australia's victory in the second Test became inevitable. Robbed by the storm in Brisbane, they were not to be denied here after bowling England out in three hours on the first day, although they lost three wickets in making the 64 they needed and batting continued to demand razor-sharp reactions on a pitch which has cost the Australian Cricket Board an estimated £90,000 in revenue lost over the last two days.

The Waugh brothers saw Australia safely to the one–nil lead they deserved despite a wicket each for Gough, Mullally and Tudor, whose first Test appearance has been the main consolation in an England defeat which leaves them with little realistic chance of regaining the Ashes. The end came at almost exactly the halfway point of the scheduled playing time, after 47 overs on the third day.

By batting for just on four and a half hours for his 47 not out, Ramprakash displayed once again his grit and watertight technique. Introvert that he is, he is content at five or six in the order but there is a case for his promotion to number three where, perhaps, he might be in a position to prevent a crisis starting rather than reacting to the one which has occurred.

Hick again batted boldly yesterday, enjoying some luck on the way to the highest score of the match. A top-edged hook and an elegant off drive off Glenn McGrath took him to 50 off 54 balls. He had been booked on a flight home last night but he will stay for the rest of the tour now and very probably take part in the remaining matches. His has been an extraordinary career from the start and by his resolute attacking batting here he has extended it again. Graham Thorpe's back condition is still giving cause for concern.

Whatever Hick's shortcomings have been, only a batsman of genius could pull a bowler of Gillespie's pace off the front foot as he did on Sunday. But Gillespie provided the final thrust when, coming on for McGrath after he had bowled nine testing overs from the River end, he hurried Hick over another attempted force off the back foot and a thick edge flew to third slip.

Dominic Cork, despite being late on a hook and sustaining a black eye as the ball lodged between his helmet peak and grille, kept Ramprakash spirited company for ten overs until he missed an inswinger of full length. Gough lasted one ball, Tudor two and Mullally, somehow, four, before falling to a feckless slog played from a foot outside his leg stump. This was the man who had batted for 78 minutes at Cairns and said afterwards: 'We have got to get runs down the order. It turns games.'

Despite this sorry cave-in, England were not in the final analysis humiliated, but they have no excuses. Had they fielded first when the pitch was slightly damp after a brief and unnecessary late watering, it just might have been a different story but Stewart admitted yesterday that he would have batted in any case had he won the toss and conditions were not that much more comfortable for batting on the third afternoon than they had been on the first morning. Eight more wickets fell in less than three hours of cut and thrust cricket yesterday.

Australia hit back from being one down in England last year to win three matches in a row and England showed a similar resilience last summer when one behind against South Africa but it is hard to see them cracking the Brazil nut hardness of Australia's cricket now. With two good pitches expected in the next two Tests at Adelaide and Melbourne before the spinners get their chance at Sydney in early January, England's best chances may already have gone.

So far only their bowlers have performed at their best. For this match at least they could have done with Andrew Caddick's mean bounce in place of Cork's relatively innocuous swing but it is in batting and fielding that Australia have been so clearly superior. England lost by playing strokes inappropriate to the uniquely bouncy WACA pitch and, once again, by coming a poor second to Australia in the decisive area of close catching.

It has happened far too often, in both countries, for it to be a matter of chance. In two Tests to date, the first of which they deserved to lose, the second of which they did, the number of catches missed and half chances not accepted is already well into double figures. At Brisbane Michael Slater dropped a catch at mid-wicket; here Steve Waugh was unable to cling on to a stinging hit to his left in the gully. Otherwise Australia have been infallible.

This, really, was the difference at the WACA, where the slips and gullies were in constant expectation of the fast flying edge. A three-innings match over five days might have become a real cliff-hanger! Nine of the 13 Australian wickets were caught behind the wicket on the off-side as it was. Until Gillespie blasted out the tail yesterday with three wickets in an over and four in six balls, 13 England wickets had fallen in the same area. Hick took a fine low catch yesterday and Atherton, having stood at first slip throughout, held a blinder high to his left, the only chance he got all match. But Ian Healy, Mark Waugh and Mark Taylor are all so sharp they would catch horseshoe bats at dusk.

Much rubbish has been written in the Australian press about England. In the Rupert Murdoch-owned newspaper *The Australian*, one writer said they were 'psychologically devastated', another that 'their ineptitude has been breathtaking and should lead to the inquisition to end all inquisitions'.

Mark Taylor is better informed and much more realistic. He said: 'We're in a good position. I thought Perth and Brisbane would be the two pitches to suit their bowlers so I'm delighted to be one up but there are still three Tests to go. We've got the momentum at the moment but that can change so it's very important we don't let that happen. The one thing we did better than England in this game was to hold our catches.

'We've definitely got a psychological advantage, there's no doubt about that; we've built it up over ten years; but England played well at times in this game. Tudor did a very good job. I was hoping for a bit of loose stuff but he didn't bowl it.

'Provided we keep playing as well as we can I think we're going to be very hard to beat. It's almost a belief that you know you're going to go out there and take a wicket or you know you're going to get through a tough period when you're batting. If you don't have that belief it won't happen. I think player for player we're a better side than England but that doesn't mean we'll always win series or win matches.'

Having won this match they will surely also win this series, or at least not lose it. Tudor's emergence as an opening partner for Gough has long-term significance, however, if England can somehow keep them both fit.

8

The Groundsman's Story

CHARLES DE LISLE

At twenty-eight, Richard Winter is young for a head groundsman, and even younger for the very demanding job into which he was thrown in May 1998. It is Winter's task, as 'Head Curator' at the WACA, scene of the second Test, to restore Perth's reputation for producing the world's fastest, bounciest and truest wickets. Over the past decade and a half, WACA surfaces have generally fallen well below the very high standards set by the late Roy Abbott, Head Curator from 1951 to 1981. His wickets helped launch Dennis Lillee's career in the 1970s; it was on a flint-hard Abbott pitch that Roy Fredericks smashed 169 for the West Indies, reaching his century in 116 minutes, off 71 balls, against Lillee and Jeff Thomson at their fastest, in 1975–6. Since the mid-1980s, the Perth pitch has been unpredictable. Its most dependable feature was the emergence of spectacularly wide cracks after a day or so of play. During the West Indies' victory over Australia here in 1996–7, Curtly Ambrose was run out after his bat became lodged in a giant crack. There are genuine fears that Perth will lose its automatic right to a Test each year, in the face of a big push from Hobart for extra Tests, unless the wickets improve, and matches last long enough to please the crowds, the marketing men and the sponsors.

What makes the Perth wicket unique in the whole cricket world is the high clay content of the local soil. Known as 'Harvey River' soil, it is 80 per cent clay, whereas Australia's other major grounds are all between the high 50s and the high 60s. As a result, the WACA wicket bakes a lot harder. The process is intensified by the climate, with more sunshine than other cities, less rain and stronger winds – notably the 'Fremantle Doctor', the breeze which blows diagonally across the ground each afternoon. It is an excellent growing environment, one in which couch grass ('warm season' grass) grows vigorously. But Harvey River soil is very difficult to work with, and things can easily go wrong. None the less, these ingredients, combined with tailor-made preparation methods, provided the recipe for surfaces that have the commentators dipping into the vocabulary of other sports – from tennis courts to trampolines.

If Richard Winter is a good name for a groundsman, Richard Spring would be perfect for the one in Perth.

Old hands in Western Australia (WA), such as John Inverarity, say that these bouncy wickets are 'not just a WACA phenomenon, they're a Perth phenomenon'. Inverarity, who captained WA as well as representing Australia as an all-rounder, is now headmaster of Hale School, Perth. *His* curator is the illustrious John Maley, formerly of World Series Cricket as well as the WACA. 'Our wickets at Hale School are very, very similar to those at the WACA,' says Inverarity. 'If John Maley was asked to prepare a wicket for a Test here starting on Saturday week, he would produce a wonderful bouncy wicket which everybody would rave about and which would last for a week. It's as simple as that.'

The situation Richard Winter inherited was unpromising. His predecessor, David Crane, had departed by mutual agreement a couple of weeks before the Test against New Zealand in November 1997. A farmer, he was regarded as a good, but not outstanding, curator over his three or four years in the job. But he resented what he saw as interference from Chris Smith, the South African-born former England opener who was then chief executive, and resigned. So desperate were things that Les Burdett, Australia's leading curator, had to be called in from Adelaide to take over final preparation of the Test wicket. In Dennis Lillee's view, the WACA wickets that season were 'an embarrassment'.

Pitches are mysterious things and opinions vary as to why recent curators have found it impossible to recapture the hard, fast surfaces of the Abbott era. Some believe it was a result of the total rebuilding of the playing arena in 1985, in which the square used since 1962 was relaid and realigned 18 degrees to fit the view from a new stand; others blame the damage done by winter sports staged at the ground. The introduction of a full programme of rugby league matches in 1995 was particularly bad for cricket. A canopy designed to protect the square between games that winter had, in some ways, the opposite effect: algae flourished underneath it.

Winter, who has a nice, open face and an engaging manner, has about as much experience of making wickets as anyone could have packed into twenty-eight years. Born and brought up in Canberra, he is the son of Ron Winter, who was for many years head curator at the capital city's main ground, the scenically attractive Manuka Oval, where the wickets are similar to Sydney's (low and slow for Australia, offering turn). At eighteen, Richard Winter succeeded his father in the job, and from 1994 to 1998 he was assistant groundsman at Eden Park, Auckland. There he introduced couch grass and succeeded in putting some bounce and pace into traditionally low, slow surfaces.

Although his father taught him the essentials of his trade, Richard Winter is more a protégé of Les Burdett, 'oval manager' at the Adelaide Oval. When he was only seventeen, Winter junior's ambition was such that he made his first major trip away from his birthplace, driving four-teen hours from Canberra to Adelaide in his first car. He was to work under Burdett for a week for free, a slice of work experience arranged by his father. Richard Winter's slender resources were drained in Ade-laide by unforeseen repairs to the car – so much so that he could not afford petrol for the journey home. Burdett offered him a day's work at A$70 (£28), operating the famous scoreboard. He arrived back in Can-berra with an empty tank and A$3 in his pocket. He had made a good impression. 'Richard is very likeable, has a good work ethic, presents himself well and knows the business,' says Burdett, who recommended him for the Auckland and Perth jobs. Winter returns the compliment. 'Working with Les was the best experience I've ever had,' he says.

We are talking, forty-eight hours before the Test starts, on a typically bright, sunny Perth morning at the 'players race', the gate through which the batsmen will pass on their way to cope with Winter's first Test wicket. As we look out towards it, the ground buzzes with the pre-match activity of players, reporters, photographers and camera crews. Winter, as tanned and healthy-looking as you would expect a grounds-man to be, seems a touch overwhelmed by all the attention, speculation and requests for interviews. However, he does not lack confidence in his creation. 'I think it'll play very well,' he says. 'I've got a very good feel-ing about it. It might assist the bowlers, as it should, on the first day. It's forecast to be fairly warm then, so it should dry out fairly quick, and generally get harder and bouncier as the day goes on. On days two and three I think it'll be excellent for batting, and the way it's looking it should hold together very nice. On days four and five I'd like to see it deteriorate a little bit so that the spin bowlers come in: I like to see every aspect of the game involved.'

The pitch which Winter and his assistant Rohan Matthews have selected for the Test is one of two contenders, on a square which has ten wickets altogether. They originally earmarked wicket No. 7, on which Australia beat New Zealand by an innings and 70 runs in four days in 1997–8, but then wicket No. 3 – which has not been used since it was relaid late in 1997 – rolled out nicely. 'We worked on No. 3 and No. 7 for a while to see which was going to perform better,' says Winter. 'We knew No. 7 was going to crack because it's always had that characteristic, whereas No. 3 hasn't shown any signs of cracking at all, so that's a very positive sign. So we took a gamble, I guess, and decided a week ago to play the Test on No. 3. I think it's paid off. It's looking pretty good.'

As the Test drew closer, Winter and his team of six stepped up a gear, working an average of twelve hours a day, seven days a week, in recent months. Winter admits he has had an easier time of it than some predecessors. There is now only one winter sport – Australian Rules football – played at the WACA, rugby league, rugby union and soccer having departed; and the last Aussie Rules game of the season was, unusually, back in June, giving the groundstaff much more time to get the square into decent shape after the footballers had finished churning it up. Nor has Winter's preparation been hampered by unpredictable weather. With the Test taking place in late November, rather than the usual Ashes timing of February, there is next to no danger of the thermometer shooting up to 40 degrees in the lead-up to the game and causing cracking.

So nervous is Winter on the opening day that he is at work by 5 a.m., an hour earlier than necessary, 'stomach churning', anxious to 'get things going'. The covers come off at six, and there follow two or three hours' frantic activity as the wicket is cut and the ground prepared for play. The outfield looks superb, the turf so immaculate that one can see why people sometimes wonder if it is artificial.

To celebrate his achievement as one of the youngest Test curators – in modern times, only Burdett, at twenty-seven, has prepared an Australian Test wicket younger – Winter has invited 'some mates' in for a breakfast barbecue. This is held in the middle of his base, the 'turf shed', amid mowers, rollers and all the other impedimenta of his trade. Winter's friends knock up sausages, bacon, fried eggs and grilled tomatoes. Alec Stewart loses the toss, is asked to bat by Mark Taylor and calls for the heavy roller (the only one requested during the game). At 10.25 a.m., five minutes before the start of play, Winter and his chums race into the nearby Members' Shelter, to take up position for what he calls 'the big moment – the first ball'. Not that the Head Curator has his own seat – he has to take pot luck along with everyone else. But he is instantly identifiable by the groundstaff's new sponsored uniform – black shorts, a black and gold polo shirt and a blue and green cap. The wicket looks good too. It is in beautiful condition, without a mark on it.

Mark Butcher fails to make contact with Glenn McGrath's opening delivery, which is cleanly taken down the legside by Ian Healy. For the crowd, it is a small anticlimax; for Winter, it is a huge relief. It is already clear that his wicket has high bounce and good 'carry', the qualities he has been striving to rediscover. Soon the degree of sideways movement will be apparent. By lunch, England, albeit in challenging conditions (it is also a humid day), are 76–6. Hussain and Stewart are out to fine deliveries, one moving in and the other out, but Atherton, Hick and, after the interval, Ramprakash need not have played at theirs, had they adjusted to the unique conditions. Later in the day Taylor (61) gives an expert demonstration of batting at the WACA, leaving many straight good-length balls, confident that they will pass safely over his stumps – something which batsmen reared in soggy Manchester, London or even Zimbabwe are instinctively fearful of doing.

During play, there is not a lot for Winter and his team to do except enjoy the cricket and be ready for work during the next interval, or break between innings, when the wicket will be swept and remarked. Unusually, Winter finds himself watching almost all the action. The Test is full of exciting, aggressive cricket – cricket with a real edge to it. This is particularly clear when Alex Tudor surprises the Australians with his pace, line and movement in their first innings, when Graeme Hick goes after Jason Gillespie in his second-innings 68, and when the Waughs are trying to regain the psychological advantage over Tudor at the end.

The verdict on Winter's efforts is positive. This is, it is generally agreed, the best Test wicket Perth has produced in more than a decade. It is quick, true and bouncy; there is some grass, which gives seam movement for the new ball, especially on the first morning when the grass is damp – Winter, worried that it is drying out too fast and may crack, had administered a light watering ('only a bit of a squiff') twenty-four hours before the start of the match. It is a watering which some seasoned observers regard as quite unnecessary – perhaps a sign of Winter's inexperience.

Even before the Test starts, however, Dennis Lillee, now a pugnacious newspaper columnist, has written a glowing notice in the *West Australian*. 'Richard Winter has managed to produce a WACA square reminiscent of the old days – chock full of bounce and a dream for the fast men.' After two days' play, Malcolm Conn in *The Australian* is describing the pitch as 'a surface fast bowlers dream about before considering even Elle Macpherson'. (One wonders whether 'The Body' would con-

sider it a compliment to be compared, unfavourably, to a 'surface'.)
After the match Lillee declares: 'The WACA wicket was a beauty and
you can't tell me, despite his denials, that Stewart wouldn't have asked
Australia to bat had he won the toss. The problem with the Poms is that
they simply didn't know which balls to leave alone – just ask Ian Healy.'

The fact remains that the match has only gone just over half the
scheduled distance. Once the Waugh twins have eased Australia to her
seven-wicket victory, curious spectators walk out to inspect the con-
crete-hard surface which has delivered a result all too quickly – not least
for those who have travelled thousands of miles to see the game, as well
as those who look after the bottom line (abbreviated Tests have become
a Perth speciality). The wicket has dried out a lot during the match.
There are some very fine cracks in it, which appeared yesterday but had
no bearing on the game; there were also some puffs of dust – a rare sight
here – as Colin Miller turned his off-breaks out of left-armer Alan Mullally's footmarks. An English Minor Counties umpire, discussing the
strip with some Australian friends, shakes his head and declares it unfit
for a five-day Test. At the press conferences after the match, however,
neither captain criticises the wicket. Mark Taylor does say, in what
could be interpreted as a polite criticism, that it is in a 'transitional'
phase and there is more work to do, while England clearly blame themselves for their batting inadequacies.

John Inverarity confirms the widespread impression that this was
almost a wonderful wicket. 'It was just a whisker outside the ideal,' he
says. 'Batting was more difficult than would ideally be the case. There
was probably a little too much movement for the good of the game. It
was certainly fast, with very good bounce, and was within the range of
typical WACA wickets of the 1970s. But on average they offered less
sideways movement than this one. On the other hand, this was a consistent wicket – something which has not been the case here for some
years.'

On what would have been day four, Winter and I meet again for a
post-mortem. This time the venue is the turf shed. 'Classy, isn't it?' he
remarks as we seat ourselves on weather-beaten old sofas, next to the
barbecue, our conversation interrupted once or twice by the sound of a
roller coming or going. He is clearly disappointed by the early finish, but
the wicket has played pretty much as he forecast: on the second and
third days it was very good for batting. He does not accept that it
offered bowlers too much lateral movement. 'It was always a concern

that England would roll over fairly quickly if they batted first,' he says. 'But I didn't think it would be that quick [all out for 112 in 39 overs]. Some players couldn't handle the wicket.'

Winter argues that if he had left less grass on the wicket, it might not have lasted five days. 'The amount of grass we leave on it, and the amount of moisture in it, is all a recipe to keep it going for five days.' However, he concedes that, given another chance, he might leave a little less grass on the pitch. He does not bow an inch to criticism of the light watering on the eve of the Test. 'Within half an hour we were rolling the wicket again,' he adds. 'The water wouldn't have penetrated deep into the pitch. It might have just wet the top 2mm of soil.'

He is sure that it was right to use wicket No. 3, rather than No. 7, which 'would have cracked open, no matter how much grass it had on it'. And if Australia had batted first? He feels they would probably have made 300 or so in a day and a half, and then had England in serious trouble as the wicket became harder and bouncier on day two. 'I don't think it would have mattered a huge amount whether England batted or bowled first.'

What he has found gratifying is the 'very good' reaction from former cricketers, and WACA members, who have been telling him the ground is looking the best it has in ten years. They shared his delight in seeing steep bounce and good 'carry' restored to Perth. 'I love seeing the 'keeper taking the ball real high,' says Winter. The reception for his wicket was such a marked change from all the criticism there was of wickets at Eden Park that, he says, 'this is probably the first time in my career I've not been blamed for the performance of a team'. He remains thrilled to have fulfilled his long-held ambition of producing a Test wicket. 'I could die now and be happy.'

His work at the WACA has been helped by the fact that, according to those close to State cricket, Winter has been given a 'far freer rein' than his predecessor. This has helped him stamp his authority swiftly on the place. 'Richard has quickly established a reputation for being a good and fair boss,' says one veteran grade cricketer. 'He's doing a fine job.' Burdett too is impressed by his pupil's start, and the fact that he recognises privately there is 'always room for improvement'.

Oddly enough, just as the WACA square is looking more familiar, Winter finds himself asked to prepare something more like somewhere else. Western Australia have just been bowled out for 58 by New South Wales in a Sheffield Shield match on a Sydney turner. 'The coach has asked me to try and prepare a spinning wicket in the practice area,' he says. 'We won't be able to do that with our clay so we may have to put some sand in it, or even get some clay over from Sydney.' And what of England? Maybe they should ship home some of that Harvey River soil, in the hope of producing a pitch that would help them develop the skills needed for batting at the WACA? Sadly, Winter says this is a non-starter. 'Our clay wouldn't be any good in your climate. It wouldn't dry out as fast. With all the rain falling on it, the wicket would probably end up being a big bog.'

As our conversation closes, Winter is looking forward to spending a quiet Christmas with his wife, Sharon, whom he met in New Zealand and married in April 1998. Does his own lawn get the attention it should? 'Not from me,' he replies. 'My next-door neighbour mows it! In return I bring home some fertiliser for his lawn. My neighbour does a good job. I don't even have a lawn mower.'

9

Backs, Bets and Bribery

CHRISTOPHER MARTIN-JENKINS

Part One: A Chance to Draw Breath

In the days when England teams in Australia were known as 'MCC', when managers wore suits and I Zingari ties, when it was possible for an England batsman to go down in the scorebook of a first-class match as 'absent bathing' and there were definite, although by no means always contentious, distinctions between the amateurs and the professionals, cricket was only the major part of a touring team's itinerary. Until the Second World War at least, it was 'tour' as much in the sense of Grand Tour as Cricket Tour.

Even in the early 1970s, when the 'voyage' meant a day and a night in an aeroplane rather than three weeks in a ship, there was still a clear pattern to the programme in each of the major cities. First there was a country match involving a long journey to and from a small town surrounded by bush, or a relatively isolated coastal place. (MCC were expected to win and almost always did.) Next, a four-day match against the State side would be played before substantial crowds, many of them putting faces for the first time to cricketers they had hitherto known only as names. The less experienced of the visiting players themselves would get the chance to learn the idiosyncrasies of the ground on which the Test match would be played, and local heroes the opportunity to have a go at the Poms and perhaps make cases for their personal advancement. Then, and only then, after a decent interval for recuperation, would come the major game. Half-way through it, too, there would be Sunday, the day of rest.

On the last Ashes tour of the century there was barely a day of rest until the series was over, let alone one in the middle of a match. It was therefore some consolation to the players, if not to the cricket authorities of Western Australia and the Australian Cricket Board, that the Perth Test should have been over in three days. (But for Graeme Hick's resistance on the second afternoon it might have been two, which would have been quite a double for England in the year in which they had also taken part in the shortest Test match ever, the one abandoned after fifty-nine minutes in Kingston because of a dangerous pitch.)

The Australians had earned two extra days with their families. For those who had been on the whole trip to Pakistan there had been not much time for drinks on the terrace or bedtime stories for the children; and the likes of Steve Waugh, seen travelling on aeroplanes with his wife Lynette and three-year-old daughter Rosie more than once during the Ansett Australia Test series, had a tour of the West Indies to contemplate as soon as the final ball of the Carlton & United triangular one-day series was done and dusted.

Even Graham Gooch, apostle of the work ethic, saw the sense in giving the players two free days in Perth before the sixth of their twenty flights to, from and around Australia. He set a formidable example himself which neither Scrooge nor Mr Gradgrind could have faulted for industry or dedication. But, having conducted a gentle and admirably frank unofficial press conference whilst seated on a sofa in the foyer of the Burswood hotel, he took himself off with eleven other members of the touring party for some golf at the Jondaloop Golf Resort, a thirty-minute drive to the north and a few miles from the invitingly named Sunset Coast.

Lancashire's two single-figure handicap golfers, John Crawley and Warren Hegg, were the stars of the day, but Nasser Hussain, having driven into the nearest lake at the first hole, recovered with customary resolution to produce the best stableford score. Meanwhile, the quietly determined Peter Such, about to be rediscovered as a cricketer, found in the rough-hewn and zealous Yorkshire physiotherapist Wayne Morton a partner capable of helping him to better the combination of Cottam and Gough. If Yorkshire's blue-eyed boy was wayward, he was not in the same league for the variety of his hooks and slices as Derbyshire's captain, Dominic Cork. This was not surprising: his left eye was badly cut and almost closed from the blow it had taken between the grille and peak of his helmet in the instant after his unwise decision to attempt a hook against the menacing Jason Gillespie.

At least Cork could play: there was too much hazard in golf for two other keen and capable players, Atherton and Thorpe. The former was not prepared to risk a relapse, having managed to play two Tests despite his spondylitis; the latter was beginning to wonder if his back was going to force him out of a tour which he had had every reason to contemplate with relish. Keeping England's bowlers fit was one thing; the batsmen were more of a problem.

Graeme Hick is another whose back has caused him problems in the past, not least when it forced him to come home early, and still in a mood of indignation, before the Adelaide Test four years before. In the previous game Atherton had declared England's second innings closed when Hick was 98 not out, a decision he later regretted, although it was encouraged at the time by Gooch, then the senior pro.

That tour ended early for Hick; this one had started late but he was intent on making up for time lost, time which would otherwise have been spent on preparing his 1999 benefit at Worcester. He had already persuaded the England players to play in a golf day during the World Cup, but, accomplished golfer though he is, the morning of his first day off in Perth was spent brushing up his batting technique in the indoor nets with the former South African Test batsman Peter Carlstein, with whom Hick had played for Zimbabwe when he was still an ingenue.

Hick was one of what had temporarily become a playing party of eighteen who was certain to play in the match against Victoria at Melbourne which separated the second and third Tests. With only four first-class matches left after that, there were bound to be some disappointed cricketers when the team was chosen, some of them wondering, perhaps, why they were being paid some £30,000 for endless sessions of nets and physical training. Thorpe, who stood for much of the flight eastwards to try to prevent his back from stiffening further, did not exactly look comfortable, but he knew he had to play if he were to be considered for the Adelaide Test.

Warren Hegg got a game to enable Alec Stewart to concentrate on his batting but Such felt, along with everyone else, that his tour was as good as over when he was left out. Ben Hollioake, the only man not yet picked for a first-class game, was more fortunate this time. So were Angus Fraser and Dean Headley, both straining to justify a recall to the Test side.

They were no more in need of wickets than were Stewart and Atherton of runs. The captain so far had only 101 first-class runs on the tour at an average of 12.6 and Atherton, with 122 at 15, was hardly less embarrassed. Stewart's tutorial with his father in Perth and the fact that Victoria had taken a leaf out of the book of too many counties and rested seven senior players for the game against the touring side gave him every chance of making a return to form and confidence. England were playing against a state whose priority was to try to hold on to its lead in the Sheffield Shield, with matches coming up against Queensland and New South Wales.

In particular they were not yet to renew acquaintance with Victoria's captain, Shane Warne, who had so far managed only eight wickets from the 94 overs he had bowled in a variety of matches since the operation to repair ligaments and the cuff of his right shoulder. They were able to practise against wrist spin, however: the young Lancashire leg-spinner, Chris Schofield, in whom much hope is invested, bowled at them in the nets throughout the Victoria game and impressed several with his tall, snappy action. Briefly, too, they had a chance to play against one of the great modern exponents of the art. Abdul Qadir was playing club cricket in Melbourne and cheerfully accepted the invitation to the nets beside the car park at the MCG.

Meanwhile, another sub-continental bowler with a distinctive action, Muttiah Muralitharan, was creating ripples. Darrell Hair, by common consent Australia's best umpire, decided voluntarily to rule himself out of matches involving Sri Lanka in the second half of the Australian season. In a word which was becoming familiar after President Clinton's public admission of at least some guilt in the Monica Lewinsky affair, Hair acknowledged that the publication of the book in which he had criticised Muralitharan's action as 'diabolical' was 'inappropriate'.

Ahead of him lay punishment by either the Australian Cricket Board or the ICC for breaching the code of conduct. For the bowler himself, about to arrive in Australia with the Sri Lankan team to prepare for the one-day series, there was more trouble ahead. So there was for England, but first they had a chance to regroup.

Daily Telegraph, Monday, 7 December
The more that tours and Test series are contracted, the more people are inclined to say that matches like the present one between Victoria and England at the MCG are surplus to the requirements of the age. It is sad that anyone should think so and the players certainly would not agree. Those on the fringe of the Test side need such games to press their claims and to justify their travelling expenses; those in the team need the rest and recuperation.

They are right, too. Cricket tours simply cannot consist only of big matches and potential money-spinners if young players are to learn and established ones are not to burn themselves out completely. Not only has this match for the Menzies Trophy been relatively well attended – although the 50,000-seat Southern Stand is closed – but some young Victorians have had their first experience of first-class cricket and more than one English performance has been encouraging with the Adelaide Test in mind.

Alec Stewart's commanding century, only his second in 48 first-class innings this year and his first of a tour which had hitherto yielded four ducks and only one fifty, was the most significant performance, of course, but Dean Headley yesterday bowled with markedly more penetration than Angus Fraser on a pitch of fairly easy pace and England's fielding was sharp.

Since dropped catches at Brisbane and Perth are largely responsible for their being one down in the Test series with three to play, this was good news, although it is whether the catches stick when the stakes are really high that counts. England's coach, David Lloyd, was sensitive enough about the matter to walk up to the media area yesterday and seek out Dean Jones, Test cricketer turned television pundit, in order to assure him that England's fielding routines lack nothing by comparison with Australia's.

Jones had been critical, probably unfairly, but the proof of the pudding is in the eating and in view of the hot water Lloyd found himself in after his argument with Geoff Boycott outside a broadcasting box last August over comments about Muttiah Muralitharan's bowling action (for which he was subsequently severely reprimanded) he would have been wiser, no doubt, to wait until England have outfielded Australia in a Test match.

Graham Gooch, as manager, was subsequently obliged yesterday to repeat comments already made by both himself and Lloyd to the effect that the slip catchers practise assiduously almost daily, taking edges from both short and longer range as the staple routine amongst many. Thorpe, Atherton, Hussain, Hick and Butcher, specialists in this crucial area, are all good catchers: inner confidence is the real reason the Australians have upstaged them and that is something which comes from being part of a winning team.

Stewart took a catch off the outside edge in Headley's incisive new-ball spell yesterday and Graham Thorpe held a fine catch low to his right at first slip. Soon afterwards Headley hit the single stump he had to aim at from mid-on to run out Jason Arnberger, the most experienced of the young Victorian batsmen. Had another swift pick-up and throw from Headley in the same position not hopped straight over the stumps when Peter Roach was stranded, the partnership of 90 which rescued the home team from a perilous 87 for five would have been terminated in its infancy.

As it was, Roach, a right-handed wicket-keeper/batsman, stayed to play some fine shots, hitting five fours across a lush outfield, and the left-handed Shawn Craig battled with much determination after Robert Croft had claimed Jason Bakker from a drive struck low in the air to mid-on. There was some turn for Croft, as there had been for his rival off-spinner, John Davison, on Saturday, but in a long spell from the Southern End he came close to a wicket only once more when Stewart almost brought off a deft stumping with a back flick from a rebound off Craig's pads.

Stewart's innings had been the centrepiece of the first day and, of course, it was a timely performance. He came in after John Crawley had edged a ball wide of his off stump and Nasser Hussain had been caught at short-leg off the towering Ashley Gilbert. At six foot ten and with size 16 feet, Gilbert is probably the tallest first-class bowler there has ever been. He looks like Angus Fraser on stilts and he naturally gets tricky bounce but the action is open and less fluent and his pace unexceptional.

Stewart hit 14 fours and it would be marvellous if it were to prove the start of one of his purple sequences. It was helpful too that Michael Atherton looked equally assured before falling to a fine gully catch, driving at Matthew Inness, who is 20, left-arm and bustling. Thorpe played with no apparent discomfort from his back before driving at a ball turning away from well outside his off stump.

Mark Ramprakash, however, is rapidly becoming the Ken Barrington of his era. For 256 minutes he played yet another correct and patient innings, sharing hundred partnerships with both Stewart and Graeme Hick who, despite coming in against the second new ball, looked every bit as confident and dominating as he had been in the second innings at Perth. They had added 48 more runs with some elan yesterday morning when in the space of three overs Ramprakash was caught off his outside edge, playing forward to a ball which left him late, Ben Hollioake was lbw flicking to leg and Hick was also given out, playing forward to a ball bowled from a wide angle, having hit seven fours and a six.

Hollioake had some revenge later in the day when he removed Brad Hodge, Victoria's captain and best batsman, with an inswinger of full length to which he padded up but he was too often hit for runs to leg after that and so, most unusually, was Fraser.

Not everyone is in form, therefore, by any means but Mark Butcher's strained groin muscle is now the only fitness worry England have and he had a long net yesterday with Lancashire's promising young leg-spinner, Chris Schofield, who is playing in Melbourne club cricket. Schofield will travel to Adelaide with the team tomorrow evening to prepare them for the return of Stuart MacGill. No similar invitation was issued to Ian Salisbury when he appeared in Perth earlier in the tour, which suggests that the management have transferred their dreams of finding a successful Test wrist spinner to the 20-year-old from Rochdale.

Another of the slow-bowling fraternity, Peter Such, had long ago learned that the greatest virtue of his profession is patience. Fourteen years older than Schofield, he was about to come into his own, although a match against a school side in Melbourne during which he was carted for two sixes by the opening batsman hardly suggested an immediate recall to Test cricket. The value of a good team man on a long tour, however, goes beyond bowling figures and batting averages. During one of the relatively relaxed evenings in Melbourne, Such was the main producer of an unusual version of the ITV Saturday night favourite *Blind Date*. It did wonders for the morale of a team which needed all the boosting it could get.

It is traditional for those travelling on an England tour for the first time to put on some sort of show for the older lags and Such wrote a script which managed to poke fun without causing offence. The main targets were Gooch, Gough and Cork, portrayed by Hegg, Hollioake and Such himself as three 'blind' suitors of a gorgeously dressed girl looking suspiciously like Bob Cottam. In the role of Cilla Black was one Alex Tudor, lacing his part as compere with plenty of 'pet's and 'chuck's. By all accounts, and this was strictly a players-only evening, the result was genuinely hilarious.

Whatever the wisdom of leaving out the talented semi-misanthropes, Phil Tufnell and Andrew Caddick, this was one England team which never looked likely to tear itself apart socially. They were all men who worked hard at their game and although there were in Headley and Butcher a couple of men who make the most of any party and others like Such and Ramprakash who are not averse to an evening in their own company, they got on well throughout.

The pattern throughout the tour was for the team to meet en bloc in the team room provided by every hotel half-way through each match. On other evenings players would eat out together ad hoc and although a firm friendship developed between Ramprakash and Tudor, who became regular dining companions, there was a healthy mixing of company. This was one of the useful legacies, perhaps, of players having their own rooms rather than being socially tied to their assigned room-mate as they often had been in the past.

There were not many team evenings like the world première of 'Blind Date' once Tudor and Hollioake had had their twenty-first birthday parties early on the tour. Hollioake, invited to smell how good his cake was, had innocently done so and had his face thrust into the icing to comical effect, but generally they were a sober bunch who kept their minds on the reasons for travelling to Australia. Gone were the days of serious practical joking beloved of Ian Botham and Allan Lamb; but gone, too, the potentially disruptive cliques of those days. As Such said when the tour was over, 'We didn't achieve our goals but at least we stayed together and pulled together.'

There was one unfortunate exception. On the final day of the Victoria match the decision was taken to send Thorpe home to nurse his bad back. Who can guess what difference a fit Thorpe throughout the tour might have made to England's chances in both the Ashes series and the one-day internationals which followed? His record pronounced him to be the most successful of the England batsmen against Australia with his Test average of 49. To my mind, he had become, with the possible exception of a fully fit Atherton, simply the best batsman in England.

Thorpe batted forty minutes for one not out on the third afternoon against Victoria before retiring hurt with further debilitating stiffness. The decision became virtually inevitable then, although he was given twelve hours to see how the injury settled down. Wayne Morton initially put an optimistic slant on this latest setback, saying that Thorpe's rehabilitation after surgery in the 1998 summer had probably gone better than expected. But he added: 'Mercurial back pain like this is frustrating for Graham, for me and for the management. The problem when he's batting is that he can't shift his weight from the front or the back foot.'

Thorpe was averaging 87 on the tour, but by the time the third Test started he was watching on television from his home in Surrey. His wife, Nicky, who was six months pregnant, must have had mixed feelings about that and there were those amongst the decision-makers in the party who felt that Thorpe himself was insufficiently determined to keep going. One of them even said privately one evening as we made our way to a restaurant on Melbourne's chic and fashionable South Bank that he would not be surprised if he retired early and took the insurance money.

That seemed to me a monstrous slur on a man who had proved himself tougher than most of his colleagues when the heat was turned on in Test matches and who was fearless against quick bowling. It is true that Thorpe seems more prone than most to catching coughs and colds and is inclined to enjoy a good discussion about whatever is ailing him, but he was the best judge of how fully he had recovered from the cyst on a facet joint, loosely described as disc trouble, which had first caused him serious pain in Barbados the previous March. The cyst was removed by a surgeon in July after he had broken down again during the third Test of England's series against South Africa at Old Trafford.

The decision to send him home now deprived England of Thorpe's services not just in the remainder of the Ashes series but in the minimum ten one-day internationals which followed in the new year. Because England were intending to use these games as part of the long build-up to the World Cup, it began to look as though this most versatile of middle-order strokeplayers might also have to be ruled out of a competition for which he would normally have been one of the first to be picked. He was averaging 40 from his forty-four one-day internationals and 46 from his last ten.

There was positive news, too, from the third day's play at the MCG, not just because England's lead of 280 promised an interesting final day with a minimum of 67 overs remaining. Dean Headley's five for 58 was only the second five-wicket analysis for England on a tour which was approaching its pivotal match this weekend. He bowled very well, too, although nine no-balls cannot have pleased Bob Cottam, who had apparently more or less cured what has been a recurring problem in Headley's career.

Headley's rhythm and nip off a good, hard but not especially quick pitch was in marked contrast to Angus Fraser's vain attempt to find anything like his best form. Despite some turn for Robert Croft, it took England an hour to part Victoria's sixth-wicket pair for a partnership of 130. Extra bounce finally enabled Headley to have Roach caught at cover in his second over with the new ball but Craig stayed to play the longest innings of his life and he was threatening the slowest hundred by a Victorian against a touring side when he ran out of partners in the tenth over after lunch. He had kept his head down for six and a quarter hours.

Crawley showed increasing signs that he had regained his fluency towards the end of his 164-minute innings in the afternoon but there was sufficient playing and missing outside the off stump to suggest that Hick would now be preferred if England decided to revert to five bowlers at Adelaide. He had taken a brilliant low left-handed catch at second slip to earn Headley his fifth wicket and, like Ramprakash and Stewart, he batted fluently on a good wicket afterwards, but Atherton fell to a top-edged hook once more – he was skilfully held overhead at long-leg off the pacey Brad Williams – and Nasser Hussain was the victim of his own tendency to misjudge a run.

The cricket held its interest throughout a shortened final day as Victoria's weakened eleven did their best to respond to a properly challenging overnight declaration. Lest there was not sufficient interest in the cricket itself (there was), Mark Ramprakash added spice to the last few overs by engaging in an unnecessary verbal duel with the towering Gilbert.

As one England official said, it was a case of 'handbags at dawn'. Gilbert made a comical sight when approached by Ramprakash for elucidation on what he had just said in reaction to a bouncer from Headley. Their brief but all too obviously hostile discussion was a legacy of the previous day when Gilbert had made a stupidly provocative remark after dismissing a batsman in a different class to himself. There was inevitable speculation that the remark might have been racist but lofty disdain is the best reaction at such times, even if Ramprakash could hardly be lofty in the shadow of this particular giant.

Stewart had asked Victoria to make 281 in 67 overs but England hardly deserved to win because their bowling on an essentially true and easy-paced pitch was largely disappointing and their over-rate deplorably sluggish even on a day when it was in their interests to bowl as many overs as possible. Angus Fraser, sadly, bowled like a man who had lost faith in himself. Whenever he was hit for four, which was far more often than usual, his next ball was quicker and more menacing. It is unthinkable that he was not trying his hardest all the time because he does that by nature, but the flesh on this occasion seamed weaker than the spirit.

Headley, by contrast, managed an early wicket again with the new ball, the catch off Jason Arnberger's outside edge being deftly taken not by Stewart, who was having a run about in the field and nursing a minor bruise on his once notoriously vulnerable right index finger, but by Warren Hegg, who had been given special dispensation by the Victorian captain, Brad Hodge, to keep wicket as a substitute for Thorpe. He later supported Croft with a catch standing up and a proficient offside stumping but the statisticians will include none of these dismissals amongst his first-class victims on the grounds that he was not a member of the original eleven.

Ben Hollioake picked up his second wicket of the tour when he took over from Fraser at the Southern End, with the help of another good, low catch at second slip by Hick, who was starting to look like a man on the verge of an Indian summer. He did not, however, bowl and Ramprakash, the second of the three would-be off-spinners in the side, was lightly enough worked by Stewart to suggest that Croft was more likely to play at Adelaide than not. When, subsequently, the selectors thought hard about how small a threat the ebullient Welshman had posed, they decided on a sudden change of policy.

It was great and surprising news for Such, called in on the eve of the third Test. But Australians hardly noticed. All they could talk about were Shane Warne and Mark Waugh.

Part Two: A Breath of Scandal

As scandals in public life go, the one which erupted around two of Australia's most revered cricketers in the two days before the Adelaide Test was small. After all, the President of the United States was about to be impeached for serious crimes and misdemeanours and when the charges of perjury and of inappropriate relations with a young female intern at the White House failed to stick with a sufficient majority to unseat him, it was forcibly argued by William Rees-Mogg in *The Times* that if only the chief prosecutor had instead concentrated on Bill Clinton's alleged financial corruption he would not have survived.

Because of the semi-sanctified state of Australia's leading sportsmen, however, the revelation that two outstanding cricketers in a highly successful era for Australian cricket had received money from Indian bookmakers during a tour of Sri Lanka and Pakistan four years before was a bombshell. The admission that they were fined for giving information to bookies was forced on the Australian Cricket Board by a radio leak which came just in advance of detailed stories in the press.

The timing was ironic and highly sensitive because, after his three-month investigation in the Lahore High Court, Judge Mohammed Malik Qayyum was just putting the finishing touches to a report to the President of Pakistan on the alleged involvement of Pakistani cricketers in match-fixing. It had been due the following week but was long delayed as a direct result of the news from Australia.

The origin of the accusations which Justice Qayyum had been questioning was a claim by Warne, Waugh and Tim May that they had been offered bribes by the then Pakistan captain, Salim Malik, to throw a one-day international in Colombo in September 1994. They gave sworn affidavits to the ACB when they returned to Australia but until the 1998 tour of Pakistan, no Australian player had given direct evidence to a Pakistani court.

An earlier judicial inquiry in Pakistan in 1996 by Justice Fakruddin Ebrahim cleared Malik of bribery but the judge indicated at the time that he was acting without the benefit of questioning Malik's accusers directly. This time it had seemed more likely that charges would be proved, following extensive questioning of a number of present and former Pakistani players and officials, some of whom had substantiated Australian claims of bribery and corruption.

Rashid Latif, one of Pakistan's many sometime captains, claimed that Malik had offered him money – 'I was offered ten lakh rupees' (£15,000), he testified in evidence subsequently published in the Delhi magazine *Outlook* – to assist in the losing of a one-day international in Christchurch in 1994. He claimed to have slept on the matter and to have been reprimanded by Malik for taking a catch. He also accused Wasim Akram of bowling deliberate wides and no balls.

According to Sarfraz Nawaz, the ex-Pakistan fast bowler, incidents went back as far as a Test in Calcutta in 1978–9 and Justice Qayyum had already said outside the pink stone High Court building in the centre of Lahore: 'The allegations levelled in the past were not baseless.'

Australian involvement with bookmakers had been a closely guarded secret, apart from the notorious incident in 1981 when Dennis Lillee and Rodney Marsh made money out of a bet on an England win when their hapless opponents were 500 to one against during the Headingley Test. There was never any suggestion that the two stalwarts had given anything less than their usual 100 per cent.

Betting on cricket in the sub-continent is rife but it was clearly the view of the executives of Australian cricket in 1995 that Warne and Waugh had compromised themselves by accepting money for information, in Warne's case immediately after losing A$5,000 at a casino in the basement of a building in a dimly lit street in Colombo one evening during the Singer Cup limited-overs series, played between four nations – India, Pakistan, Sri Lanka and Australia – in September 1994. It was in this moment of embarrassment, even for the wealthiest cricketer in Australia, that a man who had already introduced himself as a bookmaker and cricket fanatic offered full repayment 'as a gift'.

Thus was Warne enticed into the web of the Indian 'businessmen', actually illegal bookies who were present at that casino and traded on many a match involving Sri Lanka, India and Pakistan. Now, four years on, he and Waugh were finally obliged to face the consequences publicly. But they had already been punished after a secret ACB inquiry in February 1995, which had fined Waugh A$10,000 and Warne A$8,000 for giving information on pitch and weather conditions in return for payments of, respectively, A$6,000 and A$5,000. The ACB, whose chairman was then the respected Sydney solicitor Alan Crompton, chose to keep the inquiry a secret. They informed the ICC's chief executive, David Richards, and the president, Clyde Walcott, but asked them not to disclose the information.

The subsequent judicial inquiry in Pakistan in 1996 therefore took place with Australian accusations against Salim Malik central to the case against him, yet without the full co-operation of the ACB. They withheld the information about their own internal inquiry and the suspicion must be that they had dissuaded Warne and May from travelling to Pakistan to give evidence (as opposed to swearing affidavits) in order to keep their own embarrassment a secret.

The two Australian players had allegedly been approached by Malik, three weeks after the casino incident, at the Pearl Continental hotel, with offers of A$100,000 each to bowl badly on the final day of the first Test. On the evening of the approach Pakistan, chasing 315 to win, were 155 for three. Although the bribes were rejected, Pakistan got the runs after a last-wicket partnership of 57. The winning runs were four byes, let by a mortified Ian Healy after he had missed a stumping off Warne. The wicket-keeper, the toughest and most loyal of all Australia's renowned competitors, was above suspicion.

This thrilling finish was typical of a mercurial season for Pakistan. They had won all but one of their international matches on their tour of Sri Lanka (the one they lost was a surprising defeat by seven wickets) but had then lost every match in the Singer Cup. Now they had beaten Australia, a victory which proved sufficient to win the series when the remaining two Tests were drawn.

There have been differing accounts of exactly when the Australians were offered bribes. According to a report in *The Age*, the first time officials heard of any irregularities was when Mark Waugh made a dressing-room remark in jest and Colin Egar and Bobby Simpson, the manager and coach, began asking questions.

The Age was reiterating the substance of an unpublished interview with May, who had told a reporter for the magazine *Inside Sport* that he had been sharing a room with Warne in Karachi when the phone rang late on the evening of the last day of the first Test. One of the Pakistan players asked to talk to the two spinners. May was dozing so Warne went, returning white-faced to the room a little later to announce: 'They've just offered us US$200,000 to basically bowl badly tomorrow. I told them to piss off.'

By coincidence, May ricked his neck overnight and was unable to bowl effectively the next day which might explain why Warne took five wickets, May none.

Later in the tour a 'certain Pakistani player' got the same negative reaction at an official function on the eve of a one-day international when, according to May, he offered himself, Warne and the Waugh twins A$50,000 each 'if you put in a stinker'. In the event Mark Waugh made a big century and Australia a large score but Pakistan knocked off the runs with amazing ease. Going back into the dressing-room, Mark Waugh joked, according to May's account: 'We would have been better off taking the bribes, guys.'

The manager and the coach were there and asked what they were talking about. According to May, 'there was an investigation and let's just say the players involved in that particular thing felt very let down by the administrators at the time . . . The ACB said: "Don't say anything, don't say anything, whatever you do, don't say anything."'

Daily Telegraph, Thursday, 10 December
A rash of righteous indignation broke over Australia yesterday when it became clear that there had been an official cover-up over the connection of two national heroes to the allegations of bribery and corruption in cricket. Blame seemed to be attaching itself less to Shane Warne and Mark Waugh, for accepting money for passing on basic cricketing information to an illegal bookmaker in Sri Lanka in 1994, than to the Australian Cricket Board for keeping their subsequent investigation a secret.

The belated disclosure that Waugh and Warne had been fined 10,000 and 8000 Australian dollars respectively (£4000 and £3200) for taking cash from an illegal bookmaker in Sri Lanka four years ago has 'damaged the high reputation of Australian cricket' according to the ACB chief executive, Mal Speed, who was not in office at the time.

Speaking after the two players had read out virtually identical prepared statements before a packed media conference at the Adelaide Oval, Speed admitted that with hindsight it would have been better not to have kept the matter from the public, particularly in the light of the two judicial inquiries in Pakistan into alleged involvement by their players in match-fixing for money. A judge in Lahore is expected to make his report to the President of Pakistan on Tuesday week.

Mark Waugh was not asked about his own acceptance of money, nor did he disclose it, when he gave evidence to Justice Malik Mohammed Qayyum in Lahore two months ago during Australia's tour of Pakistan. Waugh repeated evidence he had given four years earlier that the then Pakistan captain, Salim

Malik, had offered him US$200,000 to play badly on the 1994 tour. Warne and Tim May both testified to similar offers and Dean Jones has stated that on a 1992 tour of Sri Lanka he refused an offer of US$50,000 in a cake tin to give information.

The amounts involved in alleged match-fixing were far in excess of the sums which Waugh and Warne received, respectively £2400 and £2000, for giving information about weather and pitch conditions to a bookmaker based in Delhi. The two players completely denied giving anything less than their best for Australia in any match or even divulging team tactics or who would be selected. Speed added that they had also denied betting on cricket.

According to a statement read out by Speed on behalf of Alan Crompton, chairman of the ACB at the time of their inquiry into rumours early in 1995, the players had voluntarily offered a full account of what had happened when asked to do so. As one journalist expressed it yesterday, 'they were honest about being dishonest'.

Waugh and Warne were told when they were fined that they had been 'naïve and foolish in the extreme'.

Both players reaffirmed yesterday that the information they provided, 'on a handful of occasions' was 'mundane, and exactly the same as any pre-match media interview'. It is easy to see how tempting such money must have seemed. Speed, who said he knew only the first name of the bookmaker involved, admitted that the ACB had not attempted to track him down to see whether he would deny or corroborate the evidence given by the two players.

A former cricketer, Salim Pervez, now 51, who played in a single one-day international for Pakistan in 1980, told the judge in Lahore that he had paid Salim Malik and Mushtaq Ahmed US$100,000 to lose a match against Australia in the quadrangular tournament in Sri Lanka in 1994, the same tournament in which it now transpires that the two Australians were given money for information.

Details of the board's findings were conveyed in confidence in 1995 to the International Cricket Council, whose chief executive, David Richards, was formerly chief executive of the ACB. Since then these two organisations and the Pakistan Cricket Board have tended to pass the buck to one another but Speed said that the whole issue of match-fixing, which he believes has now ceased, will be on the agenda of the ICC at their next meeting in Christchurch, New Zealand, in January. He promised greater 'transparency' in future over serious matters of discipline.

The world of cricket now awaits the verdict of Mr Justice Qayyum. Whatever it is there is likely to be a move to give the ICC more formal powers to investigate any suggestion of corruption in international matches. The very idea of it would once have seemed totally absurd.

The heat was taken out of the witch hunt which was starting to envelop the two stars when Taylor conducted his own press conference at the Adelaide Oval twenty-four hours later. His moral strength, never pretentiously flaunted but evident in all he did as Australia's captain, was never better demonstrated. When Taylor said that he truly believed that there were no other skeletons in the Australian cupboard, all were inclined to believe him.

'My feelings about Shane and Mark are exactly the same as they were at the time,' he said. 'They made a mistake and admitted that mistake. The ACB handled the matter in the way they thought it should be handled. The ramifications would have been the same if it had been made public at the time. It would have created the same media storm then.

'As their captain then and now I have no problem in playing with either player. Their records show that they have been great players for Australia and I certainly hope that continues for a lot longer yet. It worried me at the time because they had compromised themselves by what they did, but I knew they hadn't done anything to try and harm Australia's chances.

'People are allowed to make mistakes, but it's not fair to put Mark and Shane in the same bracket as what's been going on in Pakistan. They spoke to a certain person on the phone, giving the same sort of information as I've just given the press about Ian Healy's fitness, and they received some money for it. As soon as that was found out they were told to stop it and they haven't done it since. Mark and Shane have always liked to have a bet, so they were an easy target.

'People can always find a case against the Australian evidence but the most damning evidence throughout the whole case has come from the other Pakistani players. An ICC investigation sounds very good but I don't think the individual countries will be prepared to make the ICC the judge and jury.'

The ACB and the two main culprits were strongly criticised in the summary of a two-month investigation which they ordered in December 1998 from a senior Australian lawyer, Rob O'Regan, QC. He concluded that Warne and Waugh should have been suspended and that their fines should have been made public. He said of the two players: 'I do not think it is possible to explain their conduct away as the result of merely naïvety or stupidity.'

O'Regan found that Waugh provided information to an unidentified bookmaker on ten occasions over five months, including a tour of the

West Indies: it was not clear whether any of the instances occurred after his fine. He was warned by a senior player in 1994 to stop, but continued until 1995.

O'Regan also said he was puzzled that the ACB did not link the involvement of the players with bookies to the bribery allegations concerning Malik: 'I came to the conclusion that there was a distinct possibility of a connection between the two matters. I don't know how the ACB concluded they were separate.'

10

In the Heat Consuming: The Third Test

CHRISTOPHER MARTIN-JENKINS

Having spoken with his usual common sense on the matter of the bribes, Mark Taylor could turn his attention to Australia's attempt to win the third Test match and the Ashes. Adelaide was being grilled by a heatwave and although Les Burdett, the senior statesman of Australian curators, had given his Test pitch a good dousing not much more than twenty-four hours before the match started, it was all too evident to the trained eye that this was essentially a dry pitch with only a feeble cover of grass. Australia duly picked both Miller and MacGill and waited to see whether Taylor's fortune with the coin would continue. It did. Like the earthly passions in Charles Wesley's holy flame, the heat was about to consume lingering English hopes.

Their first and chief destroyer was a little man of no great reputation whose time had been a long time coming. Justin Langer was about to justify his right to a full series in Australia for the first time. He had turned twenty-eight on the second day of the Brisbane Test but six years after making a memorably plucky first appearance against the West Indies he was about to play only his fourteenth Test, albeit his sixth in a row after a successful tour of Pakistan.

This was the kind of inconsistent treatment from national selectors familiar to many a promising young England player, but the explanation both for his failure to establish a regular place earlier and for the chance he now had to do so lay in the nature of his place in the batting order: number three. It is a problem spot for many teams and stability often follows when they find the right man.

Langer was one of five players who had been chosen at three in the three seasons since David Boon, the hairy little stalwart, had announced his retirement from international cricket and devoted the considerable fruits of his talent and experience to two relative cricketing outposts: his native island of Tasmania and the north-eastern fastness of Durham.

The selectors, the coach, Geoff Marsh, who had opened with Boon before Taylor came on to the scene, and finally Taylor himself had slowly appreciated that Langer might be the man to play the pivotal role required of what the Australians call the 'first drop' man. He has to be able to drop anchor when seas are rough, but sail on briskly when the wind is in the right quarter.

Formidable Australian number-three batsmen run like a golden thread through the country's Test history, and many of them have been small men: Clem Hill, Charlie Macartney, Don Bradman, Lindsay Hassett, Neil Harvey, Ian Chappell, Boon himself. Now Langer was bedding down after experiments of varying success with Mark Waugh, Greg Blewett, Matthew Elliott and Ricky Ponting.

Boon had averaged 43 for Australia when he decided that 107 Test matches were sufficient for one man's career. Between them, despite Elliott's brilliance in England in 1997, he, Blewett, Ponting and Waugh had managed to average only 28 from the combination of their 47 innings at number three. Langer, however, was still vulnerable when he started the series in Pakistan in October with a duck, leg before to Wasim Akram in his only innings; and only a divine providence saved him from becoming the victim of another leg before decision when he was late on his first ball from the ferociously fast Shoaib Akhtar in the second Test in Peshawar. Reprieved, he stayed with Taylor to make his maiden Test century and he finished the series averaging 42.

Even now there were doubters. His 74 at Brisbane had, after all, been merely a matter of gliding serenely along in Michael Slater's slipstream. But there was a glint in Langer's eye when he greeted me on the Adelaide Oval outfield on the morning before the match, with an unspoilt friendliness which world-weary cricketers do not always accord passing journalists. With the dressing-room behind him and the Richardson gates beckoning in front of the vivid gardens on the other side he gazed towards the pitch and said with all the confidence of a prophet: 'It'll be a good one. They always are here. It's a lovely place to bat; a lovely place to make a century.'

Langer was on his way to practise; I was intent on getting as much as possible of my work completed before treating myself to an uplifting afternoon in the melancholy power of Siegfried, part of Australia's first ever full cycle of Der Ring des Nieberlungen. It was the only part which schedules allowed me to fit in, although Bob Willis, a somewhat unlikely Ring anorak (or should that be Loden?), managed, despite television commentary duties, to attend all four parts: some eighteen hours' worth. It was a chance to fill a gap in my education and those who have devoted many hours of their lives to an appreciation of this hugest of operas say that it was right up to scratch. Certainly to my relatively untutored ears the singing and orchestral playing seemed beautiful. It is an expensive luxury, though, this opera-going, wherever you are. The programme alone cost £25, about the same as the single round of smoked-salmon sandwiches had set me back when my wife and I went to Covent Garden shortly before it closed its doors for refurbishment and reappraisal.

I did not see the cognoscenti from Sky television (Mark Nicholas was also at the Festival Centre in search of knowledge) during the interval, but in the stifling heat and wan sunlight on the concrete steps outside the capacious, comfortable and mercifully air-conditioned auditorium I did bump into Donald Rich, sometime chairman of Hampshire County Cricket Club and member of the MCC committee. He was seeing the whole of an Ashes series in Australia for the first time. But this was his thirteenth *Ring* cycle and he would have flown to Adelaide to see it even if there had been nothing else to watch 400 metres away just across the River Torrens. He bought me a cool orange juice and we feared for the well-being of the cricketers on the morrow in sapping heat like this. Even to stand about for a matter of minutes was like being weighed down by an invisible blanket.

Daily Telegraph, Saturday, 12 December

The weather in Adelaide dominated everything on the opening day of the third Test. It was no more suitable for cricket than it might be on a freezing April day in Leeds. It was like playing inside a huge oven or the middle of the Sahara and no one could blame a large portion of a hardy crowd of 13,600 for going back to their air-conditioned homes as soon as the match began to be shown on television after tea.

The players swallowed an estimated six litres a man in energising drinks. Justin Langer suffered from cramp almost throughout his painstaking first Test hundred on home soil, Dean Headley limped off for a while during England's long, slow baking and Peter Such, a surprise selection and heroic throughout an 18-over afternoon spell in temperatures reaching 130 degrees Fahrenheit in the middle, was running in on aching feet long before the end.

Australia held the aces from the moment that Mark Taylor won an almost priceless toss, but in conditions close to being inhumane England kept going with admirable stamina and discipline. A wicket with the second new ball for Darren Gough just before the close was a bonus but a brace of missed catches in the morning made this yet another imperfect performance. Between them, Langer, Taylor and Steve Waugh made sure that the advantage gained by the fall of the coin was not wasted.

It was no perfect day for Australia either, however. The cloud over the younger Waugh twin's head followed him to the true and welcoming pitch and showed no sign of lifting during eight distinctly uncomfortable overs from Gough and Such which ended in a caught and bowled, gleefully accepted and richly deserved. The story of the villains who had taken tainted money from a bookmaker still rumbled like distant thunder on this blistering day.

Indeed it was somehow appropriate to the suddenly bruised ego of Australian cricket that the chairman of the governing board should have been doing his best to defend the honour of his administration during yet another press conference even as Taylor and Langer were taking 33 off the first four overs after lunch, the only period when the batsmen really got on top.

The day's true pattern was rather one of slowly attained control by an Australian side who would be the first to acknowledge their good fortune in winning a potentially crucial toss, the third out of three in the series so far. The pitch is slow but it will undoubtedly turn and keep low as it wears. With two specialist spinners in his side, all Taylor had to do after the national anthems, it seemed, was to bat first, see Australia through the first two hours without serious mishap and make sure that either he or one of his colleagues made the century which somebody simply had to score.

Langer was the man, working his way assiduously to an admirably single-minded second Test hundred, his first against England. It was a milestone of great importance to him, sandwiched between two seasons of county cricket, one for Middlesex and the other, if negotiations are sealed, as Somerset's new captain.* He is a player very much in the idiom of Allan Border and David Boon: patient, painstaking and dogged. He plays the ball from under his nose and only when he occasionally chased and missed a ball wide of his off stump did he look anything other than secure yesterday during an innings which began in the 12th over as the mercury was rising towards its peak.

By now Taylor, before he had scored, had escaped a half-chance, a thickish edge low in front of second slip where Graeme Hick and those either side of him were standing a yard too deep. It is a wonder Gough has any hair left after six weeks of beating edges or glancing them only for the close fielders to fail him. Slater was also dropped, cutting hard but virtually straight to Mark Ramprakash at cover point in Dean Headley's first over.

Four balls later he was gone, playing forward to a good-length ball which left him and apparently nicking it thinly to the wicket-keeper. But Taylor remains a tower of strength for Australia and in his completely uncomplicated way he saw his side to lunch without further mishap, leaving what did not need

---

*Langer decided, like Angus Fraser, who was also talking to other would-be employers, to stay with Middlesex, despite the departure of the genial Queensland-based coach, John Buchanan.

playing, defending what did and driving or pulling whenever anyone's length strayed.

The two left-handers ran the short singles smartly, although John Crawley would have run Taylor out when he was 47 had his throw from mid-wicket hit the stumps. His fifty soon followed and he now has more runs for Australia than any man except Border. If you want to know a Test batsman's true worth, look at his scores in the first innings. Taylor's in this series have been 46, 61 and, yesterday, 59 before Such, now very much in the groove from the River Torrens end, employed Nasser Hussain for an exclusively Essex dismissal. It was a neat catch from a cut low to slip.

The third Essex man, Mark Waugh, deserved no sympathy from England and got none. Such gave him nothing, while Gough, quickly recalled by Stewart, responded with a hostile spell which gave him no chance to settle. Very nearly caught and bowled once, Waugh drove a second time at a ball which hung invitingly and dragged it back to his former team-mate.

Steve Waugh restored his family's good name with another formidably good piece of batting. He made his mark quite soon against Such by getting down on one knee to mow him towards the gardens for the only six of the day. After that he occasionally leaned into a drive or rocked back to hit hard off the back foot but otherwise, like Langer, he watched and waited for the scoring chance as Stewart drove Such until he dropped and kept the three fast bowlers going in relays from the Cathedral end.

It would be an insult to Zephyrus to call the assistance they got a breeze. It was more like the hot breath of Zeus. But, despite it, Gough had the spirit to produce another quick and well-directed spell with the second new ball and when Waugh got the edge this time, Hick's large hands gobbled a fine, low catch to his left.

So, with honours almost even, to the swimming-pool. A mere forty-eight hours later, however, English supporters – and there were many who had been attracted by Adelaide's beauty and the prospect of something heroic – felt more like taking a tram to Glenelg and throwing themselves into the briny in their despair. There was no English Langer (or Barrington, or Steele, or even Tavare); no English McGrath; and certainly no English MacGill.

Daily Telegraph, Monday, 14 December
The bells of St Peter's Cathedral rang out across the Adelaide Oval soon after the close of play on the third day, summoning the faithful to evensong but simultaneously tolling the knell of England's parting dreams. Australia were 314 ahead with nine wickets in hand and two days left. They remain far superior but it is England's own incompetence which has surrendered the Ashes for

a sixth successive series, barring a rearguard action every bit as remarkable as the one at Old Trafford against South Africa last summer.

Such recoveries seldom come more than once a year: would it were the same with England batting collapses. After an admirable partnership between Nasser Hussain and Mark Ramprakash which had reached 103 when McGrath broke through (as great bowlers will when the need is also great) the last seven wickets went down for 40. This year alone England have collapsed disastrously in Antigua, at Lord's, at Old Trafford and now to a greater or lesser extent in successive matches at Brisbane, Perth and Adelaide.

In each case the batting frailties have been compounded by disastrously fallible catching. Two more chances went down yesterday afternoon as Australia built on a first-innings lead of 164. That makes 15 chances spurned in three matches. It is irrelevant that the fielding was faultless last week against Victoria because it is on the big occasions that a side's true mettle is tested.

Langer battled through a difficult time when England's off-spinners were turning the ball away from him out of the rough, with a well-guarded off-side field making attacking shots risky. Before he had reached double figures, he was missed at mid-off by Mark Butcher as he juggled with a sliced drive off Peter Such and then by Alec Stewart off the outside edge off Mark Ramprakash.

When essentially good fielders make errors as often as England's have, good and bad luck is subsumed. England will deserve no better fortune until they learn the secret of holding their catches and holding fast when a wicket falls. The bowling has been excellent, by and large, but the batting and catching hopelessly inconsistent despite hard work and genuine efforts to develop a cohesive spirit on the part of the captain, the manager, the coaches, the psychologist and the players themselves.

The soft underbelly of the batting was gobbled up in a hurry by Stuart MacGill yesterday after McGrath had made the first incisions. First he produced a ball of extra bounce and pace to have Ramprakash caught at second slip off the splice; then he hit John Crawley's off-stump. The ball cut back through a weak defensive stroke, played off the back foot to a good-length ball.

Hussain alone provided any style or substance after this as Damien Fleming belatedly got his chance of easy wickets. England not only lost their last seven wickets for 40 but their last five for 17 in only 21 balls. It was pathetic. Scant reward, too, for Hussain, who had cover driven superbly throughout an almost faultless innings of four hours and 23 minutes.

To English eyes the disappointment was all the greater for the good all-round performance on Saturday when the bowlers combined well until Langer was dropped by Ramprakash at square-leg off the hapless Darren Gough. It helped Langer complete a triumphant innings by enjoying a last-wicket partnership of 37 with McGrath. It took a brilliant low catch by Stewart, diving right, to end England's day and a half in the field in a temperature which, although more unpleasant than unbearable on Saturday, did not drop significantly until the evening.

A total of 391 was a little better than par for Australia, given the huge advantage of winning the toss. Yet England seemed to have got over a sticky start when Atherton was out in controversial circumstances. He had started to play somewhere near his best after Butcher had been given out, padding up to an off-break from Miller bowled from round the wicket. The same fate befell Taylor against Such yesterday.

The decision against Butcher was debatable but Atherton should not have been given out. He had played unnecessarily at a leg-break from MacGill and stabbed it towards the feet of Taylor at slip. The Australian captain scooped the ball up with his finger-tips and (whatever he said immediately afterwards) claimed the catch urgently as he took the rebound, with Ian Healy in voluble support. The inexperienced third umpire, Paul Angley, gave himself far too little time to make a rational analysis of replays which, over the next half hour or so, suggested that the ball might have bounced a fraction before it reached Taylor.

Alec Stewart has always been a very unconvincing starter when he has come in against decent spinners and he was caught at short-leg off an inside edge much as he had been against Mark Waugh in the second innings at Brisbane. 49 runs from five innings is the sum of Stewart's batting in this series, 346 from 19 innings in Tests in Australia overall. It is truly a dismal record, unworthy of his talent and character. To give himself a better chance in the last two games of the series, whatever transpires in the second innings here, he should be batting at six.

Hussain and Ramprakash dispelled the developing crisis with some admirably positive batting against the spinners, Ramprakash batting bareheaded and taking the attack to Miller's unexceptional off-breaks with delightful freedom. Twice yesterday morning he got down on one knee to swing Miller into the George Giffen Stand in front of square-leg and, like Hussain, he played shrewdly against MacGill's fizzing leg-breaks. But instead of waiting for the new ball as expected, Taylor recalled McGrath with the old one, which had reverse swung for him the previous evening. Very soon the skid had started.

Michael Slater led the way in Australia's second innings in an innings marked by sparkling footwork. Once Gough's testing six-over new-ball spell had been negotiated by himself and Taylor, he scored his runs shrewdly, running every one of them like a startled rabbit except when, moving down the pitch to Ramprakash, he struck an immense six over long-on, a carry which must have been well over 100 yards.

The need for quick runs was not so great as it had been for Australia in the first Test at the Gabba and this time Slater was kept to heel by some disciplined bowling by Gough and Alan Mullally before the spinners took over. They were helped by a cracked pitch which has roughed up much more than the hard and perfectly even Brisbane surface. It took a storm to rescue England there; it will need a miracle this time.

Such a shame. Even most Australians must have felt so. The struggle for the Ashes, the real business of the tour, was going to be over almost as soon as it had begun. Australia had played, and were playing, very well once again but it was galling that England should have given them so much assistance, especially after keeping going so nobly in the burning fiery furnace on the first day. Now that they were doomed, it was only human nature for some of those in the team to berate their ill fortune at losing the toss, but I was amazed by the vehemence of one man from the visitors' dressing-room, the leg-spin guru Peter Philpott.

I strolled back with him from the ground towards the team's hotel across the river. As he walked, with a slight limp from an arthritic hip (legacy of goodness knows how many balls delivered as bowler and coach), 'Pepper', as they called him in the England camp, was taunted by guttural cries from a pursuing spectator: 'Traitor, Philpott; you bloody traitor, Philpott; you're a bloody traitor, Philpott.'

But the target of this abuse from an offended fellow countryman hardly seemed to notice. He was too busy telling me all about the disgraceful nature of the Adelaide Oval pitch. It was, he felt, a win the toss, win the match sort of surface. Well, certainly so, given that Australia had two specialist spinners. Perhaps if England's selectors had not originally picked two off-spinners for the tour and had, instead of either Croft or Such, opted for at least one bowler who specialised in turning it the other way – Tufnell, Giles or Salisbury – their enterprise would have been rewarded by better luck with the tosses. As it was, and for the first time, some of them were starting to blame fate instead of their own inadequacies under pressure.

It struck me as slightly humorous, sympathetic as one had to feel that the green had rubbed the other way again, that the whinger-in-chief in the England dressing-room turned out to be a former Australian leg-spinner. Philpott, genial fellow though he normally is, raged privately not only about the pitch but also about the decision against Atherton.

Third umpires have to be experienced – not newcomers with experience of only two first-class matches like Angley, the unfortunate young man who gave Atherton out far too hastily when there had to be some doubt about whether Taylor had unwittingly knocked the ball up on the half volley. Equally, all who are to be given this arbitrary role in future need to be given a thorough tutorial in the various nuances of the television director's art. Not until a borderline incident has been studied from a sufficient number of angles to enable the third umpire to make a decision on grounds of virtually irrefutable evidence should he press the relevant button.

If he is not sure, he has to say not out, observing the time-honoured principle that the batsman gets the benefit of the doubt. Atherton himself will go to his grave utterly convinced that he was not out. 'I *saw* it bounce,' he said with no equivocation when the incident had been virtually forgotten several weeks later. By his own later admission, Taylor, appealing instinctively in the instant after he had grasped at the ball, was subsequently not so sure. As Ramprakash had said to Darrell Hair, walking past him after being given out at Lord's the season before, these things can turn a man's career. It earned Ramprakash a fine and a suspended one-match suspension for an offence caught by the television cameras and therefore deemed to be public dissent, but if he had made the remark at a different time and place few could have argued with him. It is still widely accepted that if Don Bradman had been given out caught by Jack Ikin off Alec Bedser after a similar debate about whether the ball had bounced, early on England's first tour of Australia after the war, he might not have resumed his Test career. I dare say that the reactions of England's fielders at the time might have been seen as constituting dissent had they been shown in a present-day televised match.

That Angley should have been criticised, correctly, for not applying the benefit of the doubt convention was to have important repercussions when Michael Slater was given not out by the third umpire at a crucial stage of the final Test. Poor old Poms.

What England still hoped might be the start of a long march to freedom started on a fine summer's morning before a remarkably good last-day crowd, considering that Australia needed only six wickets to secure the Ashes for a sixth successive time.

Knowing that Taylor (even the unconventional Taylor) was bound to start with his two specialist spin bowlers, Ramprakash resumed batting in a broad-rimmed sun-hat and Stewart in his England cap. All spin and no helmets allied to the lingering air of gentility at the Adelaide Oval made for a pleasantly old-fashioned start to the day and England squeezed through the first half hour without further mishap.

It was by no means plain sailing, however, with both Miller and

MacGill getting turn and bounce from the worn surface. Both batsmen were positive to the point of occasional recklessness, Stewart driving and missing when MacGill gave the ball air and Ramprakash getting an inside edge close to his leg stump as he came down the pitch to Miller.

Taylor brought Fleming on after 11 overs and a firm cover drive brought Ramprakash a richly deserved fifty after 168 minutes' batting. Not long after, however, a lethal inswinging yorker, bowled by Fleming although it might have been the work of Waqar Younis, unlocked the England door again. It knocked out Ramprakash's leg stump and the disintegration afterwards was swift. The only surprise was that MacGill, turning the ball too much to find the edge, was not directly involved in it.

Taylor called for the second new ball six overs before lunch, and with only three balls of the morning session left, McGrath once again drew Crawley into a shot he did not need to play. The edge flew to second slip where Mark Waugh made a low catch look simple. He had missed a couple of half chances at silly point off MacGill when Stewart was 38 and 45, which helps to explain why it was that the fast bowlers did the job which the spinners would eventually have accomplished anyway. Stewart batted to no apparent plan but he played pluckily and he was overdue some luck.

Hick was fatally late in playing the first ball of the afternoon, bowled by McGrath on a full length just outside the off stump. His bat still crooked, Hick steered it almost casually to third slip, as if he did not want to be seen to be in any haste. He waited more in hope than conviction for the umpire's decision. The only surprise after that was that Alan Mullally made his first runs of the series from a snick through the slips off the formidably fast and accurate McGrath, who seized four of the last five wickets despite a stomach ailment which was to keep him in doubt until shortly before the Boxing Day Test.

Thanks not a little to this man's marvellously balanced action and unrelenting menace, Australia had regained the Ashes twenty-four minutes after lunch on the fifth day of only the third Test. The series was still alive but this had been a game which they never looked like losing. The difference in the end was 205 runs, a margin which reflected all too clearly the gulf between the two sides.

It was a disparity less of natural talent than of the way in which Australia made the most of their players whilst England continued to underachieve. Incredibly, Hick's was the eleventh first-ball duck by an England batsman in 1998.

Stewart's third Test fifty in Australia sweetened a bitter pill, but only marginally. 'We came here with the intention of trying to regain the Ashes,' he said. 'We didn't play well enough against the best side in the world and really we've been beaten pretty convincingly in the two games that we've lost.'

Australia, as Taylor remarked, had not been that much more effective in the first part of their innings but he added significantly: 'We've got a mental edge and it shows in the two different tails. We can go from five for 250 to 400; they go from five for 250 to 270. And we expect them to.'

This was the first time the Ashes had been won in Australia before Christmas. Australia had further improved their record against England in the last six series to 31 matches played, 19 won, 8 drawn and 4 lost, three of them after the Ashes had been decided. England had actually subsided from 221 for five to 237 all out, losing their last five wickets for 16 runs. They had lasted six overs and one ball longer than they had in the first innings, when conditions for batting were far preferable. It showed where the match was really lost: on the third morning when they threw away their position of equality at 183 for three. It was not good enough and when the dust had settled on the spirited revival which followed after Christmas one of the oldest of sporting clichés applied once again: too little too late.

Taylor, who had not lost a series to England in a decade as a Test cricketer, admitted that winning the toss on the first day had been significant. 'In 90 per cent of the Tests I've played the toss has made no difference but this was a very important one to win. It gave us an important advantage before the game even started.'

Winning sides, however, really do seem to make their own luck. The four Ts – teamwork, toughness, technique and Taylor – had been at the heart of Australia's triumph, one which was all the more satisfying for the embarrassing revelations about Warne and Mark Waugh. No wonder Taylor said bluntly, afterwards, 'I just don't think they are as good as we are at the moment.'

Stewart, deliberately wearing his England cap at a post-match press conference, subtly disagreed: 'What has disappointed me is that we haven't played as well as we are capable of playing. To compete against Australia we had to play to our full potential. We've failed to do that and because of that we're two–nil down. We've worked very hard in the nets and on the practice grounds but when it really counts out in the middle we haven't done it. We haven't batted as a group and we've dropped catches in matches. The bowling has been, so far, pretty good, but the other two parts of our game have not been up to the standard expected.'

England had failed also in the fourth, unseen, ingredient of consistent success in cricket: moral fibre. Individually that might not have been so in the case of most of the players, but the signs during the second half of the South African series that a stronger team ethic was developing, one in which the sum could begin to exceed the parts, had gradually faded again.

England were still wilting too often under fire, whereas Australia knew how to sustain pressure in the field for long periods, and to hang on in tight situations when they were batting. It was not just against England that, like the West Indies at their peak in the 1980s, they were becoming accustomed to taking one wicket and following it in a hurry with several more.

Taylor had now captained Australia in more matches than anyone other than his predecessor, Allan Border, and his record was extraordinary: twenty-five Tests won, twelve lost and, to his delight, only eleven drawn. He had achieved, he said, everything that he wanted to as Australian captain and he added: 'I'm only playing now because I really enjoy it.'

He did not realise it at the time, but the moment to bow out while he was still on top was just round the corner.

The Crowd

CHARLES DE LISLE

'You're a beautiful guy for an Australian, Ben.' If you were born in Melbourne and have also lived in Perth, but are now playing for England, you expect this sort of barracking. Well, certainly if you are out in the middle. But Ben Hollioake, who is destined to play in none of the Test matches, is simply having a net at the Adelaide Oval on the third afternoon of the Test when a teenage Aussie spectator shouts out this backhanded compliment. England's most glamorous young player carries on unruffled, batting against Robert Croft's off-spin. Although Hollioake ignores most of the remarks, the barracker and his friend keep up the chat: 'Give us a cover drive, Ben.' Then, when Hollioake drives the ball beautifully straight at them, he is rewarded with a patronising 'Good shot, Ben'. A couple of poor shots later, he is ridiculed again. Australia 'got rid of' him because he was 'no good' as a cricketer, and so on. The spectators may be merely creating tea-time amusement for themselves. In doing so, they show how seriously Aussies take their barracking. They have to have the last word.

The third Test, starting on 11 December, has begun in a highly charged atmosphere. 'Baggy green shame' is how the normally sober broadsheet *Sydney Morning Herald* titled a front-page report on this week's revelations that Shane Warne and Mark Waugh received payments from an illegal Indian bookmaker for providing information about match conditions during Australia's 1994 tour of Sri Lanka. The following year both players had been secretly fined by the ACB after admitting to their misdemeanours. John Howard, the cricket-mad Prime Minister, has expressed 'an intense feeling of disappointment' at the disclosures. 'Australians love their cricket,' he said, catching the national mood, 'and anything that looks as though it is knocking cricket off its pedestal is something that does deeply disturb Australians.'

As it happens, conditions for this match are hardly conducive to calming everyone down. Adelaide, the capital of Australia's driest state, is in the grip of a heatwave, and on the first day the ground resembles an oven, with temperatures reaching 42° Centigrade, the city's warmest

December day since 1987. Out in the middle, the top temperature is heading for 50°C. Even though Adelaide heat is relatively dry, it is exceedingly uncomfortable. No wonder many of the 22,000 people with tickets for the first day stay away, reducing the attendance to 13,600 (the ground capacity is 30,000).

Despite the oppressive heat, it is a delight to return to the Adelaide Oval, arguably the world's prettiest Test ground, sixteen years after first seeing an Ashes Test there. (England lost that one, too.) The Oval has changed little. It is not unlike watching cricket at Worcester: there is a sedate, intimate atmosphere, a cathedral and an old-fashioned, almost rural feel. Whereas the gates open at 8 a.m., the car parks in the parklands adjoining the ground open at 6 a.m., so that cricket-goers can start the day with a barbecue.

The Oval has, as its name suggests, long straight boundaries and short square ones; it also has picture-postcard stands, a magnificent Edwardian scoreboard, some wonderful trees, the last grass hill to remain unconcreted at an Australian Test ground, and the superb backdrop of the Adelaide Hills. There is only one problem: the three retractable floodlight towers which have been left standing since an accident in March 1998, when the fourth of them suddenly collapsed into rubble, injuring two workmen. Not until the official report has been completed can the remaining floodlights be lowered into the ground, as originally planned. Even so, the towers are so much narrower and more discreet than their counterparts elsewhere that the Oval still looks fantastic.

The big talking point on day one, once Mark Taylor has won a crucial toss and elected to bat, is: how will Mark Waugh be received on his first appearance on a cricket ground since the 'bookie scandal' broke? Taylor has predicted that the batsman may have a warmer reception than usual, but for once he is guilty of wishful thinking. Around the Oval there are clues in some of the banners run up for the occasion by Aussie supporters. 'I DON'T HAVE TO PAY $6,000 TO KNOW HOW HOT IT IS TODAY,' reads one. 'HEY, MARK, THE CASINO'S DOWN THE ROAD,' reads another. 'ONCE A CONVICT, ALWAYS A CONVICT', on a large banner bearing the names of Warne and Waugh (as if they were needed), is presumably a Pommie effort.

The noisiest part of the ground is the Hill, the grassed area underneath the scoreboard, where there must be eighty-five men for every fifteen women. Here the 'Barmy Army', consisting of a hard core of about

200 and another 200 who do not join in with their singing, is trading insults with a much larger, but less organised, group of 'ocker' Aussies. It is, as a colleague puts it, a scene reminiscent of a 'mediaeval tournament': rival fans with Australian or St George flags jostle for position, and attention. For the locals, the main battle cry is 'Aussie, Aussie, Aussie, Oi, Oi, Oi'. Their song book is limited, with 'Waltzing Matilda' to the fore. The 'Barmy Army's' favourite chant, of course, is 'Barmy Army', which can go on for twenty minutes at a time. Other favourites are 'God Save *Your* Gracious Queen', a pointed reminder of Australia's constitutional status, two digs on the economic front – 'Three dollars to the pound' and 'We're richer than you' – and 'Jerusalem', to which they often turn when things are going belly-up for England. A new addition, for Mark Waugh's benefit, is 'We still hate cheats'.

As the home side takes command of the game on the first afternoon, some Aussie fans rub it in by parading a coffin draped in the flag of St George and bearing the inscription 'RIP English cricket Australia 1998–9' under the noses of the 'Barmy Army'. Within a few minutes a detachment from the army is dancing a conga in front of everyone on the Hill, pursued by hundreds of plastic cups hurled at them by the ockers. Dozens of balloons are pushed to and fro by rival fans. One wonders how the five people operating the famous scoreboard maintain their concentration amid the uproar beneath them!

There is no shade, and the only way to escape the fierce sunshine is to make a trip to the bar. This is positioned on the ground floor of the scoreboard, with screens erected to prevent patrons standing at the bar, watching the game and knocking back beer after beer. Drinks are served in plastic cups – for the simple reason that they are harmless when they are turned into missiles – and there are only three options: local Rhine Riesling, for which there are few takers, mid-strength local West End ale, with an alcohol content of just 2.7 per cent, and mineral water. Beer and water sales are brisk all day. The mid-strength draught ale, incidentally, was originally brewed specially for the Oval after a one-day international a few years ago during which the authorities lost control of an inebriated crowd and fifty or sixty fans were arrested.

My immediate neighbours on the Hill are half a dozen ockers who cool down by removing their pointed bush hats every so often, and pouring cold water into them. At the lunch and tea intervals, they join overheated spectators queueing at taps around the ground, sating their thirst and dousing their heads and clothes in the running water.

The big moment arrives at 2.48 p.m. when Mark Waugh walks on to the field to a pretty hostile reception – and not just from the Poms, on the Hill or elsewhere. He is greeted by whistling, booing and hooting, as well as some polite applause. Cries of 'Cheat! Cheat! Cheat!' ring out from the Hill. A few shouts of 'rupees!' follow as Waugh plays his first few balls. As his discomfort becomes obvious during a brief stay at the crease, my neighbours speculate on the mileage England's players may be making out of the affair. 'If you were a Pommie,' says one, 'you'd be giving Waugh heaps of shit about this, wouldn't you? And really keeping on with it.'

Meanwhile, the ockers are doing their best to strike back, and undermine England's morale and concentration. Gough, fielding just in front of them on the boundary, becomes the target for personal abuse. 'Darren Gough is a wanker.' He looks unfazed – a wise response at any time, but particularly after the Brisbane Test, when Angus Fraser lost his cool with taunting spectators, an incident which led directly to his dropping a vital catch off Ian Healy, from Gough's bowling. As he licks his wounds in the dressing-room, Mark Waugh must be secretly thankful that he fields close to the wicket: the 'Barmy Army' would have given him 'heaps' had he been stationed in front of them.

The battle on the Hill remains good-natured, even when one or two fans who have had too much to drink are hauled off by the police. However, the police and security staff fail to respond quickly when something potentially nasty develops: Aussies start hurling cans and bottles of Coca-Cola at the Poms. 'Two or three times,' says Dave Peacock, the army's self-styled 'General', 'I've had a massive thud on the head from Coke cans or bottles. One of the other guys' girlfriend has got a big cut from a full bottle of Coke which hit her. The police aren't doing anything about finding the culprits and throwing them out of the ground.'

As play ends, and the speakers belt out this season's new official battle tune, 'Go Aussie Go', one mild-mannered Australian on the Hill reckons his fellow supporters have 'wiped the floor' with the Pommie ones today. In terms of minor injuries, that must be true. But the 'bookie scandal' has left England fans with the high ground. As one puts it, *sotto voce*: 'Morally corrupt, these Aussies, always have been, always will be.' The locals have also had to put up with the disappointment of seeing Australia take the field without a single South Australian in the side, Jason Gillespie having been omitted in favour of Colin Miller. Just as bad, Justin Langer's century has saved his place, which had been under pressure from Greg Blewett and others.

Day two, and the searing heat does not abate until a 'cool change' comes through mid-afternoon. But it is a Saturday, and today's crowd is better: 16,372. Over in the Members', the atmosphere – if not the attire – on the lawns and in the marquees behind the stands is reminiscent of Wimbledon. The marquees actually stand on the grass tennis courts used by members of the South Australian Cricket Association (SACA). The ivy on the backs of the George Giffen and Mostyn Evan stands adds another familiar touch.

Gaggles of schoolgirls in sundresses flit about, occasionally popping into a stand, though more to be seen, than to see, one suspects. Meanwhile, small boys play their own Tests on the lawns in front of the marquees. Ruddy-cheeked farmers and their wives lunch from a menu including crayfish, juicy big prawns, oysters and, of course, strawberries and cream, all washed down with delicious wine from the nearby Barossa Valley. Others down the only beer on the ground which is actually full strength: only the members are trusted with the real thing, but perhaps it is a privilege they have earned – the waiting list is twenty-one years long. 'They can get smashed,' explains Terry Davies, SACA's marketing and membership manager. 'But we like to think they won't jeopardise their membership by misbehaving.'

For all their essential gentility, and their appreciation of good cricket, SACA members made their feelings about Mark Waugh plain yesterday, a minority booing and making hostile comments as the batsman made his way through them to the middle. Today, though, few are prepared to discuss this. A farmer from Port Pirie, down for the first three days, is probably representative, not least in withholding his name. 'I didn't boo Waugh,' he says firmly, 'but I didn't clap him either.' A new banner elsewhere in the ground is perhaps more reassuring. 'DON'T WORRY, MARK,' it reads, 'IF YOU'RE DROPPED BY THE AUSSIES YOU CAN ALWAYS BECOME A WEATHERMAN.'

It would be wrong to think that Aussies only barrack Poms. When Colin Miller is brought on to bowl at England's openers on the second afternoon, someone on the Hill, voicing local anger at his selection ahead of Gillespie, shouts out: 'We don't like you, Miller. Go back to Tasmania.' Barbs like these – and compliments like 'We love ya, Heals!' – are clearly audible by the players in the middle. Miller's response is swift: he quickly makes the breakthrough for Australia, removing Mark

Butcher for six. 'You're out, Butcher, you sucker!' bellows Miller's critic, turning his tongue on the old enemy. Later, when Atherton pulls McGrath stirringly for four, the 'Barmy Army' is so wrapped up in its own battles that few applaud – a shame. As England wickets tumble under grey skies on the third morning, and the Ashes slip away, Australians celebrate the removal of each batsman by jumping in the air and banging on the advertising hoardings at the front of the Hill. It is not a pretty sound, but it somehow underlines the hopelessness of England's position.

Not all Aussies are reaching for the sky. 'I'd like to see Australia beaten,' says one of those pleasant sixtysomething Anglophile ladies more likely to be found in the SACA enclosure than almost anywhere in Australia. Why? 'Because they're too cocky.' She and her husband, an Oxford graduate, also wish to see a close contest for the Ashes. After lunch, I watch the start of Australia's second innings with other SACA members, in the covered Mostyn Evan Stand. Next to me is a family with two small children, including the most charming – and best-behaved – spectator at the match. Jesse, a five-year-old with mousy hair and a denim pinafore dress, appears to have cricket in her blood – her mother says she herself used to imitate Merv Hughes's elaborate warm-up routines – and is enjoying her day so much she wants to skip school tomorrow and return. She is intrigued and puzzled by the mob on the Hill, studying the scene with her miniature binoculars, then pressing her fingers into her ears to keep the noise out. Her mother bats away questions about these funny people singing 'Rule Britannia', and urges little Jesse to concentrate on the game. It works. 'I want to be a cricket umpire,' announces the little girl.

Jesse may want to continue her cricket education tomorrow, but many spectators in the crowd of 19,720 – the best of the Test – are finding the contest tediously one-sided. After tea, hundreds desert the stands, some heading home, others back to the marquees, which become jam-packed. The spectators who stick it out are subdued, their cheering moderate; many members even join a Mexican wave, albeit with a few prompts. There is even muttering about Michael Slater's uncharacteristic rate of scoring. By the close he has taken four hours over his unbeaten 74.

In the hotel lobby on the fourth morning, English stoicism and humour are called upon yet again. 'See you in the morgue,' says one supporter to another, with a resigned smile. A third wonders aloud in the lift if today will witness 'the last rites'. At the ground, the theme is continued. 'IN THE CITY OF CHURCHES,' proclaims yet another fresh banner, 'ENGLAND DOESN'T HAVE A PRAYER'. To make matters worse, many of the British package-tour contingent have been allocated seats in the temporary Eastern Stand, which is completely open to the elements. This was almost unbearable early in the match, when the large gaps in the stand suggested that many members of the white floppy-hat brigade had taken refuge in their special marquee behind. There they could watch the game on television and take their time over their packed lunch – part of the deal, it included a chicken sandwich, custard pie, piece of fruit and choice of soft drink. For my money, though, the best liquid refreshment is the iced coffee to be found at a facility unimaginable at an Australian ground a decade ago – the cappuccino stall, behind the Bradman Stand.

Meanwhile, for this fourth day, the 'Barmy Army' has repositioned itself, moving forward so that instead of standing all day in front of the scoreboard its members are now sitting right on the boundary. According to Dave Peacock, it is an attempt to evade Aussie missiles. 'It's our way of getting round having a punch-up on the Hill,' he says. 'It also means the Aussies can't come in and wave their flags in the middle of us.'

I have neglected so far to mention three of the best spots from which to view an Adelaide Test. The first is the grassy bank at the Cathedral end, known as the 'dry area', right next to the rowdiest zone. You have a fantastic view down the ground, your neighbours will not irritate you, and if you do not want to sit on the grass all day, you can bring a deckchair or a rug; there is also plenty of shade under the trees at the back. Another good place to stretch out and sunbathe is the opposite corner of the Oval. This bank, which also has some shade, tends to be the preserve of a younger, less macho element. There are plenty of attractive young women in bikinis, confident of avoiding the sort of ribald comment that would greet them on the Hill (though even Adelaide men no longer hold up signs giving passing female spectators marks out of ten).

The atmosphere in this quiet corner is one of gentle Australian humour, minus the raw aggression and eardrum-blasting sound effects of the madhouse at the other end. As Glenn McGrath walked to the wicket on the second morning, and the tannoy announced the arrival of the 'next Australian batsman', my neighbour observed: 'The next Australian bunny, you mean!' The third excellent spot is next door: the Sir Donald Bradman Stand. The only modern stand at the Oval, it fits in superbly with the existing architecture and offers wonderful views down the ground, for the media among others, from the River Torrens (city) end. Sir Donald himself is, unusually, not at the Test. At ninety, he is said to be too frail to attend, although he has been able to receive the Bedser twins, and Mark Taylor, at his Adelaide home.

As England's second innings subsides on the fifth day, only the members' area is reasonably full, and the ground is hushed. Alec Stewart's half-century gives visiting fans something to cheer. For half an hour after it is all over, a group of seventy-odd 'Barmy Army' people stay in position, chanting 'Barmy Army – Alec Stewart'. It is a loyal, defiant and futile gesture, which echoes around an arena which is rapidly emptying (unlike in England, there are no public presentations at the end of each Test, only at the end of the series).

Terry Davies professes himself pleased with a total crowd for the match of 72,156, including a good fourth-day figure of 14,817. 'We budgeted for 70,000, so considering the heat on the first day and a half, it's a good result. And there's been very little crowd trouble.' This is confirmed by the South Australia Police Department. 'It's been a very peaceful match,' says Inspector Bronwyn Killmier. 'Two or three people were arrested on the first day when they tried to re-enter the ground after being ejected for things like throwing ice.' And the 'Barmy Army'? 'We thought they were great. Great slogans, and they were obviously enjoying the match. A couple were ejected but generally they were well behaved.'

It is lunch-time the day after the third Test has ended in bitter disappointment for England supporters. It is also the day after the 'Barmy Army's' Adelaide party. Forty core members are nursing hangovers at a backpackers' hostel in the city centre. No wonder Dave Peacock, the army's tall, broad-shouldered 'General', looks exhausted. He was up until three supervising the gathering – a well-organised affair held at the Old Adelaide Gaol, of all places – and then he, his wife Ceri and some others went to a strip club. They got to bed at five. In the tranquil garden of the Cumberland Arms Hotel, an old-style Aussie pub with stained timber everywhere, Peacock and his missus order steak and chips.

The party, which attracted 650 guests paying A$5 (£2) each, succeeded in at least two of its aims. True, no England players turned up, but four thousand dollars was raised for leukaemia research and will be donated towards Ian Botham's next charity walk for that cause; and there was a fair response to the predominantly male army's invitation to the 'ladies of Adelaide' to be part of an 'evening to remember'. How much of it anyone can remember is uncertain, but by Peacock's estimate about 100 Adelaide girls turned up, and fifty did not leave alone (even before the party, one 'Barmy' had moved in with a local woman he met at the Cumberland). One woman present for purely professional reasons was a pretty local radio reporter, who went cheerfully back to work clutching a rather artificial tape of 'Barmies' singing solely for the benefit of her microphone: Peacock and the others are good at manipulating the media.

The outfit has come quite a long way since some backpackers who had become friends and formed themselves into an organised singing/barracking group while following the last Ashes tour as individuals were christened the 'Barmy Army' by the Australian press. Now the name is registered as a trademark, a mailing list of 4,000 is serviced and song sheets are distributed at matches. This time, their T-shirts, polo shirts and other merchandise are being marketed through the official shops at Test grounds, as well as on the pavement outside. As before, the profits help to pay the travelling expenses of the 'Barmy' leaders. Like their lobster-pink followers, they are generally people in their twenties and thirties who have given up good jobs to lend England the most vociferous, most boisterous support it has ever enjoyed, home or away. There is a pretty even balance of white- and blue-collar workers, from all over England. Professionals include the odd banker, a few engineers, one or two policemen, university graduates taking a year out, and at least two solicitors on sabbatical, Ceri Peacock and her friend Andrea Francois, who is selling T-shirts outside the grounds with her boyfriend Gary Taylor. The hard core – that is, those going to all five Tests – totals some eighty, compared with forty in 1994–5. It includes one man currently banned from Surrey matches, and one MCC member, Jack Hyams. At seventy-nine, he holds the record for the highest number of runs in a career in any form of cricket (120,000 at the last count).

Although the 'Barmy Army' has attracted criticism aplenty, especially in Britain, it has also attracted praise. After the series, *Wisden Cricket Monthly* chose these supporters for its 'Man of the Month' (or rather 'Mob of the Month') slot, arguing that England's Ashes tour wasn't really short of heroes: it's just that most of them were in the stands. The army, however, is explicit about the fact that its number-one aim is to 'have fun'; supporting England takes second place. However noisy, mindless and boorish its detractors find the 'Barmy Army', the 'soldiers' can always point to the fact that the England team has long been publicly and privately supportive. Alec Stewart thought so highly of their efforts that he took the side over to the Sydney Hill at the end of the series to salute them. Players clearly feel they have more in common with this type of fan than with the middle-aged tour groups. 'The players are the same age as us,' says Peacock, a thirty-one-year-old from Bedford who resigned from his job as a contract manager with Manpower to undertake this tour. 'We're all on tour, we play cricket, the only difference is that they're playing for England.' He adds: 'The players are a little bit isolated in their five-star hotels. They want to know how we're getting on, how we afford it – and how many women the lads have pulled.'

It is also clear that the 'Barmies' – whose favourite players are Stewart, Darren Gough and Dean Headley – see themselves as striking back, on behalf of their England heroes, at the rubbishing meted out to them by Aussies. 'England players get sledged mercilessly out in the middle, and players like Goughie got heaps of abuse on the boundary in Adelaide,' says Peacock. 'What we can do is equalise that situation.' Unfortunately, this means they sometimes go over the top. Some of the remarks which Peacock shouted at Mark Taylor in Adelaide over his part in covering up the 'bookie scandal' were pretty personal, unnecessary and probably slanderous. Words such as 'disgrace' and 'cheat' featured strongly.

On the other hand, Peacock believes that as a unit the army puts on a show which even many Aussie spectators appreciate: 'I'm constantly amazed at how, at the end of a day's play, people come up and shake our hands and say, "Thanks for a brilliant day's entertainment. It's great that you're here. I just wish you luck in the next game."' He goes on: 'They love the "Barmy Army" over here. It's fun, they've taken us to their hearts but I suppose to a certain extent the Aussies feel a little bit sorry for us. Although they love the singing and the atmosphere that we generate, what really appeals to them is the fact that we're following a losing team.' There is no doubt about that; and if the 'Barmy Army' is still around when England next win a series in Australia, we shall find out how much the Aussies really like them.

The army is acutely conscious of its image, which Peacock believes (with some reason) has improved markedly since the last Ashes tour. Efforts have been made to break away from 'football-style support', eliminate songs including swear words and widen the repertoire. 'We've cut out the constant, incessant chanting of "Barmy Army",' he says, mentioning the new emphasis on 'magnificent songs' – yes, 'songs' – such as 'Jerusalem'. Peacock is also at pains to stress that most of his footsoldiers do not, as a rule, get drunk at the match. Sure, they have a few 'strong beers' in the pub at lunch-time, but the serious drinking is left until the evening, back at the hostel, when they can be heard singing until the early hours. 'At the ground,' he says, 'the Aussies outdrink us, no problem. They get really tanked up. But then, it may be their one day of Test cricket for the year.'

Peacock maintains that, whatever Australia's superiority on the field, the team's supporters are a pretty unimaginative bunch. 'They're fairly ignorant, they've got no sense of humour, no songs. If they supported their team like we do ours, they'd be absolutely crucifying us with songs and jokes and humour about how poor our team is. As it is, we can always win a song contest.' One-eyed though this view is, there is something in it: unlike in Britain, there is not much of a tradition of singing or chanting at Australian sports events; hurling insults comes more naturally. Given that Peacock, whose booming voice makes him an ideal cheerleader, has been singing, chanting and shouting for the past five days, it is hardly surprising he has almost lost his voice.

What impact does the 'Barmy Army' have on England's fortunes? It is impossible to judge, but they like to think they contributed to Mark Waugh's first-innings failure in Adelaide, and in a very close match, such as the Melbourne Test, their passion and optimism may even have helped tip the scales – they were singing 'We're going to win the Test' long before England had an outside chance of doing so. And Peacock and his mates do seem to combine being genuine cricket lovers with an interest in the other delights Australia has to offer. Asked what he likes about the country, he replies 'the culture'. Then he remembers his lines, and adds: 'If they've *got* any culture. Their way of life, their attitude to life, their emphasis on enjoying themselves, the beaches, the weather. It's a beautiful country, there's so much to see and it's easy to travel around. It's a great place.' Not that you would know it from some of his public outbursts.

12

The Prime Minister's XI

CHARLES DE LISLE

'It's almost a religious experience to go to the first day of an Ashes series,' said John Howard, Australia's Liberal Prime Minister, as the campaign opened in Brisbane. Sharing the experience was Kim Beazley, the Leader of the Labor Opposition, who was sitting contentedly a few seats away in the Australian Cricket Board's box. It was less than two months since they had been locked in daily combat in a tough Federal election campaign. Three weeks later Beazley chose to spend his fiftieth birthday at home in Perth, watching the Adelaide Test on television. On to the deciding Test of the series, and John Howard was at the Sydney Cricket Ground (SCG) for almost the entire match. It was noticeable, as he came and went from various boxes, at one point having a glass of beer courtesy of the ACB, how little ceremony attends an Australian Prime Minister. Then, when Mark Taylor announced his retirement from international cricket, Howard paid him the sizeable compliment of interrupting a Cabinet meeting to make a public tribute 'on behalf of all Australians' to 'a very great captain'. Finally, just in case fellow Australians had forgotten him amid all this excitement, Bob Hawke, the ex-Prime Minister, put in a surprise appearance on the Sydney Hill during the first one-day final.

There is one occasion in the cricket calendar, however, when the Prime Minister has the stage to himself. It is the annual match between his own XI and the touring team, held at the attractive tree-lined Manuka Oval in the national capital, Canberra. This time it took place on 17 December, two days after Australia retained the Ashes in Adelaide: perfect timing for a Prime Minister. Although Howard is genuinely passionate about cricket, he is not unaware of the political advantages to be derived from a day-long cricket-fest televised live across the nation, albeit only on 'pay' television. At times it seemed as if the cameras from Channel Seven's cable service spent almost as much time filming the pin-striped host/number-one spectator as they did the action on the field. And as if to underline the value to the game of Prime Ministerial patronage, Howard announced during his lunch party in the

Bradman Pavilion that his Government would make a grant of A$1 million (some £400,000) towards the cost of upgrading facilities at the Oval. The lunch was, needless to say, covered by crews from the main evening news television programmes, which also ran brief highlights of the match.

Unlike its English counterpart, Australian cricket has long enjoyed support in the higher echelons of politics. Whereas John Major was the first British Prime Minister since Sir Alec Douglas-Home to take a deep interest in the game, cricket in Australia has been blessed with passionate support at the top for half the post-war period, the contributions of Sir Robert Menzies (PM 1949–66) and Bob Hawke (1983–91) being acknowledged in stands named after them at Manuka. And there could hardly be a greater contrast between the enthusiasm and feel for the game and its traditions of John Howard and the indifference of Tony Blair, whose real love is, of course, soccer.

'Cricket here has political support in high places,' says Richard Cashman, general editor of *The Oxford Companion to Australian Cricket*. 'It always has had that support. And that is one way you can locate cricket in Australian society.' Cashman believes the robust political backing has been 'tremendously important' to Australian cricket, which has a very expensive structure to maintain. Certainly the Hawke Labor Government is entitled to – and duly claims – some of the credit for the renaissance in the nation's cricketing fortunes since the mid-1980s. It played a significant part in setting up the Cricket Academy in Adelaide, 60 per cent of whose funding comes from the Federal Government (most of the rest comes from its sponsor, the Commonwealth Bank). The Hawke administration also backed the establishment of 'Kanga' cricket in schools; more than a million primary schoolboys and girls now play this simplified form of the game, which emphasises participation and teaches children a range of basic skills.

Regardless of an Australian politician's personal tastes, it makes political sense for him or her to court and support the cricketing fraternity. Cricket is the country's only truly national team sport; it has an extremely high profile, dominating the sports pages (and even some front pages) throughout the summer; its appeal cuts across class, age and regional barriers – it is particularly strong out in the bush – and some, though by no means all, ethnic barriers as well; and it is seen by millions as a force for good, a force for national unity and a source of national enjoyment and pride. Moreover, a small majority of Aus-

1a The commanders:
Alec Stewart (left) and Mark Taylor, who won five tosses out of five in his last series as skipper.

1b–e Strike force (left to right):
Glenn McGrath and Jason Gillespie for Australia, Darren Gough and Alex Tudor for England.

2a

2b

2c

2a Stuart MacGill started poorly in Brisbane but by the end of the first Test was almost a match winner.

2b Mark Butcher acknowledges the applause for an excellent first hundred against Australia; Graham Thorpe also played well, but another back injury forced an early return home.

2c Nasser Hussain at second slip reprieves Steve Waugh on 68, off the bowling of Gough, needless to say.

2d Hussain redeemed himself with the first of his four Test fifties.

2e Mark Ramprakash, holding England's lower order together.

2f A typically flamboyant stroke from Michael Slater – on the way to the first of three centuries in an Ashes series, for the second time in his career.

2d

2e

2f

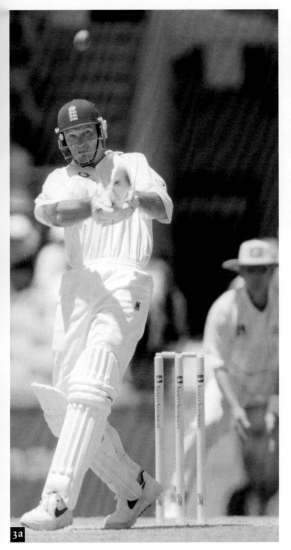

3a Graeme Hick pulling Jason Gillespie for six during the innings that averted a two-day finish on the fastest pitch in the world – Perth.

3b John Crawley is picked up at short leg by Justin Langer off Colin Miller. Crawley's tour never entirely recovered from his mysterious mugging in Cairns.

3c Yet another escape for Australia as Gough – for once the perpetrator not the victim – drops a straightforward catch at long-leg from a Ponting top-edge off Alex Tudor.

3d Bullseye! Dominic Cork suffers the consequences of being late on the hook.

4a Bob Hawke, the former Australian Prime Minister, who was once 12th man for Colin Cowdrey's Oxford side, at the SCG.

4b Richard Winter, the WACA's youthful new curator, produced a fast, bouncy pitch which kept close catchers of both sides busy.

4c Umpire Darrell Hair calls for a decision by the third umpire using the TV replay.

4d BSkyB commentators (left to right): Bob Willis, Paul Allott, Mark Nicholas, Ian Botham and Allan Border.

4e The Barmy Army goes down noisily on the Adelaide Hill. They were still chanting half an hour after the Ashes had gone.

4f Australian authorities tried to ban the Mexican wave after crowd trouble at a Melbourne one-dayer.

5a Glenn McGrath, never one to exchange pleas-
antries with the England batsmen, bowls Crawley for
five in the first innings at Adelaide.

5b Justin Langer's unbeaten 179, made in stiflingly hot
conditions, cemented his place as Australia's No. 3.

5c Alec Stewart walks off as Australia celebrate the retention of the Ashes in Adelaide, McGrath having just
dismissed England's No. 11, Peter Such.

6a As he started to run out of partners in Australia's first innings at the MCG, Steve Waugh improvised audaciously, this time against Headley. He made 122 not out.

6b Ian Healy watches as Stewart drives on the way to his first Test century against Australia.

6c A tireless Headley, bowling England towards an astonishing victory in Melbourne, appeals once more. It was the longest session in Test history.

6d Gough leads the celebrations after finishing off Australia's second innings.

7a Mark Waugh claims his 100th Test catch: Hussain at Sydney.

7b Technical perfection: watched by Warren Hegg, playing his second Test, Mark Waugh creams the ball as he marches towards his century.

7c Gough took the first Ashes hat-trick by an Englishman this century. MacGill was the middle victim.

7d Heir apparent or usurper? Shane Warne, back in the side at Sydney, casts a wary glance towards Stuart MacGill, who filled his boots so effectively.

7e As Mark Taylor holds the Ashes replica trophy aloft, Lord MacLaurin, ECB Chairman, ponders his next move in the campaign to end England's dismal run.

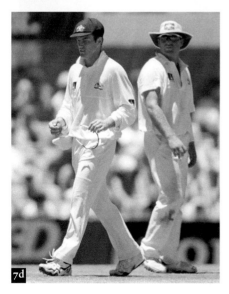

8a

8b

8c

8a Gough and Mahanama collide as the pressure rises during Sri Lanka's controversial one-day victory over England in Adelaide.
8b Muttiah Muralitharan shows an apparently straight arm to umpire Ross Emerson, whose decision to no-ball him for throwing led to a 14-minute walk-off by the Sri Lankans and to legal repercussions.
8c Graeme Hick, scorer of three one-day centuries, cools down with an ice-pack.

tralians still attach great importance to high achievement in cricket. 'The performance of Australia's cricket side,' noted a leader in *The Australian* when it selected Taylor as its Australian of the Year, 'undoubtedly has an important effect on the national mood.' Or, as Cashman puts it, 'We're a small country. We don't make a big world impact in politics, science or technology, so sport has always been a way in which Australians can stride the world stage, as it were.'

It is hardly surprising, therefore, that support for cricket also slices across political boundaries. A game that is perceived by many in Britain as old-fashioned, middle-aged, 'stuffy' (to borrow an adjective from cricket's new paymasters, Channel 4), predominantly Tory and not very successful has so broad an appeal in Australia that no serious politician is frightened to be associated with it. Equally, politics seems to attract a good number of people who are or have been actively involved in the game. They range from Rodney Cavalier, a left-wing Labor politician who is a trustee of the SCG, to Cheryl Kernot, former national leader of the Australian Democrats and one of the first women in Australia to umpire a men's grade game, and the right-wing Ian McLachlan. A free-striking batsman reckoned by Keith Miller to have had 'the straightest bat in Australian cricket' in the early 1960s, McLachlan was 12th man for Australia in the fourth Test against England at Adelaide in 1962–3, and was Defence Minister in the Howard Cabinet until his retirement from politics last year.

It is also worth mentioning that it is still – just – considered acceptable for a Prime Minister to plan official visits to London around the date of the England–Australia Test at Lord's. Howard did so in 1997 and Hawke did so in 1989; in another era, Menzies – his country's last truly Anglophile leader – did so almost as a matter of course. Another indication of the place cricket still occupies in society came in 1990 when John Hewson, then Leader of the Liberal (that is, conservative) Opposition, declared in the Sir Robert Menzies Lecture at Melbourne's Monash University that 'whatever happens, we [Australians] will always speak English, play cricket and honour the Anzacs'.

Against this background, the existence of a Prime Minister's XI at the end of the twentieth century looks less odd. The tradition of such matches survived even the turbulent premiership of the aggressively republican Paul Keating (1991–6). The smooth, highly articulate Keating had no time for cricket, preferring the company of the arts world, but dutifully persisted with the match – even though he can have recognised no more than a few faces on either side. John Howard, by contrast, could give you an accurate precis of every player's recent form. A traditionalist in the Major mould, the bespectacled Howard, fifty-nine, can claim a comparable lifelong love of the game. As a nine-year-old, he sat with his father on the SCG Hill and watched Sir Donald Bradman's second-last first-class innings, a carefree 53 in sixty-five minutes. This season, Howard, never much of a player himself, was labelled a 'cricket tragic' by Taylor. You might have expected Howard's spin doctors to be horrified; but with the Australian captain explaining that this was simply his way of conveying his belief that the Prime Minister loved the game more than he himself did, Howard was flattered. Soon afterwards, asked by the *Sydney Morning Herald* to name his favourite books of 1998, Howard underlined his priorities by nominating Dickie Bird's autobiography as one of two choices. It is probable that cricket in its way reinforces Howard's own strong monarchist views, and not entirely fanciful to mention one small additional drawback of a republic, from his point of view: an Australian head of state might well wish to field his own President's XI against touring sides.

The Prime Minister does not choose his own XI but has some say, effectively becoming a fourth member of the Australian selection panel for the occasion. The choice of Taylor to lead a PM's XI which, as usual, sought to give opportunities to players on the fringe of national selection was apparently a Howard one. The Prime Minister's other 'duties' included spinning the coin for the toss – which Taylor, for the only time all summer, lost to Alec Stewart – hosting that lunch for eighty and selecting the man of the match.

Among Howard's guests was Alex Allan, the British High Commissioner, who had the honour of handing Taylor the coin for the fateful Adelaide toss. Allan takes a keen interest in cricket, even though he is first and foremost a yachtsman. The street-smart forty-eight-year-old is a high-profile appointment to Canberra, even for a post which ranks in the Foreign Office's second tier, equal with Rome, and below Washington, Moscow, Paris, Tokyo, New Delhi and the other leading postings. Allan is not a diplomat by training, having made his career at the Treasury. His last job was the top one for an official at 10 Downing Street: Principal Private Secretary to the Prime Minister, a role in which he served Major capably for five nerve-stretching years and Blair for a few months, before packing his bags for the sun. 'The job', says a former colleague, 'was seen as a suitable reward for five tough years, often working fourteen-hour days. I hear they had to calm him down a bit in his early weeks in Canberra!' Allan, who will return to the Treasury after the Olympics, has a special qualification for this post: his wife, the printmaker Katie Clemson, is Australian.

Were it not for this game, touring teams would never visit the purpose-built capital city carved out of the bush between the wars, which would be a shame. Manuka retains a rural atmosphere, a feel underlined by one or two of the attractions to be found behind the stands – for example, there was a 'Petting Paddock' where small children could make friends with a few sheep and a goat. The contest drew a capacity crowd of 9,500 on a hot, sunny day, and the entertainment included a Father Christmas who, making no pretence of impartiality, shouted repeatedly: 'Aussie! Oi! Aussie! Oi! Aussie! Oi!' However, the players took things seriously and the ambitious young Aussies were doubtless glad to go home with a 'Prime Minister's XI' cap bearing a close resemblance to the 'baggy green' of the national team.

The present series of PM's matches dates from 1984, when Bob Hawke revived a tradition which had started and finished with the Liberal Menzies. The original matches were essentially social affairs, the idea being to boost the game in the Canberra region by bringing in international players, in the days before they could all be seen on television. Before the first match, against John Goddard's West Indians in 1951, Menzies briefed the umpires that no one was to make a duck. But when the former Test opener Jack Fingleton was caught behind, the umpire was so startled that instead of calling 'No Ball', he gave him out. So an embarrassed Fingleton had to go. During MCC's 1962–3 tour Bradman made a rare return to the crease, at the age of fifty-four. Batting at five for the Prime Minister, he began cautiously and had made four when he played a defensive shot to Brian Statham. The ball bounced off his body on to his foot, then on to the wicket, knocking off a bail. Again a stand-in umpire – Alan Davidson – was so bemused that he forgot to shout 'No Ball', and, to the huge disappointment of the crowd, off Bradman went.

During the 1998 match there were shocks of a quite different order *off* the field. With Parliament not sitting, there had appeared to be no danger of the PM's day at the cricket being interrupted by official business. However, at 9 a.m. Canberra time, the United States and Britain launched a series of cruise missile and bomb attacks on Iraq that lasted, on day one of Operation Desert Fox, until 3 p.m. Although Australian diplomats in Washington were only informed after the offensive began, Howard felt it his duty as a staunch American ally to make a statement strongly supporting the attempt to cripple Saddam Hussein militarily. Accordingly, he slipped away shortly before noon to give a press conference. Standing outside his parliamentary office, in front of two furled Australian flags, Howard cut a more American figure than Tony Blair, radiating gravitas outside 10 Downing Street, with only a Christmas tree for decoration. While Howard's remarks gained wide coverage across Australia and on CNN, the striking thing was that a major world event should have merely caused the Australian Prime Minister to miss an hour of his own cricket match. 'Australia is a small player internationally,' said one member of the Canberra diplomatic corps. 'But don't forget that she sent quite small but nevertheless symbolic military forces to the Gulf in 1990, and again earlier this year.'

By the time Howard returned, England, after an embarrassing start (26–4 after seven overs), had recovered to a point where, with one of their allocated 50 overs to go, they were 209–8, not far short of setting the PM's XI a decent target. Sportingly, Mark Taylor brought himself on. Bowling slow round-arm lobs, he conceded 16 runs, including two sixes by Angus Fraser. Once England had also taken early wickets, Alan Mullally taking one in each of his first two overs and coming back twice later to keep matters under control, they always looked like winning, although Rodney Marsh's son Daniel played a fine attacking innings and was just starting to look dangerous when he sliced a drive to extra cover off Hick, to be out for 74. England ran out winners by the exact number of runs Taylor had conceded off his solitary over; it was a match which a struggling touring side could not have afforded to lose. After making Marsh man of the match, Howard visited the England dressing-room, and then his own, for a 'couple of quiet beers'.

The strange thing about Howard's strong identification with cricket is that, during his first spell as Opposition Leader, in the 1980s, his passion for the game made almost no impression on the public consciousness. This may well have been because although he has known the likes of Colin Cowdrey for years, he was operating in the shadow of the charismatic Hawke. A sports enthusiast with the common touch who wore his emotions on his sleeve – more than once, as Prime Minister, he broke down in tears on television – Hawke had a knack of turning up at any national sporting triumph. Bobby Simpson, then Australia's coach, tried to correct the imbalance, suggesting to Howard that he send the side a telegram every now and then, and 'not just when we win – as Bob Hawke does'. Regular 'good luck' messages were soon on their way from the Opposition Leader's office, but public impact was minimal.

Hawke was also a cricketer of some note. He played first-grade (the level below the Sheffield Shield) for several seasons in Perth, and while a Rhodes Scholar was 12th man for an Oxford side captained by Cowdrey, in 1954. As he put it in *The Hawke Memoirs*, he 'realised every young cricketer's dream by fielding at Lord's for a day'.

As the international season drew to a close, I went to see Hawke. We met one morning in his office, a large, bright room overlooking the ever-expanding Sydney skyline. Apart from a small photograph of him with an arm round George Bush, there was little sign that he had ever been Prime Minister. An evocative painting of an outback cricket scene added a nice Australian touch. As his assistant prepared coffee in superior mugs, Hawke said how 'disappointed' he had been with England's fielding in the Test series. On the desk in front of him was a small pile of large cigars – one of which he soon lit – and a pair of rimless spectacles, a reminder of the pair which was smashed when, as PM, he mistimed a hook shot in a game against the Canberra press gallery.

A relaxed, likeable figure who is now a business consultant in Asia, Hawke does not look his sixty-nine years. He is tanned, fit and lean: he works out at a gym at his harbourside home. Now that he is free to do as he pleases, the tightly coiffured silver hair of his days in office has been released, a big wave falling roguishly over the right side of his head. That, too, makes him look younger. A small man (he was a wicket-keeper in first-grade, though he was also a decent batsman), he speaks slowly and deliberately, with plenty of gesticulating, occasionally thumping the desk with his fist to emphasise a point.

For the first twenty minutes or so we discussed politics and the international scene, Hawke fondly recalling 'some mighty rows, epic battles' over South African sanctions with the most powerful Pom of the 1980s – 'Margaret'. When I shifted the conversation on to cricket, his eyes visibly brightened. The revival of the PM's match, I already knew, had been one of his first decisions on winning office, taking him just twelve days. The ACB, he said, had been 'mad keen' on his idea, and he was helped by the fact that Lawrie Sawle, with whom he had played cricket at the University of Western Australia, soon became chairman of the national selectors. 'So we had a good connection,' Hawke added. He remains proud of the money which the matches raised for various levels of the game, and of the players – such as David Boon, a century-maker against West Indies in 1984 – who made their first big mark in the PM's colours.

'Did you have any hand in selection?' I asked innocently. 'Bloody oath!' cried Hawke. 'I'd tell the selectors what I thought, I had some ideas, but I'd also ask them if there was anyone they particularly wanted to test. So it was a combined effort.' He likes to think that in Australia there is some connection between a love of cricket and longevity in office, noting with a cheeky smile: 'Fraser, Whitlam and Keating wouldn't have known one end of the bat from another, but the enduring Prime Ministers, Menzies and Hawke, had a genuine passion for the game.' Did that mean John Howard was going to be around for a long time? 'No,' he added smoothly, again the old pro. 'I hope he'll be the exception to the rule.'

Offered a loosener on the reasons for current Australian supremacy, Hawke cover drove expertly for four. 'I can't overstate the importance of the Cricket Academy,' he said. 'I think the quality of Australian cricket has gone up enormously as a result. You only have to look at the statistics to see that.' However, there was one aspect of the performance of the Ashes-retaining side which troubled him. Although himself noted for a colourful vocabulary, Hawke said he would like to see the team cut down on the 'sledging'. 'I still think it's important to play fair,' he said. 'I don't think our blokes have played unfairly, they've not cheated, but they push things reasonably hard on the pressure and at times they've gone over the top. For example, I've got enormous admiration for Glenn McGrath. He's a marvellous young man and a great bowler. But I think at times he does himself a little bit of a disservice by excess belligerence in a personal sort of sense.'

With that diplomatically phrased rebuke out of the way, Hawke readily conceded his good fortune in getting to know many of the leading Aussie players of the post-war era, including the most admired Australian of all. 'I think,' he said, talking very slowly, 'I can genuinely call Bradman a friend. I rang him on the occasion of his ninetieth birthday and we talked briefly. Wished him a happy birthday. Hope he does the ton!'

What about all the fuss currently being made of Mark Taylor, and the captaincy? Taylor had 'done much' to deserve the adulation, and 'in terms of public estimation' the position from which he had just resigned was, as often claimed, second only to that of the PM. 'The captain of the Australian cricket side,' he added, 'is a pretty important bloke!'

Two days later, Hawke reminded us that he was still a not unimportant bloke. He had been invited to the first one-day final between Australia and England at the SCG as the guest of a company. It so happened that the only way for him to reach their box in the O'Reilly Stand was to make his way through the ockers and the 'Barmy Army' members doing battle on the Hill. Not many retired politicians would relish such a journey. But many people cheered 'Hawkie', some stopped to shake his hand, someone offered him a cup of beer, the match almost came to a halt – and he was back on the evening news bulletins. It was Hawke-as-man-of-the-people revisited.

As a cricketer, Kim Beazley – who attended the 1998 Perth Test in a private capacity – ranks somewhere between Hawke, his old political patron, and Howard. Beazley played a lot of cricket as a schoolboy, his great hero being his fellow West Australian, the Test bowler Graham McKenzie. Day after day Beazley would run into the crease, legs pumping, trying to imitate McKenzie's long, loping action. 'I was like all my friends,' Beazley told his biographer, Peter FitzSimons, a former rugby Test forward, 'in that I wanted to play for Australia.' The fast-medium bowler never came close, but a hat-trick for the Cottesloe Cricket Club 4th XI, at the age of sixteen, was some consolation. Not only did it earn him a hat-trick trophy presented by none other than McKenzie himself, but it was accompanied by the memorable words: 'I haven't got one of these.' Meanwhile, in a fiftieth birthday interview in the Melbourne *Age*, Beazley showed he was not going to be out-cricketed by Howard. A voracious reader, he mentioned that his presents included a copy of a biography of W. G. Grace.

While it is reassuring for Australian cricket to know that the alternative Prime Minister is as great a cricket lover as the present one, one or two shrewd observers began to wonder if towards the end of his captaincy Mark Taylor was not being used by the PM. The chief cricket writer of the *Sydney Morning Herald*, Malcolm Knox, even gave this as one of a number of reasons why Taylor should step down when he did. 'There is no doubt that Mark Taylor and John Howard share a genuine mutual liking . . .' he wrote in the paper on 1 February 1999. 'But everything a politician does in public is a political act. The Prime Minister's office has derived great surface glamour from exploiting the Howard–Taylor relationship.' Knox went on: 'Taylor has allowed himself to be used as a de facto Howard endorsement . . . Taylor has allowed the office of Australian cricket captain to be used politically.

The impact of that decision on the office, over the long term, is questionable.' That may be so, but the Australian media's adulation of Taylor and 'hyping' of the captaincy seem to pose equal potential risks for his successors in this 'office'. How is Steve Waugh to make a true success of replacing a man who, by the end, was being routinely described as a 'statesman', someone who – as Mike Coward of *The Australian* rather neatly put it – had 'the ear of the Prime Minister, the country's other leader'?

13
Nadir and Zenith: The Fourth Test

Christopher Martin-Jenkins

England's performances immediately before and after Christmas were about to encapsulate the strange inconsistency, the Jekyll-and-Hyde nature of their cricket, which had been typical for too long. Had they batted, bowled and fielded at Adelaide with the inspiration they were finally to summon up on the altogether extraordinary final day of the Melbourne Test match, they might have overcome the disadvantage of losing the toss. Then, not only the series but the Ashes too would still have been at issue during the final game of the rubber.

That in the real world they once again left their best until too late was immensely disappointing, even to many Australians, but the manner of their imminent revival at the MCG was unforgettable and genuinely heroic. At the same time it was frustrating, because it proved what might have been if only those crucial catches had stuck during the first three matches.

What transpired in the final phase of the series might be the subject of a major psychological study. The Australians, the main prize won, tried no less hard to assert their superiority but the motivation was not quite so intense and metaphorically they took their eye off the ball just long enough to allow their opponents to record an amazing victory. In England's case there was more than a hint of the cornered animal in the way that the team came back from the desperate probability of a defeat which would have put an utterly different complexion not just on the immediate press reaction but, to some extent, on the tour itself.

The burning fiery furnace was already being stoked after the appalling conclusion to the match in Hobart three days before Christmas. It would have consumed many an international career had not Alec Stewart and Dean Headley forced a reappraisal. But they did; and it created an unexpectedly dramatic climax to the series.

Before the zenith, there was a nadir, almost as embarrassing to England supporters as the games on the previous tour when the young cricketers from the Adelaide Academy twice utterly outplayed Mike Atherton's side in one-day matches. Oddly, however, the match in Hobart against an accomplished collection of Test reserves playing as an 'Australian XI' actually started rather well for the touring team and not least for Atherton himself, who had reassumed the captaincy for four days.

Several of the central figures, Alec Stewart and Nasser Hussain included, had taken the chance to have some time off with their wives and children in the gentlest of all the Australian capitals. After the rush of the major cities on the mainland, Hobart is a gentle haven, a lovely place in sunshine at any rate, and throughout the team's pre-Christmas stay the weather was cool, fresh and mainly bright. Not surprisingly, since it was born as a community at about the same time early in the nineteenth century, and because its latitude is the same, the Tasmanian capital has the feel of one of the ports of New Zealand's South Island. It is manageable in size, unsophisticated, even a little hick. People do not worry too much what they wear here and when I went to the morning service on Sunday in the largest Anglican church in town, both the atmosphere and the size of the congregation were akin to a small country parish church in England.

It was pouring with rain outside on that particular day and it often is when England teams visit. This, indeed, was the first time in my experience of Hobart Decembers that there has not still been some snow left on the top of Mount Wellington, the most accessible of the rugged hills which rise above the River Derwent towards the 4,000-foot peak of Mount Cook. Hobart itself is seldom short of water from above but Tasmania has recently been worryingly dry, yet another symptom, it seems, of the disease of global warming.

The river is more than just the heart of Hobart; it is the reason for the town's existence. It is not hard to guess why it was christened the Derwent: at a glance the broad estuary might easily be one of the larger lakes of Cumbria and throughout supper one night with friends whose house on the edge of town (a mile or so past the Real Tennis court) is separated from the water only by trees and shrubs, the only sound was the clear, beautiful and unmistakable sound of a blackbird's melodic warbling. According to one of my hosts, a retired member of the State orchestra, the species had spread after an original blackbird had escaped from a cage. One wonders if Browning had the song in his mind when he penned 'Oh to be in England now that April's there'. That purest of sounds was an instant link between a Tasmanian summer and an English spring.

In the Tasmanian Museum and Art Gallery there are pictures by the dozen of Derwent landscapes, mostly the work of the Victorian artists who came to appreciate the scenic beauty which lay behind Tasmania's early reputation as a brutal penal colony. One of many sympathetically restored sandstone buildings in the middle of Hobart, the museum is an easy stroll from the quay which was about to be cleared of its trawlers to make way for the annual return of the boats from the Sydney to Hobart yacht race which starts every Boxing Day in that other and still grander harbour to the north. This time, alas, the boats which limped home reached safety only after a severe mauling from high winds and hideous swells in the Bass Strait which claimed the elderly yacht *Sir Winston Churchill* and the lives of six sailors.

Leading England for the first time in a first-class match since his resignation in Antigua in March, Atherton scored a chanceless and commanding 210 not out, the highest score of his career, against what was clearly billed by the national selectors as Australia's second eleven. In bowling, although definitely not in batting, however, they quickly became a spent force.

Coached for this one-off match by Allan Border, who twice willingly took the field as a substitute, they had lost the services of the off-spinner Gavin Robertson because of back spasms before the game started. Paul Reiffel then broke down with the first new ball, having already bowled four no-balls in an over and a half, and Michael Kasprowicz did so with the second when a hamstring twanged.

A benign, true pitch and an attack thus reduced by injury to a single specialist bowler gave Atherton the opportunity to bat with a mastery which, thanks mainly to McGrath, had eluded him in the Test matches. If it was a somewhat bloodless conquest it was nevertheless a timely reminder of his talent and determination and he was one of the most cheerful members of a touring party entertained by the press on the second evening of the game at one of several enticing fish restaurants created out of warehouses on the harbour's edge.

Opportunities like this for informal get-togethers between players and press are rare in the high-pressure world of contemporary international cricket. Players are on the fringe of the media themselves, many of them loosely involved and likely to be more so in future; but journalists are viewed with natural suspicion, not all of them deemed to be sufficiently knowledgeable or understanding and to a man obliged to be alive to the possibility of any story which might be a little different.

Conversation this time was free enough. Amongst the discussions I had were one with Dominic Cork on the exact meaning of the word 'philandering'; another with John Crawley about whether he had been wise to abandon his natural penchant for on-side strokes; a third with Atherton and Angus Fraser about whether the venerable bowler should have been given the help of a fierce wind when he opened the bowling with the tyro Alex Tudor; and a fourth with Darren Gough and Peter Such about the mind-boggling treatment they had received before, during and after a molly-coddled round of golf at Melbourne's Crown Casino. They had been offered the use of any from a wide selection of the most expensive and up-to-date sets in the world, then played on immaculate fairways with not another soul in sight and caddies to cater for their every whim.

For a time, it seemed that the match against the Australian eleven was to be a similar cakewalk. After Atherton came Hick, despatching the occasional bowlers with lordly ease to compile one of the quickest and easiest of his first-class hundreds. This was the 104th and soon after he had battered 75 from his last thirty-seven balls, Atherton declared England's first innings at 469 for six to give his bowlers 11 overs with the new ball. Thereupon the embarrassment of this powerful-looking Australian eleven was eased by the solid start made by Matthew Elliott and Greg Blewett.

Atherton, though he hit some magnificent strokes through the covers, had scored only 65 of the 195 he added with Hick for the fourth wicket after Butcher and Crawley had got themselves out and Ramprakash had made his now almost routine 65. He was beaten by Michael Bevan's flipper but, well set as he was, should have made a century. All three of the batsmen who had made a start were obliged to hearken to a favourite dictum of Graham Gooch: 'After your own batting, it's watching someone else bat and then fielding.' In other words, don't give it away.

There was a background issue during the game concerning England's other, and official, coach. Outwardly, at least, David Lloyd reacted with genial equanimity to a suggestion in a Sunday newspaper that he would be sacked before the tour had even reached its one-day stage. Privately he was shortly to admit to a temptation to stand down after the World Cup so that he could resume the far less stressful business of commentating. But if ever a man blew hot and cold, it is Lloyd: he was quite capable of changing his mind after further thought and when he returned home he tried to talk the ECB into a lengthy extension of his contract before deciding, in the absence of any long-term commitment from the board, that he would pass on the reins.

The facile conclusion after the disappointments of the early part of the series were that his conscientiousness has not been enough and that the batting performances of the team had too often been a poor advertisement for his abilities as a coach. But there had been an unmistakable improvement in organization and morale since Lloyd's appointment in 1996. His second contract had originally confirmed him in the post until the end of the 1999 season.

It was soon apparent on the third day at Hobart that the pitch was so unusually perfect for batting that it would be impossible to get a result without the kind of contrivance which was once so common in three-day county cricket on covered pitches. England's regular bowlers fared not much better than the Australian eleven's part-timers as Blewett (newly signed by Yorkshire in lieu of Darren Lehmann, who was expected to play in the World Cup whilst Blewett was not) scored his fifth and highest century in a total of eighteen innings against England. His formidable excellence was displayed in the knowledge that Lehmann, not himself, had been chosen to replace Ricky Ponting in the Boxing Day Test at Melbourne.

Lehmann declared four overs after tea when the Australians were still 176 behind England. Blewett had dominated a first-wicket partnership of 206 with Matthew Elliott and both had played with great assurance on a pitch which at that stage had already yielded more than 120 runs per wicket. Yet it had been relaid by the curator, Peter Apps, in a climate almost as cold and wet as England's and on a square over which Rules football is played all winter, stopping only six weeks before the cricket season begins. Apps believes that a natural scarifying by the studs of winter sportsmen would do most tired squares much more good than harm: food for thought for English groundsmen.

Still relatively early in an Australian Summer, however, this particular pitch was lacking the life which would have made for a closer contest between bat and ball. Butcher and Crawley took full advantage of the continued absence through injury of three of the Australian bowlers to strike a rapid 119 off 21 overs before Crawley, having hit eleven elegant fours, was given out leg before, apparently as a punishment for attempting a reverse sweep. Butcher went on to 85 not out.

The unfortunate Ben Hollioake even managed 17 before becoming

Elliott's ninth first-class victim, caught at slip. He had at least had the satisfaction of dismissing Elliott himself, and also Corey Richards, in the same over; but Blewett, looking younger than twenty-seven, soon deflated the twenty-one-year-old with four superlative fours in five balls: a pull, a drive on the up through extra cover, an off drive and another pull. It was merely the aperitif.

Daily Telegraph, Wednesday, 23 December
Now even the bowlers have failed, and with a vengeance. England could not win 'the sixth Test match' even after scoring 469 for six and 199 for three. The combination of a very flat pitch, rudderless bowling and wonderfully dominating batting by 23-year-old Corey Richards and Greg Blewett, who is playing like Bradman, made a complete nonsense of what in other circumstances might have been a challenging declaration.

Blewett, slim and fit as a whippet, batted quite brilliantly and however poor the bowling it is a pity that Graham Gooch dwelt upon what he called the 'totally abject' performance of England rather than on the strokeplay of two batsmen who were not considered for the fourth Test in Melbourne later this week.

The Australian Eleven won by nine wickets with absurd ease. They had 22 overs and four balls in hand after scoring at a rate of almost seven runs an over. This against an international attack which failed in every bowler's case to maintain the consistent line and length which alone would have exerted some pressure and thereby, perhaps, obliged the Australians to lose wickets by chasing against the clock.

Gooch was blunt and upset in the aftermath of a defeat which leaves England exposed to ridicule again, three days before Christmas and four before a Boxing Day Test which threatens further embarrassment or, worse, humiliation. 'It was,' said the manager, 'a very poor performance. I don't like to see England lose in this manner. They bowled both sides of the wicket and their performance was not up to the standards we'd expect. Credit to their two guys; they played really well and it was a very flat wicket but you'd have expected an international side to make them work much harder.'

He might have added that the bowlers had such a poor day collectively – although to some extent they bowled only as well as the conditions and the coolly assertive Blewett allowed – that there were no clues as to who should join Gough and Mullally in the attack at Melbourne. Headley and Croft did well, perhaps, to miss this game.

Blewett took his average against England in three innings to 525. When he reached 38 he became only the sixth batsman to make more than 1000 runs before the end of December in an Australian season, joining Bill Ponsford, Bobby Simpson (twice), David Hookes, Graham Yallop and Allan Border. Strange indeed that this is one list on which the name Bradman does not appear.

Blewett has now scored 1175 runs in 10 innings, including six hundreds, the last four of which have exceeded 150. His was an astonishing tour de force on a relaid pitch which is slower than the usual Hobart belters and as heavily loaded in favour of the batsmen as the ratio of 1337 runs in the game to 14 wickets suggests.

It should not be overlooked that England lost after two declarations, as many sides have before. But their batting success in this game had to be seen in the light of the injuries to three of the Australian Eleven's four specialist bowlers. By contrast the home side's domination underlined the quite extraordinary strength of contemporary Australian batting. Has any country at any time had so many batsmen of Test class?

Mark Butcher was given time to complete perhaps the easiest hundred he has ever made, losing Dominic Cork to a run out at the first attempt on his hundredth run, before Mike Atherton declared, half an hour into what turned out to be an unnecessarily extended day's play. As events transpired England could have batted another 45 minutes and set the Australians 430.

Blewett set out at once with the assurance of an evangelist. The path ahead of him at the moment seems both straight and broad, except, of course, the one which leads to the Australian dressing-room. He drove on the up and pulled with level-headed ease, his weight staying on the front foot, such was his trust in a pitch of evenly covered black clay and completely reliable bounce.

Many a past county game has demonstrated how games of this nature can be hard for any fielding side to pull back when two batsmen get set. Blewett and Richards were soon in control once Tudor had bowled Matthew Elliott off his body as he missed a pull at a short ball. Anything short thereafter from Tudor was comfortably and correctly defended by the impressively orthodox Richards and pulled away with disdain by Blewett.

It was the experienced bowlers who deserved the greater censure, however, and there was no excuse for Fraser, Cork and Such. Richards took an instant liking to Such. In successive overs he danced down the wicket to drive him over mid-on, drew back to force him past cover, whipped him through mid-wicket and, off consecutive balls, swept him for four and six.

Fraser, when all was lost, proved that it was not an impossible task to contain batsmen on this pitch by beating Richards twice in succession after tea with balls which left the right-hander off a good length. But by then Richards had completed his first hundred against England and his fourth in six matches. Believe it or not, he was picked for this game partly because the national selectors, rating him highly, suspected that with Taylor, Slater and the Waugh twins back in the New South Wales side, Richards might not have been picked for the Sheffield Shield game against Victoria. Slater and Mark Waugh both duly scored hundreds.

Blewett played throughout this match with the same merciless attacking intent as Bradman must have done, looking to score off almost everything bowled at him, and with an equally contemptuous yet equally unboastful ease. Blewett's scores this season have been: 175, 47, 31, 36, 143, 51, 158, 152, 169 not out and, yesterday, 213 not out. Only four other batsmen have scored a double hundred and a 150 in the same game – Arthur Fagg (two double hundreds against Essex in 1938), Warwick Armstrong, Maurice Hallam, who almost did it twice, and Zaheer Abbas, who actually did it twice. Only Zaheer and Blewett have been not out in both innings. Gloucestershire's fondly remembered 'Z' scored 215 not out and 150 not out against Somerset in 1981.

Blewett said afterwards that he could not remember hitting the ball much better than he is at the moment. 'I've just tried to play really straight, which is one of my strengths,' he said. He has been an opening batsman most of his life but he has batted for Australia at three and at six and he is happy to do so anywhere. It is inconceivable that he will not get back eventually.

The England team flew to Melbourne, some to meet up with the wives and families now gathered there and most of them smarting from the anger of their manager and full of remorse for their own lack of professionalism. They had a day off to ponder their failure and to try to think of Christmas as well as cricket.

It was out of this unlikely and wretched background that the sensational climax to the Test series emerged. Regular followers of England should not have been surprised, perhaps, because the team had in recent times made something of a habit both of throwing away promising situations and of coming back when all seemed lost.

There was intense interest in the Test due to start on Boxing Day and some twists and turns in the narrative before the game even started. After assiduous nets on Christmas Eve, Alec Stewart turned up for a press conference originally intended to be a low-key affair for the benefit of travelling English writers. In the event he was confronted not just by Australian cricket journalists too, but by newsmen and women interested in the wider story of a stricken side apparently close to real sporting humiliation.

Outwardly, Stewart took them all in his stride. Privately he was smarting at the embarrassment of having to account for the unprofessional performance in Hobart. It had been unacceptable on the last day, he said, and his own batting form was in urgent need of improvement. He would probably carry on keeping wicket, although there was just a chance that he might give the gloves to Warren Hegg and revert to his favourite role as an opening batsman . . .

*

Christmas Day came and went, as Christmas Days do. The two teams had light practice sessions in the morning and England's players had a game of football during which Alex Tudor apparently triggered the minor hip strain which was to give Stewart the excuse he needed to make the change to which he had alluded.

It was listlessly hot when the faithful emerged from a majestic Sung Eucharist in St Paul's Cathedral, over the road from Flinders Street Station and the fashionable South Bank. There had not been a vacant pew beneath what is claimed to be the second-tallest spire in the Anglican Church. Salisbury's is 123.2 metres (404 feet) high; Melbourne, built in the Gothic transitional style between 1880 and 1891, 96.7 metres. Sadly, it is now dwarfed by the skyscrapers all around it.

If such juxtaposition of modern and traditional is typical of Melbourne, so was the Christmas weather. It had become suddenly cool and blowy by the time everyone emerged from their lengthy lunches, the England team and their families after a merry party at their hotel which had included entertainment from a choir, a jazz band and a magician, the journalists and their families – some of them at least – after a no less merry and much more bibulous lunch at a French restaurant which had produced roast turkey worthy of home and hearth.

The morning after dawned grey, with drizzle in the air. As the huge crowd gathered, praying that the forecast for rain would be wrong, there was extraordinary indecision behind the scenes in the dressing-room. Seasoned players said later that they had seen nothing like it. Half an hour before the game began Hegg was strolling about with a cup of coffee in his hands, blithely unaware that he was about to be awarded his first Test cap. Tudor's withdrawal, a decision which seems to have been made for him – 'If it had been a one-day match he could have played' – meant not only that Stewart would open but that Fraser would, after all, get at least one more Test in Australia.

No sooner had the toss been made before a crowd expected to grow to 70,000 than it started to rain and continued to do so throughout Boxing Day. It was expensive for the cricket authorities, who had to return the ticket money, and a miserable anticlimax for everyone. I felt sorriest of all for the BBC's cricket correspondent, Jonathan Agnew, a home-loving man who had made the long journey back to his village in rural Leicestershire between the third and fourth Tests, missing the Hobart débâcle, seeing his wife and family, picking up a roaring cold and leaving his loved ones on Christmas Eve in order to be back on duty in the *Test Match Special* commentary box early on Boxing Day morning.

At least the match he was about to see, although he could not have guessed it through the gloom of 26 December, was a classic which would be followed by an even more compelling game in the new year. Rain on the first day of the Boxing Day Test was nothing less than a violation of a Melbourne ritual, but from the moment that Australia struck their first blow in the still pervading gloom of the following day, the match – and England – made up for lost time.

Daily Telegraph, Monday, 28 December

Alec Stewart's decision to open the batting again, made only half an hour before the toss on Saturday when Alex Tudor was declared unfit, paid him a handsome and thoroughly deserved dividend yesterday in the form of an admirable and long overdue first Test hundred against Australia. Hitting 16 fours with the precise timing and bristling resolve which has marked each of his previous eleven centuries for England, he gave his team the positive lead they so badly needed.

Strip from their mercurial first innings of 270 the 59 conceded in ten overs by the tyro Matthew Nicholson and you have another batting performance which gave the England bowlers no margin for error; but Darren Gough did his best to make the total seem bigger on a hard, grassy but remarkably dry pitch with another exceptionally fast opening spell.

The feeling at the end of a grey, blustery day, when paper-bags blew about like snowflakes and leaded bails were needed to keep wickets intact, was still one of renewed frustration on England's part. At 200 for three, with Stewart and Ramprakash batting superbly, they had the Australians beneath their feet for the first time in the series, but they wriggled free mainly thanks to the wiles of Stuart MacGill and poor technique against leg-spin which Peter Philpott's clinics seem to have done nothing to cure.

The cricket so far has been as capricious and unpredictable as Melbourne's notorious climate: four seasons in 48 hours and 12 wickets in one elongated day. An extra hour has been scheduled for the last four days to make up as much as is reasonably possible of the time lost on a first day of pouring rain. There should be a result now, but over £500,000 is the estimated loss of income including the refund of tickets to a first-day crowd of 61,800.

Tudor's was one of those late withdrawals in which England so specialise. If anyone genuinely knew exactly when his 'hip niggle' developed, no one was saying. His misfortune was Fraser's and Hegg's good luck. Hegg, 30, has been a hard-working, companionable and unselfish member of the touring party but he is not the answer to England's perennial problem of a proper balance between batting and bowling. His sudden promotion, ahead of John Crawley, whose career average of 50 is virtually double that of his Lancashire colleague's, cannot be more than a temporary expedient.

The two Lancastrians chosen fell to outside edges so thin that they might each have survived on a luckier day. The bottom line, however, in both cases, was that they were playing without the intention of scoring a run at balls pitched outside their off stump. Nothing so underlines the difference between English and Australian batting in this series than the greater ability of the Australians to judge when and when not to play a stroke.

Atherton should have left the fifth ball of McGrath's first over yesterday, but he did not and he was given out despite the fact that the only definite sound was that of the inside edge brushing his front pad. So, 24 hours after losing their tenth toss out of the last 13, and, incredibly, their tenth in eleven Ashes Tests, England also lost their first wicket before the Atherton/Stewart opening partnership could be properly relaunched.

There were perhaps only half of the eventual crowd of 25,099 present in the cavernous stands when McGrath followed up with Butcher's wicket in his second over. The ball cut back at England's new number three, took the inside edge and flew to the right of Justin Langer at short-leg. Out went Langer's right hand and in came Nasser Hussain, one place lower than usual but no later in the innings.

Captain and vice-captain stopped the rot. Stewart started a little streakily against Fleming, with fours off first the outside then the inside edge before facing McGrath for the first time as late as the ninth over. Soon he was scoring with authentic front foot strokes and showing his class with one remarkable stroke off a ball from McGrath which lifted just outside the off stump: somehow Stewart got his wrists high and jammed down on to the top of the bounce to send the ball skimming past gully.

Hussain, starting with a smooth off-driven four off Fleming, joined in even more willingly when Nicholson came on, looking like a quicker but less controlled version of Martin Bicknell. He was punished for failing to bowl a length. 19 came from his first two overs, 26 from three and when MacGill joined him from the Southern End at 67 for two, Stewart almost immediately advanced to loft him over mid-on.

The captain's first fifty came off only 66 balls, with eight fours across an outfield a good deal quicker than expected. But the last thing Taylor does in these sorts of circumstances is to lose his nerve. Keeping Nicholson going when most captains would have taken him off, he was rewarded when Hussain pushed at a ball outside his off stump and edged to give Healy his 350th Test catch.

The next 29 overs, either side of lunch, raised the serious question of whether Taylor's judgement had for once been wrong when he chose to put England in. He has won 25 of his 49 tosses and this was only the fifth time he has chosen to field first. Yet the bounce of the pitch was even, swing negligible and sideways movement off the seam slight. Ramprakash was soon playing with as much confidence as Stewart and apart from a lucky moment straight after lunch when the captain, then 78, edged a force off Nicholson and only his right boot saved him, the partnership blossomed like a vibernum in winter.

Ramprakash has himself come out of a cautious kind of hibernation in the last few weeks. He played beautifully and with an enterprise befitting a Test batsman of his class and experience. Nicholson and Fleming were dominated in turn and ten overs after lunch Stewart at least reached the moment for which he has striven so long: his first hundred against Australia and, of all places, at the Melbourne Cricket Ground. He saluted all points of the Coliseum after square-cutting MacGill for his 16th four.

Six overs later, he aimed a sweep at a ball which had not yet pitched. It dipped, bit and turned back to hit his leg stump. Australian batsmen do not try to sweep leg-spinners. More culpably still, Ramprakash, trying not to lose impetus, aimed an on-drive at Steve Waugh's medium pace in the next over and, a fraction too early, lifted the ball tamely to mid-on. Waugh followed up by claiming Hegg and all that was left of the glory that might have been was a spirited innings by Hick and a staunch effort by Headley, which roused McGrath and Healy to melodramatic ire for which both were warned by Steve Bucknor.

Having played himself in before tea Hick played some fine shots after, including a commanding hook off McGrath and a huge swing for six off MacGill. Again the leg-spinner had his revenge, however, flighting the ball into the wind for Hick to strike, from a yard down the pitch, to deep mid-on.

Australia were left with a theoretical 27 overs but bad light at the end reduced it to 18. Gough bowled at a speed scientifically measured at around 90 mph from the Northern End, showing, said Stewart pointedly later, 'what English bowlers can do when they've had a rest'. In his third over, Slater stepped across his stumps to a ball of full length and was leg before; in his sixth Taylor pushed at a ball angled towards his off stump and Hick held the thick edge low to his right.

It took all Langer's feisty temperament and tight technique to see Australia without further mishap to the close of a day of vivid cricket.

A whitening pitch, burgeoning sunshine and the easy elegance of Mark Waugh's batting all augured well for the home side next morning, but Darren Gough had bowled so well and with such little fortune throughout the series that justice demanded a major haul. On a surface offering him encouraging pace and bounce he kept the game in balance with bowling of great pace and no little guile.

Just before the end of the first hour of a two-and-a-half-hour morning session, Fraser claimed Waugh lbw as he walked in front of his stumps to work a good-length ball to mid-wicket. He had executed the stroke of the match so far, a crashing drive through extra cover played over a bent front knee in Gough's five-over opening spell, but Fraser bowled with good rhythm and his usual steadiness in two morning spells which gave Gough the chance to attack from the other end.

Steve Waugh settled in with typically organised vigilance, and Langer rode some luck, but forty-five minutes from lunch he aimed a square drive in the first over of Gough's second spell and sliced it hard to the gully where Hussain clung on safely.

Lehmann's first Test run in Australia came off his legs in the same over and he carved Gough over point soon after but he was if anything overconfident and an attempt to repeat the stroke was fatal, giving Hegg his first Test catch and Gough four for 46 at that point.

The contest remained even until tea as, on a clear, cool, sunny day, a crowd of 43,353 basked in the glow of close combat. Waugh, 77 not out at the second interval, had batted impeccably, but Gough had taken his fifth wicket just before the break with an inswinging yorker which up-ended both Nicholson and his stumps. The new ball was due, Australia were eight wickets down and they were still 18 runs behind.

Once again these perfidious sons of Albion seemed now to count chickens before they were hatched, going through the motions but, deep down, believing the hard work was done. Until tea the bowlers had been purposeful and only one catch had gone down, a hard one to Hick's left off Headley before Fleming had scored.

Waugh, hitherto playing a shrewd, careful and immaculate percentage innings, shrewdly took some chances against the new ball in pursuit of his seventeenth Test century and in MacGill, no batsman really at this level, he found a partner with a good enough eye and the right sort of cricketing nous to hang around. England's cricketing discipline failed them again as the counter-attack developed and, at 319, with MacGill stranded in mid-pitch as Hussain picked the ball up at mid-wicket, not only did his throw miss the stumps but Hegg failed to get up to them to receive the ball.

Twenty-one more runs were added before the breakthrough came, leaving England with a deficit of 70 and, due partly to the extra hour's play and partly to their own disgracefully slow over-rate, with an hour and a half's batting. Stewart, quite unable to conjure anything up as a captain in the field, nevertheless batted with skill, courage and defiance to reduce the Australian lead to five; but Atherton, his technique and confidence as hopelessly lost as they were at different stages of the two previous winter tours, might have been out twice before Fleming squared him up with a leg cutter and hit his off stump.

By contrast, Butcher was freakishly dismissed after a promising start. Going down on one knee to smite on the up and with the spin, he struck the ball from the meat of his blade straight at Slater, fielding very close at short-leg. It could have killed him. Instead, as he ducked and turned, the ball stuck underneath arms thrust across his chest in self-protection.

When the players went off fifteen minutes later, they and their spectators were emotionally drained, let alone physically. They had been at the ground for some ten hours, watching cricket which had itself lasted almost two hours longer than the scheduled six. But we had not seen anything yet.

Daily Telegraph, Tuesday, 29 December

Of all the belated English victories against the trend of a series; of all the heroic fourth-innings efforts in their recent, apparently interminable years of struggle, this was the most astounding and the most emotional. At the last it was sheer character and inspired fielding, the two ingredients which seemed to have prevented this enigmatic touring team from making the most of its abilities and opportunities, which carried them to a 12-run defeat of Australia.

Australia, needing only 175, failed on a very good batting pitch and that was the essential point. At one stage they were 130 for three and coasting but wins can come from the blue in cricket and this Australian side has demonstrated several times that they are vulnerable when chasing runs in the fourth innings. In an atmosphere of frenzied excitement – no longer the breathless hush of poetry – England took their last seven wickets for 32.

Only against South Africa in Port Elizabeth in 1997 have Australia successfully chased a serious fourth-innings score in their recent history. At The Oval against England in the final match of the 1997 series they failed to get a much smaller total of 124, but that was on a surface whose top had gone.

Taylor said that he had fielded first after winning the toss – only the fifth time in 25 that he has put an opposition in – because his experience of Melbourne was that pitches tend to get easier to bat on as matches progress. There was only minimal movement and some bounce yesterday to encourage England's hero, Dean Headley, but five of his six wickets for 60 were taken for only 26 runs in a marvellously well-sustained second spell from the Southern End.

This was all the more remarkable for the fact that Mark Waugh had cut two long hops for four in an over costing ten when Stewart brought Headley back after four innocuous overs from Fraser. He would have taken him off again if a catch of inspired brilliance by Ramprakash at square-leg had not given Mullally deserved reward for an admirably controlled ten-over spell of probing swing bowling. Headley responded with a maiden over and then with four wickets for four in his next 14 balls.

He was made man of the match, although Steve Waugh, who took a fateful decision to play an extra half hour to finish the game on the scheduled fourth day when England wanted to come off, was once again undefeated. He never looked like getting out, having come to the middle with 72 needed.

Waugh actually made two misjudgements as the game reached its thrilling climax. With advice from Taylor conveyed by the 12th man, Miller, he opted to stay in the middle despite the lengthening shadows which made the light difficult for batsmen coming in. Notwithstanding the contrast of sun and shadow, it was the obvious decision because the force was with Australia then, Nicholson was batting well as Waugh's eighth-wicket partner and Stewart was only too keen to get England off for a night's rest after three hours and 20 minutes in the field.

Both captains said that the new ICC regulations to increase playing hours for matches when play has been lost to rain needed further revision. In this case the long final session – it stretched in the end to just over four hours with three drinks breaks – was extended both because the England innings ended 29 minutes before the tea interval, which was therefore taken early, and because of the provision for an extra half hour which either captain could have claimed in order to win the game.

Waugh's second error was to run a single off the first ball of what turned out to be the final over bowled by a fired-up, but still coolly accurate, Gough. MacGill, whose first-innings stand with Waugh seemed to have won the match, was castled by a ball fired towards his blockhole and two balls later McGrath was leg before.

England, all out for 244 after, praise be, a last-wicket stand of 23 by Mullally and Fraser, had seemed to be 50 runs short of the target required to give Australia their notorious fourth-innings jitters, but Steve Waugh's prediction that 150 would take some getting proved prophetic. Perhaps it even sowed seeds of doubt which normally do not enter Australian minds.

Events proved that England had eked out their second innings just long enough and the last-wicket runs were crucial. They were potentially expensive, also, for McGrath, who has sailed close to the disciplinary wind all series and was finally and belatedly given a suspended fine of 30 per cent of his match fee by the referee, John Reid, for crude and abusive language to Mullally. The fine of about £1000 will only be paid if he repeats the offence in the next four months.

England's innings was always a struggle yesterday from the moment that Headley, the night-watchman, was bowled through the gate. But Hussain and Hick both played fine, positive innings which wasted no scoring opportunities after Stewart, having reached his valuable fifty, had been caught at silly point off pad and bat.

Hussain hit eight fours, including two late cuts in succession off Damien Fleming, and Ramprakash supported him well in an excellent fourth-wicket partnership of 49 but Nicholson came to Taylor's rescue with three wickets either side of lunch. Ramprakash played round a ball on his off stump, Hussain cut hard but straight to cover point and Hegg, having played one deliberate uppercut, heedlessly attempted another despite the posting of a fly slip.

Running in from that position, MacGill held the awkward catch well but Hick, meanwhile, had been playing with an air of command, driving handsomely and powerfully and punishing MacGill with fierce cuts when he dropped short. Suffering from a hamstring twinge, although it was no more apparent when he was bowling than was Healy's broken finger when keeping wicket, MacGill turned the ball a good deal but he is not Shane Warne when it comes to accuracy. He soon had Gough caught at short leg but it was Fleming who bowled Hick as he hit across the line of a ball of full length in pursuit of a ninth four.

Australia set out purposefully in search of 175, but sketchily too. Slater sliced Gough over third slip's head in the first over and was perilously close to lbw to Headley in the second. Hit again by a ball which cut back and kept low, one of only two to do so all day, Slater walked before umpire Bucknor, who has had two excellent games, had lifted his finger.

But Australia had 31 by now and eight overs had gone so it was a considerable bonus for England when, ten runs later, Taylor hooked in the air to long-leg. Langer was missed by Hick, low to his right at second slip, off Mullally's next ball and, switching from over to round the wicket, Mullally continued to confine both left and right hander to careful defence.

But Langer and Mark Waugh had added 62 patient runs when Langer pulled hard to square-leg where Ramprakash dived sideways and held a fabulous catch in his right hand. Taylor felt this was the turning point. In fact the Waughs had reduced the target to only 45 before Mark went back to a good-length ball and Hick took the first of two good catches at second slip.

The collapse had really started now. Lehmann was judged to have got a thin inside edge, driving, Healy pushed firmly at a ball outside his off stump and Fleming was leg before to a ball of full length before Nicholson helped Steve Waugh add 21. Two came from overthrows off the innocent Nicholson's back as Headley came close to running him out. With 14 runs still needed by Australia Headley had him caught behind instead and in an atmosphere of feverish excitement Gough completed the job in the next over.

Fraser, lacking zip and therefore the weak link in England's attack, never stopped encouraging Headley and if this proves to be his last Test, as it probably will, he has gone out on a high note. Mike Atherton, too, may have only one more match left for England. Amongst his opponents in Sydney this weekend may be Shane Warne: the Australian team will be named this morning.

It was duly named and Warne was duly recalled, after a press conference at the ACB headquarters a couple of boundary hits from the MCG in Jolimont Street. All the old Warne charm was there as he told of the difficulty of deciding whether to have his shoulder operation in the first place and then of the long haul back to fitness, demanding daily physiotherapy and a tedious routine of exercises. It was worth it, however. 'I feel like I'm starting my Test career all over again,' he said.

Sydney was a great place for him to do so, mainly because of the pitch, but also because of the tremendous expectation. The fair city was buzzing with its customary turn-of-the year vitality and the morning after the New Year's Eve fireworks gave me a chance to play the New South Wales golf course, magnificently situated at La Perouse above Botany Bay where the whole Anglo-Australian adventure had started with Captain Cook. My captain for the day was none other than Ian Botham and if pulling him out of the hat as my four-ball partner was typical of the fortune which lay ahead in 1999, it promised to be a good year. Having seen the new year in with his usual limitless capacity for fun and alcohol, the greatest English all-rounder of his generation showed not a sign of a hangover as he went round one of the most demanding courses in Australia in two over par.

14

Tour Groups

CHARLES DE LISLE

There may not be as many England supporters as expected at the fourth Test in Melbourne, but this bar at a four-and-a-half star hotel is not big enough for two very different groups. For more than an hour John Jameson, the rumbustious former England opener who is now assistant secretary (cricket) at MCC, has been patiently answering questions from the dozen-strong package-tour group which he is 'hosting' for the evening. He has been struggling to make himself heard above the cries of 'Barmy Army – Alec Stewart' from five or six well-lubricated fans standing by the Metro Inn's bar, celebrating the England captain's first Ashes century earlier that day, the first day of actual play in the Test.

Eventually, at about 8.30 p.m, a dark-haired woman in her forties slips away from Jameson's group. It turns out that she has gone to complain to hotel staff about the noise. It works: five minutes later the rowdy group has departed, and the question-and-answer session is proceeding smoothly again. 'I can't stand bad behaviour,' she explains later. 'I said to reception: "I had the choice of staying here or at the Hilton. The Hilton wouldn't allow this, so why do you?"'

This small party, mostly from the West Midlands, is travelling with Tana Travel and will go on to the Sydney Test. Tana is one of about twenty specialist firms which have flown in a total of some 1,500 supporters for the Melbourne match, Australia's answer to the Lord's Test. The majority are couples in the forty-five to sixty-five age bracket; there are also groups of young single men, and occasionally women, as well as solo travellers, and people old enough to have seen Bradman at his peak (one man, aged eighty-three, suffered a heart attack in Sydney but is making a good recovery at the time of writing). A further 1,500 or so have made their own arrangements. Add in the 'Barmy Army' and the expatriates and you can see why 'Pom' support is estimated by ground officials as totalling 4,000-plus people on each day of the match. It sounded like many more: as Alec Stewart was to say, after England's astonishing victory, the team felt as though it was playing at home –

even though the crowd in the vast stadium on that fourth and final day numbered 29,000.

The Tana group, which includes one MCC tie and one turquoise tank top (they have separate owners, you will be glad to hear), is being shepherded by Stephen Newman, who has made it a condition of his recent sale of the company that he still be allowed to take charge of the Christmas/New Year tour. A man who knows his cricket, he puts his finger on the fragility which makes the life of an England supporter a nerve-stretching one. 'You don't follow England session by session, or even over by over,' says Newman. 'You follow ball by ball. Every ball from which nothing goes wrong for England is a relief.'

Every tour group has its 'anorak' – the cricket fanatic who scores every ball of every day's play – and in this party his name is Martin. A Mancunian who is a member of Nottinghamshire as well as Lancashire (whose jacket he sports with evident pride), he is retired from Unilever. Today he has braved the Melbourne cold and gloom to score every ball of the day's action (England 270, Australia 59–2). 'I'm scoring every ball "rough",' he says. 'I'll transfer it to the computer when I get home.' He admits he came unprepared for the weather in a city known for its 'four seasons in a day'. On the first, washed-out day he bought a sweatshirt at the ground but he still froze today. Some members of the group returned to the hotel during the lunch interval, warming up with a shower and steaming coffee, and returning with blankets; not Martin.

The man in the turquoise tank top is Dave, a shy, intelligent bachelor of about forty who works for a construction firm. Why is he forking out £3,125 (including a hefty single supplement) for an eighteen-night tour? 'I'm on my own, so it's nice to have a holiday with company,' he says. 'I came to the Brisbane Test four years ago, under my own steam, but I'm much preferring travelling this way.' Although he has only been in the country for four days, he looks sunburnt – or is it windburnt? He has been impressed by the Aussies' professionalism in the nets on Christmas Day. All agree that this contrasts with England's preparation. As Jameson, referring to the last-minute injury which forced fast bowler Alex Tudor out of the side for this Test, puts it: 'What the bloody hell was Tudor doing playing football in the middle of a major cricket tour?' It is a typically pungent observation from a player of the old school.

On Boxing Day, the star attraction at a reception given for clients of Sport Abroad is Merv Hughes, the former Test player better known for his moustache and his raw aggression than for his fast bowling (though that was pretty good). About a third of the firm's 190 guests here have opted to attend a show billed as 'Big Merv at the Hilton'. The event, held at the hotel where the Australian team is staying, has a younger feel: there are one or two Premiership shirts, and only one MCC tie. With no cricket today, the punters – predominantly male – are still talking about their Christmas lunch out in the bush. At Emu Bottom Homestead, they were treated to demonstrations of sheep-shearing, boomerang-throwing and horse-riding, as well as a huge lunch, including turkey, and plenty of alcohol.

To guide them through the cricket, they have the services of former England players Pat Pocock, John Edrich and Bob Taylor. At regular intervals, these 'hosts' join their clients in the stands, garnishing their own opinions with the latest insights and gossip collected in chats with one-time colleagues and adversaries during visits to the media centre (which is insulated from the weather, a bonus even these hardened crick-eters appreciate in Melbourne). It is a pleasant enough winter occupa-tion for those players who have not graduated to the commentary box – and a few who have. The ex-players are not generally paid, but a free trip for their families and themselves, plus expenses, represents fair remuneration.

'Welcome to Manchester!' says master of ceremonies Barry Richards, to laughter. Smooth, polished and likeable, Richards is one of those who combines commentary work with 'meeting and greeting' on the sup-porters' circuit. He introduces Hughes as 'a bit of an icon in Australia'. 'Big Merv', appearing in his home state, does not disappoint. 'Just go out and get absolutely legless tonight,' he urges the audience. 'Bank on a sleep-in because it's not going to stop raining for a long time.' He is proved wrong there, but when he returns to the theme of hard drinking, he gets his best reaction of the evening. All it takes is a fresh angle or two on the well-known story of how David Boon drank 52 cans of beer en route from Sydney to London for the Ashes tour of 1989, breaking Rod Marsh's Australian team record for the booziest flight to Blighty. The only member of the current set-up ever likely to challenge this, Hughes implies, is Colin 'Funky' Miller. It is a reminder of how far the present Australian team has moved from the drinking culture of the 1970s and 1980s.

Hughes, wearing a snappy dark blue suit and psychedelic tie, neatly summarises the intense emotions involved in an Ashes series. 'If Australia loses to the West Indies,' he says, 'you lost to a better side. But when Australia loses to England, that's not acceptable.' He adds, to sad nods of agreement around the room, 'And it's the same for England when they play Australia.'

Hughes is also interesting on what he terms 'the art of sledging'. He concedes that he 'copped a fair bit of flak in England' for the way he played the game. As far as he is concerned, every Test batsman is technically a good player, 'but if he's mentally weak and I don't try and put pressure on that side of his game, then I'm not doing my job'. Apart from his weakness for that old sporting cliché 'at the end of the day', Merv is a pretty original and entertaining act, with trenchant views. He also lifts his audience's spirits with a prediction that England will win the Sydney Test, and rounds off with a Viagra joke.

On the third evening of the Test, another slice of Middle England gathers at the Hilton for a 'State of Play' party jointly organised by *The Cricketer* magazine and ITC Sports, which handles arrangements for its tours. Although some of the wives find better things to do with their precious days Down Under than watch the match, one middle-aged woman arrives exclaiming: 'What a wonderful day's cricket.' Among the hosts is the Sky commentator Paul Allott, who has rustled up two members of the England party: David Lloyd, the coach, and Warren Hegg, the wicket-keeper making his Test début. Supporters are impressed that the Lancastrian pair has turned out, especially given the extremely long day's play, and Hegg's unfortunate afternoon behind the stumps. Some England players approach such occasions – if they attend at all – with trepidation, fearing an earful from disappointed fans, but as Allott says, Lloyd, a sociable man, is 'quite good at fielding the flak'.

Also presiding is the man who was probably cricket's original 'celebrity host'. Trevor Bailey has been steering parties around Australia since Ray Illingworth's 1970–1 campaign. 'In my playing days [the 1950s],' he says, directing me towards another of the rather sophisticated canapés, 'we would have one or two supporters following us around. Certainly the number was in single figures. There was no question of these tours when it took us twenty-eight days to get here by sea.' Bailey says that although he is one of *Test Match Special*'s summarisers at this Test, he still takes the trouble to 'go over and see the punters. They like that, and I enjoy it.' About half the faces, he says, are familiar from previous trips. 'Trevor knows some of these people so well,' says Helen Tabois, the tour manager, 'it's like a house party.' Not that his role is entirely social. His duties here include collecting clients' tickets for the rain-ruined first day and organising their refunds.

The eighty-odd clients at the party – which lasts until 10 p.m. – include three solo travellers who have elected, at a cost of £6,000, to witness all five Tests on *The Cricketer*'s 'Grand Tour'. Arthur Haygarth, a retired insurance liability claims inspector from Merseyside, is one of them. He is not regretting his outlay. A pleasant, red-faced man, he says it has always been an ambition to follow an Ashes series. He is 'thoroughly enjoying' the experience. He loves having people to watch and discuss the game with, there is a lot of camaraderie in the party, and there is the fun of star-spotting at the Australian team hotel. Among those taking a shorter trip is a former NatWest employee who has raided his recent voluntary redundancy pay-off to fulfil what is also, for him, a lifetime ambition. He is unashamedly thrilled that David Lloyd has confided England's probable intention of retaining Hegg, and recalling Tudor, for the Sydney Test.

Another former England player with juicy morsels to offer the punters is Alan Butcher, one of their hosts, and the father of the England opener Mark, who is married to Alec Stewart's sister Judy. 'People sometimes say cricket is a soft game,' he says, 'but tonight I saw my son going into a bearpit.' A new recruit to host work, the genial Butcher seems well suited to it, appearing unfazed and even amused by an insensitive and ill-informed remark from one punter, to the effect that his son's freakish dismissal an hour or two earlier was due to his 'playing an inappropriate shot for the time of day'. Butcher, being good with people, relishes the work; his second wife and their two small children are evidently enjoying their Christmas in the sun.

I ask Paul Allott, a director of both *The Cricketer* and ITC Sports, what supporters want from their expensive tours. 'Besides the fact that they're in a foreign country watching cricket – which is their passion – one of the things they *really* like is meeting a current England player,' he says. 'They only have to do it at a cocktail party, and they only have to do it once, but it makes the trip.' How does he find the punters? 'They're generally pretty knowledgeable about the game, willing to learn, and they don't ask too many silly questions. They're fairly resilient about England's performances. They've spent their money; the cricket is their prime reason for coming here but there are plenty of other things they can do.' Does he enjoy entertaining them? 'Yes. It can get a bit tedious, at times, when you've been at the ground for ten hours, like today, and you're bombarded with questions, but I don't mind it.'

Although one would not know it out here, most firms have had a dispiriting response to their efforts to drum up Ashes business this time round – even with the pound worth a tempting A$2.70. According to Barry Dudleston, whose Sunsport Tours has been in this market for five years, the final turn-out on organised tours represents only about 50 per cent of the industry's expectations. 'This has been a disaster for everybody,' he says. One operator, Mike Burton, cancelled its tours altogether, so weak was demand; other companies have dropped certain packages and gone ahead with reduced numbers on others. However, Nick Hunt, Sport Abroad's tour manager, says his numbers – peaking at 330 for the Sydney Test, and totalling 700 for the whole tour – show small if slightly disappointing growth compared with the Ashes tour of 1994–5, when the total was 650. John Snow, the former England fast bowler, says his tours are fully booked, with 120 clients in Sydney and 200 carried overall.

Most operators agree that the tour schedule has done them few favours. With the first Test starting within eight months of England's hugely popular Tests in Barbados and Antigua, many supporters had neither the money, the inclination nor the time off for another cricketing trip so hard on the heels of the last. Moreover, this time the Perth and Adelaide Tests have been scheduled before Christmas, when many people are reluctant to go away, rather than at the end of January/beginning of February, when there is nothing many would rather do.

Other factors cited by Dudleston – a first-class umpire – include the fact that many fans prefer to come to Australia under their own steam: unlike in the West Indies, the grounds are big and tickets easy to obtain, and many more people have friends and relations to visit. The economic slowdown, England team performances and what Dudleston diplomatically terms 'England team PR' are also widely blamed. What he and others are driving at here is that on some recent tours package-tour supporters have sensed little or no appreciation of their loyalty, finding the more prominent England players, in particular, remote and unfriendly around the hotels and bars. 'A few can be extremely surly,' says one veteran supporter. 'They don't even say "good morning" to you.'

Of the current team Darren Gough is indisputably the best with all types of fan, as he showed during the Adelaide Test when he walked into the bar of the Hilton hotel. He found it half full of Brits – the sort of scenario some players dread. By the time Gough left, he had spoken to most of them. At the other end of the spectrum, Alec Stewart, Nasser Hussain, Mark Ramprakash and Graham Thorpe do not exactly court the package tourists, whereas Angus Fraser and Robert Croft (especially if he is in the Test side) can be very good, Warren Hegg is invariably friendly, and the likes of Graeme Hick and Mark Butcher are, for the most part, simply quiet. To be fair to the players, they respond much more warmly to 'Barmy Army' supporters, who are, after all, their contemporaries.

As far as one can judge from spending time with tour groups from half a dozen companies, most supporters make friends easily within the group, exchanging hearty banter at the ground, in the bars and on the coach ferrying them around the city's sights. Most also warm to Australia, praising its energy, youthfulness, diversity and natural beauty – the majority of itineraries include the option of visits to Ayers Rock or the Great Barrier Reef, as well as to attractions close to the major cities.

But of course the England contingent in Melbourne will also remember that after travelling half-way across the world they witnessed a famous victory in one of the great Ashes Tests. The turning-point was perhaps Mark Ramprakash's wonderful diving catch at square leg to dismiss Justin Langer, off the bowling of Alan Mullally – an inspirational moment of which the England supporters massed (together with the 'Barmy Army') in the Great Southern Stand at the MCG had a superb view. Only Dickie Bird, himself a tour host, was unmoved. His reluctance to applaud such a feat must be simply a sign of the ingrained neutrality of an umpire, two years into his retirement, rather than any lack of appreciation of a great piece of fielding.

As Dean Headley and then Darren Gough rip through the Australian batting order in the sunshine of an unforgettable last evening, many normally restrained souls sitting around me leap excitedly to their feet at the fall of each wicket, applauding wildly. 'We came out here far more pessimistic than we needed to be,' says Stephen Newman of Tana Travel after the match. 'It could have been Perth and Adelaide all over again.' Another tour manager is more prosaic: 'When the cricket goes well,' he says, 'clients forget the little grumbles. We won't be hearing much about the service at breakfast tomorrow being slow – if they make it to breakfast, that is.'

Four hours later, at around midnight, the more adventurous package tourists are joining England's impromptu victory party in the bar of the team's hotel, the Stamford Plaza (the question of where England are staying is one of those most often asked by supporters). Headley leads the celebrations. Mullally is also in the thick of things. Carrying the drinks but also very much to the fore is Angus Fraser, who orders ten 'B52' cocktails from a startled woman behind the bar. Five minutes later, Graeme Hick, of all people, comes over and orders another dozen of these deadly concoctions for his team-mates, who knock them back as quickly as they have knocked the Aussies over this evening. It is good to see Hick, a major contributor to the victory, celebrating with the new freedom which characterises his Test batting.

Amid all the smiles, the singing and the cheering, Graham Gooch, the tour manager, impatient to lay his hands on more champagne, simply bypasses the queue at the bar. Meanwhile, Ramprakash, another architect of the win, has as quiet a drink as is possible in the frenzied atmosphere with a journalist friend. As Gooch and his players cheerfully pose for photographs with fans of all types, no one could accuse them of being anything but good ambassadors for their country; and no one – at least no one British – is complaining about the noise.

15

Cricket in Excelsis: The Fifth Test

CHRISTOPHER MARTIN-JENKINS

Few days in the history of Test cricket can have been so thrilling and satisfying as the first of the Sydney Test match. All the ingredients were there: a sunny day, an excited crowd bigger than any which had packed into the stately old Sydney Cricket Ground for a Test match in the last quarter of a century, and cricket of shimmering and uplifting excellence.

Winning another priceless toss – given their superiority in spin it was virtually the passport to victory – Australia faltered early but recovered through a majestic partnership by the Waugh brothers, before Darren Gough produced a fairy-tale hat-trick and England took the last five Australian wickets for 11 runs with the second new ball.

I came away from the ground that Saturday evening wondering if I would ever see quite such a perfect day's cricket again. It was hot and dusty, the seething tide of chanting spectators leaving the SCG – they all seemed to be English – were as noisy and tribal as the jubilant supporters of an FA Cup-winning team at Wembley and there wasn't a taxi to be found for miles on the slow trudge back towards the hotel at Coogee Beach. But who cared? There had been more than a hundred runs in each of the three sessions; the first hat-trick of the century by an English bowler against Australia; the first full house in a Test at Sydney for thirteen years; another fine bowling performance by Dean Headley; and a stand of 190 between the brothers from Bankstown.

In that rough Sydney suburb, they and their two cricket-playing younger brothers, Dean and Daniel (both at one stage promising to emulate the twins), must have been raised with wisdom by their newsagent father Ken and his wife Beverley, a tennis player of skill who treasured and nurtured her sports-minded sons without spoiling them. Steve and Mark certainly spoilt those who love beautiful batting, however, after Headley and Alex Tudor, restored to the team instead of Alan Mullally but rusty-looking and lacking rhythm, had taken three wickets for 52 in the first 14 overs of the game.

Three Australian wickets before lunch had been considerable but still insufficient consolation for losing the toss, but for all the excitement of the Australian collapse at the end of the day it was already evident that England had let Australia score too many runs on a pitch so certain to turn. Bad luck played its part in this but so too did some wayward afternoon bowling and muddled thinking by the management.

Good captains are invariably lucky captains and this was the fifth time in five, and the twelfth in thirteen Tests against England, that Taylor had either called or spun the coin correctly. Having picked three spinners and left out Damien Fleming, it was just what he wanted. England's diabolical ill-fortune on recent Australian tours continued when Atherton withdrew with 'increasing spinal stiffness'.

The decision to omit Ashley Giles, who had been called to Sydney as a possible extra spinner after playing in one evening match for the newly arrived one-day squad, was, by contrast, a self-inflicted error. Much had been asked of the captain on this demanding tour but he was about to play a series of one-day matches in which he cheerfully took upon himself the triple burden of captain, wicket-keeper and opening batsman. The case for doing the same just once in a Test match of such immense importance as this – the series decider – and thereby opening up a place for a second spinner was overwhelming. It was all very well to call on Ramprakash as the second slow bowler – he spins the ball sufficiently to be treated seriously in this role – but only if he had been given far more bowling in previous matches. The real mistake, of course, had been to take two specialist off-spinners in the first place instead of treating Croft as a one-day player and picking Phil Tufnell.

For some time at least on the hot and sunny opening morning there was something in a well-grassed pitch for Gough and Headley and an excellent catch in Headley's second over kept the Melbourne spirit alive as Taylor was squared up and edged low to Hick's left.

The opening bowlers were too variable in length after that, however, and Slater and Langer scored mainly through cuts until Tudor had Langer caught behind for 12 in his first over – alas for England off a no-ball. This was another costly consequence of unprofessional cricket. Whilst Bob Cottam had been away with the limited-overs men the day before, Tudor had been bowling regular no-balls in net practice. Whichever of the two managers now in Australia had chosen to switch Cottam – David Graveney with the one-day team or Gooch with the Test players – had got the priority badly wrong.

Still, Headley was irrepressible. He came within an inch of running

179

out Langer but almost immediately afterwards dismissed Slater with a bouncer which the batsman, trying to hook, gloved to the wicket-keeper. An over later, the thirteenth, Langer failed to get on top of the bounce against Tudor and hit straight to cover point.

The Waugh brothers had already begun to turn the tide for Australia with some aggressive and classy batting before lunch. In putting on 113 in the middle session they matched each other for the majesty with which they crashed anything wide of the off stump through the covers. Shades of the Chappell brothers one glorious day at The Oval in 1972. Ian was watching from the commentary box now and as a latter-day Richie Benaud he was busy towards the end of the day writing his trenchant observations on a laptop. Greg, never quite so happy in the public eye, was the contented supremo of South Australian cricket and an expert on healthy living through the right diet and exercise.

Unlike the Chappells, the Waughs did not both make hundreds on this occasion because Steve, looking for the boundary which would have secured the century, was beaten by a perfectly flighted off-break from Such, nine overs into the evening session. The amount the ball turned was ominous for England, but that was temporarily forgotten in the ecstasy over Gough's subsequent hat-trick.

His dressing-room nickname, 'Dazzler', suggests meretriciousness; but there is substance and skill as well as something of the showman in the best Yorkshire fast bowler since Fred Trueman. (Paul Jarvis promised as much but the inner drive was not as great as the talent.) Gough had sweated hard and often to conquer a succession of injuries and at twenty-eight he had reached his peak. How long he will be able to sustain it remains to be seen: both the amount of cricket he plays and the vigorousness of his action make great demands even on his sturdy physique.

Of the twenty-three hat-tricks in 112 years of Test cricket, four had been taken by bowlers involved in the current Test series, but this was the best deserved. Gough had performed magnificently since the tour started, fuelled by a burning desire to win back the Ashes for England and, that mission having failed, some respect for the old country. Australians do not think much of some of England's cricketers, but they esteem this one. He had come back with such a vengeance from the drubbing he received from Slater in the second innings at Brisbane that since his one for 185 there he had taken 19 more wickets at 23 runs each.

Only four overs of the day remained when Healy shaped to play his favourite cut shot to the fourth ball of Gough's seventeenth over, but it lifted and cut back, cramping the batsman, who nudged it to the wicket-keeper. Being Healy, every bit a competitor, he walked to the side of his crease, head down, hoping the umpire had been looking the other way. No such luck.

Gough gathered himself for MacGill, whose 43 in the first innings at Melbourne seemed to have turned the match Australia's way. Now he was unable to get his bat down close enough to a 90 m.p.h. yorker which ripped out his middle stump.

'I've been on a hat-trick a few times in Test cricket. This time I was more relaxed,' said Gough later. He ran in at full bore as usual and produced for the unfortunate Miller another searing yorker which, this time, swung away late to hit the off stump. Delirium from the crowd; joy unconfined for Gough and his team-mates. He had become the first Englishman to take a hat-trick in an Anglo-Australian Test since J. T. Hearne at Headingley in 1899; and only the eighth England bowler ever to get a hat-trick in a Test.

The last to do it, Dominic Cork, 12th man here, came on with a drink and congratulations. The Saturday morning when he took wickets with the first three balls in the day against the West Indies at Old Trafford in 1995 represented a heady triumph for Cork; too heady, perhaps. Gough, simple, smiling, happy, friendly fellow that he is, has never lacked confidence, like Trueman before him, but any boastfulness in him is not of the kind that self-destructs.

Proud patriot that he is, he revelled in the moment of joy when Miller's castle fell and might have drunk a toast afterwards to Dean Riddle, the softly spoken New Zealander whose fitness regime had helped him to this new level of well-being. At a stage of the tour when others were looking weary, Our Darren was positively shining with health, whether sprinting towards the bowling crease or pacing the breakfast room at the team's hotel in Coogee beside his wife Anna Marie and his tiny replica son Liam.

This was the first time that he had managed to get through a five-Test series without an injury and there were twelve one-day matches off the reel still to come. The chances are that he will never bowl quite so fast, for sustained periods, as he did in Melbourne and Sydney.

Daily Telegraph, Monday, 4 January

The fifth Test so far has encapsulated the 1998–9 series: Australia a tough, talented, versatile and resilient team; England improved, not as bad as they are often portrayed, but still down on their luck, technically inferior and not quite good enough in the little things which add up to big ones. After two days Australia, 115 ahead with all second-innings wickets intact, were in complete command. Stuart MacGill was a hero, Shane Warne was back and English euphoria after Gough's hat-trick had evaporated in the shimmering Sydney heat.

Before Mark Waugh had scored on Saturday, a ball from Dean Headley bounced, hit him on the glove and just evaded the grasp of John Crawley, diving at full stretch to his left at short-leg. It was another case of almost but not quite; so near and yet so far. How long, oh Lord, how long?

Nor did these things change yesterday. Hussain batted doggedly and well for almost three hours for 42 and Crawley justified his inclusion by hitting five fours and playing the spinners with finesse but the fact remained that although seven English batsmen got to double figures, the biggest partnership was 49 and no one got to fifty. Stewart, who, as it transpired, might just as well have kept wicket because he began batting after a night's rest, was out chasing a wide ball from McGrath and both Ramprakash and Hick failed to keep attacking shots along the ground.

Generally, too, there was too much block or bash about the England batting. As the former Australian captain and coach, Bobby Simpson, was quick to observe, they failed to work the ball into the gaps for singles, thereby increasing the pressure on themselves and decreasing the disruption to the spinners. That was not a mistake which the Waugh brothers had made during the glittering partnership of 190 for the fourth wicket which followed Australia's shaky start and preceded the spectacular Saturday evening collapse against Gough and Headley.

It would have been asking too much for yesterday's play to match the high intensity of Saturday's. Australia, however, had scored more than a hundred in each session and they soon had England and their supporters down from their cloud yesterday. Their spinners were too good for fretful batsmen on a turning pitch, as they were always likely to be once Mark Taylor won the toss, and might well have been even if he had not.

MacGill has been their find of the series and although Warne was in the thick of the struggle from early on the second day it was his fiery little assistant who proved the hardest spinner to handle during an England decline which proceeded by slow but inevitable degrees from the moment that Butcher went back to Warne's fourth ball and was given out leg before.

MacGill's five for 57 improved on the five for 66 he took against Pakistan at Rawalpindi. As usual, he spun his leg-breaks viciously; further than Warne, although not with the same formidable ability to give the ball a tweak without losing length or direction. He has come a long way in a short time.

Miller bowled his off-breaks well wide of the off stump with the intention of hitting it, varying his pace and trajectory cleverly. Warne took two good catches in addition to his wicket and although his flight deceived no one and he bowled few variations, this was not at all a bad performance considering that he has not played a Test for ten months. It is too early to say with certainty that he is not the bowler he was, but for the moment he is only Australia's second-best leg-spinner.

He had a hand in the two England wickets before lunch during a tense morning's cricket. In the seventh over a hitherto restrained Stewart was tempted by the cunning McGrath to drive at a wide ball with his weight not fully committed and the result was a fast edge to Warne at third slip and McGrath's 200th Test wicket.

As he has throughout his topsy-turvy series, Butcher, not selected until Michael Atherton withdrew on Saturday morning with further stiffness of the spine, played McGrath better than anyone but he had his awkward moments against Miller, who switched from outswingers and off-cutters to slower off-breaks after six overs with the new ball from the Randwick end.

MacGill was called upon first by Taylor but at 52 for one Warne was called up to take over from Miller and all Australia paused in anticipation. Butcher went down on one knee to lift his second ball boldly to the mid-wicket boundary, then right back to the fourth ball which spun from middle stump and might just have grazed the leg.

Ramprakash started impressively but lost his timing after lunch and drove McGrath on the up low to wide mid-off, whereupon Graeme Hick gave England their only period of command. After a patient reconnaissance he began to strike the ball with clean assurance, removing Warne from the attack with a fiercely pulled four followed by a straight driven six. But MacGill bounced a long hop higher than he expected and he carved low to short extra-cover.

Fatally, Hussain was caught off pad and bat off a ball pitched well outside his off stump – Mark Waugh's 100th Test catch – in the 50th over and it was a matter of time after that. Warren Hegg and Alex Tudor did well but they were out of their depth. Both were close to being stumped off MacGill before Hegg was bowled through the gate and Tudor off his pads by a googly. Crawley, by contrast, got a leg-break which spun sharply to give the redoubtable 'Tubby' his 156th slip catch for Australia.

England looked doomed again but gloom was inappropriate after a weekend's cricket like this. Australia had been given both a fight and the occasional fright since Christmas and the home spectators had loved it as much as the many and vociferous England supporters. 81,041 was the aggregate attendance after two days and no one was anticipating a fifth.

Daily Telegraph, Tuesday, 5 January

A great innings probably won the final Test for Australia yesterday. If Michael Slater's 123 out of 184, an innings replete with brilliant strokes and dazzling footwork, turns out not to have been a match-winning effort, someone will have to bat equally exceptionally for England today. Either way this will have been an epic cricket match, watched by the biggest Sydney crowd for a quarter of a century. If England lose narrowly, the moment when Slater appeared to be run out for 35 when Australia were 52 for two, but was reprieved by the third umpire, will inevitably be seen as the most significant of the turning points.

It has been a wonderful cricket match and when the bails were plucked off on a golden summer evening, England still had a theoretical chance of getting the 287 they needed to win and level the series. Of their six specialist batsmen, however, two had already played their final innings of the series, 183 were still required and the odds remained heavily on an Australian victory.

Cricket is a game of chance and umpiring error has always been a part of it, so too much fuss should not be made of the run out. Simon Taufel, the third umpire who had to judge on a direct hit on the stumps by Dean Headley from deep mid-on, is a young official who is highly regarded although he had stood in only nine first-class games when this season started. He looked at replays from two different angles, the most important of which unfortunately had Peter Such, waiting behind the stumps for Headley's throw, obscuring the view of both ball and stumps. Taufel eventually ruled not out although everything suggested that in the days before television replays the square-leg umpire, in this case Steve Dunne, would have lifted his finger.

An experienced English umpire, who was in Australia as a travel guide and has done the television adjudication job in Tests in England, said that Slater should have been given out on the evidence of the two angles. 'It is not necessarily a matter of judging on just one angle but on the evidence of them all,' he said. Fixed cameras square to the stumps at both ends, so far unique to Lord's, could only help in future. Television commentators watching the head-on camera replay, however, eventually spotted movement at the base of the stumps just before Slater's bat reached the crease.

How magnificently he cashed in on his good fortune is evident from the fact that only one man has ever scored a higher proportion of a completed Test innings: Charlie Bannerman in the first innings of the first Test ever played, at Melbourne in 1877. 'There was some really good bowling today and batting conditions were really hard,' said Slater at the end of the day. 'Once we got 200 ahead every run felt like two. We're quietly confident. 280 odd should be enough if we bowl well.'

Slater was out of the Australian side for 20 Test matches, including the six in England in 1997, because the selectors deemed him to be too rash. In this series, as in the last against England four years ago, he has made three fine hundreds, all, it is true, in the second innings once a first-innings lead had been gained. But there is a man for every situation in the Australian side, except, the evidence shows, when they themselves are in the sort of position England now face, of chasing a fourth-innings total on a wearing pitch.

Analysing his eleventh Test century and his seventh against England, Slater added: 'I kept telling myself to wait for the ball I knew I could hit where I wanted to; to keep it simple and not get too far ahead of myself.' His driving was unstoppably powerful and well timed, mainly through or over extra cover whenever a fast bowler overpitched but also, three times, over the boundary off Peter Such from well down the pitch. The first of his three sixes was swept into the O'Reilly Stand at mid-wicket, the other two were driven straight.

At the other end all was struggle and strife. Darren Gough sprained an ankle in the first over of the day but still dismissed Mark Taylor with his sixth ball, angled across and edged low to first slip, before Dean Headley and Such took over as the bowlers on whom Alec Stewart relied. Headley, a cricketer with a big heart who has gained new and higher stature in a single week, had two more wickets before lunch, with some more straight, fast, authoritative and rhythmic bowling.

He trapped Langer on the back foot and then outwitted a fluent looking Mark Waugh with a second successive short ball, pulled to square-leg and expertly caught by Ramprakash. Such's first wicket came from an even better reaction catch by John Crawley, who clutched the ball to his chest at silly-point off the face of Darren Lehmann's bat.

Such bowled throughout the hot afternoon session from the Randwick end, never afraid to flight the ball, turning it sharply, albeit quite slowly, a fact which gives England a grain of hope. Two of his remaining wickets were caught close to the bat, the other two – Warne and McGrath – at mid-wicket. Headley bowled Steve Waugh with a beauty which swung in and left him off the pitch and finally got Slater, eighth out after tea, cutting.

England had bowled and fielded with spirit and control. Stewart directed the field well, notably when blocking Steve Waugh's favourite scoring areas after he had been obliged to drop to number seven because of a hamstring injury, but he was too reluctant to give Alex Tudor a second chance. His straight, brisk morning spell had restrained Slater as well as anyone.

When England's long march to freedom began, four overs after tea, Australia looked with confidence not just to Warne and McGrath, with 515 Test wickets between them, but to MacGill and Miller. But England went out with guns already removed from the holsters and soon they were smoking.

Butcher stroked three offside fours in McGrath's first over, a reprise of the way he had batted when England chased 247 and won by eight wickets at Trent Bridge last season, albeit on a far better pitch than this one. Stewart's first ball from Miller was driven with conviction through extra cover.

There were 28 on the board already when Miller switched to his slower style, 39 when MacGill joined him and 55 when Warne was summoned for the 14th over to put a stop to all this upstart English enterprise. This time it took him a full over to account for Butcher. With the cunning of experience he sensed Butcher's naive eagerness to get down the track and delivered a top spinner from wider – so wide that he cut the return crease and should have been no-balled. Umpire Dunne did not spot it and Butcher was stranded, much as he had been against Muttiah Muralitharan at The Oval in August.

Stewart played several bold lofted strokes to leg in his determination to hold the initiative but there was a desperate air to some of them. Having struck five fours and made his 42 off only 55 balls he, too, was beaten by a leg-break as he danced out to pull-drive, and Ian Healy had the bails off with unerring speed.

Hussain, outstanding in the field earlier, survived with Ramprakash to the close and, despite the length of the odds, no English supporter could be utterly without hope after what had happened at Melbourne. The prospect of one final day of dramatic events was appealing, but for cricket correspondents as well as for players back-to-back Test matches can be a strain. To my embarrassment, the demands of the job obliged me to make only a very late appearance at a special dinner that third evening of the match to celebrate, albeit a few months too late, the eightieth birthdays of the Bedser brothers.

The survivors of the 1948 side, the 'Invincibles' as they were now affectionately and routinely dubbed, had also been fêted at a dinner, missing only the most invincible of all, Sir Donald Bradman. More in demand than any member of the royal family but the Queen and now in his ninety-first year, the Don these days received visitors at his home in Kensington Park in Adelaide rather than making public appearances, but there are museums in his honour both at the Adelaide Oval and in his old home town of Bowral, paintings depicting him still do the rounds of the charity dinners and he had made a fine recovery both from the death of his beloved wife Jessie and from an illness which at one stage four years before had appeared likely to be mortal.

All through the series there had been breakfasts and dinners linked to the cricket. The Australian passion for sport is not confined to its contemporary heroes; nor, indeed, is it restricted to Australians alone. The Bedsers, Alec and Eric, have long been honorary Australians anyway, so two generous parliamentarians, Lloyd Lange and Roger Wotton, hosted an evening at Parliament House in Macquarie Street which was swarming with familiar faces from the past. One of them, the urbane Ken Archer, gave an outstanding speech. It was worth the long taxi ride from Coogee even for the cheese and port.

The following day England managed to add only 84 more runs for their last eight wickets, going down twenty-one minutes after lunch before another healthy attendance which swelled the overall crowd to 142,282. They saw high-class leg-spin bowling hastening Australia to their expected victory but it was demonstrated not so much by Warne as by MacGill.

Once the understudy, now very much the leading man, the hero of the hour displayed extraordinary calm for one with a reputation for volatility. Like all artists, he made it look simple, overwhelming the batsmen not with mysterious variations or unfathomable flight but simply by the sheer viciousness of his spin, achieved with an action which looked as gentle as a rider reaching up to stroke the neck of a favourite horse.

MacGill's seven for 50, a career best, gave him 27 wickets in the four Tests he had played in this series and 47 in eight matches for Australia. Only Hussain, determined to be positive according to the team plan, played him with any lasting success but he was seventh out, miscueing a drive shortly before lunch and the tail lasted only seven overs in the afternoon. The last wicket was outrageous, Such falling to a deflection off the boot of Michael Slater as he took evasive action from a full-blooded and rather handsome stroke. It was the final misfortune for England, the ultimate triumph for MacGill and his team. Victory by 98 runs in this match and three to one in the series reflected Australian superiority faithfully enough.

Jim Higgs, the former Test leg-spinner who was one of the selection committee which first took a chance on the talent of Warne, continues to express the theory that any country which does not itself possess spin bowlers of high quality will not produce batsmen who play them with authority. That was the first thing for England's administrators to ponder as the post-mortem began; not that it was anything they did not already realise.

MacGill (initials SCG) was suddenly a national hero and a hot commercial property. In the twenty-four hours after the game his manager received endorsement offers worth almost a quarter of a million pounds. In the end he had taken more wickets in the series even than McGrath, whose domination of Atherton and general excellence had been even more fundamental to Australia's success.

Once more on the final day McGrath had taken a vital wicket, having probed expertly around the off stump in the first few tension-filled overs. With his sixteenth ball of the day he drew from Ramprakash a weak half-cut at a ball lifting just outside the off stump. The snick travelled very low to first slip where Taylor grasped his 157th catch in 104 matches. The new Test record had fallen to a fielder blessed with rare hand-to-eye coordination and powers of concentration which had been especially remarkable in the last four years, given all that a captain has to think about. Off quick bowlers he was equally good low to the ground and above his head. Off the slow ones he was no less sharp: he took thirty catches off Warne to only twenty by Healy. (The ball turns that much in Australia.)

The statistician for The Cricket Society, Keith Walmsley, had revealed at the start of the series that only nine other fieldsmen in the history of Test cricket had a higher percentage of catches per match than Taylor's 1.49. Curiously, the only other contemporary players were both New Zealanders and both specialist slips: Bryan Young and Stephen Fleming. Eknath Solkar of India headed the all-time list with an average of 1.96 catches a match, but forty-eight of his fifty-three catches were taken off spinners, whereas Taylor, uniquely, had a virtually even balance between catches off fast and slow bowlers (that balance held by eight taken off medium pacers). It was an illustration not just of Taylor's versatility but also of the enviable variety of the Australian bowling attack during his career.

Taylor did not at once announce his retirement, but he had no regrets when, several weeks later, he did so. His batting (but emphatically not his catching and captaincy) had probably lost a little of its authority, so he was wise to go whilst the applause was still ringing around him. Meanwhile, he gave one more exemplary press conference; from a position of strength as usual and wearing his baggy green cap, just in case it *was* for the last time. Then he returned to the dressing-room and for several hours joined the players of both sides over drinks and reminiscences which showed that, whatever the appearance of ill-feeling in the heat of combat, English and Australian cricketers respect and like each other still. They are, after all, players, not warriors.

All concerned with cricket in England had to ask again why it was that they had foundered once more on the Australian rock. Superficially they had paid both for bad luck with the two important tosses and for their own mistakes. They could be faulted not for any lack of industry or determination but for errors of judgement and execution.

Deep down, however, they were victims of a superior system as well as of a better team. Since 1989 and the combination of Bobby Simpson as coach, Allan Border as captain and Lawrie Sawle as a far-sighted chairman of selectors, Australia had stuck to a formula of calculated aggression with bat and ball, supported by fielding of the highest standard. Players had been picked for their character as well as their talent and since Warne's emergence against the West Indies in 1992–3 they had possessed the finest leg-spinner in the world.

Simpson gave way to Geoff Marsh, Border to Taylor, Sawle to Trevor Hohns, in the first two cases reluctantly but at the right time. The high standards never faltered. So it was not just in the lower reaches of their cricket that Australia developed an excellence which was constantly under revision.

Nevertheless, the top works only because the base of the pyramid is so sound. In schools and at youth camps, potential international cricketers are spotted early, nurtured physically and mentally, and slowly baked hard in the oven of the competitive cricket which exists at every level. It is easier, too, for Australians to focus on the ultimate dream of getting into the national side because of the passionate patriotism which is part of the national psyche.

Even the Australians cannot be complacent. Malcolm Speed, the chief executive of the ACB, brought into the job from a similar role in basketball, speaks of the need to market the game against 'increasing rivalry from other sport and leisure pursuits'. There has to be constant vigilance about the marketing of the game here, just as in England, but Australia have the priceless advantage of role models to capture the minds of the young.

Their playing resources are not infallible. England proved at Melbourne, not for the first time, that Australians will fold under the pressure of tight bowling and fielding like any other team, and although Taylor's successor, Steve Waugh, made the elimination of such occasional fallibility a prime objective of his captaincy, he is by nature more cautious and unlikely therefore to press home so many winning opportunities.

There are ample batting reserves for the established five of Taylor,

Slater, Langer and the Waughs – Lehmann, Ponting, Elliott, Blewett, Richards, Bevan, Law, Hodge, Lee, Harvey – and a mature and talented batsman/wicket-keeper replacement for Healy in Adam Gilchrist. But McGrath is the only world-beating fast bowler and, curiously, Australia have only two leg-spinners who regularly get into a first-class team. Fortunately both Warne and MacGill are exceptional by any standards.

No doubt others are being bred below because the climate and the hard pitches encourage wrist spin. In Britain they do not, but ECB coaches have belatedly started a process of searching, region by region, for young wrist-spinning talent and then giving special treatment to the most promising. Two seventeen-year-old leg-spinners went to the Australian Academy in Adelaide early in 1999 at the behest of the Brian Johnston Memorial Trust to widen their education. For the moment, England selectors had only two specialist leg-spinners, Ian Salisbury and Chris Schofield, to choose from.

England could claim in the end that Gough had almost cancelled out McGrath, but they had no one to match MacGill (or Warne) and throughout Australia had batted and fielded more reliably than England. They made four totals over 300, England only one, in the first innings of the first Test. Even then, their tail collapsed. To rise from seventh position in the world rankings, England had to find a batsman or two who, like the Waugh brothers, can bowl usefully (Andrew Flintoff and Graeme Swann have the potential) and a bowler or two who can bat usefully.

The additional hardness of the Australians was most obvious not in the occasional, unpleasant and unnecessarily overt aggression of the superbly methodical McGrath but in the way they finished the jobs they had started well. Of the sixteen Australian batsmen who reached 50, eight made centuries; of 15 England batsmen who reached 50, only Alec Stewart and Mark Butcher got the other half. Not half enough.

Only Nasser Hussain scored more than 400 runs; for Australia, Steve Waugh, Michael Slater and Justin Langer did so and Mark Waugh made 393. In a low-scoring series, a reflection of pitches which, other than the Gabba, always gave the bowlers some help, England made 22 ducks to Australia's 15 and there was a ten-run difference of runs per wicket overall: Australia 2,703 runs at 33, England 2,243 at 23. Not surprisingly, therefore, only one English bowler, the burgeoning Dean Headley, took his wickets at a cost of under 25, as against five Australians.

All this might have been different but for the fallible catching in the first three Tests. The final count of possible chances missed by the two sides was twenty-two by England, nine by Australia. It was impossible to calculate the loss of confidence and morale on the part of the bowlers, or the encouragement given to reprieved batsmen.

16

The Umpires and Referee

CHARLES DE LISLE

'I'm one of the tough old bastards,' says John Reid, discussing how he approaches his work as an International Cricket Council (ICC) match referee. During this Ashes series, however, Reid has not proved quite as tough as he likes to think: it took him until the fourth Test to punish Glenn McGrath, the most persistent 'sledger' on either side. We are talking in the umpires' room at the Sydney Cricket Ground (SCG), at 9.30 a.m., ninety minutes before the start of play on the second day of the fifth Test. It is a long, thin room at the side of the beautiful Victorian Members' Stand, on the first floor. It has no view of the playing area. Nor does it have a television set. It does have a large white board which anyone officiating in a first-class match here is invited to sign. Dickie Bird's signature (top left, of course), recording his one Test appearance (Australia–Pakistan, 1995–6) here as a 'neutral' umpire, is also a reminder that the odd 'whitecoat' – as they like to call umpires in Australia – can become a big name in his own right.

As befits the man in charge, Reid sits at the head of a long wooden table – a table large enough to accommodate all twenty National Grid international umpires. Along the table his fellow officials make themselves comfortable, chatting over a cup of tea and some biscuits. The only one with a face that would be recognised in the street is Darrell Hair. Australia's best umpire has been in the news all summer. In his memoirs, *Decision Maker*, published on the eve of the series, Hair reignited the controversy over the action of Muttiah Muralitharan, Sri Lanka's off-spinner. Hair, who had no-balled Muralitharan seven times for throwing during the Melbourne Test in 1995, described his action as 'diabolical' and said he could have called him twenty-seven times. As a result of these comments, the forty-six-year-old umpire has been pressured by the Australian Cricket Board – which does not accept that he had any right to publish a book – into standing aside from Sri Lanka's ten qualifying matches in the one-day series.

Hair's colleague out in the middle for this Test is Steve Dunne. The moustachioed Dunne, fifty-five, has also been in the headlines lately. By giving Mike Atherton not out caught behind off Allan Donald when he had made 27 of his match-winning 98 not out in the fourth Test against South Africa last season he inadvertently made a lot of new friends in England. Appropriately for a New Zealander, Dunne counts the balls of an over with a sheep counter. Dunne and Hair enjoy working together – this is their fourth Test as a pair, their bond initially being forged during that emotional Melbourne Test of 1995. They share a good sense of humour, something you must need as an umpire.

The third umpire is Simon Taufel, handling TV monitor duties for the third time in a Test match (and the third time at Sydney – the third umpire is always a local official). At twenty-seven, he is the baby of the team; he is a bit baby-faced too. This game, in front of the largest Sydney Test crowd since Taufel was a four-year-old, is the biggest challenge in his short career. The Playing Control Team, as it is officially known, is completed by Peter Hughes, the 'fourth umpire', another local official. He acts as a '12th man' for the others, making the tea being one of his duties. Like Hair and Taufel, he lives in Sydney, and commutes to the SCG from his home; Reid and Dunne are staying at the same hotel as the Australian team, the Quay West.

As you would expect, the atmosphere in the umpires' room is calm. There are no interruptions, but then a strictly worded notice on the door forbids entry to anyone (and that includes irate players), in the hour before or after play, without the referee's permission. Behind the chat, the officials are quietly preparing themselves mentally for the seven or so hours of intense concentration that will be required on another hot Sydney day, in front of another magnificent crowd (38,917 to be precise). There is a lot at stake. The pressures on umpires in a final Test are often the fiercest, and with England having created an unexpected chance to level the rubber 2–2, this is already proving a tense, unpredictable game, full of passionate, attacking cricket. Add to that the fact that, given the way the ball turns here, Sydney asks even the best umpires difficult and unusual questions. Today, with England facing an Australian attack including two leg-spinners, Warne and MacGill, and an off-spinner, Miller, Messrs Hair and Dunne will be confronted with constant appeals against uncertain batsmen. In Hair's view, leg-spin is the hardest type of bowling to umpire. For one thing, the angle, with the stock ball spinning across the right-handed batsman towards first slip, makes it very difficult to see deflections off the bat; and, as with any slow bowler, an umpire has no time to relax, take a deep breath and regain his composure between deliveries.

While umpires are in some ways a breed apart, they share some of the preoccupations of players. They talk about their 'game' and their 'form'. They worry about having a bad Test, being heavily criticised in the media, and in the captains' and referee's reports, and not being selected for the next big game. Although Hair is being paid A\$5,800 (£2,300) for this match, he umpires just two home Tests a year, as well as several abroad in his role as an ICC 'neutral' official (this is only his twenty-eighth Test in all). His book apart, he has almost no other source of income.

An hour or so before the start, a large plate of fruit is brought in. There is melon, watermelon, bananas, grapes. The umpires tuck in. Although aware of its calming properties, I express interest that Hair and Dunne should face the heat – in all senses – with such healthy fuel inside them. Hair explains that the fruit, as well as a regular supply of ice-cold water and energising drinks during the day, helps him ward off dehydration. 'If you get dehydrated,' he says, 'it affects your concentration levels, and then there can be a breakdown in your skills.' But, he adds with a smile, 'it's a very different scene here at the end of the day. It's more a question of beer and meat pies.' Hair, who towers above his colleagues (he is 6' 4" and broad with it), comes across as the most laid-back umpire. With only forty minutes to go, he has still not changed into his black trousers and white shirt – because of the heat and humidity, he and Dunne, who have to look the same, have agreed to leave their ties behind – and he is still doing the crossword. It is Hair's way of relaxing, of finding 'the right frame of mind'. At lunch-time, incidentally, relaxation takes the form of changing into a pair of shorts and putting his weary feet up on a chair for twenty minutes.

By 10.55 a.m., Hair is ready to start the day's proceedings. There is no bell at Sydney, so by tradition the umpires simply go downstairs, knock on the door of the England dressing-room, inform the captain they are about to go out, cross the Members' Bar, and do the same at the Australian dressing-room. Then it is out on to the field, via their own special gate. Meanwhile, John Reid is settling into the third umpire's room alongside Taufel. They do not exactly have the best seats in the house. They occupy an anonymous box at mid-wicket, at the top of the Brewongle Stand. True, it is air-conditioned, and it has a good view, but, as Reid remarks, they would rather be looking straight down the wicket; and it takes so long to get back to the umpires' room that their tea – scones, cream, jam and cold drinks – has to be brought to them by Peter Hughes. Reid sits on the right, Taufel on the left; Reid bids me pull up a seat between them. To Taufel's left are two television monitors, one above the other. One shows the 'ground feed' from Channel Nine, the other has the coverage as seen by the viewer at home: in other words, interrupted by commercials and race meetings. If both sets fail, the third umpire illuminates the white light in front of him, signalling to everyone that, because of a technical failure, all decisions must for the moment be made by the men in the middle.

Also right in front of Taufel are the other two buttons which he will press to signal – on the lights just in front of this box – his decisions to 38,000 pairs of eyes around the ground: red for 'out', green for 'not out'. The other crucial piece of equipment, when a tight decision is referred to the TV umpire, is the telephone. On the receiver, just in case it is forgotten under the pressure of events, is written the extension number of Nine's outside-broadcast director. Oddly, given that what is said out in the middle is one of the referee's greatest concerns, the officials do not receive any 'feed' from Nine's stump microphones. Each does have a pair of binoculars, and there is a 'walkie-talkie' for communicating directly with their colleagues in the middle. 'Hello, mate' is Taufel's customary walkie-talkie greeting to Hair.

Before play starts, Taufel explains what happens when Hair or Dunne makes the fateful shape of a television screen with his hands. 'You play director,' he says. 'You dial up the Channel Nine director, and request the pictures you want [from any of ten cameras]. You ask him to slow it down, you ask to see the incident from other angles, and slow them down. It's important to take a reasonable amount of time to get a good feel of all the evidence available. That can take three minutes.'

As England's first innings gets under way, it is the routine aspects of the job which catch the eye. Taufel uses a 'clicker' to count the number of balls in each over, though there is nothing he can do if he sees an umpire about to allow a seven-ball over – unless he is asked on the 'walkie-talkie'. He also makes a note of all appeals, successful or not, a note to which the men in the middle may need to refer when assessing their own performances. Reid, using a selection of coloured felt tips, fills in various records of the play. Dubious decisions by an umpire are noted down, for mention in his confidential end-of-match umpire's report to the ICC. In this two-page document Reid will first assess each umpire's performance under four headings: 'correct decisions', 'coping with pressure', 'attitude to players' and 'players' respect for umpires'. Reid will tick a box to rate each official as 'good', 'OK' or 'poor' on each count; the captains follow the same procedure in their reports. The referee and captains then have to compare the overall performance of Hair and Dunne, ticking boxes to rate them 'equal', or one as 'slightly' or 'much' better than the other. In the next section, Reid, Mark Taylor and Alec Stewart are asked to detail any specific criticisms they have of an umpire's decision-making in the following areas: lbw, caught behind, bat–pad catch, use of the third umpire, bouncers/beamers, no-balls, wides and the umpire's own positioning. Details of any shortcomings in the areas of coping with pressure, attitude to players and players' respect for umpires, or any other failings are also required. The third umpire's game is scrutinised too, at least by the referee.

'If an umpire is not up to standard,' says Reid, 'I detail those decisions which were wrong. But I also commend good decisions. On a wicket where it's turning, I might say "so-and-so" had a very good match and gave some good bat–pad decisions.' The referee may also take the opportunity to mention any bad behaviour the men in the middle may have overlooked. Says Reid: 'If an umpire hasn't reported an alleged breach of the ICC Code of Conduct – a case of "sledging" or barging, say – and I think he should have done so, he gets a black mark in my report.' Shortly after the Test, Reid's report will be faxed to the ICC in London, together with the captains' reports. Oddly, if they wish to say anything about the TV replay umpire, they have to scribble it on as an extra item. In his report after this game, Alec Stewart will surely have scribbled fairly furiously about one of Taufel's decisions. Taylor and Stewart, incidentally, are both known to take trouble over their reports, something which is by no means true of all Test captains.

During the match, Reid also keeps a record of each over bowled, including allowances for time lost to each interruption of play, be it the fall of a wicket, a drinks break or a batsman calling for a change of bat; for some reason Michael Slater's elaborate celebrations on reaching a century do not count as an interruption, which is hard on England. After making appropriate allowances and checking with the scorers, Reid calculates at the end of each day's play whether each side is ahead of, level with or behind the 15 overs per hour required, and by how many overs. Before play next day, he hands each captain an 'over-rate sheet' setting out the latest position, allowing them to hurry up their bowlers if necessary. At the end of the match, Reid calculates whether a fielding side should be fined a proportion of its match fees for failing to maintain the required 15 overs per hour (there are, it turns out, no over-rate fines in this series, though England would have been punished after the last, pulsating, day in Melbourne had Australia's second innings lasted a couple more overs – fifty in total).

Reid, who also refereed the last Ashes series in Australia (a more acrimonious affair), was an aggressive middle-order batsman who captained New Zealand to its first-ever Test victory, over West Indies in 1955–6. A retired businessman aged seventy, he is fond of saying of players: 'These guys have got to realise I'm not here on holiday. I have a job to do. The captains know the rules. They have to control their players on the field.' That means, among other things, keeping what Reid terms 'yapping', 'mouthing' or 'mouthing off' to a minimum. Likeable and somewhat cynical, he has an infectious laugh. In normal circumstances, the only time he is seen out in the middle is when he supervises the toss. Here, Stewart called 'heads' for the fifth time in the series, and when Reid picked up the coin, he found that for the fifth time the England captain had called wrong. Stewart then asked for a closer look at the 1953 South African five-shilling piece which had been used for all but one of the tosses. 'Alec spun it four times, and it came up "heads" every time,' says Reid. 'So he couldn't complain about my coin.'

Taufel, meanwhile, cannot complain about his luck. He has just become the youngest member, by a decade, of Australia's nine-strong national umpires' panel, from which all Test and one-day international appointments are made, and is about to make his international début out in the middle, in a one-dayer. A promising right-arm quick bowler who played for the NSW Under-19s before a back injury curtailed his career, he has been a first-class umpire since 1994–5, earning consistently good reports from captains. Possessed of a confident manner, he is still employed as a plant manager at a printing firm. His name, by the way, is pronounced 'tow-fel' and does not, as some England fans are to suggest, rhyme with 'awful'.

Reid is very conscious of how the players' behaviour will look to the millions watching on television. When a boundary is hit, he makes a point of watching the bowler's reaction, rather than following the ball to the fence. After ninety minutes' play, I ask whether anything has caught his attention so far today? 'No, everybody's behaving themselves – even McGrath,' he replies. In Melbourne a few days ago, McGrath became the first player on either side to be disciplined by Reid for violating the

ICC Code of Conduct, his thorough 'sledging' of Alan Mullally (so geed up that he finally made some runs) on the last day earning him a fine of 30 per cent of his match fee for using 'crude and abusive language'. At the hearing, conducted by Reid and held at 9 p.m., because of the match's late finish, video evidence of the incident was, as usual, screened. Mark Taylor defended McGrath's behaviour, saying it was 'just a couple of number elevens having a go at one another'. Reid, who had hauled both captains out of the showers the evening before to issue a 'friendly warning' about 'sledging', took a more serious view, though McGrath was given a partial reprieve which one or two fellow referees felt undeserved. 'The big saving grace', discloses Reid, explaining why the fine was suspended for four months, 'was that McGrath said he was working on his attitude. He recognises that he bowls better when he's not talking. That's why he got a suspended sentence.' Mullally, who was not blameless either, was also spoken to by the referee, though he has not been selected for this game.

Although all seems quiet this morning, Reid emphasises that 'things can blow up very quickly, and when they do they can be very big'. Taufel and Reid certainly cannot risk missing a ball so, like their colleagues out in the middle, they must have strong bladders. There is certainly no hint of a repeat of an alleged incident at a Test in England. An experienced third umpire was discovered, when asked his opinion of a tight run out, to be watching a race on television. By contrast, only once in the four hours I spend in their eyrie does Taufel even leave his chair, and then it is just to stretch his legs in the box, between overs. There are no unexpected visitors, though there might have been. If a team is not happy with the performance of the umpires, it is entitled to complain to the referee, and there will be a knock on the door from the manager, possibly even the captain. 'It happens very seldom,' says Reid. 'The batting side might want to ask me to talk to the umpires about no-balls not being called, or the fielding side might want to know why a run out wasn't referred to the third umpire.'

By the evening of the second day (Australia 322 and 13–0, England 220) it is clear what a busy match *this* third umpire is having. Where the TV replay umpire would expect to make just one or two decisions over five days, Taufel has already made three. All were tight. On the first morning, Taufel judged from the replays that Justin Langer, on 25, had just beaten a direct hit from Dean Headley, swooping in from point. On the second afternoon, Warren Hegg, on one, and Alex Tudor, on 14, were also given the green light after appeals for stumpings by Healy off MacGill. None of the reprieved made much of their good fortune, so the effect on the game was minimal.

On the third morning, with the match delicately poised, Taufel is presented with an even more difficult decision. Mark Waugh hits Peter Such to deepish mid-on and his partner, Michael Slater, tries to turn an easy single into a two. Headley, again fielding brilliantly, throws down the stumps, and the fielders, the crowd and the batsman himself seem certain, looking at the big screen replay, that he is out. But after three very long minutes, Taufel presses the green button. He has decided, on the basis of unsatisfactory video evidence, that the batsman must be given the benefit of the doubt. Only two camera angles are any use, and he asks to see them both in slow motion twice. The big problem is that in the side-on view, from a camera in the Ladies' Stand (and one not in line with the wicket), the stumps are obscured by Such; the moment they are broken by the throw can only be seen in the end-on picture, which suggests he is out. Taufel does ask for a shot from a camera at the other end, on the top of the Bradman Stand, but it is apparently of no use, and is not relayed to him. As he put it to me after the match: 'I had to make up my mind based on two camera angles, one of which was unhelpful. You have to make the best decision you can with the evidence you're given. With more resources, the decision might have been different.' He added, with understandable emphasis, 'What would you say of an umpire on the field who made a run-out decision from mid-wicket?'

This time a Taufel decision has a potentially decisive influence on the game, for Slater, then on 35, goes on to make a delightful 123 out of Australia's second-innings 184. In all the ensuing discussion, it is almost unanimously agreed that Australia should follow the lead taken by South Africa, and by Lord's, and install four side-on cameras, one on each side of each end of the wicket. However, a more experienced third umpire might not have needed extra technology. By putting the two images together, he could have given Slater out on the available evidence. If you look at Such's position in the end-on view, as the ball breaks the stumps, and then look at the bowler side-on, when he is in the same position, you can see that Slater is just short of his ground at the crucial moment. 'You have to be 100 per cent sure, but Taufel could have been,' argues an experienced umpire watching the game, adding: 'There's no excuse for mistakes by the third umpire. It's not a difficult job.' On the other hand, it is not easy for Taufel to do this job properly on a ground equipped with only one side-on camera.

At 5.15 that afternoon Taufel, who looks unshaken by the Slater saga, is on the line to the Nine director once more. 'It's me again,' he says, asking for replays of an appeal by Healy against Mark Butcher for a stumping off MacGill. Within thirty seconds, and without saying a word to either of us with him in the box, Taufel is reaching for the green button. 'That was an easy one, Simon,' says Reid. 'You shouldn't take any pay for that!' 'I'll take as much pay as I can,' replies Taufel, probably thinking that he is overdue a simple decision – it was a ridiculous appeal. As he explained later, in his matter-of-fact way: 'I was happy with the shots I saw.' Despite the intense concentration required throughout the match, the third umpire and the referee are still able to enjoy the occasion. They remark on the 'sheilas' picked up by the cameras and keep up a running commentary on the play. When Stewart, leading England's pursuit of an almost impossible victory target of 287, charges MacGill and is stumped, Reid exclaims: 'What *was* he trying to do there? Oh well, I don't know, I committed suicide often enough, playing the wrong shot at the wrong ball!'

What do the officials do in the evening? One thing they do *not* do is watch the highlights on television. Those are in the post to Darrell Hair anyway: the ACB requires Test umpires to review their own performance on video after the match. They have to look afresh at every appeal from their end and write a self-assessment report. And his partner? 'I've seen a few clips of this game on the news,' Dunne said afterwards. 'But if you want feedback on a particular decision, you can get it from the third umpire. During this Test I've glanced occasionally at the big screen, but not when I've made a decision: it might distract me from the next ball. I'll have a look at a decision by my partner, or a brilliant piece of fielding. I had another look at the great catch Ramprakash took in front of me, to dismiss Mark Waugh.'

On the third night of the Test all five officials dine together, an event organised by Reid to promote team spirit. They gather beforehand in Reid's hotel room, where duty-free whisky is dispensed. The venue is the Waterfront, an expensive restaurant in Sydney's historic Rocks area, with superb views of the harbour from a position close to the Harbour Bridge. No doubt the party of seven – 'wives and lady friends' are also invited – perused the menu and made its decisions faster than most. 'We talked about cricket, our family lives, news affairs and the world,' says Dunne, adding: 'It's very important that umpires get on *off* the pitch. It makes the job a heck of a lot easier if you know how your colleagues think. You develop confidence in the way they operate.' Says Hair, who was accompanied by his 'lady friend' from Nottingham: 'The main concern was relaxation. We discussed what was happening in cricket generally, but not this match. We do that as soon as play finishes.'

For Reid, the drink he has one evening with Peter Burge, a fellow referee, is also typical. There is apparently a lot of the sort of banter Australians and New Zealanders exchange. The two discuss their other great shared passion – fishing – with Burge proudly telling the story of how he has just caught his first salmon trout. As for cricket, there is an element of machismo in the private conversation of referees. There is talk of having 'done' this or that player for this or that transgression. The officials are, with some reason, proud of the part they play in ensuring, as the ICC puts it, that 'the spirit of the game is observed'. Reid acknowledges, however, that his role is to support the umpires and not, as the ICC underlines, 'in any way interfere with their traditional role'.

On the fourth morning, Reid runs into McGrath as they are leaving the hotel. 'I shook his hand,' says Reid, 'and said, "Congratulations on your 200" and he thanked me and said, "I haven't said a word all match, ref." That shows a good attitude – no hard feelings.' As the last day of a generally good-natured series opens, Reid says he is 'very pleased with the spirit and attitude in which it has been played'. He believes this has something to do with the uncompromising way in which he set out his stall seven weeks earlier, before the first Test in Brisbane. He was motivated partly by a strong feeling that referees in some recent series around the world had been too lenient. In a headmasterly letter to the management of each side, three days before the match, Reid emphasised that a very tough line would be taken on dissent – 'a shake of the head or a tap on the bat is not disappointment!' – and on other breaches of the ICC code: 'sledging, chat abuse, crude language, gestures', intimidation of umpires, bringing the game into disrepute and illegal advertising on equipment or clothing. 'Mr Manager, Gentlemen,' Reid rounded off, 'there will be millions of cricket fans, young and old, watching this series in many countries. You are their cricketing heroes – your conduct should set an example of how this great game should be played.' Reid was delighted that having asked Graham Gooch, the England tour manager, and Geoff Marsh, Australia's coach, to read out his letter at their next team meetings, the Aussies went one step further and copied it to each player.

Once Australia has won the match, Reid feels free to comment on Taufel's performance. 'He's excellent,' he says. 'And in giving the batsman the benefit of the doubt he's been consistent.' But Reid is still unhappy with the ACB's selection as third umpire in Adelaide of Paul Angley, who had never previously been a TV umpire at any level. It was he who hastily gave Mike Atherton, who was playing very well at the time, out caught behind for 41. 'It was a pathetic appointment,' says Reid, who added his authority to Gooch's formal complaint to the ICC about it. At his press conference after the Sydney Test, Alec Stewart makes clear, in a good-humoured way, England's disbelief at the Slater run-out decision. He also says that 'more experienced' third umpires are needed in Australia. Despite his good marks for Taufel, Reid concurs, saying that the TV umpire should be an experienced Test official. 'A whole match', he adds, with surprising candour, 'can revolve around a crucial decision, like the Atherton catch, or this run out.'

And what of Messrs Dunne and Hair? They kept a potentially explosive match under firm control. Steve Dunne professes himself satisfied with his performance but will have mixed memories of his first Sydney Test (and thirtieth overall). He had a very moderate game. Gough was unlucky to be given out lbw by him in the first innings – he was a long way forward – and so was Langer in the second: it looked high but Dunne's left index finger soon despatched him. Darrell Hair, with infinitely more experience of Sydney behind him, had a good match, and he knows it. 'I was happy,' he said a few days later. 'It was a tense match, one of the toughest Tests I've stood in.' But he is feeling good about his work this season, and was relieved to call three very faint edges – Mark Waugh in the first innings, off Headley, and Hegg and Headley in the second, off MacGill – correctly. Hair also mounts a plausible defence of the lbw decision against Butcher which gave Warne his comeback wicket in his first over – a decision which he is aware some observers have tried to 'pull to pieces'. And John Reid? He too had a good, if unexacting, game, even if for a few unimportant seconds his eagle eyes failed him. On the third afternoon he failed to spot Atherton running an errand on to the field – in his training gear.

However, long after the many rights and few wrongs of the umpiring are forgotten, this Test will linger in the memory. 'The atmosphere and the crowd were phenomenal,' reflected Hair. 'The players were just so keen to be out there. I remember Darren Gough saying to me during the game: "If you could just play cricket at the SCG and at Lord's, wouldn't life be wonderful?"' Gough must have momentarily forgotten Heading-ley, but in the excitement of taking an Ashes hat-trick, even his fellow Yorkshiremen might be prepared to forgive him that.

17

Colour and Controversy:
The One-Day Series

CHRISTOPHER MARTIN-JENKINS

There are forty-four matches in all in the 1999 World Cup, a tournament for twelve teams which, since it takes place only once every four years, might be forgiven an element of overkill. By contrast, the Carlton & United Series which followed the Tests during January and February hardly merited such indulgence. No fewer than eighteen matches were planned to decide the winner from only three contestants. In the event, the eighteenth game, the scheduled third final, was not played because Australia outplayed a weary England in the first two finals to prove themselves just as clearly the better side in 50-overs-a-side cricket as they had been in the five-day, two-innings variety.

Glenn McGrath was the common denominator. He took 27 wickets, most of them at decisive moments in matches which might otherwise have taken a different course. With Curtly Ambrose's star waning fast, only Allan Donald of South Africa could challenge McGrath as the supreme fast bowler in the world, whatever the length of the game, when the winter's cricket was finally played out.

The good news for England was that Darren Gough was not far behind, but there were too few world-class cricketers around him. As Shane Warne, Adam Dale, Ricky Ponting, Michael Bevan, Darren Lehmann, Adam Gilchrist and Mark Waugh all proved themselves during January and February to be potential matchwinners against any opposition, it was apparent that only South Africa – or, in certain conditions, India – would start the World Cup with a better chance than Australia.

For both sides, and the third one, Sri Lanka, the tournament was played as if in the shadow of the major world event to come. The reigning World Cup holders did not do themselves justice partly because they were determined not to risk Aravinda de Silva, their most inspirational batsman, in many of the matches after he had torn a thigh muscle in a warm-up game. Equally significantly, their phenomenally successful Test off-spinner, Muttiah Muralitharan, was again hounded by controversy.

Ironically he had to stay behind in Australia when his colleagues had gone home, for minor surgery to his bowling arm.

That much-discussed and photographed limb was the cause of a combustible cricket match between Sri Lanka and England which ended in bitterness and led to an ICC hearing at which the game's administrators, not for the first time, were routed by lawyers. This unseemly but by no means unprecedented international row overshadowed some exciting cricket which kept turnstiles clicking throughout Australia from the opening game on 10 January to the finals five weeks later.

England had been accorded every chance of success by the itinerary. The separation of the first-class and limited-overs sections of the programme enabled them to fly fresh players in after Christmas, men whose skills were deemed to be better suited to the peculiar demands of the instant game. They said goodbye to Atherton, Butcher, Cork, Fraser, Hegg, Ramprakash, Such and Tudor; and welcome to Mark Alleyne, Mark Ealham, Neil Fairbrother, Adam Hollioake, Ashley Giles, Nick Knight and Vince Wells. A new physiotherapist, Dean Conway, flew in too, to learn the touring ropes from Wayne Morton, an enthusiast whose bowling had improved so much by firing away in the nets all day at England batsmen on previous tours that he had produced a career-best bowling performance for his Yorkshire club in 1998 at a time when he should have been some way beyond his peak as a medium-pacer.

David Graveney took over as manager from Graham Gooch and for some time he was able to ride on the same cloud of satisfaction which had followed the England one-day side in Sharjah when, late in 1997, they had overcome India, Pakistan and the West Indies in a four-nation tournament. If that proved that they could be a force in one-day cricket overseas as well as on their own pitches at home, the challenge now was to beard the Australian lion in his den and that had not been achieved since the 1986–7 tour when Mike Gatting's side had swallowed every prize in sight.

England's status as the tournament started lay somewhere between the small but genuine triumph in Sharjah and the listless incompetence which had typified their wretched failure in the 1995–6 World Cup in India, Pakistan and Sri Lanka. Determined though they were to finish their long visit to Australia on the right note, there was a longer and more important agenda. Having reached three previous World Cup finals and lost them all, England's fervent objective for the last year of the century was to find a side capable of going one better this time.

Everyone knew how much good for cricket in Britain might flow from the successful attainment of that ambition and the selectors could therefore be forgiven for using the matches in Australia to test a few more pieces in what they hoped might turn out to be a perfectly complete jigsaw by the time the World Cup started in England in May.

Alleyne and Wells were the new faces, although neither was in any way new to first-class cricket. Both in their thirties, they were being rewarded for county careers which had recently blossomed, Wells as a strong presence in the confident Leicestershire team, Alleyne as the leader of a frequently underestimated Gloucestershire. Mainly a batsman, he had nevertheless taken 68 first-class wickets in the last two seasons. It was evident from the start, however, that with Ealham virtually certain to occupy one of the all-rounders' places in the final World Cup eleven, the elder Hollioake strongly placed to claim another, and Matthew Fleming and Dougie Brown still hoping to remind the selectors how well they had done in Sharjah, there could not ultimately be room for them both.

Alleyne and Wells were both chosen for the opening match in Brisbane in which England started with a seven-run win over Australia. The pitch at the Gabba was disappointingly slow and England managed only 178 for eight in their 50 overs, Fairbrother immediately making his mark with 47. Mullally, however, was the matchwinner, taking the first four Australian wickets for 18.

This was the first of only three defeats for Australia over the five weeks in which the three teams criss-crossed the country on the mercifully efficient and punctual planes of the Test sponsors, Ansett Australia. As the home team grew in confidence, their own World Cup line-up became increasingly clear, the picture blurred only by confusion over the most fundamental position of all: the captain's. Steve Waugh had pulled a hamstring muscle badly enough during the later stages of the Sydney Test to miss the start of the tournament and to play only a walk-on role subsequently. Shane Warne, his peccadilloes rapidly forgiven, proved such a flexible and intuitive alternative leader that it was evident to all but the Australian selectors that he should have been awarded the World Cup captaincy too.

Waugh's promotion to lead the one-day side ahead of Mark Taylor in the previous season had been a contentious decision but it had been proved right. There was some logic, therefore, to maintaining Waugh in his position for the World Cup even after he had been chosen ahead of

Warne to assume the Test captaincy; but there was a better case for continuing to divide the responsibilities, leaving Warne to fight for his Test place against MacGill; and Waugh to contest a batting position in the one-day side.

To do so, had he been one of the ranks, Waugh would have to have been preferred to Damien Martyn, the confident West Australian who, despite an opening duck against Mullally, eventually replaced him with success in the Carlton & United matches. Martyn had once himself been ear-marked for the national captaincy and after being cut down to size by the hard realities of the Australian system it was good to see this spirited character displaying the necessary maturity to make the most of what was once a precocious talent. When decisions had to be made about the World Cup party, he was preferred to both Greg Blewett and Michael Slater, which spoke volumes for the extraordinary depth of talent available.

Australia got off the mark in the tournament by beating Sri Lanka easily in Sydney on the back of a dashing century by Gilchrist. Already England had also inflicted a defeat on Sri Lanka, winning by four wickets in the last over of the second of the Brisbane games. Fairbrother top-scored again. He is a brilliantly inventive batsman and proved in this tournament an able substitute for Graham Thorpe. But it is no mystery that Thorpe has proved the better Test batsman. During the remaining games Fairbrother was always more at ease against the Sri Lankan bowling than he was when confronted by McGrath's menacing mien and pace.

McGrath took the key wickets when Australia comfortably avenged their early defeat by England in their second meeting at Melbourne, but England at least scored off him more freely than they did off his opening partner. In this as in every match, Dale's impeccable straightness, and his ability to wobble the white ball, proved invaluable to his side in the early stages of an opponent's innings.

England experimented in this game by sending in Ealham at number three to try to disrupt McGrath and Dale by unorthodox hitting. He made 21 off 19 balls but Ealham was not to be confused with a right-handed version of Jayasuriya and, in any case, England do not bat well enough or deep enough to throw caution completely to the winds in the first 15 overs while all but two of the fielders are confined to the circle.

Australia lost only one wicket in knocking off the 179 required to win, Mark Waugh making 83 not out and Ponting 75 not out. A crowd of 82,299 became bored with the one-sidedness of it all and the behaviour of some (perhaps those who did not realise that not every one-day game boils up to a thrilling finish) became so unruly, throwing rubbish on to the outfield close to fielders, that Stewart asked Warne (the home captain in his home town) to go out and placate them.

When the two sides met again in Sydney two days later Dale could not be collared (10–0–26–0) but it was in this game that England produced their best performance of the tournament, making 282 for four on a slow SCG turner thanks to the first of four outstanding innings by Hick. Going in early after Nick Knight (who had a disappointing tournament all round), Hick was able to build an innings in the proper manner and Nasser Hussain appreciated the same opportunity during a third-wicket stand of 190. It was Hussain's first one-day international fifty after nineteen previous matches and when he and Hick were both out with six overs still to be bowled, Fairbrother and Adam Hollioake kept the momentum going admirably. Although Australia looked capable of reaching their demanding target while Lehmann and Mark Waugh were together, they fell seven runs short.

England beat Sri Lanka in Melbourne three days later, Hick scoring a comfortable 66 not out after Gough had removed four fine players – Jayasuriya, Kaluwitharana, Atapattu and Tillekeratne – in a devastating new-ball spell. England were therefore well on the way to the finals, and Sri Lanka desperate for a win, when the two teams arrived in Adelaide for the notorious match of 23 January.

It should have been a classic of its kind on an Adelaide pitch back to its fast, true best and but for the intervention of one of the umpires, Ross Emerson, it would have been. Having been put in as usual by Sri Lanka's proud, canny and fearless captain, Arjuna Ranatunga, England got off to a rollicking start through the generally disappointing opening pair, Knight and Stewart, who paved the way for Hick's commanding and powerful 126 not out. From the first 43 balls had come 50, but Knight was run out by Muralitharan and when the bright-eyed off-spinner came on to bowl Emerson called him for throwing from square-leg an instant after he had delivered the fourth ball of his second over, the nineteenth of the match.

Pandemonium ensued. Ranatunga, having challenged Emerson's decision aggressively, wagging his finger and poking it towards the umpire's chest, led his team to the edge of the outfield, staying there for a quarter of an hour during animated discussions between Sri Lankan officials. What had happened was half-expected from the moment that Emerson and Tony McQuillan were named as the umpires for the match. Both men had no-balled Muralitharan on Sri Lanka's previous tour of Australia. Emerson had done so seven times during a one-day international against the West Indies in Brisbane, shortly after Darrell Hair had called him for throwing in a Test. Hair had ruled himself out of the current series in the wake of the controversy over a book in which he had described the Sri Lankan off-spinner's action as 'diabolical'.

Emerson, the forty-four-year-old private investigator from Perth, who had, it transpired, recently been suspended from his job on medical grounds because of stress caused by a personality clash, had been on the Australian umpiring panel for five years, but had never stood in a Test and after this match, rightly or wrongly, he never will. There is something to be said for the belief that he was being morally courageous in sticking to his view that, despite the verdict of an ICC panel in Muralitharan's favour, the action was illegal. The majority opinion, however, was that this was a small man victimising a great bowler and that Emerson should have been content to accept the filmed evidence which the ICC panel had studied to their satisfaction. The Sri Lankan manager, Ranjit Fernando, said pointedly at the end of the game: 'Someone out there decided to play God today.'

It was by no means the end of the nastiness. Ranatunga told his off-spinner to go round the wicket and then ordered the umpire, with an all too obvious challenge to his authority, to stand closer to the stumps, as if to obscure any further view of the arm which, because of a minor deformity, has a permanent slight kink in the elbow. The ICC panel's verdict, although it was not a final one and remained under review, had been that Muralitharan's arm does not straighten before delivery as the law forbids and that his rare power of spin comes from the exceptional flexibility of his wrist.

England scored 53 off their last three overs (Murali, for once, was expensive) and set a formidable target of 303 to win. In reply the Sri Lankans lost two wickets for eight runs in the first four overs but the wristy brilliance of Sanath Jayasuriya (51 off 36 balls) kept them in the hunt and Mahela Jayawardene played a glorious innings in his wake. The rattled Emerson should, however, have given him run out for 39, or at least called for the replay, on the evidence of which the third umpire would have condemned the batsman. When, at the climax of the game,

Roshan Mahanama changed direction deliberately as he ran a quick single in order to impede Gough as he followed through, the unfortunate Emerson rejected what looked like a legitimate appeal for obstructing the field.

These incidents tarnished a superb effort by Sri Lanka to get past England with two balls to spare and in the end not many of the players or officials emerged from the game with credit. Stewart, furious after the barging incident, could not resist a niggly little brush of the shoulders with Mahanama soon after. It rendered rather hollow Stewart's charge, picked up by a pitch microphone, that Ranatunga's behaviour had been 'appalling for a country's captain'.

He had certainly made a calculated public exhibition of himself, almost as if he had been expecting trouble. There were two views of his conduct, as there were of Emerson's. On one hand, he was clearly in breach of one of the game's essential tenets, expressed in the introduction to Law 42: *The captains are responsible at all times for ensuring that play is conducted within the spirit of the game as well as within the laws.* On the other, Ranatunga obviously saw himself as the defender of an unjustly harassed bowler. It did not justify in any way his all too public contempt for the umpire, but it explained it.

The Sri Lankan Cricket Board had hired a firm of lawyers and a public relations company after the acrimony of the 1995–6 tour but it did not prevent Muralitharan being harried, wherever he played during this next visit, by cries of 'chucker' and 'no-ball' from sections of the crowd.

The referee, however, agreed with Stewart when it came to an official verdict. Peter van der Merwe summoned Ranatunga to a disciplinary hearing three days after the game, having sought the advice of the ICC chief executive, David Richards. It was clear enough that the Sri Lankan captain had broken the Code of Conduct under which all cricketers are obliged to play and he was actually charged with five breaches of the regulations. Two lawyers representing the Sri Lankan captain were present at the hearing, along with two from the ICC and when the verdict was announced, a suspended six-match ban and a £65 fine (75 per cent of his match fee), it was Ranatunga who appeared to have won.

Van der Merwe, shaking with emotion, told journalists afterwards that the disciplinary panel had been compromised by the lawyers. 'In future,' he promised, 'the ICC will take the lead to ensure that lawyers will not be present at hearings.' He added: 'His [Ranatunga's] every action will be very, very closely monitored over the next twelve months

. . . Respect is something both he and I will lose by this decision.'

Between their victory on the field and this painless defeat in the 'courtroom', Sri Lanka, emotionally and physically drained no doubt, were beaten by Australia at Adelaide. So, two days later, were England who, despite good innings by Mark Waugh, Lehmann, Martyn and Lee, seemed to be well on target on a slower surface whilst Hick was blazing towards his third hundred in four innings. He bats at his best to the sound of cathedral bells and his best is majestic. Once again, however, McGrath changed the course of the game, this time by defeating Hussain and Fairbrother in quick succession. Warne bowled superbly and deployed the fielders shrewdly, Hick kept losing the strike and was run out, backing-up, and the innings disintegrated.

England at least avenged one of their Adelaide defeats by bowling the Sri Lankans out for 99 at Perth (Ealham five for 32) after Fairbrother had enjoyed himself on the quick Perth pitch to make 81 not out and thereby to make sure that, whether or not Thorpe was fit to take his place in the World Cup fifteen, the left-handed Lancastrian would be there too. Ironically Fairbrother himself was soon to succumb to his longstanding problem of brittle hamstring muscles, but England were now certain of qualifying for the finals.

Sadly, they had already produced their best cricket. Sri Lanka beat them again, this time in Sydney, to confirm that the opening match of the World Cup at Lord's on 14 May would be one between well-matched teams. Australia also recorded another superfluous win, achieved by four wickets despite resting McGrath, so England had managed to win four of their first five qualifying matches and to lose four of their last five. Foolishly, once qualified, they did not give Gough the rest he deserved and Stewart had only one match off, despite a sore finger which had contributed towards some untypically sloppy wicket-keeping. Giles and Ben Hollioake were especially badly treated.

McGrath was fresh again for the first of the best-of-three finals, also played at the SCG. Despite a wayward opening spell by Mullally and a typically masterful 69 not out on a slow pitch by Bevan, Australia, constrained by the medium pace of Ealham and Wells, managed a total of only 232 for eight. In reply Stewart set an aggressive tone, lifting the miserly Dale over square-leg for six and striking McGrath for four fours in five balls, the last of them a top-edged hook over the wicket-keeper's head. The subsequent exchange of views showed how badly both sides wanted to win.

It was a certain overheatedness, indeed, which did for England in the end. Dale subsequently got both Knight and Stewart in yet another excellent new-ball spell, but Hick and Hussain were progressing well when Hick was run out by a direct hit on the stumps by Ponting. Hussain, partially to blame, made amends with an innings which ought to have steered his side home. But against Warne he, like others after him, was obsessed with the sweep. Warne taunted him for this but, curiously, it was only when Hussain finally middled one and sent it soaring towards the mid-wicket boundary that he got over-excited. With Wells batting well at the other end, only 35 needed from eight overs, and six wickets in hand, Hussain tried to drive a leg-break over extra-cover, missed his tremendous flail and was stumped.

Hollioake tried to sweep his first ball and was dubiously given out leg before, whereupon Wells, straight driving Shane Lee's skilfully used slower ball towards the sightscreen, was beautifully caught after a forty-yard run from mid-off by Brendon Julian. England still needed 35, but now with only three wickets in hand, and Warne still had overs from McGrath up his sleeve. Back he duly came to fire out Ealham and Gough and the game was up.

The second final three days later was an embarrassment. Australia scored 272 for six on a true and lively pitch, Lehmann making 71 off 75 balls in the absence of Bevan, who had dislocated a finger in the previous match. It was not an unassailable total, but Knight ran himself out in the second over, Hick carved his second ball to third-man, Hussain was given out first ball and Fairbrother was more clearly caught behind off his second. Not long afterwards, Australia won by 162 runs. Game, set and match, indeed.

18

The Winning Culture

CHARLES DE LISLE

'If Australia's 3–40,' says Dean Jones, 'and you wonder what they're saying in the dressing-room, they'll be looking at golf magazines, or watching golf on television. That's how the players deal with the pressure.' A wonderfully watchable batsman, Jones is in his first season away from the pressures out in the middle: he retired in March 1998, still only thirty-seven. We are talking during the supper break of England's last qualifying match in the one-day series, against Australia at the SCG, scene of many a decisive Jones contribution in the compressed form of the game. The venue is Jones's new place of work, the ABC Radio commentary box. Still something of a folk hero in his native Victoria, 'Deano' is a boisterous, extrovert character, very Australian in his banter, his aggression, his swagger, his unrelenting search for the psychological edge, his ability to create and withstand pressure – and in the outspokenness which probably cut short his international career (he played the last of just fifty-two Tests in 1992). And his mobile telephone conversations really are punctuated with endearments like 'Champ'.

As fellow commentators digest the airline-style meals provided for the media, Jones mentions what he sees as one of Australian cricket's chief strengths. 'The senior player mentality in the first-class game here is very, very good,' he says. 'Team culture comes down to the senior players, like Ian Healy. They set the tone. They clip someone's ear if they get too full of themselves, or they lift someone up.' Jones believes that the tied Test against India in Madras, in 1986, when he made a courageous 210 in the most appalling heat and humidity, was 'the game that created the new culture of Australian cricket' because it taught the players – including David Boon and Steve Waugh – how tough cricket can be.

Jones, who has played for Durham and Derbyshire, argues that young Australians also benefit from a well-organised system of 'mentors'. Senior players – not least in the national side – not only look after younger ones, they give them 'honest and proper appraisals of how they're going, whether they like it or not'. Jones himself matured into an international batsman under Allan Border's tutelage, achieving career averages of 46 in Tests and 44 in one-dayers, having earlier relied heavily on his father and Keith Stackpole, the former Australia opener.

Much of this, however, is part of successful teamwork in any sphere. What else makes Australia such an extraordinarily tough and effective fighting unit? To my mind, the Aussie tradition of 'mateship', forged in the desperate struggles of the colonial days, is a major factor. Jones agrees. 'Mateship is very important,' he says. 'Mateship's all about getting over conquests and problems and all that type of thing. You can't do it singlehandedly. Not everyone's perfect. Everyone goes through different emotional strains and stresses, and you need your mates to help you out.' The 'bookie affair' is surely an example. Without the very strong bonds in the Aussie team, and particularly those between Mark Taylor, Shane Warne and Mark Waugh, the damage to Australian cricket's reputation and image could have been much worse. At several critical junctures between 1995 and late 1998, Taylor stood right behind his players, not just as a captain and a human being, but as a mate supporting mates in trouble.

However, when Ricky Ponting was knocked unconscious in a fight at a Sydney night-club in January, he was largely left to fend for himself. There was a feeling that the senior players with whom he had been socialising elsewhere earlier on should have done more to look after him, but it was essentially Ponting, who was left with a black eye, who was portrayed as letting down his mates. After all, he was still out, pursuing a pretty financial analyst, four hours after the 1.30 a.m. team curfew which applies on the nights of floodlit games; and, as he subsequently admitted, he had a drink problem, for which he would undergo counselling. 'My problem with "Pont",' says Jones, 'was not that he got hit, because you can get cleaned up anywhere. And I'm not worried about him having a drink. My problem was: what the hell was he doing up at quarter to six in the morning when in seventy-two hours he was going to play the biggest match of his season – the one-dayer in front of his home crowd at Hobart? "Pont" was shitting on his mates, the guys he works with. That's the worst thing you can do in a team.' The ACB appeared to agree, banning Ponting from three one-day games and giving him a suspended fine of A\$5,000 (£2,000). Quite a few cricket lovers felt that, compared with Warne and Mark Waugh, he had been treated harshly, and wrote to the newspapers saying so. 'Q: What is the difference between an unethical payment and a black eye?' asked

Luke Tannock, from Sydney, in *The Weekend Australian*. 'A: One you can cover for four years, the other you can't cover for four days.' But what lay behind Ponting's night out? One perceptive commentator argued that it was really 'all about pressure. Part of the pressure that Ponting is struggling with [at the age of twenty-four] is that he is considered a future Australian captain.'

Geoff Marsh, the coach, also tried to put the incident in context, emphasising that his players drink much less than those of ten or twenty years ago. 'These players now rarely drink,' said Marsh. 'They'll have a drink when they win, but during matches and the lead-up to matches they hardly touch a drink . . . money is a reason. Guys are earning a lot of money now. In the goals they set at the start of the year they said they had to behave themselves in public and do those things that professional sportsmen have to do. Unfortunately, Ricky went wrong. But most of the guys are good.'

As it happens, Ponting excels at the one activity to which the team invariably turns for relaxation: golf. 'He's the best golfer in the side by a street,' says Jones, another fanatical golfer. Ponting plays off a handicap of one, Greg Blewett off two, Taylor (a right-hander at this game) off seven, and most of the others off eights, nines or tens. 'Their handicaps are heavily scrutinised,' adds Jones (8.8), hinting at the competitiveness within the side on the golf course. He laments, however, that his successors do not socialise as much as did his generation. Today, as he says, most players tend to go straight from the ground to the hotel, have a swim or go to the gym, have a couple of quiet drinks in the bar, then go to a film, or have a room-service supper in front of the television. The days of 'a few beers' with their opponents in the dressing-rooms after play are largely over. 'It's unfortunate,' says Jones. 'You learn a lot from those chats.'

On the whole, though, Jones is full of praise for the current Aussie side: 'Old cricketers very rarely say: "Oh, Jeez, they're better players than we were." Cut it out! I think we should wake up and smell the coffee. These guys now are better and tougher than we were. They're fabulous players.' He adds: 'In the last three years standards in the one-dayers have risen 3 to 5 per cent.'

There is something almost tribal about Australia's team culture. When you hear Healy offering that constant encouragement to bowlers after every ball ('Bowled, Warnie' or 'Bowled, Shane'), it drives home what a tremendous spirit and feeling of togetherness binds the side. No matter how many horses are selected or discarded for particular courses, this powerful team ethos prevails. It seems irresistible, whatever a player's background.

The culture has its flipside. In his controversial memoirs, the umpire Darrell Hair observes that when Kepler Wessels returned to the Test scene as the first captain of the 'new' South Africa, the legacy of his spell in Australian colours in the 1980s was all too clear. Wessels, he says, had 'inherited the Australian way of whingeing about decisions . . . it is [always] out when you are bowling, but never when you are batting'. There is also the Australian way of 'sledging'. Overt verbal aggression directed at batsmen by bowlers and close fielders was close to getting out of control in Allan Border's time as captain, but Taylor curbed most of the excesses.

The pride in wearing the 'baggy green cap' is now taken so much for granted that it is a cliché. It is a tradition which the present group of players has been self-consciously developing. It was actually Steve Waugh's idea, three years ago, that every player should take the field for the first session in his cap. As Waugh expressed it recently: 'It gives the team power and a bit of aura and unites everyone to let the opposition know that we're all heading in the one direction. It's a symbol of our unity more than anything else.'

When Bobby Simpson, one of the architects of Australia's decade of success, became the national team's coach in 1986, the prevailing social climate was quite different. 'We were going through a poor era as regards wearing the baggy green cap,' says Simpson. 'It wasn't cool to appear enthusiastic, it was considered old-fashioned. We really had to get through that barrier and get the players to express their passion. So, yes, we had to overcome the apathy in society about being proud to play for Australia.' One measure taken was the reintroduction of a team blazer as standard wear whenever Australia travelled, home or away; another was an intense concentration on improving fielding, partly with the aim of getting home crowds firmly behind the team; a third was an attempt, also successful, to restore the peer influence which had dropped away during the Chappell years. Overall, Simpson's principal objective was to reintroduce a work ethic, while ensuring that the players started to enjoy their cricket – and win matches.

We meet in a North Sydney hospital, where Simpson has just had a long-mooted knee-replacement operation. So busy is he with various commitments – he is a coaching consultant to India's World Cup squad

– that this is the only time he can fit in an interview. He is not one to be carried away by another successful Ashes defence. He thought Australia's Test form 'a bit in and out'; believes the selectors should be concentrating on fewer players, and giving them more of a run; and is 'very worried' about the next generation of batsmen. 'There are some problems in the top levels of fifteen- to twenty-year-olds,' he says. 'Technically, things are not healthy at all.' Not that he finds very much to applaud at the other end of the world. 'The thing that used to make England Test teams so great was their patience. That's disappeared.' He adds, with an enigmatic smile: 'It sounds disrespectful, but we no longer take any notice of how well our players do in England, from a selection point of view, and we haven't for some time. It's always our blokes on top, isn't it?'

If that sense of proportion is a valuable asset in Australia's efforts to stay on top, so too are the very positive – at times uncritical – attitudes emanating from most of the Australian media. Tony Greig, although not a disinterested observer, believes, rightly I think, that television and radio coverage of the national side has helped reinforce the players' positive approach, and given good performers extra confidence. 'On Channel Nine,' he says, 'we really sell cricket hard. We *really* get behind good players, so much so that we turn them into millionaires. We don't hold back at all. If someone's good, boy, we unashamedly make 'em the best in the world!'

As Greig says, television is the principal means of selling the game. And this season the ratings, like the crowds, were very good. Test cricket's ratings were up 17 per cent compared with the previous summer's matches against New Zealand and South Africa, and the full one-day figures, yet to be finalised at the time of writing, were expected to show a similar increase. The evening sessions of preliminary day–night games were generally attracting national audiences of between 2 million and 2.8 million viewers (that is, one in every six or seven Australians), enough to outperform almost all other programmes, even the main evening news. In the first week of the Carlton & United series, four of Australia's fifteen most popular programmes were matches in that series; and figures for the sixteen to thirty-nine age group (so crucial to the game's future, as well as to advertisers) were not much lower. One must remember, though, that most one-dayers were screened in the January 'silly season' when there was not much else worth watching.

Greig cheerfully concedes that it is not simply those who broadcast cricket ball-by-ball, or the print media, who help to create this favourable climate around the Australian team. Other television and radio stations devote a lot of airtime, in news and other programmes, to cricket; you even hear the personalities and play being discussed on rock-music stations with youthful audiences. 'We're all talkin' "Tubby" at the moment,' said a jaunty disc jockey on Sydney's 2MMM, a few days after Taylor's retirement. 'It's like he's died or somethin'.'

And what of the crowds? The party atmosphere of the one-dayers attracts a lot of people, from a fairly Americanised society, who do not have much interest in cricket. They come along to have an evening out with their friends, see what is going on in the crowd, check out the 'Barmy Army', and blow off steam on a hot night. This type of patron is typified by the eighteen- to twenty-five-year-olds whom the ACB's marketing department categorises as 'entertainment seekers'. Importantly, half this segment of the audience is female. Of the entire one-day audience, the proportion of women varies between 30 and 40 per cent; at Tests it is a still respectable 20 to 25 per cent. Ticket prices are very reasonable, especially to English eyes: an adult can get into a one-dayer for as little as A\$22 (£8.80) and a Test for as little as A\$18 (£7.20).

Many newcomers to international grounds soon discover that they are not the ideal place to 'party'. For one thing, if you want to have a cigarette you are now only allowed to light up *behind* the stands. The authorities do not make exceptions, even for 'legends' such as Doug Walters, regularly seen puffing away behind the stands at Sydney – this season he actually boycotted the stand named after him in protest at the ban. The aggressive anti-smoking regulations now in force at Test grounds and other open-air venues show how Australia is still in some ways moving in an American direction; in Britain, cricket remains happy to take Benson & Hedges' money, their sponsorship having been transferred to the new Super Cup through to completion of their existing contract at the end of 2000.

The intense media focus on the international season of 1998–9 was profoundly irritating to some Australians not interested in the game, who must have felt nearly as overwhelmed as many people in Britain do by soccer's huge profile. On the morning after the Sydney Test finished, the *Sydney Morning Herald* gave one writer a platform to redress the balance. 'Consider the average SCG crowd,' wrote Pilita Clark. 'We are not talking United Nations here. Worse, look at the Test team itself.

Other mass-appeal sports, such as Aussie Rules football, rugby or even tennis (none of which is covered with the same intensity as cricket), have managed to diversify. Aborigines and people from non-English-speaking backgrounds have played at the highest levels of these sports for years, unconsciously sending a message of inclusion and unity to millions.

'But,' she continued, 'not Australian cricket. Here, we still have a bunch of overwhelmingly Anglo-Celtic boys from the suburbs who, together, look nothing like today's Australia. And yet summer after summer, year after year, the news media treat them as if they are not merely representative of the culture, but cultural representatives.'

One cannot argue with most of Pilita Clark's facts. Very few players have yet to emerge from the inner-city, ethnic suburbs, where soccer and basketball are much more popular. But she has overlooked the large number of players from the bush, where cricket is still very strong. These include Taylor and Slater, who hail from Wagga Wagga, NSW, some six hours' drive from Sydney; McGrath, who cut his teeth bowling at an oil drum on his father's sheep-and-wheat farm near Narromine in New South Wales's west; Healy, the son of a bank manager in a sports-mad Queensland town; and Matthew Elliott, who grew up in a fruit-growing area of Victoria, playing his first strokes on a half-length concrete pitch laid by his father, a secondary-school teacher.

Such men, reared in some of Australia's most traditional, conservative areas, may seem old-fashioned – some look like players from the 1930s – but they do represent an important strand of Australia, and one appreciated more now than it was in the 1970s or 1980s, when a brasher, flashier style was preferred. These are people with whom many Australians can identify as easily as they do with urban 'larrikins' such as Shane Warne, with his bleached hair, earstud and red Ferrari.

Craig McGregor, author of the recent book *Class in Australia*, sums it up well. 'The accents of Aussie cricketers are very rarely posh,' he says. 'A lot speak in broad Australian accents, the typical accent of working-class Australia. Mark Taylor, for example, has quite a broad accent. Others speak in "general Australian" – the accent of the middle class.' McGregor sees McGrath as a quintessentially Australian figure. 'He's the *typical* Aussie grown-up boy – you know, short hair, freckles, thin, bit gawky, sticky-out ears, good bloke and a very good sportsman. Australia's been producing people like that in all the sports for a bloody century!'

One reason for the lack of 'posh' accents is that over the past thirty years the leading private schools, for all their first-rate facilities and good coaching, have produced very few Test players. Two current exceptions are Greg Blewett, who attended St Peter's College, Adelaide, and the quick bowler Matthew Nicholson, who was at Knox Grammar School, Sydney; Warne was also privately educated, though he won a scholarship to Mentone Grammar, a minor private school in Melbourne. There is not thought to be any prejudice against the products of private schools, which have turned out some outstanding players, notably Ian and Greg Chappell, whose school, Prince Alfred College, Adelaide, has had more first-class players than any other Australian school. But some coaches believe that because talented cricketers at private schools keep on playing fellow schoolboys until they are eighteen, they fall behind their contemporaries in the state sector, who compete against fully grown men in first-grade from the age of sixteen.

The leading Australian players are in fact a pretty good social – if not ethnic – mix. It is a broader church than in England, where the professional game is more middle class and public school in character. But then the strong working-class base of Australian cricket, in terms of both players and followers, is one of the reasons for the game's special place in the Australian psyche. And while the national team may not be as multicultural as it should be, you could point out that this is not the only respect in which it is scarcely representative of Aussie society in the late 1990s. It appears to contain no homosexuals – and they are a very large community Down Under. There is no suggestion of homophobia at the top of the cricket tree but, as in so many sports, the culture of the national team is ruggedly heterosexual. When Stuart MacGill went public, in a women's magazine interview in January, with his search for 'Ms Right', he was billed as 'the only romantically unattached member of the Test team'. Maybe he should have gone clubbing with Ricky Ponting.

19
Emerald City

CHARLES DE LISLE

As increasing numbers of people from around the world will soon discover, Sydney is a great city, as cosmopolitan as you will find anywhere, with an almost unmatched natural beauty. It is no longer, as Mark Twain said, 'an English city with American trimmings', but distinctively, charmingly Australian. Sydney, which hosts the XXVII Olympic Games next year, seems certain to be the focus of more world interest than any other metropolis in the year 2000.

The 'Emerald City', originally a convict colony founded in 1788, combines the sophistication, bustle and buzz of a big city with the laid-back feel and outdoor life of a holiday destination miles from high-rises, noise and fumes. Even when you are perspiring in the city centre – Sydney is very humid – you are only a few minutes' walk from a harbour-side café overlooking the Opera House and that magnificent coathanger of a bridge, and within half an hour of a dip in the surf at Bondi – or a swim from a harbour beach should you prefer something gentler.

One of the joys of a truly uplifting city is the sizeable proportion of the 200 miles of foreshore which has not been built on, leaving plenty of unspoilt parks and areas of bushland in which to walk, jog, picnic, read, loll, soak up the sun (which shines for 342 days a year) and enjoy scintillating views. The harbour is Sydney's greatest attraction, and, though it is tempting fate to say so, it acts, I think, as its own wonderful insurance policy, bestowed by nature, against the ravages of progress and human greed. It would be almost impossible to ruin the place.

For the great majority of Sydneysiders, the last Australian Summer of the century meant – as well as coping with life's daily worries – choosing which of their remarkably unspoilt seventy beaches to go to over the weekend, or whether to go to Bondi or Coogee for a surf before work. For huge numbers it also meant other strenuous activity. Possibilities, apart, of course, from cricket, swimming and surfing, included rollerblading, sailing, windsurfing, paragliding, tennis, golf, basketball, baseball, bushwalking and rock climbing (in the nearby Blue Mountains). For seriously strong swimmers, there was the two-kilometre Bondi

Beach Cole Classic, a 'hardy annual' which attracted a field of 2,300 and was won by an Aussie Olympian.

This summer, Sydney's fittest had their first chance to pit themselves against the Harbour Bridge. For A\$98 (£39), rising to A\$120 (£50) on weekends, patrons tackle a 134-metre climb which has, for the bridge's sixty-seven years, been restricted to bridge workers, a few official visitors and the odd, usually inebriated, trespasser. Climbers, each wearing a safety harness and attached to one another, are taken up in a group, by a trained guide, and it takes three hours all told. A breath test is administered to every climber beforehand, just in case. Even so, there have already been more than fifty proposals of marriage at the 'summit'. Although it is not a challenge recommended for the tourist suffering from vertigo – or the nervous would-be bridegroom (or bride) – the opportunity of vigorous exercise and a fresh harbour view drew an average of 1,000 people each weekend over this first summer. And there is a long list of people wanting to make the ascent in blustery conditions.

The scramble to catch Sydney's latest, most fashionable view was well observed in a line from *Emerald City*, an incisive, witty 1980s play about corruption in the city, by David Williamson, a leading playwright, which had a brief London run. 'In Melbourne all views are equally depressing, so there is no point in having one . . . No one in Sydney ever wastes time debating the meaning of life – it's getting yourself a water frontage. People devote a lifetime to the quest.' I was lucky enough to work as a journalist in Sydney, from 1984 to 1987, and even luckier to find my water frontage – at least, a delightful flat in Darling Point, overlooking the Opera House and bridge, two minutes' walk from the water's edge – within four months of arriving. Once you have that view, you feel compelled by the city's beauty and climate to explore as much of it as possible on foot, by ferry and by boat, assuming you are fortunate enough to know someone with one.

Such are the natural splendours that Sydney is the only place where I have entered a fun run – the nine-mile City to Surf, held during the winter, which took 30,000 runners past Kings Cross, through the eastern suburbs bordering the harbour, and along the rugged clifftops overlooking the Pacific to Bondi. I finished, too, albeit in 10,000th place, and the certificate recording my finishing time – and the expression on my face as I crossed the line – is one of my prouder possessions.

Returning to Sydney last November for the first time in three and a half years, I was struck, as everyone is, by the increased traffic conges-

tion: enormous improvements are being made to the road system of this
sprawling city to bring it up to standard for the Olympic invasion. For
the moment this means long delays for everyone, starting with the drive
in from the airport, which is itself a building site. Fortunately, at least
some Sydney cabbies are still patient, and a pleasure to talk to. This is
quite something, given that they are also having to cope with worsening
crime. The latest figures show that NSW accounted for most of the
recent overall national increase in criminal activity, with record rises
compared to other states in the categories of assault, armed robbery and
unlawful entry, among others. As a result, many cabbies have been
forced to take a leaf out of New York's book, and erect security shields
between themselves and their fares. But, this being egalitarian Sydney,
the passenger seat really is a passenger seat, so you can still look your
driver in the eye, through the perspex, as you chat. And when he dis-
covers you're from London, he may well still say, self-deprecatingly:
'Oh, we're just a country town compared to *London*.'

The Sydney 2000 Olympics, and the massive investment generated by
the event, have created great optimism, and a great deal of work for the
construction industry. This goes way beyond the building of Olympic
venues, a big enough job in a city which, unlike Australia's other major
centres, conspicuously lacked top-level sports facilities. Round every
street corner a new skyscraper is going up – not much fun for pedestri-
ans, but most of the buildings will be worthwhile additions to an attractive plate-glass skyline (and finished modern buildings are surely to be
preferred to the 'black holes' which disfigured the city streets in the
1980s). Some big names have commissions in Sydney: the Italian architect Renzo Piano has designed an office block and neighbouring apartment block for Macquarie Street. Quite a few of the new towers in or
near the city centre are apartment blocks, complete with gyms, swimming pools and parking – another Manhattan touch in a city where low-
rise suburban living and a large garden have long been the norm. One
advantage is that, with people again living in the city centre, street life is
flourishing once more. Such is the pace of development that even when
you have long known Sydney well, there are moments when you feel at
sea. There are so many new hotels, for a start. One, the Park Hyatt, has
grabbed a spot in the historic Rocks area, bang opposite the Opera
House. It made a fabulous setting for an old friend's fortieth birthday
party in February. Meanwhile, many areas have been given major face-
lifts for the Games.

What else has changed? Well, lots of things. Barristers taking silk have (since 1992) become Senior Counsel (SC), not Queen's Counsel, an indication of the strong republican sentiment in Sydney (in the other states, Queensland apart, QCs are still appointed). Some of Sydney's many commercial radio stations now routinely describe it as 'the world's greatest city', a sign of the population's growing confidence that their town really *has* arrived. And the rough-house of state (that is, New South Wales) politics has finally thrown up a woman leader. After an early summer coup, Kerry Chikarovski was anointed Leader of the NSW Liberals, putting her one step away from being only the third female state premier in Australian history. And if Mrs Chikarovski, a charismatic blonde, defied long odds to take her party to victory in the 27 March election, she would become the first Australian woman elected premier in her own right – with the additional prize of hosting the Olympics. Can it really, I wonder, be five and a half years since Sydney beat Beijing into second place and Manchester a distant third, and some locals, having anxiously set their alarm clocks for 4 a.m. to hear the news from Monte Carlo, jumped out of bed and rushed spontaneously down to the Opera House to celebrate?

One thing that has not changed is the average Sydneysider's sense of humour. As they survey their building sites and their fledgling freeways, they start to ponder life after the 'green' Games. After all, goes the joke, if all the promises made by the politicians and the planners in the 1990s were true, the city should be a 'bloody perfect' place to live in come the day the circus leaves town.

The separation of Tests and one-dayers, while admirable, meant that England's cricketers did not spend a night in Sydney, let alone glimpse that famous turning wicket, until they had been in Australia for ten weeks and the main tour was almost over. This is rather like scheduling a tour of England and only writing London into the itinerary in August. Anyway, on 30 December, England's seventeen-man party and their families flew in, still flushed with the excitement of the Melbourne win, and they were joined the next day by the one-day specialists, still jet-lagged after a Boxing Day flight from the UK and a game in Queensland. The one-day contingent, who would need to be up at 6.30 a.m. on New Year's Day to board the coach to another warm-up match, this time in the beautiful setting of Bowral, did not have long to prepare for Sydney's biggest night of the year.

On New Year's Eve, nearly a third of Sydney's 3.8 million population gathered expectantly around the foreshores of the harbour. They came to watch the biggest firework display in their city's history, and to attend one of the world's larger New Year's Eve parties – and 'party' is the word Sydneysiders use for the occasion. However, those 1.2 million people – 400,000 of them packed into a tiny area bounded by the Opera House, Circular Quay and the Harbour Bridge – were not merely seeing in 1999 in traditional Sydney fashion. On a typically warm summer's night people turned out, with family or friends, to play their part in the opening round of what could legitimately be called a two-year party. For the A$2 million (£800,000) pyrotechnic extravaganza was, as the media kept reminding everyone, but the 'dress rehearsal' for the millennium celebrations, the Olympic Games and Australia's 100th birthday on New Year's Day, 2001. In between, there would be so many other public and private celebrations – some regular features of the Sydney calendar, many not – that even the most energetic party animal in this hedonistic city would, at times, be drooping.

The 'dress rehearsal' went well. The main display, traditionally held at 9 p.m. for the benefit of those with young families, was launched by Kylie Minogue, the pop star who made her name as an actress in the Australian soap opera *Neighbours*. The huge crowds – a genuine cross-section of this melting pot of a society – squeezed into every available spot around the edge of 'our 'arbour'. They had a good, but not too good, time (some recent New Years had been marred by aggressive drunkenness). And although it was cloudy, there was no rain. For some forty minutes, the people of Sydney – a demanding audience – saw their great city, its skyscrapers and its waterways, brilliantly illuminated by five tonnes of explosives detonated from two barges, one placed either side of the bridge. The climactic moment, as local custom dictates, came when the bridge was transformed into a stunning 'Niagara Falls'. Most spectators – an estimated 1.1 million had somehow travelled into the city centre – were delighted with the show, although some complained that low cloud and smoke obscured their views.

This year, or rather last year, those who stayed on – and they included the England players, one of many groups enjoying the spectacle from the comfort of a boat – were treated to a reprise. At ten seconds to midnight, there was a second eruption of explosives. Nearly 1,600 firework shots lit up the arch of the Harbour Bridge alone; meanwhile the 'sails' of the Opera House were swathed in golden light. Photographs of the fireworks went round the world. Because of the setting, they caught the eye more than shots of New Year's Eve fireworks at Time Square in New York, say, or the Parthenon in Athens or Berlin's Brandenburg Gate; and the pictures from Sydney, which had the added advantage of arriving on picture editors' computer screens first, were duly published quite widely abroad – or 'overseas', as Australians always say, with logic on their side.

Meanwhile, Sydney City Council, which pays for the fireworks, was congratulating itself on another sound investment. It was the latest step in a carefully calibrated five-year programme to stage a more impressive show each New Year's Eve – at least until the one after next, when the centenary of Federation of the six British colonies as a sovereign nation on 1 January 1901 will be celebrated. The millennium fireworks, said the council, would be three or four times the size of this lot, the budget A$4 million (£1.6 million), the anticipated crowd 2 million.

Even those figures will be pretty small beer by the standards of Ric Birch, whose company Spectak has the contract for the Sydney fireworks. Birch is used to big tableaux, casts of thousands and audiences of billions: he produced the opening and closing ceremonies of both the Los Angeles and Barcelona Olympic Games. Now, almost inevitably, he is master of ceremonies for the Games in his home town. None of the thirty-odd applicants could match his reputation as a man who can make a ceremony sing. His LA opener of 1984 is remembered, as one admiring journalist put it, for its 'Hollywood flash grand pianos played by gents in tails, preened-up movie starlets and the loudest, brassiest marching band ever to blast its way on to an arena'. He has even been described as the world's greatest special events organiser.

Birch, fifty-four and already in the post four years, has a big title – Director of Ceremonies for the Sydney Organising Committee for the Olympic Games (SOCOG) – a big budget (A$37 million, £14.8 million) and an even bigger task: to present Australia, a young country still groping towards a settled national identity, to the world. And he must do so in a way that does justice to her biggest single achievement: building a stable, peaceful, democratic, successful multicultural society in an unstable part of that world. Birch and his team will need to tread carefully between the claims and cultures of Australia's indigenous people, the Aborigines, and the continent's many other communities – no fewer than 160 countries are represented, and seventy languages spoken, in the population of 18.5 million.

The perils of the job became even clearer at the Atlanta Games of '96, when Birch contributed a seven-minute 'teaser' for Sydney to the closing formalities. His decision to include a group of schoolchildren riding bicycles with colourful, rubber kangaroos on the back caused weeks of heated debate back home. Birch explained it away as a harmless example of Australian self-parody – 'likeable larrikinism' was his phrase – but many Aussies felt they might have looked kitschy in the eyes of the world, and have yet to forgive him for using the national symbol so lightly. No wonder he has all but ruled out the suggestion that the Olympic flame should be lit by a flaming boomerang that would somehow come whirling through the night sky on 15 September 2000.

We meet a few weeks into the New Year at SOCOG's headquarters, a short cab ride from the city centre. Outside in the bright sunshine, a seventy-strong media throng awaits a lunch-time press conference at which Michael Knight, the state Olympics Minister, will be put on the spot once more about the bribes scandal which has seriously tarnished the city's Games. Inside, Birch cuts a well-dressed but relaxed, casual figure, in a white dress shirt with white T-shirt underneath, pin-stripe trousers (but quite natty ones – more Beatles than Savile Row) and black leather shoes. He is short with grey hair and, having lived in the United States for a decade, comes across as quite American: his accent is mid-Pacific, and he uses the word 'cops' a lot. A television producer by training, he is an engaging companion, intelligent, thoughtful and, of course, original.

It is soon clear that he derived genuine pleasure from spotting interesting multicultural vignettes at the fireworks. 'I saw one group of eight or ten teenagers arm in arm,' he says proudly. 'There was an Indian girl with a white Australian boyfriend, two Chinese girls with Chinese boyfriends, a Chinese girl with a white boyfriend, and a couple of kids that were maybe Korean. I guess they were all probably schoolfriends. It was really terrific. The way people mix in Sydney is more obvious than in any other major Australian city.'

To underline this, he mentions two of the 'kids' on his crew that night. One, called Jessica Wong, has a Chinese father but actually looks very like her mother, who is Irish; one might assume that the other girl, Donna McMahon, is Irish too, but in fact she is a Buddhist who looks very Thai. 'That's a very Australian thing,' says Birch, and you see exactly what he means.

Birch has compared Sydney 'the party city' with cities famous for their carnivals – Port-of-Spain, Trinidad, and Rio de Janeiro – as well as with Mediterranean Italy, France and Spain. 'It's a lot to do with the geography and a lot to do with climate,' he said after a previous fire-work show. 'I guess it comes from generations of people who are used to taking their clothes off and jumping into the water.' He still sees things through the same lens. 'It's hot,' he says, 'and Sydney's all about bodies. And on New Year's Eve, when you've got the added excuse of alcohol and the expectation of making an idiot of yourself, it's the perfect place to party. I passed a lot of kids in the street saying "Happy New Year" to everyone. They were pissed as parrots but quite well mannered with it. They were there to celebrate, have a good time and laugh, basically. That's part of the Sydney ethos, too.' He goes on: 'Sydney's a very hedo-nistic place. There's a fair bit of body worship. There are the beaches and the colours, the T-shirts, the short skirts. Sydney really does cele-brate the body and that shows itself in the celebration.'

Once they had recovered from New Year's Eve, Sydney people had plenty of other excuses to carry on celebrating. The first, of course, was the Test (2–5 January). Largely due to England's stirring comeback in Melbourne, the last 5,000 tickets for the first day's play sold on New Year's Eve, and the last 5,000 for day two vanished on day one. But, as the Olympics approach, ACB executives detect a growing 'big-event mentality' among Sydney people, which they believe was also a factor in those full houses. Four of the one-dayers sold out, too, but that was not unexpected. The season's last international at the SCG ended with a typ-ical Sydney flourish. As Australia ran off, unlikely victors in the first one-day final, and the 32,640 spectators were thanked for their patron-age, the sky above was filled with fireworks. After England's deflating performance, it gave one a real lift.

There was also much for arts lovers to savour. The Art Gallery of NSW had a superb and very popular Cezanne exhibition, while the annual Festival of Sydney, featuring open-air concerts and film screen-ings, ran through January. It was a critical, if not a commercial, success. Australia Day, 26 January, saw the traditional ferry race, and more fire-works, this time at Darling Harbour, a Docklands-style redevelopment of old wharves which has transformed an eyesore into a waterfront shopping, museum and entertainment complex with good modern architecture. The crowds watching some relatively modest pyrotechnics were more multicultural, less Anglo-Celtic, than those of New Year's Eve.

Next up, in February, was the Sydney Gay and Lesbian Mardi Gras

Festival. This was a month-long extravaganza, including 130 events, culminating in an exuberant televised night-time parade through the city and along Oxford Street, Paddington – an exotic area (close to the SCG) where sights such as a drag queen with a poodle dyed to match her out-rageous spotted outfit are not unknown on any day of the year. At Mardi Gras, 600,000 gay and straight people jostled for the best views of 200 floats, one of them tastelessly called 'Saving Ryan's Privates'. The parade also featured four dozen Shirley Bassey impersonators and 250 'Dykes on Bikes'. As usual, the spectacle attracted thousands of families with young children, as well as their unshockable grandparents. Next day, the gay community held its customary 'recovery parties' all over the city.

Although things would calm down during the winter, there were dates aplenty to put in the diary. High on the coveted list were tickets to the official opening on 12 June, with appropriate fanfare, of the new Olympic stadium, at Homebush Bay, eight miles from the city centre, with the Socceroos (in other words, Australia) taking on a FIFA world team expected to include Brazil's Ronaldo. The opening's promoter, by the way, is Dean Jones, the recently retired Test batsman. Fast forward, through numerous Olympic 'trial' events at sparkling new venues, to December, and you have the Christmas party season all over again, fol-lowed by another great outdoor event, the start of the Sydney–Hobart yacht race, on Boxing Day.

The 1998 race was tragically marred by the death of six yachtsmen in appalling storms. This was by no means the only aquatic tragedy during the summer. There was a spate of drownings in NSW, particularly on Sydney beaches. By the end of January, to the horror of the dedicated and professional surf life-saving community, over thirty people – more than double the average number – had drowned on the state's beaches. Some of the deaths in Sydney were blamed on sheer bad luck, others attributed to over-enthusiastic swimmers or inexperienced surfers ignor-ing clear warnings and taking needless risks on sections of beach not patrolled by life-savers, and being caught in 'rips' (undertows). A dis-proportionate number of the victims on these notoriously difficult Pacific beaches were tourists, Asian migrants or young people. One sea-soned life-saver told me he and his colleagues were convinced, although there was no official evidence to support this, that alcohol was partly to blame for some of the fatalities: certainly a number of people rescued were found to be quite drunk. Surf life-savers, fearful that the influx of tourists for the Olympics could spark another series of drownings, started to lobby the state government, urging ministers to push safety leaflets into every hotel lobby in time for the Games. Mercifully, a wet February kept many people off the beaches, undoubtedly saving lives.

Spending January and the first half of February in Sydney reminded me how adept most Australians are at making the most of their time off, especially in the holiday period, when it is probably fair to say that even those at work are under less pressure than most Brits in August. But then Aussies take their leisure hours seriously, a point which Ric Birch, if not his own driven lifestyle, underlines. 'For us – and in a way this should be reflected in the Olympic ceremonies – our leisure time is just as important as our work time,' he says. 'A lot of Australians work much harder at their leisure time than they do their working time.' Another reason, surely, for the country's great sporting record.

Birch's Olympic opening ceremony, which will take place at night, will last, says the ringmaster, for three hours and twelve minutes, 'give or take a minute'. What does he hope to see characterise the Sydney Games? 'All being well, a feeling of being looked after by a people who are generous with their time and proud of their city and wanting to share it.' He pauses and adds: 'I think the best thing about Australia is that Australians are not particularly formal people. They're prepared to be laid-back, they don't take themselves too seriously, but are genuinely friendly. We accept strangers very willingly. We're very tolerant. I hope all that comes over at the Olympics.'

Birch pauses again, and then hints at his faith that he and his compatriots will stage as successful a Games as is now possible, given the scandal. 'Beneath that kind of laid-back, louche, "she'll be right, mate" kind of attitude,' he says, momentarily adopting a real Aussie twang, 'there is actually a great deal of professionalism. It's just that no Australian would wish to create the impression that he or she is actually very, very good at what they do. It's much easier to project a calm, casual attitude,' he adds, 'because then when you pull it off, it comes as such a surprise, it's so much more successful. People think: "If this surfie drugged to the eyeballs is able to pull this off, imagine what he could do if he really tried."' No wonder Alexander Downer, the Foreign Minister, is fond of observing that Australia is the most Irish country outside Ireland, though many Americans would disagree. Expanding on the theme of the Emerald Isle, and the many Aussies of Irish descent, Birch says: 'Australia's personality is based very much on the Irish . . . we follow lost causes. I just wish Australians had the gift of the gab.' (I cannot help thinking: if only they played cricket like the Irish.)

This seems the moment to ask Birch – whose problem it is for the next eighteen months – about the subject which must sometimes keep him awake at night. What's the state of play on the Australian national identity? 'It's really difficult,' he says. 'It comes up all the time with ceremonies. How many Englishmen have to define themselves? It's in your bones.' It is the same, he adds, for other Europeans; and now even Americans seem to have done with defining themselves. 'Australia is still looking for its national identity, which is a symptom that we're still coming to grips with ourselves as a nation.' Interestingly, though, he does not like having the national identity defined, because it then becomes 'dangerously easy' to say whether or not an individual fits the national stereotype. Such judgements, he says, go against the grain of Australianness, which is about tolerance and latitude.

What does he hope the Olympics – with all that they should mean in terms of increased international recognition, Sydney's growth as a financial centre, and the extra tourist, convention and other business – will do for the Emerald City? Intriguingly, given his central role, Birch expresses not a hope, but a fear – that Sydney will become 'very crowded and that some of its charm and character will be destroyed . . . that it'll become callous and uncaring and will forget the human and personal scale'. He goes on: 'There will be pressure after the Olympics, as Sydney's sheer physical beauty is exposed to people around the world. We'll have to make sure that hard-nosed Americans who come here to do business know how to relax as well as do business.' Is there any danger, as some people believe, of Sydney becoming a Manhattan of the southern hemisphere in the twenty-first century? 'I can't see that ever happening,' replies Birch, 'because people in Sydney won't wish to spend their entire waking hours pursuing their careers. People here would always want to go surfing and take the weekend off and go sailing and get a bit pissed at a party and take a "sickie" next day from work.'

20

Whither the Lucky Country?

CHARLES DE LISLE

A week or two after England went home, Malcolm Turnbull, chairman of the Australian Republican Movement, had a gentle crack at the team. 'The republican cause is not an anti-British thing,' he said, '. . . and given the poor performance of their cricketers it is hard to whip up any anti-British feeling. It simply is a pro-Australian movement.' He was quite right to say that being a republican does not make you anti-British; but if his movement is to surmount longish odds and win the referendum in November, it will be due to the support of many anti-British Australians as well as the more moderate, floating, voters he was endeavouring to reassure.

Much of the 'Pommie-bashing' is good-natured, and some of it is justified. After England's dropped catches on the opening day of the first Test, the joke doing the rounds in Brisbane next morning was typically to the point. 'Have you heard?' it went. 'England are walking to the Gabba today. They can't even catch a bus!' Later in the summer a Sydney acquaintance, describing some incompetent colleagues, observed playfully: 'They're amateurs – like your cricket team!' Behind such mild banter, there sometimes lies strong feeling.

Just ask some of the 'whingeing Poms' who have been moving back to the UK at the rate of seventy a week (3,737 left Australia in 1996–7). 'It's a staggering rate,' says Barrie Hunt, president of the United Kingdom Settlers' Association, which has tried to discover the reasons for the exodus. According to a survey of 200 British settlers conducted on the association's behalf, 35 per cent believe the Australian media runs negative stereotypes about Poms; 39 per cent believe they are discriminated against compared with Aussies of non-British origin and 37 per cent feel that complaints lodged by them are not taken as seriously as those raised by other ethnic groups. Even so, 74 per cent are glad they migrated, which is perhaps not so surprising given Australia's many blessings. For Hunt, the findings confirm a perception that Australia is 'anglophobic'.

Jim Potts, the British Council's director in Australia, believes attitudes have softened a good deal. When he took up his post in 1993, he says, the local press was engaged in a 'fairly systematic devaluing of the relationship with Britain. There was a lot of very sardonic, really quite hostile, commentary – not just the jokey cricketing-type banter, which is taken in good spirits.' His recent press surveys (some sports pages apart) are much more encouraging, an improvement which he ascribes largely to the 'New Images' campaign in which he was a central figure; he thinks the fact that Paul Keating, the Labor Prime Minister who argued passionately for a republic, lost office in 1996 may also have lowered the temperature. The genial Potts, whose personal enthusiasm for the country is obvious, sums things up thus: 'There's huge admiration and love for Britain here. But at the same time there can be this other reaction, the chip on the shoulder . . . Brits can have a hard time.' Earlier, surveying the cultural scene as a whole, he observes: 'There's still a strong Australian nationalism, which is redefined constantly.'

If the 'whingeing Poms' who spoke of discrimination were thinking of the work-place, I would not be surprised. Although I never encountered discrimination in my years on Australian newspapers, some areas of broadcasting, for example, are a different matter. Aussies, who are great consumers of news bulletins, now generally prefer their news presented to them by someone with a strong, clear Australian accent, or someone multicultural; so an identifiably British accent is, these days, generally a handicap.

Much of this, of course, simply reflects welcome changes in the land of the 'fair go' over the past twenty-five years or so: the broadening of society, the disappearance of the 'cultural cringe', and growing national pride and self-confidence. And in many fields Australians are, with good reason, proud of their achievements. Take the film industry. Although the country has enjoyed regular Oscar success since 1980, the past four or five years have seen an extra degree of Hollywood recognition. This year brought no fewer than seven Academy Award nominations. As Cate Blanchett remarked after hearing of her best actress nomination for *Elizabeth*: 'Per capita, we must have the highest proportion of nominees of any country. It's pretty incredible.'

Despite these accomplishments there is still, I think, a small – if declining – proportion of Australians who feel a need to niggle at their British cousins in order to express their own identity. And the haughty, patronising attitudes of some Brits are partly responsible. In an article in *The Australian* of 28 January 1999, titled 'Time to wipe the amused disdain off English faces', Paul Ham, who lived in London for fifteen years, argued that Australians were 'kidding themselves if they think the country to which they are constitutionally linked holds them in high regard'. He went on: 'There is a good reason why Australia should sever her constitutional links with Britain: the British, and chiefly the English, find us contemptible . . . no number of Sir Don Bradmans, Dame Joan Sutherlands and Patrick Whites will budge the notion in the English brain of Australia as the witless, cultureless progeny of a giant prison, conceived and built by ex-public schoolboys on an extended holiday.' Ham was seriously overstating the case but there is something in it.

However, the chances are that, even allowing for an anticipated late surge in republican support, the referendum will be narrowly defeated. Any change to the constitution must be endorsed by a majority of voters overall, and a majority in four of the six states. The two most cosmopolitan, NSW and Victoria, are expected to vote republican – Australia's president, incidentally, would be elected on a bipartisan basis by Parliament and would assume the Governor-General's powers – but the likelihood of two of Queensland, South Australia, Western Australia and Tasmania following suit has receded lately. In January, a national poll for *The Australian* found 48 per cent of people favouring a republic, as against 35 per cent backing the status quo – the narrowest gap since late 1994. The recent defection of Dame Edna Everage to the republican camp is not expected to be a decisive blow.

The republican cause will undoubtedly suffer from the splits in its own ranks, the fact that the Liberal Prime Minister, John Howard, a monarchist, will have an influence on the campaign, and the innate conservatism of voters, who have a record of rejecting referenda, invariably so when the proposal has not had the backing of both major parties. Many Aussies are practical, down-to-earth people who are proud of their country but cannot see the point of a symbolic change. The 'if it ain't broke, don't fix it' argument appeals to them. As Howard has put it, 'You don't trip on the crown every morning.' The former Chief Justice of Australia and leading monarchist Sir Harry Gibbs has argued thus: 'We are a self-governing democracy, completely independent of any external control in all aspects of our affairs, and the Queen has no power to influence the formation of policies or the conduct of government in Australia. The argument that we should convert to a republic rests solely on sentiment.'

Although the debate is given a lot of space in serious newspapers, most of which are republican, it is not yet high on the agenda of the majority of voters. As Howard, the archetypal Aussie 'battler', observed early in the summer, the republic is 'never raised by Australians I mix with'. They include that other well-known battler, Mark Taylor, a declared sceptic about constitutional reform (they take the views of recent captains on these matters quite seriously Down Under).

Moreover, some people with republican sympathies will vote monarchist. Many voters are instinctively suspicious of a president chosen by politicians, and would prefer to bide their time in the hope that a popularly elected head of state will one day be on offer. But if Australia does vote 'yes' this year, the president will take office on 1 January 2001, the centenary of Federation, leaving the 2000 Olympics to be opened, almost certainly, by the Prime Minister. Under the Olympic Charter, it should be the Queen, but that has long been ruled out; and Labor's preference for the job to be done by the Governor-General is unlikely to prevail. Like most Prime Ministers, John Howard likes to appear presidential, and knows how to wrap himself in the flag – particularly the Australian part of it. For some reason, when he addresses the media, standing in front of the national flag, the Union Jack section tends to be furled away, leaving the stars of the Southern Cross to catch the television viewer's eye.

There remains a powerful case for Australia – despite her unsettled national identity – to replace the Queen with her own head of state. The republican argument is essentially that the monarchy is an anachronism in a multicultural society in which millions have no British ties whatever, and whose future lies largely – if not as much as seemed to be the case a few years ago – in the Asia-Pacific region. Australians, they say, should be represented by an Australian. In any case, becoming a republic can be seen as a logical step in the nation's progress, no more rebellious an act than, say, a young person deciding that the time has finally come to give up the bedroom in the parental home out of which he or she actually moved several years ago.

The former Labor Prime Minister Bob Hawke, as proud an Aussie as any, has long been a moderate republican. 'I just find it basically insulting', he told me, 'that we use another country's head of state to be our head of state.' He went on: 'There's an argument going on in your country about whether Charles can marry Camilla and Camilla can become the Queen – well, you're arguing about who our King and Queen of Australia will be. And I don't want you bloody Brits – as much as I love you – to be making that decision for me, thank you very much!'

On a three-month visit to Australia, one cannot gain a complete picture, but the sense of uncertainty, even desperation, about the imminent plebiscite was emphasised by republican attempts to alert the electorate to the alleged dangers of missing this red bus. Malcolm Turnbull, who made his name in his early thirties representing the former MI5 official Peter Wright in his *Spycatcher* court victory over the Thatcher Government (a classic 'Pom-bashing' exercise), argues that Australia would be a better society with an Australian head of state and believes with 'even more conviction' that it will be a 'much worse' society if she votes to keep the monarchy. He adds: 'Those who are unconvinced of the merits of changing the constitution should contemplate the dangers of not doing so. Conservatives, unthrilled by republicanism, should bear in mind that even Howard is of the view that, if we do become a republic, "the fabric of the Australian community is not going to be, in any way, damaged or hurt by the process".'

Now a wealthy merchant banker, Turnbull also urges voters to think of Australia's image beyond her shores: 'What will the world say if, on the verge of the millennium, the centenary of our life as a nation, Australia signs up for another 100 years of the British monarchy? What will it say about our belief in ourselves, our confidence in our own people, if we reaffirm that no Australian is good enough to be our head of state?' If the republicans do lose, their dream may have to wait a decade or so – giving the 'Barmy Army' several more Ashes series in which to taunt the old enemy with renditions of 'God Save *Your* Gracious Queen'. On the other hand, a vote for a republic would take Australia into the millennium, the Olympics and her own centenary on a high.

As the 'Lucky Country' prepared to make a choice that has taken other nations to war, Sydney saw the début of a project which bitterly divides Europeans. While some believe the euro will help ensure that western Europe never sees another war, others believe just as passionately that it will prove disastrous, and could provoke new conflict. On 4 January, time zones and a public holiday in New Zealand gave Sydney the honour of launching the first day of full trading in the new currency. More internationally minded Australians may have reflected that, even outside the single currency, Britain, as a member of the European Union, has less sovereignty in a number of important areas than Australia, republic or not.

Questions of national identity are by no means the only reason why some Australians – despite their relief at the defeat of Hansonism, despite anticipation of uplifting public events, and despite retention of the Ashes – are not feeling as good about themselves and their country as they would like. Reconciliation with the Aboriginal people is another sensitive issue, especially with the international spotlight hovering.

The subject was tackled frankly but delicately by the Governor-General, the avuncular Sir William Deane, in his Australia Day address. He said it was 'one of those plain truths' that true reconciliation would not be achieved until 'we further address appalling problems of material disadvantage which oppress Australia's indigenous peoples'. Deane drew attention to the fact that an Aboriginal baby girl born that day would, on current statistics, have a life expectancy twenty years shorter than a non-indigenous baby girl born on the same day, and the chance of her dying in infancy was three times greater. He welcomed the 'considerable' progress already made towards reconciliation but also spoke of Australia's need to face up to her responsibility for the 'problems of the spirit' experienced by Aboriginals.

A week or two later the respected political columnist and author Paul Kelly examined the state of the nation. Writing in *The Weekend Australian,* Kelly acknowledged that the economy had performed excellently in the 1990s, and that the country had 'opportunities for dramatic self-realisation' over the next few years. But he also spoke of a national mood, by and large, of 'apprehension and uncertainty amid growing wealth and opportunity'. Australia, he wrote, often seemed to be a 'confused, insecure nation, pessimistic about its future'. Among the reasons, he argued, were growing numbers of broken families and drug addicts, and globalization, which was 'dividing the nation along a new class fault of winners and losers'. Above all, there was pent-up frustration over a sense that shared community values were being eroded and contested. Symptoms of the malaise, said Kelly, included a decline in respect for many institutions and 'fresh uncertainty about our history and our identity'.

Apart perhaps from the last point, however, these problems are hardly unique to Australia. Many other advanced Western countries are struggling with many of the same blights; and Britain is also beset, in the eyes of many, by a crisis of the nation state. But if Kelly was right about the turmoil in society, it would help to explain why Australians did not yet appear in quite the mood to take the big step of completing the process of national independence. It was also significant that while rugby league was listed amongst institutions suffering diminished respect, cricket was not: an indirect affirmation of the game's continued high standing in what remains a vibrant, energetic, youthful and notably cheerful country.

As the summer ended, those in charge of trying to engender a proper sense of occasion in Australia's beginnings as a nation, in the lead-up to her 100th birthday celebrations, reached once again for this trusted symbol of Australianness. 'What kind of country', asks a government advertisement, referring to the original England–Australia series of 1877, 'would have a cricket team before it had a Parliament?'

As Australia wrestled with her social and other problems, she would be relying even more heavily on cricket in the future, both as a showcase for traditional Australian values, and for the stability, national unity, pride and pleasure the game provides, from the MCG to the most parched paddock. And if cricket could succeed in identifying and developing the best young talent across an even broader spectrum of society, there was perhaps no knowing how long the national side's winning ways might last.

21

The Pursuit of Excellence

CHRISTOPHER MARTIN-JENKINS

Great hope and a huge amount of money have been invested in England's attempt to win the 1999 World Cup. It could happen, but it is unlikely. Shortly before the one-day finals in Australia, Alec Stewart said of his team: 'This is becoming a very good side, full of spirit and confidence.' Forty-eight hours later they threw away a winning chance in the first final and they were subsequently humiliated in the second.

Sportsmen who want to succeed have to be positive, of course, and Stewart and his team in Australia could not be faulted either for zeal or effort, facts which absolved them from serious blame for their ultimate failures; but not even politicians at election time have such a talent for self-delusion as English professional cricketers frequently do. Wishful thinking does not win matches. Until the British system creates strength in depth and those who play for their country can match the Australians regularly in deed as well as in word, the aspirations to be top of the world will be unfulfilled.

There has already been, however, a belated acceptance, notably at the professional level of English cricket, of the need for a thorough change of attitude which is already bearing some fruit. There have been changes, too, although not all of them will work, aimed at the overhaul of a system which evolved without any planning in days when overseas competition was generally weaker. It is not impossible that England, seventh out of nine in the Test rankings and no better than fourth equal in the one-day list, will find the formula for more consistent success soon. In an expanding world of international cricket, with more games being played between the Test nations and others like Bangladesh and Kenya – before long, perhaps, the United States – eager to become involved, rapid improvement is essential. Speaking after the Adelaide Test, Stewart, obliged to be realistic, got nearer to the truth when he said: 'I don't believe England have declined but that other countries have got better faster.'

The answer lies in the pursuit of excellence in all aspects of cricket and at all levels. It would perhaps have needed only two more world-class players, one of them a wrist spinner, for England to have won in Australia, but great players do not suddenly appear when some Aladdin rubs his lamp. If the game in Britain is to take a permanent change for the better, it has to change the culture. The prime drive since the England and Wales Cricket Board took on the responsibility for the recreational and professional game together has been commercial, but marketing must exist for cricket, never the other way round. The emphasis now has to be on creating wider opportunities for the young at the base of the pyramid and on a drive for sustained quality at the top.

Lord MacLaurin, chairman of the ECB since it replaced the old Test and County Cricket Board in January 1997, has been the catalyst for the spate of recent decisions which may finally persuade cartoonists to put away their vision of an apoplectic colonel as the archetypal representative of English cricket. If the MCC vote to admit lady members was symbolic, those to change county competitions and increase the programme of home Tests and internationals to a total of seventeen each summer were strictly pragmatic. They paved the way for a television deal which left a feeling of unease in some parts at least of the public mind, for all the enthusiasm of the board and, naturally, the two companies who outbid the BBC. The ECB will be judged, however, on how wisely they spend the money.

From the start the burden of the ECB song has been that 'Team England' has to come first. There have been forward moves, despite the latest Ashes defeat, since David Lloyd came bustling in as the new coach in 1996 with bright new fielding routines, the introduction of more specialist coaches, the application of video technology both to coaching and to tactical planning and a new emphasis on the things which sports scientists have taught contemporary sportsmen about diet, lifestyle, specific fitness training and the right mental approach for success.

All this, however, has been no proof against inadequacies in the basic cricket disciplines: bowling straight and to a length, playing with the full face of the bat, holding catches and playing within the spirit of the game. The need now, as far as the national side itself is concerned, is for leadership – starting with the appointment of the right full-time manager – which encourages the pursuit of excellence not only by hard work but also as a goal in life. Australia turned things round in the late 1980s partly because those in charge set the right example and backed men of steely character like Mark Taylor, Ian Healy and Steve Waugh.

The South Africans have been equally impressive since political changes allowed them to return as full members of the International Cricket Council. There was an admirable dignity when they were beaten by England at Headingley in 1998, thereby losing a series which they had come close to winning. Rather than whinge, as he might have done in the wake of some unjust umpiring decisions, the captain, Hansie Cronje, looked to the faults of his own side. Cronje is one of several committed Christians in the South African dressing-room and the team's English coach, Bob Woolmer, has observed how their moral and physical strength has helped to develop these men as cricketers. Jack Birkenshaw, the Leicestershire manager, made the same comparison between Cronje's lifestyle and that of the average county cricketer brought up for generations on an assumption that the best preparation for cricket was nights spent at the bar or chasing the local totty.

Cricket has a worthy tradition of characters who sowed their wild oats, as well as sad stories of those who never fully came to terms with life outside the game's warm circle and in too many cases resorted eventually to suicide. In the post-war years of release, the likes of Keith Miller, Bill Edrich, Denis Compton and Godfrey Evans enjoyed themselves to the full off the field and provided lustrous entertainment on it. Extroverts and bon viveurs are no less necessary in dressing-rooms in the sterner atmosphere pervading professional cricket now – it is, after all, a game to be enjoyed – but the more rounded and responsible the attitude of the influential members of a team, the greater will be their ability to withstand the pressures of competition and to keep life in perspective.

This was a truth grasped by John Barclay, sometime captain of Sussex and manager of Mike Atherton's England team in Zimbabwe and New Zealand in 1996–7, who came close to being an excellent manager. He was prepared to defy an instruction from Tim Lamb, the ECB's chief executive, not to spend money on a trip to the Victoria Falls when he felt it was the right thing for the players to do and he perhaps took unfair blame for the diplomatic failings of a small-minded team; but he lost the confidence of the media by failing to deal frankly with them.

Since then, there has been a full-time media relations officer, with a brief to improve the public relations of England teams abroad and to bridge the gap between the media's constant requirement for news and the needs of players who these days are given too little time for relaxation between visits to airports and cricket grounds.

Finding the right manager – firm, moral, good-humoured, patient and media-friendly – will be essential when England players are contracted centrally to the ECB, as they will be from the start of the newly inflated programme of international cricket ushered in to attract more television money from 2000 onwards. England players are expected to play in only 15 per cent of the revamped county programme once the excessive diet of seven Tests and ten one-day internationals each season begins. Five Tests and seven internationals would have kept a wiser balance between the need to fulfil international obligations and to avoid the kind of club v. country confrontations which confuse the priorities in other sports.

There is no question of which should take greater precedence in England because the profits from international matches have long underpinned the ceaseless efforts of the county game to make itself viable. Furthermore, it has been obvious for many years that if England are to give themselves the best chance of improving their international record, they have to give their best players the right amount of cricket, keeping them sharp but fresh.

The counties, to some extent forced into a corner by ECB promptings that the system would collapse unless there was a lucrative television deal, took the wrong option when they chose a two-division championship from 2000 instead of regional cricket: a tier between Test and county cricket which would have given ambitious young professionals a fairer and clearer path towards winning an England place and established England players the right amount of competitive cricket between international matches.

The danger of two divisions is not just that some counties will get richer and others poorer – already Sussex have lost over £360,000 in two years in trying to lock horns with wealthier counties – but that money will be spent on escalating salaries rather than on the development of young players and the refurbishment of playing and spectator facilities. For generations, county cricket was serious but utterly civilised. It is some time since it has been genuinely a comfortable profession, as it is often described, at least for the majority. Some players, it is true, have learned to coast and to pace themselves, but so they always did. Two divisions will almost inevitably make games more abrasive and open to abuses such as the preparation of pitches to suit the home team, without necessarily raising playing standards. Superficially, of course, the idea of promotion and relegation involving six of the eighteen clubs every season will raise the interest for players, spectators and media alike.

Patience is required all round because so many of the attempts to make English cricket catch up with Australia are in their infancy. Since the previous Ashes tour in 1994–5 there has been a new constitution for the game; a new body responsible for both professional and recreational cricket; a decision to divide the Championship and the new 45-over 'Sunday' league into two divisions; and more money spent on development officers to reignite the game in schools, which is and always has been the only place to start.

Wealth creation is essential as the means of improvement and those who strove to sell the game more aggressively to sponsors and television companies have served the game well, mercifully avoiding what would have been a fatal decision to remove home Test matches from terrestrial television. Even the deal which gave Sky television exclusive live coverage of all the one-day internationals and one Test a season was fraught with risk, because maximum exposure of any sport to the young is by far the best way of enthusing them.

The extra income which comes to the game from the £103 million deal with Channel 4 and Sky Sports, coupled with the new sponsorships which began to flow back to the game at the start of 1999 after an anxious period due to England's poor results and the uncertainty over television coverage, gives administrators the chance to get the priorities right.

There are plenty of them to do so, because cricket administrators have sprouted like daffodils in spring of late, their numbers increasing by the week in the first year of the ECB's existence. Their annual report for 1997–8 revealed that 128 employees cost more than £4.6 million in salaries and expenses. This was justified by the new burst of energy in all departments since the maestro from Tesco brought his considerable drive and business acumen to the task of pulling together the strings of the essentially conservative TCCB and set about running cricket like a modern plc. The burgeoning bureaucracy has to be watched, however, and the marketing department cannot rest on its considerable laurels of recent times because, as MacLaurin knew from the outset, and research confirmed, cricket has lost ground to other sports and to alternative claims on the leisure time of a public which once took cricket for granted as the game of summer.

In embracing the new, however, not least the essentially warm-climate attractions of floodlit cricket, the ECB has to be wary of gimmickry for its own sake. When the sponsors of the new 45-over, two-division National League, CGU insurance, added £6.3 million, over four years, to the coffers, they became the third new sponsor of the old Sunday League in twelve years. Each, of course, was announced with a clash of cymbals but it is substance that the game requires and the firm base which comes from youngsters wanting to play cricket and people of all ages wishing to go to watch it.

At least until very recently there has been too much concern about the watching, too little about active participation. The crowds for the County Championship in 1950 aggregated almost 2 million. By 1963, the first year of the knockout cup, the pioneering limited-overs competition soon to be known as the Gillette Cup, the figure had dropped to 700,000; hence the need for something different. Only three years after the Gillette started, Championship crowds had dropped to 500,000, but by 1998 they had grown again to 525,997 and overall crowds for county matches in the four domestic competitions and in the matches against the South African touring team were 1,183,343.

Crowds have been recycled as a result of the option to watch the more instant form of the game. They have dropped overall since the post-war peak, but not perhaps to the extent that is imagined, and the staging of midweek floodlit games has proved successful in offering professional cricket to spectators at times when it suits them to go. Spot research showed that a tenth of those who went to watch floodlit league games in 1998 were paying to watch a cricket match for the first time.

If this was encouraging, other recent analysis emphatically is not. While the official research by the Target Group Index Research company into the favourite sports of British youngsters in 1998 was showing a worrying decline for cricket, the respected and assiduous cricket historian and statistician Peter Wynne-Thomas was carrying out his own exhaustive survey into the playing of cricket in towns and villages throughout his home county of Nottinghamshire. What he discovered was that village cricket in the county is dying and that in public parks, once thriving stages for recreational cricket, the game has already virtually disappeared.

This is not cricket's fault; it is the result simply of changing social trends: but it is cricket's problem, to be solved if the game is truly to be regenerated. Concerned by what he calls the 'woolly' information emanating from Lord's about the number of people playing cricket, Wynne-

Thomas traced every ground in Nottinghamshire which had staged recreational adult cricket since 1946. Of 103 village grounds in use in 1946, forty-one have disappeared; of seventy-one firms' grounds, only twenty-one remain; urban club grounds have halved from sixty-three to thirty-one; public park pitches have dropped from eighty-three to twenty-seven; and school grounds used for club cricket from twenty-five to only six.

Curiously, two other types of club ground have fallen less dramatically: of fifteen landed estate grounds in 1946, ten are still flourishing; and despite the decimation of the Nottinghamshire coalmining industry, cricket clubs associated with the mines have survived and reformed. There were thirty-six collieries in Nottinghamshire when the mines were nationalised in 1947, all with sports grounds, and when two new mines were sunk in the 1950s, at Bevercotes and Cotgrave, new cricket grounds were laid out. There are now only five working mines in the county, but twenty-two clubs which still have mining connections. Until the 1960s they still had their own colliery league.

But this is the exception to the trend. Grounds have been put to use for all sorts of different activities since their pitches fell into disuse. Thirty-two of the village grounds, for example, have become agricultural fields once more and it is no surprise that thirteen of the old firms' grounds are now housing estates. 'The sad aspect of the decline in village grounds', says Wynne-Thomas, 'is that in the 1950s virtually everyone in the county lived within walking distance of a cricket ground, so any youngster who was interested could wander down to the local ground and get involved in practice matches or evening nets and thus graduate to the local team.'

There was a grain of hope, however. Only three of the disused village grounds have become housing estates as opposed to agricultural fields. 'If there was a real upsurge in cricket,' says Wynne-Thomas, 'it would be possible to resurrect most village grounds. The survey did in fact reveal that six or seven villages have had clubs which died and were then revived.'

There seems less hope for public parks in urban areas. The Forest ground, first used for cricket in 1770, has not seen a match for five years and only a disused artificial strip still stands, unused, between two soccer pitches. Wynne-Thomas cites vandalism of pitches – the park pavilions are like 'fortified bunkers' – and the collapse of clubs connected to smaller firms and the old boys of local schools.

Nottinghamshire's experience is part of a national trend which is nothing less than a public scandal, one for which successive Governments have been castigated far less than they should have been. Whereas the vast majority of Australia's 18.5 million people have a well-used and excellently maintained ground close to where they live, England's 49 million have suffered a disastrous decline in outdoor sporting facilities. In the last twenty years the incredible number of 10,000 sports fields have been sold for development.

The Central Council for Physical Recreation was aware of 409 grounds under threat at the time of the last General Election in 1997, so it seemed to be good news when the New Labour Government issued a press release the following January from the Department of Culture, Media and Sport. Here was the promise: 'The Government will fulfil and extend its pledge to stop the sale of playing fields which schools and communities need.' In March 1998, the Education Secretary, David Blunkett, introduced an amendment to the Schools Standard and Framework Bill by which local authorities were required to seek ministerial approval before selling off school playing fields for building. Sales had to be referred to the Department of Education, whose own officials had to seek the approval of the Sports Council. *Yet by October 1998 the number of sites listed by the CCPR as being under threat had grown to 632, an increase of 65 per cent since the election.* So much for the Prime Minister's boast to Parliament two months earlier that: 'We have ended the unnecessary sale of school playing fields.'

Against this horrifying stupidity, an open invitation to misspent youth, the money fed back to cricket grounds through the Sports Council, and its new source of funds, the National Lottery, is like spittle in the wind. Efforts often have to be heroic to succeed. A special merit award was presented to Tony Moody of the Lambeth Borough Community Cricket Association by the Professional Cricketers Association for his coaching and fund-raising efforts in south London. Lambeth, it transpired, has only one cricket ground for 200,000 people – and since it is The Oval, not many amateurs can use it.

Even the immortal cricketing name of P. B. H. May was almost insufficiently alluring to create just one new ground in his memory amidst the apathy and commercial greed of London. Not until five years after the death of England's finest post-war batsman was an appeal to revive the Wadham Lodge ground sufficiently well supported by the Lottery Awards Panel to enable a new sports centre there to go ahead. The voluntary appeal in May's memory raised £2.85 million, to which the panel eventually added the necessary additional £1 million to allow building to start.

The Lottery panel proved less accommodating when it was presented with an eminently sensible approach by the King Edward VI Community College at Totnes in Devon. Founded in 1553 but a comprehensive school since the 1960s, the school made a joint appeal with Totnes Cricket Club, currently playing at an inadequate park ground, to develop an equally unsatisfactory school playing field into 'a top-class sports facility for the use of the whole community'. The whole scheme, to include the levelling and drainage of the field, a new turf square, an all-weather pitch and all-weather nets, plus two 75m x 50m pitches for junior football, was estimated at only £500,000. The school spent £4,000 on a professional presentation from a specialist company, but in the words of the school's sports master, Tony Dixon, in March 1999: 'It's increasingly apparent that the Sports Council Lottery Fund will be unable to honour any of their original promises and the local District Council refuses to endorse the scheme. Without their support, no bid has a chance anyway. Result: brilliant opportunity to deliver funding to grassroots cricket, dead in the water.'

A shortage of houses there may be in Britain in 1999. A shortage of sports grounds there most certainly is and the combination of a new commitment to organised sport in schools and the provision of decent facilities for playing it both inside and outside schools would cure most of the evils by which the Devil occupies the idle hands of youth. I remember with clarity speaking at a fund-raising dinner organised by the saintly John Passmore in Cape Town before apartheid was ended. Its purpose was to raise money to create a new sports ground in the midst of the dust and squalor of Langa township. What was right for the deprived youth of South Africa in 1983 has to be right for the urban teenagers of Britain now.

The situation is not all gloomy for cricket, however. The ECB's 1998 report claimed 50,000 Kwik Cricket kits in use and nearly 4,000 primary schools with Kwik Cricket teams, a total number of nearly a million primary schoolchildren thereby getting early exposure to the joys of the game. The figure for secondary-school cricketers playing the game 'in one form or another' was given as 600,000 and CGU, the new sponsors of the National League, were planning involvement in the development of a new form of instant cricket in secondary schools to bridge the gap between the game played with plastic bats and soft balls and the altogether tougher one wherein the leather ball can bruise and the willow bat needs to be used with proper technique if a player is to develop. The decline in the quantity and quality of school cricket since the early 1980s has already been greatly offset by an increase in the junior sections of clubs.

Talented young players, once spotted, will only be successfully developed by improved coaching as well as the provision of better facilities. In the 1998–9 winter the ECB's technical director, the former Glamorgan and England opening batsman Hugh Morris, launched the Rover National Coaching Scheme by which volunteer coaches will be guided towards courses which will give them qualifications at five levels, ranging from the teaching of basic skills at schools or clubs to advanced levels involving professional players. Morris is determined that, as in Australia, talented young players will be taught proper techniques early, given the right amount of competitive cricket to develop their abilities, and sound advice on diet and personal development.

This is the culture of excellence which alone will produce the self-perpetuating success on which Australians can now depend but which, at the other end of the scale, has been lost in the West Indian islands. In the Caribbean the supply line of cricketers was once as automatic as it now is in Australia and once was in England too. If you need a fast bowler, they used to say in Yorkshire, whistle down a mine shaft. If you needed one in the West Indies, it was a matter of combing the nearest beach for natural talent. But satellite television from the United States of America showed basketball, not cricket, tempting tall and athletic youngsters to something different. Meanwhile, the great teams which carried the West Indies to twenty-nine series without a defeat between 1980 and 1995 finally ran out of steam. Standards of technique, fitness and discipline slipped and the winning habit was lost.

England have yet to create either the habit or the plentiful supply of fully prepared cricketers which would make that possible. Part of the process is the attempt to force the more serious club cricketers to play a harder form of the essentially friendly club cricket which has amused countless generations of British cricketers. The move towards premier leagues gathered pace in 1998 with clubs playing longer hours and slimming down the size of leagues so that only the strongest teams in the area remained. In Lancashire, where powerful traditional forces urged the continuation of leagues of long standing, amalgamations were being considered early in 1999 between the Northern League and the Liverpool Competition and also between the two most famous leagues, the Lancashire and Central Lancashire. The Birmingham League had already reorganised itself to take in the best clubs of Warwickshire and Worcestershire and in Kent the start of the 1999 season saw the first prolonged experiment in England of the kind of two-day club cricket which has long been the staple diet for serious recreational adult cricket in Australia, South Africa and the West Indies.

Kent's format, backed by a three-year sponsorship, allows the side batting first on a Saturday morning to continue for two sessions, or a minimum 68 overs, leaving the other side to start its first innings after tea and continue on the following Saturday. As in Australia, the main issue is fought over first innings but an 'outright' two-innings victory is possible.

Not every region believes the idea of premier leagues will necessarily improve standards. Tony Millard, secretary of the Sussex league, reported 'a stong groundswell of opinion that two-day cricket would actually lower quality. It will take out of top club cricket the married men with families who may be at their peak at around twenty-eight or twenty-nine. It would then become the tool of nineteen-year-olds playing against fellow nineteen-year-olds.' Millard added: 'I don't think there is much wrong with the development of cricketers up to the age of nineteen. We allegedly have some of the best in Sussex, but only Jim Parks, John Snow and Ted Dexter have become regular Test players since the war, which I think is evidence that things go wrong when nineteen-year-olds join the staff, too quickly think they have made it and then shelter under the first-class umbrella and prepare for a possible benefit.'

There is much truth in this. It is in the professional game, therefore, that excellence has to be promoted with even greater determination in all aspects. There are clear signs that it is starting to happen. By employing their players all the year round and offering them help in off-the-field skills to improve their prospects of alternative employment in due course, Lancashire recently set a trend which other counties may follow if they can afford it.

England and Australia are the only countries who routinely make money from Test cricket and the new chairman of the powerful England Management Committee, Brian Bolus, is one of many who believe that the reason is that until now international cricket in England has been sensibly rationed.

Bolus promised to tread warily at first when he took over in January 1999 after defeating the former incumbent, Bob Bennett of Lancashire, by eleven votes to eight, but he could be expected to keep a keen eye on what the ECB are spending and on the discipline and public relations of the England side. Above all, as a believer in the essential worth and attraction of county cricket, Bolus wanted to stress the interdependence of England and the counties. He had no wish, he said, 'to drive any wedge between rich counties and the rest'.

Behind that sentiment lay a battle between the smaller counties, reliant on the money from the central pool, and the Test grounds, who formed themselves into a consortium in September 1998 to negotiate with the ECB for greater profits from the international matches they staged – not least so that they could reinvest in grounds which Jim Cumbes, the Lancashire chief executive, described as 'dilapidated'. All things are relative, but there is ample proof from other sports that well-appointed new stadiums invariably attract new spectators and bigger, more contented crowds generally. This too, needs to be a part of changing the culture.

Just as counties and the England players have to work together for mutual benefit in future, so does England have to fit sensibly into the rapidly changing world order. As the only Test country with a home season between April and September, England is particularly vulnerable to the dangers of overkill in international cricket and the swift burn-out of leading players. But the others are not immune. In the space of a few months in 1998 there was an Asia Cup in Bangladesh, a Sahara Cup in Toronto, a President's Cup in Kenya, a Wills Quadrangular tournament in Pakistan and the Champions Trophy in Sharjah.

For many years it has been obvious that the ICC should have been cutting back on these spurious one-day competitions, but television money and the greed of the relatively few people who make a great deal of money from them – not to mention the gamblers who exploit them – have prevented proper control of both quality and quantity. The result has been a decline in Test crowds in some parts of the world, notably New Zealand and Pakistan. In South Africa, returning to the fold when the habit of watching Test cricket had been lost, and Zimbabwe and Sri Lanka, where it had not existed until their promotion to the top flight, it is generally only the one-day internationals which attract really large crowds.

The move to create a World Test Championship – probably with a rolling league followed by play-offs every four years – may be unstoppable now, but it is essentially artificial and it would not be necessary if every Test captain played to win with the same vigour and invention of Australian sides in the Taylor era.

A simple limit on the number of Tests and, more urgently, of one-day internationals each year must be imposed upon all by mutual agreement. It has not helped, perhaps, that the chairman of the ICC after Clyde Walcott was Jagmohan Dalmiya, the Calcutta businessman who has seen nothing wrong – and much that is commercially attractive – in the explosion of one-day internationals. The fact remains that under Walcott, Colin Cowdrey before him and MCC presidents for many years before, no one was prepared to see the danger of overkill, to draw a line in the desert and proclaim 'thus far and no further'.

At least the ICC is now trying to do that as far as the conduct of matches is concerned. The growing evidence that there was match-fixing for a time in certain matches in the 1990s belatedly obliged the ICC to set up its own independent commission of inquiry and the world body is now officially empowered to deal with serious disciplinary matters like this.

The hearing after Arjuna Ranatunga's violation of the Code of Conduct in Adelaide, however, demonstrated that more needs to be done to ensure that cricket can regulate itself without being dominated by lawyers. Peter van der Merwe was the independent ICC referee who found himself unable to administer the punishment he felt appropriate to the Sri Lankan captain's behaviour. Referring after the hearing to the Code of Conduct, he said: 'This little green book was drawn up by cricketers, for cricketers, to be administered by cricketers. However, in this instance it was a great disappointment, and very complicated, to find that legal people were in prominence at this hearing. I have no doubt that the ICC will take heed of how this hearing had to be conducted and that this green book will find a lot of amendments in the next edition.'

A seven-point preamble defining the spirit of the game will precede the new code of cricket laws when it is published in 2000. Stressing that any action which abuses the spirit causes injury to the game itself, the preamble will begin by reiterating the responsibility of captains for 'ensuring the spirit of fair play'.

All who play cricket from an early age will in future be reminded at the very outset of the laws that the spirit involves respect for opponents, captains, team-mates, umpires and 'the game's traditional values'. Point six states unequivocally that there is no place for any act of violence on the field of play and the preamble also forbids disputing an umpire's decision by word, action or gesture, directing abusive language towards an opponent or umpire, appealing knowing the batsman is not out and seeking to distract an opponent either verbally or by harassment with persistent clapping or unnecessary noise under the guise of enthusiasm or motivation of one's own side.

An MCC working party chaired by Lord Griffiths of Govilon, the former Cambridge and Glamorgan fast bowler and MCC president, has been engaged in rewriting the laws, with the assistance of a parallel committee comprised of at least one representative from all the Test nations. When Bobby Simpson saw the draft of the proposed preamble he asked Lord Griffiths if it would actually be part of the laws. The reply was that it would have the same effect as the preamble to any statute of English law. In the words of the committee's secretary, John Jameson, 'If anything in the laws refers back to the preamble, the preamble becomes the law.'

The initiative came from Lord Cowdrey, chairman of the MCC cricket committee which is overseeing the new code. It is due to be ratified in May 2000. No startling changes in the laws themselves are expected, although the one about the ball being lost – the seldom-invoked Law 20 which gives batsmen the right to run more than six before 'lost ball' is called – is bound to be updated. Jameson said: 'We are trying to strengthen Law 42 in respect of short-pitched bowling and beamers, but we are doing this really for 98 per cent of cricketers who do not play as professionals. Regulations for Tests or professional competitions can be drawn up to adapt or reinforce the laws.'

No one disputes that life is harder for professional cricketers now because of the invasive influence of television. First viewers see an 'incident' – possibly one which would have gone unnoticed by spectators on the ground – in close-up; then a succession of repeats, spiced by the observations of the commentators. This, however, only increases the responsibility of players to preserve the tradition of fair play which, although often honoured more in the breach than the observance, is still essential to cricket's well-being.

The MCC's attempt to put a stop to the deterioration in standards of behaviour is unlikely to put the clock back to a time when hostility on the cricket fields was both less open and also less exposed to the public gaze via the hounding lens of the television camera; but it will remind the players who set the standards, the professionals and especially the captains, of their responsibility. In the highly commercialised world of contemporary professional cricket it is self-regulation which is, in the end, the answer. If everyone played the game as Mark Taylor did, with aggression but also fairness and enterprise, there would be little need for hearings or lawyers.

Appendix

compiled by FRANK WHEELDON

The England Test Party

	Age	Caps	Tours to Australia
A. J. Stewart (capt., Surrey)	35	81	1990–91, 1994–95
N. Hussain (vice-capt., Essex)	30	34	
M. A. Atherton (Lancashire)	30	84	1990–91, 1994–95 (capt)
M. A. Butcher (Surrey)	26	14	1996–97 (Eng A)
D. G. Cork (Derbyshire)	27	25	1992–93 (Eng A)
J. P. Crawley (Lancashire)	27	26	1994–95
R. D. B. Croft (Glamorgan)	28	14	
A. R. C. Fraser (Middlesex)	33	44	1990–91, 1994–95
D. Gough (Yorkshire)	28	26	1994–95
D. W. Headley (Kent)	28*	10	1996–97 (Eng A)
W. K. Hegg (w/k, Lancashire)	30	0	1996–97 (Eng A)
B. C. Hollioake (Surrey)	20*	2	
A. D. Mullally (Leicestershire)	29	9	
M. R. Ramprakash (Middlesex)	29	29	1994–95
G. P. Thorpe (Surrey)	29	52	1992–93 (Eng A), 1994–95
A. J. Tudor (Surrey)	20*	0	

N.B. The ages in the above table are as at 1 October 1998.
The players with a * alongside their age had a birthday whilst on tour.
Tudor, 23 October; Hollioake, 11 November; Headley, 27 January.

Tour Match Details

29 Oct (Lilac Hill)
England 297–5 (50 overs, M. A. Atherton 88, A. J. Stewart 74, J. P. Crawley 64), ACB XI 296 (50, R. J. Campbell 74). England won by 1 run.

31 Oct–2 Nov (Perth)
Western Australia 334–8dec (S. M. Katich 106, J. L. Langer 85, M. Nicholson 58 n.o.; D. Gough 4–74) & 268–3 dec (R. J. Campbell 146), England 321 (N. Hussain 118, M. R. Ramprakash 81; M. Nicholson 7–77) & 192–4 (J. P. Crawley 65, G. P. Thorpe 64 n.o.). Match drawn.

7–10 Nov (Adelaide)
England 187 (N. Hussain 57, D. G. Cork 51) & 457–4 (G. P. Thorpe 233 n.o., M. R. Ramprakash 140 n.o., M. A. Atherton 53), South Australia 325 (G. S. Blewett 143, J. M. Vaughan 58; D. G. Cork 4–45). Match drawn.

13–16 Nov (Cairns)
Queensland 209 (D. I. Foley 71, I. A. Healy 57) & 124 (J. P. Maher 56), England 192 (A. J. Stewart 52; A. C. Dale 7–33) & 142–9 (M. S. Kasprowicz 6–31). England won by 1 wkt.

5–8 Dec (Melbourne)
England 373 (A. J. Stewart 126, M. R. Ramprakash 78, G. A. Hick 67) & 207–5 dec (J. P. Crawley 68), Victoria 300 (S. A. J. Craig 83 n.o., P. J. Roach 80; D. W. Headley 5–58) & 245–8 (G. R. Vimpani 72, B. J. Hodge 50). Match drawn.

17 Dec (Canberra)
England 225–8 (50 overs), Prime Minister's XI 209 (48.4, D. J. Marsh 74). England won by 16 runs.

19–22 Dec (Hobart)
England 469–6 dec (M. A. Atherton 210 n.o., G. A. Hick 125, M. R. Ramprakash 65) & 199–3 dec (M. A. Butcher 103 n.o.), Australian XI 293–4 dec (G. S. Blewett 169 n.o., M .T. G. Elliott 81) & 376–1 (G. S. Blewett 213 n.o., C. J. Richards 138 n.o.). Australian XI won by 9 wkts.

Summary:

	Won	Drawn	Lost
First Class	1	3	1
One Day	2	0	0

First Test Match
Woolloongabba, Brisbane. Match drawn
20, 21, 22, 23, 24 November 1998. Australia won toss
Umpires: K. T. Francis (Sri Lanka) & D. B. Hair

AUSTRALIA	*First Innings*		R	B	M	4
*M. A. Taylor	c Hussain	b Cork	46	135	190	6
M. J. Slater	c Butcher	b Mullally	16	40	66	2
J. L. Langer	lbw	b Gough	8	43	55	–
M. E. Waugh	c Stewart	b Mullally	31	50	65	3
S. R. Waugh	c Stewart	b Mullally	112	232	330	13
R. T. Ponting	c Butcher	b Cork	21	61	93	1
+I. A. Healy	c Mullally	b Fraser	134	229	303	14
M. S. Kasprowicz	c Stewart	b Mullally	0	3	2	–
D. W. Fleming	not out		71	108	108	11
S. C. G. MacGill	c Stewart	b Mullally	20	30	30	4
G. D. McGrath	c Atherton	b Croft	5	24	35	–
Extras (lb 14, w 1, nb 6)			21			
Total (158 overs)			485			

Fall of wickets: 1–30 (MJS), 2–59 (JLL), 3–106 (MEW), 4–106 (MAT), 5–178 (RTP), 6–365 (SRW), 7–365 (MSK), 8–420 (IAH), 9–445 (SCJM), 10–485 (GDM)

Bowling
Gough	34	4	135	1
Cork	31	6	98	2
Mullally	40	10	105	5
Croft	23	6	55	1
Fraser	28	7	76	1
Ramprakash	2	1	2	0

ENGLAND	*First Innings*		R	B	M	4
M. A. Butcher	caught and	b M. Waugh	116	236	278	16
M. A. Atherton	c M. Waugh	b McGrath	0	14	16	–
N. Hussain	c Healy	b Kasprowicz	59	99	141	10
**+A. J. Stewart	c Kasprowicz	b MacGill	8	9	13	1
G. P. Thorpe	c Langer	b McGrath	77	169	195	7
M. R. Ramprakash	not out		69	164	238	6
D. G. Cork	c MacGill	b McGrath	0	11	14	–
R. D. B. Croft		b Kasprowicz	23	48	49	3
D. Gough	lbw	b McGrath	0	23	23	–
A. D. Mullally	c Kasprowicz	b McGrath	0	1	1	–
A. R. C. Fraser	c M. Waugh	b McGrath	1	7	5	–
Extras (b 1, lb 9, nb 12)			22			
Total (128.2 overs)			375			

Fall of wickets: 1–11 (MAA), 2–145 (NH), 3–168 (AJS), 4–240 (MAB), 5–315 (GPT), 6–319 (DGC), 7–360 (RDBC), 8–372 (DG), 9–372 (ADM), 10–375 (ARCF)

Bowling
McGrath	34.2	11	85	6
Fleming	27	5	83	0
Kasprowicz	29	6	83	2
MacGill	24	5	69	1
S. R. Waugh	3	0	17	0
Ponting	3	0	10	0
M. E. Waugh	8	1	18	1

	Second Innings		R	B	M	4	6
(2)		b Cork	0	5	3	–	–
(1)	caught and	b Fraser	113	139	178	13	1
	c Mullally	b Croft	74	149	199	8	–
	not out		27	54	70	1	–
	not out		16	30	45	–	–

(b 1, lb 1, nb 5)   7
(3 wkts dec, 62 overs)   237

1–20 (MAT), 2–182 (MJS), 3–199 (JLL)

6	0	50	0
5	0	18	1
14	4	38	0
(5) 20	2	71	1
(4) 15	1	52	1
2	0	6	0

	Second Innings		R	B	M	4	6
	lbw	b MacGill	40	98	132	4	–
	c Fleming	b McGrath	28	55	59	4	–
		b MacGill	47	122	145	1	2
	c Ponting	b M. Waugh	3	8	9	–	–
	c Langer	b M. Waugh	9	27	39	–	–
	st Healy	b MacGill	14	45	39	1	–
	not out		21	37	52	3	–
	not out		4	25	38	–	–

(lb 3, w 1, nb 9)   13
(6 wkts, 68 overs)   179

1–46 (MAA), 2–96 (MAB), 3–110 (AJS),
4–133 (GPT), 5–148 (NH), 6–161 (MRR)

16	6	30	1
(3) 7	2	12	0
(2) 8	3	28	0
22	3	51	3
1	1	0	0
(5) 14	0	55	2

Second Test Match
WACA, Perth. Australia won by 7 wickets
28, 29, 30 November 1998. Australia won toss
Umpires: D. J. Harper & S. Venkataraghaven (India)

ENGLAND	*First Innings*		R	B	M	4
M. A. Butcher	c Healy	b Fleming	0	10	14	–
M. A. Atherton	c Healy	b McGrath	1	18	26	–
N. Hussain	c Healy	b McGrath	6	24	28	–
*+A. J. Stewart		b McGrath	38	29	58	4
M. R. Ramprakash	c Taylor	b Fleming	26	60	97	1
J. P. Crawley	c M. Waugh	b Gillespie	4	17	22	–
G. A. Hick	c Healy	b Gillespie	0	2	2	–
D. G. Cork	c Taylor	b Fleming	2	13	13	–
A. J. Tudor	not out		18	30	49	1
D. Gough	c M. Waugh	b Fleming	11	24	23	–
A. D. Mullally	c Healy	b Fleming	0	9	10	–
Extras (lb 2, w 2, nb 2)			6			
Total (39 overs)			112			

Fall of wickets: 1–2 (MAB), 2–4 (MAA), 3–119 (NH), 4–62 (AJS), 5–74 (JPC), 6–74 (GAH), 7–81 (DGC), 8–90 (MRR), 9–108 (DG), 10–112 (ADM).

Bowling
McGrath	16	4	37	3
Fleming	14	3	46	5
Gillespie	7	0	23	2
Miller	2	0	4	0

AUSTRALIA	*First Innings*		R	B	M	4
*M. A. Taylor	c Stewart	b Cork	61	144	188	6
M. J. Slater	c Butcher	b Gough	34	70	102	6
J. L. Langer	c Crawley	b Ramprakash	15	40	55	2
M. E. Waugh	c Butcher	b Tudor	36	128	204	4
J. N. Gillespie	c Stewart	b Mullally	11	71	85	–
S. R. Waugh		b Tudor	33	61	78	6
R. T. Ponting	c Stewart	b Tudor	11	16	30	–
+I. A. Healy	lbw	b Gough	12	7	5	2
D. W. Fleming	c Hick	b Gough	0	1	1	–
C. R. Miller	not out		3	4	13	–
G. D. McGrath	c Cork	b Tudor	0	2	2	–
Extras (b 1, lb 10, nb 13)			24			
Total (89.2 overs)			240			

Fall of wickets: 1–81 (MJS), 2–115 (JLL), 3–138 (MAT), 4–165 (JNG), 5–209 (SRW), 6–214 (MEW), 7–229 (IAH), 8–228 (DWF), 9–240 (RTP), 10–240 (GDM).

Bowling
Gough	25	9	43	3
Cork	21	6	49	1
Tudor	20.2	5	89	4
Mullally	21	10	36	1
Ramprakash	2	0	12	1

	Second Innings		R	B	M	4	6
	c Ponting	b Fleming	1	15	14	–	–
	c Taylor	b Fleming	35	56	82	6	–
	lbw	b Fleming	1	14	14	–	–
	c Taylor	b Fleming	0	5	6	–	–
	not out		47	183	270	5	–
	c Langer	b Miller	15	45	62	–	–
	c Ponting	b Gillespie	68	73	99	8	2
	lbw	b Gillespie	16	31	47	1	–
	c Healy	b Gillespie	0	2	2	–	–
	lbw	b Gillespie	0	1	1	–	–
		b Gillespie	0	4	6	–	–
	(nb 8)		8				
	(70.2 overs)		191				

1–5 (MAB), 2–11 (NH), 3–15 (AJS), 4–40 (MAA), 5–67 (JPC), 6–158 (GAH), 7–189 (DGC), 8–189 (AJT), 9–189 (DG), 10–191 (ADM)

26	10	47	0
19	7	45	4
15.2	2	88	5
10	4	11	1

	Second Innings		R	B	M	4
(2)	c Hick	b Mullally	3	15	22	–
(1)	caught and	b Gough	17	38	40	1
	c Atherton	b Tudor	7	21	40	–
	not out		17	37	57	2
(5)	not out		15	29	35	2
	(lb 3, nb 2)		5			
	(3 wkts, 23 overs)		64			

1–16 (MAT), 2–24 (MJS), 3–36 (JLL)

	9	5	18	1
	5	0	19	1
(2)	9	0	24	1

261

Third Test Match
Adelaide Oval. Australia won by 205 runs
11, 12, 13, 14, 15 December 1998. Australia won toss
Umpires: S. A. Bucknor (West Indies) & S. J. Davis

AUSTRALIA		First Innings	R	B	M	4	6
M. J. Slater	c Stewart	b Headley	17	37	52	1	–
*M. A. Taylor	c Hussain	b Such	59	124	186	5	–
J. L. Langer	not out		179	350	491	13	–
M. E. Waugh	caught and	b Such	7	30	35	–	–
S. R. Waugh	c Hick	b Gough	59	109	148	4	1
R. T. Ponting	c Hick	b Gough	5	28	33	–	–
+I. A. Healy	c Ramprakash	b Headley	13	27	39	1	–
D. W. Fleming	lbw	b Headley	12	23	29	2	–
S. C. G. MacGill		b Such	0	4	5	–	–
C. R. Miller	lbw	b Headley	11	9	13	2	–
G. D. McGrath	c Stewart	b Gough	10	27	47	1	–
Extras (lb 6, nb 13)			19				
Total (125.5 overs)			391				

Fall of wickets: 1–28 (MJS), 2–140 (MAT), 3–156 (MEW), 4–264 (SRW), 5–274 (RTP), 6–311 (IAH), 7–338 (DWF), 8–339 (SCGM), 9–354 (CRM), 10–391 (GDM)

Bowling
Gough	29.5	4	103	3
Mullally	26	5	59	0
Headley	23	1	97	4
Such	38	8	99	3
Ramprakash	9	1	27	0
Hick				

ENGLAND		First Innings	R	B	M	4	6
M. A. Butcher	lbw	b Miller	6	35	46	–	–
M. A. Atherton	c Taylor	b MacGill	41	92	108	2	–
N. Hussain	not out		89	204	262	8	–
*+A. J. Stewart	c Slater	b Miller	0	3	3	–	–
M. R. Ramprakash	c M. Waugh	b McGrath	61	120	134	6	2
J. P. Crawley		b McGrath	5	20	24	1	–
G. A. Hick	c Taylor	b MacGill	8	16	17	2	–
D. W. Headley	lbw	b MacGill	0	1	2	–	–
D. Gough	c Healy	b MacGill	7	5	8	1	–
A. D. Mullally		b Fleming	0	5	4	–	–
P. M. Such	lbw	b Fleming	0	1	2	–	–
Extras (b 1, lb 3, w 1, nb 5)			10				
Total (82.5 overs)			227				

Fall of wickets: 1–18 (MAB), 2–83 (MAA), 3–84 (AJS), 4–187 (MRR), 5–195 (JPC), 6–210 (GAH), 7–210 (DWH), 8–226 (DG), 9–227 (ADM), 10–227 (PMS)

Bowling
McGrath	18	4	48	2
Fleming	10.5	2	34	2
Miller	23	6	71	2
MacGill	28	6	53	4
M. E. Waugh	3	0	17	0
S. R. Waugh				

	Second Innings		R	B	M	4	6
(2)	lbw	b Gough	103	191	274	8	1
(1)	lbw	b Such	29	71	88	3	–
	c sub+	b Such	52	183	227	2	–
	not out		51	83	126	5	–
	c Hick	b Headley	7	22	21	–	–
		b Gough	10	30	42	1	–
	not out		7	13	20	–	–

(lb 12, w 1, nb 6) 19
(5 wkts dec, 98 overs) 278
+ sub (B. C. Hollioake)
1–54 (MAT), 2–188 (MJS), 3–216 (JLL),
4–230 (SRW), 5–268 (RTP)

22	2	76	2
16	6	18	0
18	1	78	1
29	5	66	2
12	1	27	0
1	0	1	0

	Second Innings		R	B	M	4	6
	c Healy	b Fleming	19	39	49	–	–
	c M. Waugh	b Miller	5	43	56	–	–
	lbw	b Miller	41	97	133	4	–
(6)	not out		63	122	148	6	–
(4)		b Fleming	57	173	186	2	–
(7)	c M. Waugh	b McGrath	13	53	68	1	–
(8)	c Ponting	b McGrath	0	1	2	–	–
(5)	c M. Waugh	b Miller	2	4	3	–	–
	c Healy	b McGrath	3	9	9	–	–
	c Healy	b Fleming	4	3	5	1	–
	lbw	b McGrath	0	4	6	–	–
	(b 7, lb 9, nb 14)		30				
	(89 overs)		237				

1–27 (MAB), 2–31 (MAA), 3–120 (NH), 4–122 (DWH), 5–163 (MRR), 6–221 (JPC),
7–221 (GAH), 8–231 (DG), 9–236 (ADM), 10–237 (PMS)

	17	0	50	4
	21	3	56	3
	24	1	57	3
	25	8	55	0
(5)	2	1	3	0

Fourth Test Match

MCG, Melbourne. England won by 12 runs.
26, 27, 28, 29 December 1998. Australia won toss
Umpires: D. J. Harper & S. A. Bucknor (West Indies)

ENGLAND		*First Innings*	R	B	M	4	6
M. A. Atherton	c Healy	b McGrath	0	5	3	–	–
*A. J. Stewart		b McGill	107	160	212	16	–
M. A. Butcher	c Langer	b McGrath	0	7	8	–	–
N. Hussain	c Healy	b Nicholson	19	56	83	2	–
M. R. Ramprakash	c McGrath	b S. Waugh	63	92	119	5	–
G. A. Hick	c Fleming	b MacGill	39	67	83	3	1
+W. K. Hegg	c Healy	b S. Waugh	3	8	6	–	–
D. W. Headley	c Taylor	b McGrath	14	49	52	–	–
D. Gough		b MacGill	11	14	21	2	–
A. R. C. Fraser	not out		0	2	11	–	–
A. D. Mullally	lbw	b MacGill	0	5	3	–	–
Extras (lb 7, w 1, nb 6)			14				
Total (76 overs)			270				

Fall of wickets: 1–0 (MAA), 2–4 (MAB), 3–81 (NH), 4–200 (AJS), 5–202 (MRR), 6–206 (WKH), 7–244 (DWH), 8–266 (GAH), 9–270 (DG), 10–270 (ADM)

Bowling
McGrath	22	5	64	3
Fleming	19	3	71	0
Nicholson	10	0	59	1
MacGill	19	2	61	4
S. R. Waugh	6	2	8	2
M. E. Waugh				

AUSTRALIA		*First Innings*	R	B	M	4
*M. A. Taylor	c Hick	b Gough	7	29	44	–
M J. Slater	lbw	b Gough	1	14	18	–
J. L. Langer	c Hussian	b Gough	44	103	168	5
M. E. Waugh	lbw	b Fraser	36	68	91	3
S. R. Waugh	not out		122	197	315	13
D. S. Lehmann	c Hegg	b Gough	13	23	28	2
+I. A. Healy	c Headley	b Fraser	36	55	68	3
D. W. Fleming	c Hick	b Mullally	12	30	41	2
M. J. Nicholson		b Gough	5	18	23	–
S. C. G. MacGill	c Hegg	b Mullally	43	63	98	3
G. D. McGrath		b Mullally	0	2	2	–
Extras (b 4, lb 6, nb 11)			21			
Total (98.3 overs)			340			

Fall of wickets: 1–13 (MJS), 2–26 (MAT), 3–98 (MEW), 4–127 (JLL), 5–151 (DSL), 6–209 (IAH), 7–235 (DWF), 8–252 (MJN), 9–340 (SCGM), 10–340 (GDM)

Bowling
Gough	28	7	96	5
Headley	25	3	86	0
Mullally	21.3	5	64	3
Ramprakash	2	0	6	0
Fraser	22	0	78	2

	Second Innings		R	B	M	4	6
		b Fleming	0	9	8	–	–
	c Slater	b MacGill	52	98	120	4	–
	c Slater	b MacGill	14	45	67	1	–
(5)	c Slater	b Nicholson	50	131	157	6	–
(6)		b Nicholson	14	43	66	–	–
(7)		b Fleming	60	82	123	8	–
(8)	c MacGill	b Nicholson	9	21	28	1	–
(4)		b McGrath	1	15	21	–	–
	c Slater	b MacGill	4	14	20	–	–
	not out		7	20	25	–	–
	caught and	b McGrath	16	15	21	–	–
	(b 2, lb 4, nb 11)		17				
	(80.2 overs)		244				

1–5 (MAA), 2–61 (MAB), 3–66 (DWH), 4–78 (AJS), 5–127 (MRR), 6–178 (NH), 7–202 (WKH), 8–221 (DG), 9–221 (GAH), 10–244 (ADM)

20.2	5	56	2
17	4	45	2
15	4	56	3
27	3	81	3
(5)	1	1	0	0

	Second Innings		R	B	M	4
(2)	c Headley	b Mullally	19	33	49	1
(1)	lbw	b Headley	18	23	25	3
	c Ramprakash	b Mullally	30	53	105	3
	c Hick	b Headley	43	81	116	3
	not out		30	49	108	2
	c Hegg	b Headley	4	7	11	1
	c Hick	b Headley	0	2	8	–
	lbw	b Headley	0	3	3	–
	c Hegg	b Headley	9	29	41	–
		b Gough	0	2	3	–
	lbw	b Gough	0	2	3	–
	(b 4, lb 1, nb 4)		9			
	(46.4 overs)		162			

1–31 (MJS), 2–41 (MAT), 3–103 (JLL), 4–130 (MEW), 5–140 (DSL), 6–140 (IAH), 7–140 (DWF), 8–161 (MJN), 9–162 (SCGM), 10–162 (GDM)

15.4	2	54	2
17	5	60	6
10	4	20	2
(4)	4	0	23	0

Fifth Test Match
SCG, Sydney. Australia won by 98 runs.
2, 3, 4, 5 January 1999. Australia won toss
Umpires: R. S. Dunne (New Zealand) & D. B. Hair

AUSTRALIA	*First Innings*		R	B	M	4
*M. A. Taylor	c Hick	b Headley	2	8	13	–
M. J. Slater	c Hegg	b Headley	18	35	62	2
J. L. Langer	c Ramprakash	b Tudor	26	39	54	2
M. E. Waugh	c Hegg	b Headley	121	205	294	10
S. R. Waugh		b Such	96	171	201	9
D. S. Lehmann	c Hussian	b Tudor	32	37	44	5
+I. A. Healy	c Hegg	b Gough	14	28	48	1
S. K. Warne	not out		2	7	14	–
S. C. G. MacGill		b Gough	0	1	2	–
C. R. Miller		b Gough	0	1	2	–
G. D. McGrath	c Hick	b Headley	0	2	2	–
Extras (lb 2, nb 9)			11			
Total (87.3 overs)			322			

Fall of wickets: 1–4 (MAT), 2–52 (MJS), 3–52 (JLL), 4–242 (SRW), 5–284 (DSL),
6–319 (MEW), 7–321 (IAH), 8–321 (SCGM), 9–321 (CRM), 10–322 (GDM)

Bowling				
Gough	17	4	61	3
Headley	19.3	3	62	4
Tudor	12	1	64	2
Such	24	6	77	1
Ramprakash	15	0	56	0

ENGLAND	*First Innings*		R	B	M	4	6
M. A. Butcher	lbw	b Warne	36	70	90	4	–
*A. J. Stewart	c Warne	b McGrath	3	17	28	–	–
N. Hussain	c M. Waugh	b Miller	42	126	174	4	–
M. R. Ramprakash	c MacGill	b McGrath	14	42	52	1	–
G. A. Hick	c Warne	b MacGill	23	38	55	3	1
J. P. Crawley	c Taylor	b MacGill	44	75	116	5	–
+W. K. Hegg		b Miller	15	50	52	–	–
A. J. Tudor		b MacGill	14	40	43	2	–
D. W. Headley	c McGrath	b MacGill	8	20	25	1	–
D. Gough	lbw	b MacGill	0	2	2	–	–
P. M. Such	not out		0	4	6	–	–
Extras (b 8, lb 8, w 1, nb 4)			21				
Total (80.1 overs)			220				

Fall of wickets: 1–18 (AJS), 2–56 (MAB), 3–88 (MRR), 4–137 (GAH), 5–139 (NH), 6–171 (WKH),
7–204 (AJT), 8–213 (JPC), 9–213 (DG), 10–220 (DWH)

Bowling				
McGrath	17	7	35	2
Miller	23	6	45	2
MacGill	20.1	2	57	5
Warne	20	4	67	1

	Second Innings		R	B	M	4	6
(2)	c Stewart	b Gough	2	25	30	–	–
(1)	c Hegg	b Headley	123	189	271	11	3
	lbw	b Headley	1	5	11	–	–
	c Ramprakash	b Headley	24	60	79	4	–
(7)		b Headley	8	29	37	1	–
(5)	c Crawley	b Such	0	8	12	–	–
(6)	c Crawley	b Such	5	26	36	–	–
	c Ramprakash	b Such	8	12	24	–	–
	c Butcher	b Such	6	24	46	–	–
	not out		3	9	15	–	–
	c Stewart	b Such	0	2	2	–	–
	(b 3, lb 1)		4				
	(64.5 overs)		184				

1–16 (MAT), 2–25 (JLL), 3–64 (MEW), 4–73 (DSL), 5–91 (IAH), 6–110 (SRW), 7–141 (SKW), 8–180 (MJS), 9–184 (SCGM), 10–184 (GDM)

(2)	15	3	51	1
(1)	19	7	40	4
(4)	5	2	8	0
(3)	25.5	5	81	6

	Second Innings		R	B	M	4	6
	st Healy	b Warne	27	47	60	3	–
	st Healy	b MacGill	42	55	83	5	–
	caught and	b MacGill	53	131	169	2	–
	c Taylor	b McGrath	14	46	60	1	–
		b MacGill	7	25	39	1	–
	lbw	b Miller	5	14	22	–	–
	c Healy	b MacGill	3	10	10	–	–
		b MacGill	3	21	28	–	–
	c Healy	b MacGill	16	23	25	2	–
	not out		7	16	19	1	–
	caught and	b MacGill	2	12	10	–	–
	(lb 5, w 1, nb 3)		9				
	(66.1 overs)		188				

1–57 (MAB), 2–77 (AJS), 3–110 (MRR), 4–131 (GAH), 5–150 (JPC), 6–157 (WKH), 7–162 (NH), 8–175 (AJT), 9–180 (DWH), 10–188 (PMS)

10	0	40	1
17	1	50	1
20.1	4	50	7
19	3	43	1

Averages

England

TEST MATCH BATTING	M	I	NO	RUNS	AVGE	HS	100	50	C
M. R. Ramprakash	5	10	2	379	47.38	69*	–	4	5
N. Hussain	5	10	1	407	45.22	89*	–	4	4
G. P. Thorpe	1	2	0	86	43.00	77	–	1	–
A. J. Stewart	5	10	1	316	35.11	107	1	2	11
R. D. B. Croft	1	2	1	27	27.00	23	–	–	–
M. A. Butcher	5	10	0	259	25.90	116	1	–	5
G. A. Hick	4	8	0	205	25.63	68	–	2	11
J. P. Crawley	3	6	0	86	14.33	44	–	–	3
M. A. Atherton	4	8	0	110	13.75	41	–	–	2
D. G. Cork	2	4	1	39	13.00	21*	–	–	1
A. J. Tudor	2	4	1	35	11.67	18*	–	–	–
A. R. C. Fraser	2	3	2	8	8.00	7*	–	–	1
W. K. Hegg	2	4	0	30	7.50	15	–	–	8
D. W. Headley	3	6	0	41	6.83	16	–	–	2
D. Gough	5	9	1	43	5.38	11	–	–	1
A. D. Mullally	4	7	0	20	2.86	16	–	–	2
P. M. Such	2	4	1	2	0.67	2	–	–	1

TEST MATCH BOWLING	OV	M	RUNS	WKTS	AVGE	B/B	5W	10W
D. W. Headley	121.3	20	423	19	22.26	6–60	1	–
A. J. Tudor	42.2	8	180	7	25.71	4–89	–	–
P. M. Such	116.5	24	323	11	29.36	5–81	1	–
A. D. Mullally	157.3	44	364	12	30.33	5–105	1	–
D. Gough	201.3	40	687	21	32.71	5–96	1	-
D. G. Cork	57.0	11	165	4	41.25	2–98	–	–
A. R. C. Fraser	69.0	8	229	4	57.25	2–78	–	–
R. D. B. Croft	43.0	8	126	2	63.00	1–55	–	–
M. R. Ramprakash	44.0	3	136	1	136.00	1–12	–	–
G. A. Hick	1.0	0	1	0		0–1	–	–

FIRST CLASS BATTING	M	I	NO	RUNS	AVGE	HS	100	50
G. P. Thorpe	4	8	3	438	87.60	223*	1	2
M. R. Ramprakash	10	19	3	845	52.81	140*	1	7
N. Hussain	9	18	1	724	42.58	118	1	5
G. A. Hick	6	11	1	412	41.20	125	1	3
A. J. Stewart	8	16	1	530	35.33	126	2	3
M. A. Atherton	8	15	1	438	31.28	210*	1	1
M. A. Butcher	9	17	2	396	26.40	116	2	–
J. P. Crawley	7	14	0	355	25.35	68	–	3
D. G. Cork	6	10	1	164	18.22	51	–	1
A. J. Tudor	4	5	1	68	17.00	33	–	–
R. D. B. Croft	4	6	3	46	15.33	23	–	–
W. K. Hegg	4	8	2	60	10.00	15	–	–
B. C. Hollioake	2	4	1	26	8.66	17	–	–
A. D. Mullally	6	10	2	68	8.50	25*	–	–
D. W. Headley	6	10	0	69	6.90	20	–	–
D. Gough	7	12	2	61	6.10	11	–	–
A. R. C. Fraser	6	6	2	18	4.50	8	–	–
P. M. Such	4	5	2	2	0.66	2	–	–

FIRST CLASS BOWLING	OV	M	RUNS	WKTS	AVGE	BEST	5w	10w
D. W. Headley	213.3	38	665	29	22.93	6–60	2	–
D. Gough	266.2	56	873	31	28.16	5–96	1	–
A. D. Mullally	220.3	61	509	19	28.27	5–10	1	–
R. D. B. Croft	162.0	32	488	15	32.53	3–56	–	–
D. G. Cork	162.2	35	475	12	39.58	4–45	–	–
A. J. Tudor	84.2	13	353	8	44.12	4–89	–	–
P. M. Such	169.4	33	530	12	44.16	5–81	1	–
B. C. Hollioake	44.0	3	212	4	53.00	2–55	–	–
M. R. Ramprakash	81.0	7	287	5	57.40	1–4	–	–
A. R. C. Fraser	193.0	33	630	8	78.75	3–57	–	–
G. A. Hick	5.0	0	26	0	–	0–0	–	–

Australia

TEST MATCH BATTING	M	I	NO	RUNS	AVGE	HS	100	50	C/S
S. R. Waugh	5	10	4	498	83.00	122*	2	2	–/–
M. E. Waugh	5	10	3	393	56.14	121	1	1	10/–
J. L. Langer	5	10	1	436	48.44	179*	1	2	4/–
M. J. Slater	5	10	0	460	46.00	123	3	–	5/–
I. A. Healy	5	8	1	221	31.57	134	1	–	16/3
D. W. Fleming	4	5	1	95	23.75	71*	–	1	2/–
M. A. Taylor	5	10	0	228	22.80	61	–	2	9/–
D. S. Lehmann	2	4	0	49	12.25	32	–	–	–/–
R. T. Ponting	3	4	0	47	11.75	21	–	–	4/–
S. C. G. MacGill	4	6	0	69	11.50	43	–	–	5/–
J. N. Gillespie	1	1	0	11	11.00	11	–	–	–/–
S. K. Warne	1	2	1	10	10.00	8	–	–	2/–
C. R. Miller	3	4	2	17	8.50	11	–	–	–/–
M. J. Nicholson	1	2	0	14	7.00	9	–	–	–/–
G. D. McGrath	5	7	0	15	2.14	10	–	–	3/–
M. S. Kasprowicz	1	1	0	0	–	–	–	–	2/–

TEST MATCH BOWLING	OV	M	RUNS	WKTS	AVGE	B/B	5w	10w
S. R. Waugh	11.0	3	28	2	14.00	2–8	–	–
J. N. Gillespie	22.2	2	111	7	15.86	5–88	1	–
S. C. G. MacGill	185.2	33	478	27	17.70	7–50	2	1
G. D. McGrath	196.4	53	492	24	20.50	6–85	1	–
D. W. Fleming	134.5	29	392	16	24.50	5–46	1	–
C. R. Miller	99.0	18	238	9	26.44	3–57	–	–
M. J. Nicholson	25.0	4	115	4	28.75	3–56	–	–
M. E. Waugh	26.0	2	90	3	30.00	2–55	–	–
M. S. Kasprowicz	37.0	10	110	2	55.00	2–82	–	–
S. K. Warne	39.0	7	110	2	55.00	1–43	–	–
R. T. Ponting	4.0	1	10	0	–	0–10	–	–

Test Match Milestones

1st (Brisbane)

Australia 485 (I. A. Healy 134, S. R. Waugh 112, D. W. Fleming 71; A. D. Mullally 5–105) & 237–3 dec (M. J. Slater 113, J. L. Langer 74). England 375 (M. A. Butcher 116, G. P. Thorpe 77, M. R. Ramprakash 69 n.o., N. Hussain 59; G. D. McGrath 6–85) & 179–6. Match drawn. M. A. Taylor played his 100th Test, Mullally took five wickets in an innings for the first time (10th Test). Fleming's score, in the first innings, was his highest in first-class matches.

Second (Perth)

England 112 (Fleming 5–46) & 191 (G. A. Hick 68; J. N. Gillespie 5–88, Fleming 4–45). Australia 240 (M. A. Taylor 61; A. J. Tudor 4–89) & 64–3. Australia won by 7 wkts. England's score of 112 was the lowest score they have recorded at Perth. Test début for A. J. Tudor (England) and Hick was playing in his 50th Test.

Third (Adelaide)

Australia 392 (Langer 179, Taylor 59, S. R. Waugh 59; D. W. Headley 4–97) & 278–5 dec (Slater 103, Langer 52, M. E. Waugh 51 n.o.). England 227 (Hussain 89, Ramprakash 61; S. C. G. MacGill 4–53) & 237 (A. J. Stewart 63 n.o., Ramprakash 57; McGrath 4–50). Australia won by 205 runs. Atherton reached 6,000 Test runs and Mullally recorded his fourth consecutive duck.

Fourth (Melbourne)

England 270 (Stewart 107, Ramprakash 63; MacGill 4–61) & 244 (Hick 60, Stewart 52, Hussain 50; MacGill 4–61). Australia 340 (S. R. Waugh 122 n.o.; D. Gough 5–96) & 162 (Headley 6–60). England won by 12 runs. No play possible on first day because of rain, only the sixth day's play lost in 91 tests at this venue. Débuts for W. K. Hegg (England) and M. J. Nicholson (Australia). Atherton recorded his first 'pair' in Test cricket, S. R. Waugh passed 7,000 Test runs.

Fifth (Sydney)

Australia 322 (M. E. Waugh 121, S. R. Waugh 96; Headley 4–62) & 184 (Slater 123; P. M. Such 5–81, Headley 4–40). England 220 (MacGill 5–57) & 188 (Hussain 53; MacGill 7–50). Australia won by 98 runs. Taylor won the toss for the fifth time in the series. Gough completed a hat-trick (Healy, MacGill and Miller were his victims), which was the first for England in an Ashes Test since Johnny Briggs in 1891–92, also at Sydney. Butcher passed 1,000 runs in Tests and McGrath took his 200th wicket. Taylor took his 157th catch to become the leading fielder in Test matches. The series ended without a single run out dismissal being given and with 35 ducks (Australia 15, England 20), which was one short of equalling the record for a five-Test series.

Carlton & United One-day Series

1st match: Australia v England
Brisbane, 10 January 1999
(England won toss): England won by 7 runs
Umpires: D. J. Harper and A. J. McQuillan
Débuts: V. J. Wells and M. W. Alleyne. Award: A. D. Mullally

ENGLAND			R	B	4	6	FOW
N. V. Knight	c Gilchrist	b McGrath	30	57	3	–	4–72
*+A. J. Stewart	lbw	b Dale	0	1	–	–	1–0
V. J. Wells		b Dale	10	22	1	–	2–29
G. A. Hick	c Gilchrist	b Fleming	8	14	1	–	3–42
N. H. Fairbrother		b McGrath	47	83	4	–	8–136
A. J. Hollioake	c Gilchrist	b Fleming	5	20	–	–	5–87
M. W. Alleyne	run out		2	3	–	–	6–93
M. A. Ealham	c Ponting	b Julian	14	31	–	1	7–122
R. D. B. Croft	not out		26	46	1	–	
D. Gough	not out		23	24	2	–	
A. D. Mullally			–				
Extras (lb 4, w 8, nb 1)			13				
Total (8 wkts, 50 overs)			178				

Bowling: McGrath 10–1–24–2; Dale 10–3–25–2; Fleming 10–0–33–2;
Julian 5–0–29–1; Warne 10–0–42–0; Blewett 5–0–21–0

AUSTRALIA (Target 153 from 36 overs)			R	B	4	6	FOW
M. E. Waugh	c Stewart	b Mullally	23	22	4	–	2–46
+A. C. Gilchrist		b Mullally	13	11	2	–	1–24
R. T. Ponting	c Hollioake	b Mullally	8	18	–	–	3–47
D. R. Martyn		b Mullally	0	8	–	–	5–48
G. S. Blewett	c Stewart	b Ealham	0	10	–	–	4–48
M. G. Bevan	not out		56	76	2	–	
B. P. Julian		b Croft	23	43	1	–	6–94
*S. K. Warne	run out		8	16	–	–	7–117
D. W. Fleming	c Mullally	b Croft	2	7	–	–	8–129
A. C. Dale		b Gough	4	4	–	–	9–142
G. D. McGrath	not out		1	1	–	–	
Extras (lb 2, w 5)			7				
Total (9 wkts, 36 overs)			145				

Bowling: Gough 6–0–47–1; Mullally 8–1–18–4; Ealham 7–1–16–1;
Hollioake 7–1–31–0; Croft 7–0–24–2; Alleyne 1–0–7–0

2nd match: Sri Lanka v England

Brisbane, 11 January 1999
(Sri Lanka won toss): England won by 4 wkts
Umpires: S. J. Davis and P. D. Parker
Débuts: None. Award: N. H. Fairbrother

SRI LANKA			R	B	4	6	FOW
S. T. Jayasuriya	c Hick	b Gough	1	2	–	–	1–2
+R. S. Kaluwitharana	c Headley	b Croft	58	61	5	–	2–99
M. S. Atapattu		b Hollioake	51	90	2	–	4–128
*A. Ranatunga	caught and	b Hollioake	0	2	–	–	3–102
H. P. Tillekeratne		not out	50	86	2	–	
R. S. Mahanama	c Knight	b Hollioake	2	6	–	–	5–139
U. D. U. Chandana	c Fairbrother	b Ealham	23	32	1	–	6–185
W. P. U. J. C. Vaas		b Mullally	5	16	–	–	7–200
G. P. Wickremasinghe		not out	7	5	1	–	
M. Muralitharan			–				
D. N. T. Zoysa			–				
Extras (b 1, lb 3, w 6)			10				
Total (7 wkts, 50 overs)			207				

Bowling: Gough 9–0–37–1; Mullally 10–2–35–1; Headley 5–1–22–0;
Ealham 6–0–33–1; Croft 10–0–44–1; Hollioake 10–0–32–3

ENGLAND			R	B	4	6	FOW
N. V. Knight	st Kaluwitharana	b Chandana	40	54	2	–	2–87
**+A. J. Stewart	run out		24	36	3	–	1–59
G. A. Hick	c Kaluwitharana	b Muralitharan	37	42	2	1	3–128
N. H. Fairbrother		not out	67	105	1	1	
A. J. Hollioake		b Muralitharan	1	5	–	–	4–130
M. W. Alleyne	st Kaluwitharana	b Muralitharan	18	50	–	–	5–187
M. A. Ealham	lbw	b Tillekeratne	1	2	–	–	6–190
R. D. B. Croft		not out	10	9	–	–	
D. W. Headley			–				
D. Gough			–				
A. D. Mullally			–				
Extras (lb 3, w 1, nb 6)			10				
Total (6 wkts, 49.3 overs)			208				

Bowling: Vaas 7.3–0–40–0; Zoysa 6–0–31–0; Wickremasinghe 4–0–16–0
Muralitharan 10–0–34–3; Chandana 10–1–41–1; Jayasuriya 10–1–35–0
Tillekeratne 2–0–8–1

3rd match: Sri Lanka v Australia
Sydney, 13 January 1999
(Sri Lanka won toss): Australia won by 8 wkts
Umpires: T. A. Prue and S. J. A. Taufel
Débuts: None. Award: A. C. Gilchrist

SRI LANKA			R	B	4	6	FOW
S. T. Jayasuriya	c Gilchrist	b Julian	65	62	9	–	1–95
+R. S. Kaluwitharana		b Warne	32	38	5	–	2–106
M. S. Atapattu	c M. Waugh	b Warne	18	23	1	–	3–130
H. P. Tillekeratne	run out		73	95	3	–	8–258
*A. Ranatunga	run out		26	39	1	–	4–183
D. P. M. Jayawardene	c Gilchrist	b Julian	11	21	–	–	5–214
U. D. U. Chandana		b Fleming	2	6	–	–	6–217
R. S. Mahanama	c Gilchrist	b McGrath	5	7	–	–	7–226
W. P. U. J. C. Vaas		not out	13	14	1	–	
M. Muralitharan	run out		0	0	–	–	9–259
G. P. Wickremasinghe			–				
Extras (b 2, lb 2, w 5, nb 5)			14				
Total (9 wkts, 50 overs)			259				

Bowling: McGrath 10–0–39–1; Fleming 10–0–61–1; Blewett 2–0–23–0;
Julian 8–0–42–2; Warne 10–1–44–2; Bevan 5–0–26–0; Martyn 5–0–20–0

AUSTRALIA			R	B	4	6	FOW
+A. C. Gilchrist	c Atapattu	b Vaas	131	118	10	2	2–225
M. E. Waugh	c sub	b Muralitharan	63	76	3	–	1–151
R. T. Ponting		not out	43	59	2	1	
D. R. Martyn		not out	16	24	2	–	
G. S. Blewett			–				
M. G. Bevan			–				
*S. K. Warne			–				
B. P. Julian			–				
D. W. Fleming			–				
B. E. Young			–				
G. D. McGrath			–				
Extras (lb 3, w 4)			7				
Total (2 wkts, 46.1 overs)			260				

Bowling: Vaas 6–1–43–1; Wickremasinghe 7–1–36–0; Muralitharan 10–0–49–1; Jayasuriya 7.1–0–28–0;
Jayawardene 7–0–40–0; Chandana 9–0–61–0

4th match: Australia v England
Melbourne, 15 January 1999
(England won toss): Australia won by 9 wkts
Umpires: R. A. Emerson and D. B. Hair
Débuts: None. Award: M. E. Waugh

ENGLAND			R	B	4	6	FOW
N. V. Knight	c M Waugh	b Warne	27	29	3	–	3–77
**†A. J. Stewart	c Gilchrist	b McGrath	8	16	1	–	1–15
M. A. Ealham		b McGrath	21	19	3	1	2–44
N. Hussain	c Warne	b McGrath	47	62	5	–	8–145
G. A. Hick	c Gilchrist	b Fleming	3	13	–	–	4–85
N. H. Fairbrother	c Bevan	b Dale	15	40	2	–	5–112
A. J. Hollioake	c Gilchrist	b McGrath	13	16	1	–	6–139
R. D. B. Croft	run out		2	9	–	–	7–143
D. Gough	c M Waugh	b Bevan	15	28	1	–	9–173
D. W. Headley		not out	10	26	–	–	
A. D. Mullally	c Ponting	b Bevan	2	6	–	–	10–178
Extras (lb 3, w 8, nb 4)			15				
Total (43.2 overs)			178				

Bowling: McGrath 10–0–54–4; Dale 8–2–27–1; Julian 5–0–28–0; Warne 10–0–44–1; Fleming 7–1–13–1; Bevan 3.2–0–9–2

AUSTRALIA		R	B	4	6	FOW
M. E. Waugh	not out	83	109	8	–	
†A. C. Gilchrist	b Mullally	21	28	3	–	1–44
R. T. Ponting	not out	75	99	8	–	
D. S. Lehmann		–				
D. R. Martyn		–				
M. G. Bevan		–				
B. P. Julian		–				
*S. K. Warne		–				
D. W. Fleming		–				
A. C. Dale		–				
G. D. McGrath		–				
Extras (lb 2, w 1)		3				
Total (1 wkt, 39.2 overs)		182				

Bowling: Gough 10–0–48–0; Mullally 10–2–42–1; Headley 3–0–21–0; Ealham 6.2–0–25–0; Hollioake 4–0–14–0; Croft 6–0–30–0

5th match: Australia v England
Sydney, 17 January 1999
(England won toss): England won by 7 runs
Umpires: D. B. Hair and S. J. A. Taufel
Débuts: None. Award: G. A. Hick

ENGLAND			R	B	4	6	FOW
N. V. Knight	c Gilchrist	b McGrath	0	3	–	–	1–1
**+A. J. Stewart	c Gilchrist	b Fleming	17	32	2	–	2–39
G. A. Hick	lbw	b Fleming	108	129	5	1	4–245
N. Hussain		b Fleming	93	114	6	–	3–229
N. H. Fairbrother		not out	17	15	1	1	
A. J. Hollioake		not out	22	14	2	–	
M. A. Ealham			–				
R. D. B. Croft			–				
A. F. Giles			–				
D. Gough			–				
A. D. Mullally			–				
Extras (b 4, lb 5, w 9, nb 7)			25				
Total (4 wkts, 50 overs)			282				

Bowling: McGrath 10–0–56–1; Dale 10–0–26–0; Fleming 10–0–64–3; Lehmann 4–0–20–0;
Warne 10–0–57–0; Bevan 3–0–26–0; Blewett 3–0–24–0

AUSTRALIA			R	B	4	6	FOW
+A. C. Gilchrist	c Hussain	b Gough	6	7	1	–	1–9
M. E. Waugh	c Croft	b Hollioake	85	95	9	1	3–151
R. T. Ponting	c Hick	b Gough	6	13	–	–	2–36
D. S. Lehmann		b Mullally	76	87	6	–	5–203
*S. R. Waugh	c Gough	b Hollioake	0	1	–	–	4–152
M. G. Bevan		not out	45	59	–	–	
G. S. Blewett		b Giles	32	33	2	–	6–263
S. K. Warne		not out	6	6	–	–	
D. W. Fleming			–				
A. C. Dale			–				
G. D. McGrath			–				
Extras (b 4, lb 9, w 5, nb 1)			19				
Total (6 wkts, 50 overs)			275				

Bowling: Gough 10–2–40–2; Mullally 10–0–45–1; Ealham 10–0–52–0; Giles 5–0–40–1;
Hollioake 10–0–48–2; Croft 5–0–37–0

6th match: Sri Lanka v England
Melbourne, 19 January 1999
(Sri Lanka won toss): England won by 7 wkts
Umpires: D. J. Harper and T. A. Prue
Débuts: None. Award: D. Gough

SRI LANKA			R	B	4	6	FOW
S. T. Jayasuriya	c Hussain	b Gough	1	17	–	–	1–10
+R. S. Kaluwitharana		b Gough	15	20	3	–	2–19
M. S. Atapattu	c Hick	b Gough	1	11	–	–	3–20
H. P. Tillekeratne		b Gough	0	13	–	–	4–21
D. P. M. Jayawardene	c Stewart	b Hollioake	12	38	1	–	5–48
*A. Ranatunga	run out		76	105	5	–	8–180
U. D. U. Chandana	c Wells	b Croft	50	68	3	–	6–140
G. P. Wickremasinghe		b Hollioake	8	10	1	–	7–158
W. P. U. J. C. Vaas		not out	11	15	–	–	
M. Muralitharan	c Hussain	b Mullally	1	3	–	–	9–184
D. N. T. Zoysa	run out		0	0	–	–	10–186
Extras (lb 8, w 3)			11				
Total (50 overs)			186				

Bowling: Gough 10–2–28–4; Mullally 10–2–23–1; Hollioake 9–0–46–2;
Ealham 10–0–32–0; Croft 8–0–29–1; Wells 3–0–20–0

ENGLAND			R	B	4	6	FOW
N. V. Knight	c Jayasuriya	b Zoysa	31	36	2	–	1–52
**A. J. Stewart	c Ranatunga	b Zoysa	20	35	3	–	2–53
G. A. Hick		not out	66	101	3	–	
N. Hussain	st Kaluwitharana	b Muralitharan	29	51	3	–	3–115
J. P. Crawley		not out	31	52	1	–	
M. A. Ealham			–				
A. J. Hollioake			–				
R. D. B. Croft			–				
V. J. Wells			–				
D. Gough			–				
A. D. Mullally			–				
Extras (lb 2, w 7, nb 3)			12				
Total (3 wkts, 45.2 overs)			189				

Bowling: Vaas 10–0–39–0; Wickremasinghe 10–0–35–0; Zoysa 6–1–22–2;
Muralitharan 10–0–40–1; Chandana 7.2–0–38–0; Jayasuriya 2–0–13–0

7th match: Sri Lanka v Australia

Hobart, 21 January 1999
(Sri Lanka won toss): Sri Lanka won by 3 wkts
Umpires: S. J. Davis and P. D. Parker
Débuts: None. Award: M. S. Atapattu

AUSTRALIA			R	B	4	6	FOW
M. E. Waugh	c Mahanama	b Jayasuriya	65	105	1	–	4-138
+A. C. Gilchrist		b Vaas	12	27	1	–	1-20
G. S. Blewett	c Mahanama	b Wickremasinghe	1	7	–	–	2-25
D. S. Lehmann	c Jayawardene	b Jayasuriya	51	65	3	–	3-118
S. Lee	c Chandana	b Muralitharan	18	21	–	1	5-153
*S. R. Waugh	c Jayawardene	b Jayasuriya	20	22	1	1	6-185
M. G. Bevan	c Kaluwitharana	b Muralitharan	18	23	–	–	8-198
B. P. Julian	caught and	b Vaas	7	7	1	–	7-196
S. K. Warne	c Chandana	b Vaas	5	8	–	–	9-206
A. C. Dale		not out	7	13	–	–	
G. D. McGrath		not out	1	2	–	–	
Extras (lb 2, w 3)			5				
Total (9 wkts, 50 overs)			210				

Bowling: Vaas 10-1-27-3; Wickremasinghe 8-1-20-1; Muralitharan 10-1-42-2;
Jayawardene 4-0-20-0; Chandana 7-0-44-0; Jayasuriya 10-0-47-3; Tillekeratne 1-0-8-0

SRI LANKA			R	B	4	6	FOW
S. T. Jayasuriya	run out		3	4	–	–	1-4
+R. S. Kaluwitharana	lbw	b Dale	54	82	5	–	2-120
M. S. Atapattu	run out		82	121	6	–	3-163
*A. Ranatunga		not out	45	61	2	–	
U. D. U. Chandana	c Dale	b Warne	8	11	–	–	4-178
H. P. Tillekeratne	c sub	b Warne	3	8	–	–	5-188
D. P. M. Jayawardene		b McGrath	1	3	–	–	6-190
R. S. Mahanama		b Warne	4	7	–	–	7-198
W. P. U. J. C. Vaas		not out	2	4	–	–	
G. P. Wickremasinghe			–				
M. Muralitharan			–				
Extras (lb 2, w 3, nb 4)			9				
Total (7 wkts, 49.3 overs)			211				

Bowling: McGrath 10-2-33-1; Dale 10-2-30-1; Julian 10-0-41-0;
Lee 6-0-39-0; Warne 10-0-45-3; Blewett 3.3-0-21-0

8th match: Sri Lanka v England
Adelaide, 23 January 1999
(Sri Lanka won toss): Sri Lanka won by 1 wkt
Umpires: R. A. Emerson and A. J. McQuillan
Débuts: None. Award: D. P. M. Jayawardene

ENGLAND			R	B	4	6	FOW
N. V. Knight	run out		44	74	3	–	2–139
*+A. J. Stewart	c Ranatunga	b Vaas	39	33	6	–	1–64
G. A. Hick		not out	126	118	5	4	
N. Hussain	c Tillekeratne	b Jayasuriya	6	7	1	–	3–148
N. H. Fairbrother		not out	78	71	4	2	
V. J. Wells			–				
A. J. Hollioake			–				
M. A. Ealham			–				
R. D. B. Croft			–				
D. Gough			–				
A. D. Mullally			–				
Extras (lb 2, w 4, nb 3)			9				
Total (3 wkts, 50 overs)			302				

Bowling: Vaas 10–0–76–1; Wickremasinghe 9–0–72–0; Jayawardene 4–0–24–0;
Muralitharan 7–0–45–0; Jayasuriya 10–0–43–1; Chandana 10–0–40–0

SRI LANKA			R	B	4	6	FOW
S. T. Jayasuriya	c Fairbrother	b Gough	51	36	6	2	3–68
+R. S. Kaluwitharana	run out		0	0	–	–	1–3
M. S. Atapattu	c Fairbrother	b Mullally	3	12	–	–	2–8
H. P. Tillekeratne		b Croft	28	48	1	–	4–137
D. P. M. Jayawardene	lbw	b Wells	120	111	9	–	7–269
*A. Ranatunga	c Wells	b Gough	41	51	2	–	5–223
W. P. U. J. C. Vaas	run out		5	6	–	–	6–235
U. D. U. Chandana	c Fairbrother	b Wells	25	18	1	1	8–288
R. S. Mahanama	run out		13	11	2	–	9–298
M. Muralitharan		not out	2	4	–	–	
G. P. Wickremasinghe		not out	2	2	–	–	
Extras (lb 9, w 4)			13				
Total (9 wkts, 49.4 overs)			303				

Bowling: Gough 10–1–68–2; Mullally 10–0–61–1; Hollioake 5–0–45–0;
Ealham 10–1–48–0; Croft 10–0–42–1; Wells 4.4–0–30–2

9th match: Australia v Sri Lanka
Adelaide, 24 January 1999
(Sri Lanka won toss): Australia won by 80 runs
Umpires: S. J. Davis and S. J. A. Taufel
Débuts: None. Award: G. D. McGrath

AUSTRALIA			R	B	4	6	FOW
+A. C. Gilchrist	c Muralitharan	b Wickremasinghe	41	36	4	1	1–86
M. E. Waugh	c Chandana	b Muralitharan	57	68	5	–	3–135
B. P. Julian		b Chandana	21	15	2	1	2–116
G. S. Blewett	c Kaluwitharana	b Jayasuriya	40	71	1	–	4–203
D. S. Lehmann	c Muralitharan	b Chandana	40	49	2	–	5–208
D. R. Martyn		not out	33	28	2	–	
S. G. Law	run out		8	11	–	–	6–223
S. Lee		b Vaas	20	16	2	–	7–258
*S. K. Warne	c Tillekeratne	b Vaas	0	2	–	–	8–259
A. C. Dale		b Jayasuriya	0	2	–	–	9–261
G. D. McGrath	c Mahanama	b Vaas	2	5	–	–	10–270
Extras (lb 2, w 3, nb 3)			8				
Total (50 overs)			270				

Bowling: Vaas 10–0–63–3; Wickremasinghe 7–0–45–1; Muralitharan 10–0–51–1;
Jayasuriya 10–0–48–2; Chandana 10–0–44–2; Jayawardene 3–0–17–0

SRI LANKA			R	B	4	6	FOW
S. T. Jayasuriya	c Julian	b McGrath	12	20	1	–	3–30
+R. S. Kaluwitharana	c Gilchrist	b McGrath	9	12	1	–	1–26
M. S. Atapattu	c Warne	b McGrath	0	2	–	–	2–27
H. P. Tillekeratne	c Warne	b McGrath	10	35	1	–	6–53
D. P. M. Jayawardene	c Lee	b Dale	9	15	1	–	4–40
*A. Ranatunga	c Julian	b McGrath	0	2	–	–	5–40
R. S. Mahanama		b Blewett	55	82	3	–	9–177
U. D. U. Chandana	lbw	b Lee	38	59	3	–	7–143
W. P. U. J. C. Vaas	c Gilchrist	b Lee	0	1	–	–	8–143
G. P. Wickremasinghe		not out	21	28	2	–	
M. Muralitharan		b Blewett	11	10	1	–	10–190
Extras (lb 3, w 4, nb 18)			25				
Total (41.4 overs)			190				

Bowling: McGrath 10–0–40–5; Dale 10–2–31–1; Julian 5–0–37–0;
Warne 9–0–53–0; Lee 6–0–20–2; Blewett 1.4–0–6–2

10th Match: Australia v England
Adelaide, 26 January 1999
(Australia won toss): Australia won by 16 runs
Umpires: D. J. Harper and P. D. Parker
Débuts: None. Award: G. A. Hick

AUSTRALIA			R	B	4	6	FOW
M. E. Waugh	c Hussain	b Croft	65	80	7	–	3–118
+A. C. Gilchrist		b Gough	0	3	–	–	1–1
G. S. Blewett		b Gough	4	15	–	–	2–25
D. S. Lehmann		b Croft	51	68	3	–	4–131
D. R. Martyn		not out	59	68	3	–	
S. G. Law	c Stewart	b Ealham	3	6	–	–	5–134
S. Lee	c Fairbrother	b Headley	41	53	1	–	6–224
B. P. Julian		b Headley	0	1	–	–	7–224
*S. K. Warne	run out		11	7	1	–	8–239
A. C. Dale			–				
G. D. McGrath			–				
Extras (lb 4, nb 1)			5				
Total (8 wkts, 50 overs)			239				

Bowling: Gough 10–0–51–2; Mullally 10–0–39–0; Headley 10–0–59–2;
Ealham 10–0–46–1; Croft 10–0–40–2

ENGLAND			R	B	4	6	FOW
N. V. Knight	caught and	b Warne	42	73	3	–	2–98
**+A. J. Stewart	c Gilchrist	b Dale	6	14	–	–	1–18
G. A. Hick	run out		109	119	6	2	9–223
N. Hussain	lbw	b McGrath	21	36	3	–	3–162
N. H. Fairbrother		b McGrath	10	6	2	–	4–176
J. P. Crawley	caught and	b Julian	11	23	–	–	5–193
M. A. Ealham	caught and	b Warne	4	12	–	–	6–202
R. D. B. Croft	caught and	b Julian	0	1	–	–	7–204
D. Gough	c Dale	b Warne	2	5	–	–	8–210
D. W. Headley		b McGrath	2	9	–	–	10–223
A. D. Mullally		not out	0				
Extras (lb 7, w 2, nb 7)			16				
Total (48.3 overs)			223				

Bowling: McGrath 9.3–0–40–3; Dale 10–1–35–1; Lee 3–0–23–0; Julian 10–0–44–2;
Warne 10–0–39–3; Martyn 3–0–15–0; Law 2–0–8–0; Lehmann 1–0–12–0

11th match: Sri Lanka v England
Perth, 29 January 1999
(Sri Lanka won toss): England won by 128 runs
Umpires: P. D. Parker and S. J. Davis
Débuts: None. Award: M. A. Ealham

ENGLAND			R	B	4	6	FOW
N. V. Knight	c de Silva	b Perera	13	21	1	–	2–30
*+A. J. Stewart		b Perera	0	2	–	–	1–6
G. A. Hick	lbw	b Vaas	10	19	2	–	4–38
N. Hussain	c Kaluwitharana	b Perera	0	9	–	–	3–37
N. H. Fairbrother		not out	81	119	3	–	
A. J. Hollioake	run out		46	74	2	–	5–127
M. A. Ealham	c Mahanama	b Muralitharan	16	32	–	–	6–166
R. D. B. Croft	c Chandana	b Vaas	32	38	2	–	7–221
D. Gough		not out	0				
D. W. Headley			–				
A. D. Mullally			–				
Extras (lb 6, w 8, nb 15)			29				
Total (7 wkts, 50 overs)			227				

Bowling: Vaas 10–2–38–2; Perera 10–0–55–3; Muralitharan 10–1–26–1; Chandana 8–0–39–0; Jayasuriya 9–0–47–0; de Silva 3–0–16–0

SRI LANKA			R	B	4	6	FOW
S. T. Jayasuriya	c Hollioake	b Ealham	40	58	4	1	2–65
+R. S. Kaluwitharana	c Hollioake	b Gough	5	11	1	–	1–15
M. S. Atapattu	c Knight	b Ealham	17	39	2	–	3–65
P. A. de Silva	c Stewart	b Ealham	1	5	–	–	4–67
D. P. M. Jayawardene	c Hussain	b Gough	3	13	–	–	5–71
*A. Ranatunga	c Knight	b Ealham	11	33	–	–	7–98
R. S. Mahanama	c Hussain	b Ealham	6	17	1	–	6–85
U. D. U. Chandana	c Gough	b Headley	9	19	–	–	8–98
W. P. U. J. C. Vaas		not out	0	4	–	–	
M. Muralitharan		b Mullally	1	4	–	–	9–99
R. L. Perera	c Hick	b Mullally	0	1	–	–	10–99
Extras (lb 2, w 1, nb 3)			6				
Total (33.3 overs)			99				

Bowling: Gough 8–2–15–2; Mullally 6.3–0–17–2; Headley 8–0–33–1; Ealham 10–2–32–5; Croft 1–1–0–0

12th match: Sri Lanka v Australia
Perth, 31 January 1999
(Sri Lanka won toss): Australia won by 45 runs
Umpires: D. J. Harper and T. A. Prue
Debuts: None. Award: R. T. Ponting

AUSTRALIA			R	B	4	6	FOW
+A. C. Gilchrist		b Vaas	47	45	7	–	1–62
M. E. Waugh	c Atapattu	b Wickremasinghe	12	14	1	–	2–62
R. T. Ponting	run out		39	57	1	1	4–138
D. S. Lehmann	c Kaluwitharana	b Wickremasinghe	20	37	1	–	3–100
D. R. Martyn	c Mahanama	b Muralitharan	48	56	2	–	5–205
M. G. Bevan	not out		72	65	4	–	
S. Lee	c Atapattu	b Wickremasinghe	22	26	–	–	6–226
B. P. Julian	c Kaluwitharana	b Vaas	1	2	–	–	7–268
*S. K. Warne	not out		1	3	–	–	
A. C. Dale			–				
G. D. McGrath			–				
Extras (b 1, w 6, nb 5)			12				
Total (7 wkts, 50 overs)			274				

Bowling: Vaas 10–0–51–2; Perera 10–0–71–0; Wickremasinghe 10–0–48–3;
Muralitharan 10–0–46–1; Jayasuriya 10–0–57–0

SRI LANKA			R	B	4	6	FOW
S. T. Jayasuriya		rtd hurt	50	49	8	1	
+R. S. Kaluwitharana	c Lee	b Dale	13	12	1	–	1–22
M. S. Atapattu	run out		34	55	1	–	2–126
H. P. Tillekeratne	c Ponting	b Warne	30	62	2	–	4–159
W. P. U. J. C. Vaas	c Julian	b Warne	20	16	2	–	3–153
*A. Ranatunga	c Gilchrist	b Ponting	14	21	–	–	5–201
D. P. M. Jayawardene	c Dale	b Warne	36	40	3	–	7–219
R. S. Mahanama	lbw	b Julian	4	11	–	–	6–213
G. P. Wickremasinghe	c Warne	b McGrath	10	10	1	–	8–229
R. L. Perera		b McGrath	3	7	–	–	9–229
M. Muralitharan	not out		0	0	–	–	
Extras (b 1, lb 4, w 2, nb 8)			15				
Total (9 wkts, 46.3 overs)			229				

Bowling: McGrath 8.3–3–19–2; Dale 6–0–51–1; Lee 5–0–32–0;
Julian 7–0–28–1; Ponting 10–0–41–1; Warne 10–0–53–3

13th match: Sri Lanka v England
Sydney, 3 February 1999
(Sri Lanka won toss): Sri Lanka won by 11 runs
Umpires: A. J. McQuillan and S. J. A. Taufel
Débuts: None. Award: T. T. Samaraweera

SRI LANKA			R	B	4	6	FOW
A. Gunawardene	st Crawley	b Giles	24	45	1	–	1–71
+R. S. Kaluwitharana	c Gough	b Alleyne	54	87	5	–	3–109
W. P. U. J. C. Vaas	run out		14	14	–	–	2–99
P. A. de Silva		not out	52	52	3	1	
*A. Ranatunga	c Hussain	b Gough	0	4	–	–	4–111
D. P. M. Jayawardene	c B Hollioake	b Alleyne	2	7	–	–	5–122
M. S. Atapattu	lbw	b Alleyne	4	15	–	–	6–133
U. D. U. Chandana	c Giles	b Wells	0	7	–	–	7–134
H. P. Tillekeratne		not out	13	35	1	–	
T. T. Samaraweera			–				
G. P. Wickremasinghe			–				
Extras (b 4, w 12, nb 2)			18				
Total (7 wkts, 44 overs)			181				

Bowling: Gough 9–2–35–1; B Hollioake 4–0–25–0; Ealham 9–3–30–0; Giles 5–0–31–1;
Alleyne 9–1–27–3; Wells 8–1–29–1

ENGLAND			R	B	4	6	FOW
N. V. Knight		b Chandana	58	109	2	–	5–119
V. J. Wells		b Samaraweera	26	50	2	–	1–53
G. A. Hick		b Samaraweera	0	2	–	–	2–53
N. Hussain	st Kaluwitharana	b Tillekeratne	9	24	–	–	3–74
+J. P. Crawley	c Ranatunga	b Samaraweera	13	21	1	–	4–118
M. A. Ealham	c sub	b Jayawardene	0	3	–	–	6–122
M. W. Alleyne	c Jayawardene	b Chandana	18	20	1	–	7–150
*A. J. Hollioake	st Kaluwitharana	b Chandana	13	17	1	–	9–162
B. C. Hollioake	run out		4	6	–	–	8–155
A. F. Giles		not out	10	10	–	–	
D. Gough		not out	1	3	–	–	
Extras (b 1, lb 5, w 11, nb 1)			18				
Total (9 wkts, 44 overs)			170				

Bowling: Vaas 6–0–24–0; de Silva 9–0–25–0; Samaraweera
9–0–34–3; Chandana 9–0–35–3; Tillekeratne 5–0–22–1;
Jayawardene 6–0–24–1

14th match: Australia v England
Sydney, 5 February 1999
(England won toss): Australia won by 4 wkts
Umpires: D. B. Hair and P. D. Parker
Débuts: None. Award: D. R. Martyn

ENGLAND			R	B	4	6	FOW
N. V. Knight		b Dale	3	10	–	–	1–11
+A. J. Stewart	c Lee	b Julian	25	48	3	–	3–57
G. A. Hick	c Gilchrist	b Dale	4	10	1	–	2–26
N. Hussain	c Lehmann	b M. Waugh	31	59	2	–	4–90
V. J. Wells	run out		39	63	2	–	6–143
A. J. Hollioake	c Gilchrist	b Bevan	19	26	1	–	5–124
M. W. Alleyne		not out	38	47	1	–	
M. A. Ealham	c Bevan	b Warne	33	37	2	1	7–201
R. D. B. Croft	c Gilchrist	b Kasprowicz	0	1	–	–	8–205
D. Gough		not out	1	2	–	–	
A. D. Mullally							
Extras (b 2, lb 6, w 5, nb 4)			17				
Total (8 wkts, 50 overs)			210				

Bowling: Kasprowicz 8–0–39–1; Dale 10–1–28–2; Julian 10–0–39–1;
Lee 5–0–22–0; Warne 10–0–48–1; M. Waugh 3–0–11–1; Bevan 4–0–15–1

AUSTRALIA			R	B	4	6	FOW
M. E. Waugh	c Stewart	b Mullally	27	46	4	–	2–51
+A. C. Gilchrist		b Mullally	19	37	–	–	1–50
R. T. Ponting	c Wells	b Ealham	43	71	4	–	4–158
D. S. Lehmann	lbw	b Hollioake	41	57	2	1	3–130
B. P. Julian	c Hick	b Wells	25	31	3	1	5–180
D. R. Martyn		not out	38	32	4	–	
M. G. Bevan	c Ealham	b Croft	0	4	–	–	6–181
S. Lee		not out	8	7	1	–	
*S. K. Warne			–				
A. C. Dale			–				
M. S. Kasprowicz			–				
Extras (lb 5, w 2, nb 3)			10				
Total (6 wkts, 47 overs)			211				

Bowling: Gough 5–0–24–0; Mullally 10–1–31–2; Ealham 9–0–46–1;
Alleyne 5–0–24–0; Croft 10–2–43–1; Hollioake 6–0–28–1; Wells 2–0–10–1

15th match: Australia v Sri Lanka
Melbourne, 7 February 1999
(Australia won toss): Australia won by 43 runs
Umpires: D. J. Harper and T. A. Prue
Débuts: None. Award: A. C. Gilchrist

AUSTRALIA			R	B	4	6	FOW
+A. C. Gilchrist	c Tillekeratne	b Vaas	154	129	14	4	5-286
M. E. Waugh		b Muralitharan	19	37	2	–	1-92
B. P. Julian	c Jayawardene	b Muralitharan	0	2	–	–	2-92
R. T. Ponting	c Jayawardene	b de Silva	61	64	3	–	3-213
D. S. Lehmann	c Ranatunga	b Samaraweera	27	27	1	–	4-253
D. R. Martyn	c Kaluwitharana	b Wickremasinghe	18	20	1	–	6-291
M. G. Bevan		not out	11	13	–	–	
S. Lee	run out		5	6	–	–	7-301
*S. K. Warne	c Tillekeratne	b Vaas	3	3	–	–	8-307
M. S. Kasprowicz		not out	2	1	–	–	
G. D. McGrath			–				
Extras (b 4, w 4, nb 2)			10				
Total (8 wkts, 50 overs)			310				

Bowling: Vaas 10-1-68-2; Wickremasinghe 9-0-52-1;
Muralitharan 3.4-1-15-2; de Silva 10-0-55-1; Tillekeratne 1.2-0-11-0;
Samarawcera 9-0-60-1; Jayawardene 7-0-45-0

SRI LANKA			R	B	4	6	FOW
A. Gunawardene		b Lee	75	66	9	2	2-147
+R. S. Kaluwitharana	c Martyn	b Warne	68	60	9	1	1-145
P. A. de Silva	c M. Waugh	b Lee	11	13	1	–	3-164
D. P. M. Jayawardene	run out		27	36	1	–	5-200
*A. Ranatunga	c Gilchrist	b Lee	1	3	–	–	4-166
H. P. Tillekeratne	c Ponting	b Lee	42	60	2	–	10-267
M. S. Atapattu		b Lehmann	12	19	1	–	6-225
W. P. U. J. C. Vaas		b McGrath	14	15	1	–	7-248
T. T. Samarweera		b Lee	3	9	–	–	8-255
G. P. Wickremasinghe	c Gilchrist	b McGrath	4	5	–	–	9-265
M. Muralitharan		not out	1	1	–	–	
Extras (b 2, lb 2, w 1, nb 4)			9				
Total (47.1 overs)			267				

Bowling: McGrath 8-0-46-2; Kasprowicz 8-0-45-0; Warne 8-1-51-1;
Julian 5-0-45-0; Lee 8.1-0-33-5; Bevan 3-0-15-0; Lehmann 7-0-28-1

Final Table	P	W	L	Pts	NRR
Australia	10	7	3	14	+0.538
England	10	5	5	10	+0.157
Sri Lanka	10	3	7	6	-0.667

First Final: Australia v England
Sydney, 10 February 1999
(Australia won toss): Australia won by 10 runs
Umpires: D. B. Hair and S. J. Davis
Débuts: None. Award: M. G. Bevan

AUSTRALIA			R	B	4	6	FOW
M. E. Waugh	c Stewart	b Wells	42	56	3	–	3–98
+A. C. Gilchrist		b Gough	29	30	3	–	1–40
R. T. Ponting	c Stewart	b Wells	10	14	–	–	2–67
D. S. Lehmann	c Mullally	b Wells	19	33	1	–	4–115
D. R. Martyn	c Stewart	b Ealham	21	38	–	1	5–139
M. G. Bevan		not out	69	74	6	–	
S. Lee	c Fairbrother	b Ealham	12	27	–	–	6–176
B. P. Julian	c sub	b Ealham	12	13	1	–	7–199
*S. K. Warne		b Gough	9	13	1	–	8–222
A. C. Dale		not out	1	3	–	–	
G. D. McGrath			–				
Extras (lb 6, w 1, nb 1)			8				
Total (8 wkts, 50 overs)			232				

Bowling: Gough 10–0–43–2; Mullally 7–0–42–0; Wells 10–2–30–3; Ealham 10–0–45–3; Croft 5–1–28–0; Hollioake 8–0–38–0

ENGLAND			R	B	4	6	FOW
N. V. Knight		b Dale	22	35	2	–	2–67
**+A. J. Stewart	c Waugh	b Dale	27	18	4	1	1–34
G. A. Hick	run out		42	58	2	–	3–114
N. Hussain	st Gilchrist	b Warne	58	98	4	–	5–198
N. H. Fairbrother	c Gilchrist	b McGrath	8	12	–	–	4–131
V. J. Wells	c Julian	b Lee	33	39	3	1	7–198
A. J. Hollioake	lbw	b Warne	0	1	–	–	6–198
M. A. Ealham	c Gilchrist	b McGrath	4	14	–	–	8–204
R. D. B. Croft		not out	12	12	1	–	
D. Gough		b McGrath	0	2	–	–	9–204
A. D. Mullally		b McGrath	7	11	1	–	10–222
Extras (lb 3, w 2, nb 4)			9				
Total (49.2 overs)			222				

Bowling: McGrath 9.2–1–45–4; Dale 10–0–33–2; Lee 7–1–29–1; Warne 10–0–40–2; Julian 4–0–28–0; Martyn 6–0–27–0; Lehmann 3–0–17–0

Second Final: Australia v England
Melbourne, 13 February 1999
(Australia won toss): Australia won by 162 runs, won series 2–0
Umpires: D. B. Hair and D. J. Harper
Débuts: None. Award: D. S. Lehmann.
Series awards: G. A. Hick & G. D. McGrath

AUSTRALIA			R	B	4	6	FOW
+A. C. Gilchrist	c Knight	b Croft	52	64	6	–	3–104
M. E. Waugh	c Hick	b Gough	1	12	–	–	1–11
R. T. Ponting	c Fairbrother	b Hollioake	37	43	3	1	2–92
D. S. Lehmann	c Hussain	b Wells	71	75	4	–	4–216
D. R. Martyn		b Mullally	57	80	2	1	5–244
S. G. Law		not out	20	18	1	–	
S. Lee		not out	20	9	–	2	
B. P. Julian			–				
*S. K. Warne			–				
A. C. Dale			–				
G. D. McGrath			–				
Extras (lb 10, w 3, nb 1)			14				
Total (5 wkts, 50 overs)			272				

Bowling: Gough 9–1–55–1; Mullally 10–1–53–1; Ealham 6–0–41–0;
Wells 5–0–34–1; Croft 10–0–40–1; Hollioake 10–0–39–1

ENGLAND			R	B	4	6	FOW
N. V. Knight	run out		4	9	–	–	1–9
**+A. J. Stewart	c Lee	b Julian	32	36	5	–	5–43
G. A. Hick	c Dale	b McGrath	0	2	–	–	2–10
N. Hussain	c Gilchrist	b McGrath	0	1	–	–	3–10
N. H. Fairbrother	c Gilchrist	b Dale	0	2	–	–	4–13
V. J. Wells		b Warne	23	54	–	–	7–72
A. J. Hollioake	c Gilchrist	b Dale	7	8	–	–	6–50
M. A. Ealham		b Warne	12	35	1	–	8–88
R. D. B. Croft		not out	13	22	1	–	
D. Gough	c Gilchrist	b Julian	6	15	–	–	9–100
A. D. Mullally	lbw	b Warne	9	10	2	–	10–110
Extras (w 1, nb 3)			4				
Total (31.5 overs)			110				

Bowling: McGrath 6–0–26–2; Dale 10–1–27–2; Julian 6–2–18–2;
Waugh 4–0–23–0; Warne 5.5–0–16–3

Index

Abbott, Roy, 95
ABC Radio, 72, 74, 213
Aborigines, 28, 219, 226–7, 237
ACB *see* Australian Cricket Board
accommodation, 39
Adelaide, 44, 97, 121–4, 127–8, 132–42, 208–11; description, 133–4, 136, 138; the Hill, 133–8; viewpoints, 138–9
administration expenses, 243
Age, The, 21, 115, 151
ageing, 2
Agnew, Jonathan, 72, 73, 77, 78, 161–2
Akram, Wasim, 51
alcohol consumption, 214–15, 229–30; Botham, 78, 169; Fourth Test, 170, 172, 177; Ponting, 214; Third Test, 134–5, 136, 142
Allan, Alex, 146–7
Alleyne, Mark, 205–6
Allott, Paul, 72, 75–6, 173–4
Ambrose, Curtly, 51, 55, 95
Among the Barbarians (Sheehan), 16
Angel, Jo, 40
Angley, Paul, 126–8, 202
Anglo-Celtic Australia, 25–26
Anglo-Saxon Australia, 22, 26
anti-British feelings, 13–15, 71, 232–8
Anwar, Saeed, 54
Apps, Peter, 157
Archer, Ken, 187
Arnberger, Jason, 112
Arnold, Evan, 45
Art Gallery of NSW, 228
Ashes, origins, 8
Ashton, Malcolm, 47
Asians, 26, 28
Atherton, Mike, 10, 33, 34, 51, 67; Fifth Test, 179; First Test, 55, 67; Fourth Test, 163, 165–8; Hobart, 153–9; injuries, 40, 43–44, 47–48, 55; sweepstakes, 43; Third Test, 126, 127–8, 137
Atlanta, 227
Attwood, Alan, 21
Australian, The, 6, 21, 23, 94, 145, 152, 233–4
Australian Cricket Board (ACB), 5, 7, 25,

27–28, 169, 189, 200–1
Australian Cricketers' Association, 5, 7
Australian Rules football, 18, 21, 47, 98, 219

'backyard cricket', 21–2
'baggy green cap', 22, 30, 188, 216
Bailey, Trevor, 173–4
Bangladesh, 6
Bannerman, Charlie, 184
Barbados Test, 45
Barcelona, 226
Barclay, John, 241
'Barmy Army', 133–42, 151, 170–7, 236
barracking, Internet, 18
'Battle for the Backyard Ashes', 22
Baxter, Peter, 72
'beach cricket', 21
Beazley, Kim, 17, 143, 151
Bedser, Alec, 32, 68, 139, 186–7
Bedser, Eric, 139, 186–7
Benaud, Richie, 70, 72, 78,79
betting, 6, 42, 84, 86, 113–19
Bichel, Andy, 48
Birch, Ric, 226–7, 230–1
Bird, Dickie, 146, 176, 192
Birkenshaw, Jack, 241
Blair, Tony, 15, 17, 144, 146, 148
Blake, Terry, 3, 4
Blanchett, Cate, 233
Blewett, Greg, 45, 121, 136, 156–60, 215, 220
Bligh, Ivo, 8
Blofeld, Henry, 73, 79
Blunkett, David, 246
Bolus, Brian, 249–50
Boon, David, 120–4, 172, 213
Border, Allan, 52, 131, 155, 158, 189, 214, 216; First Test, 72, 76, 80
Botham, Ian, 140, 169; Centenary Test 1977, 71; First Test, 72, 74, 75–76
Bowral, 186, 224
Bradman, Don, 25, 53, 65, 128, 146–7, 158, 170, 234; Blewett similarities, 160; Hawke friendship, 150; Oval stand, 139; popularity, 186

289

Brayshaw, Ian, 92
Brearley, Mike, 84
bribery, 6, 113–119, 120; International Olympic Committee, 9; see also corruption allegations
Brisbane, 32, 51–69, 206
Britain, 15; crisis, 237; feelings towards, 13–15, 71, 232–8; 'symbolic' relationship, 14
British Lions, South Africa, 37
broadcasting see television
Burdett, Les, 96, 97, 98, 120
Burge, Peter, 201
burning ritual, 8
Burton, Mike, 175
Bush, George, 149
Business Review Weekly, 23
Butcher, Alan, 174
Butcher, Mark, 126, 157, 159, 163, 166, 174, 183, 186, 202; First Test, 33, 34, 42, 48, 55, 58, 63, 70, 76

Cairns ground, 46–47, 48, 54
Campbell, Ryan, 42
Canberra, 143, 147
Carlstein, Peter, 105
Carlton & United Series, 204, 207, 217
Cashman, Richard, 24–25, 27, 144–5
catching, 190–1; Fifth Test, 188; Third Test, 125, 131, 149
Cavalier, Rodney, 145
Centenary Test 1977, 71
Champion, Greg, 22
Chandrasekhar, B. S., 81
Channel Nine television, 70, 71–72, 195
Chappell, Greg, 20, 180, 220
Chappell, Ian, 11, 121, 180, 220; Centenary Test 1977, 71; First Test, 50, 72, 75, 76, 78
Charles, Prince of Wales, 235
Chikarovski, Kerry, 224
Clark, Pilita, 218–19
class see culture
Class in Australia (McGregor), 219
Clemson, Katie, 147
climbing, Sydney, 222
Clinton, Bill, 106, 113
coaching, 248
Code of Conduct, 208–11, 251–3
Collette, Lisa, 74
Colvile, Charles, 72, 74
Compton, Denis, 241
Conduct Code, 208–11, 251–2
constitutional reforms, 13–15, 232–8
Conway, Dean, 205
Cook, Captain, 169

'Cool Britannia', 15
Cork, Dominic, 156, 159, 181; First Test, 48, 49, 50, 55, 60, 65–66, 68; Second Test, 93
corporate investment, 23–24
corruption allegations, 2, 113–19, 132–5, 141, 214–15, 227, 251; Taylor, 114–19, 141, 214; Warne, 114–19; Waugh, 114–19, 132–5, 214; see also bribery
Cottam, Bob, 82, 109, 111, 179
county cricket, 242–9
Cowans, Norman, 82
Coward, Mike, 64, 152
Cowdrey, Colin, 46, 148, 251, 252
Crane, David, 96
Crawley, John, 156–7, 182–3, 185; First Test, 48, 49, 50, 55; Second Test, 90, 91
Cricket Academy, Adelaide, 40, 144, 150, 153–4, 190
Cricket NSW, 28
Cricketer, The, 11, 173, 174
Croft, Robert, 48, 54, 60, 66, 68–69
Crompton, Alan, 115, 117
Cronje, Hansie, 241
Crook, Andrew, 45
crowd see supporters
culture, 19–31, 213–20, 226–7, 230–8
Cumbes, Jim, 250

Daily Telegraph, 54–69, 84–86, 89–94, 106–108, 122–7, 158–68, 182–6
Dale, Adam, 47–48, 207, 211–12
Dalmiya, Jagmohan, 251
Davidson, Alan, 147
Davies, Terry, 136, 139
de Silva, Aravinda, 204
Deane, William, 237
DeFreitas, Philip, 82
Denness, Mike, 1
Der Ring des Nieberlungen, 121–2
development, talent, 27–8, 30–1, 189–90, 213–14, 240–2, 247–9
Dexter, Ted, 27
Dilley, Graham, 82
Dixon, Tony, 247
Donald, Allan, 33, 34, 51, 55, 204
Douglas-Home, Alec, 144
Downer, Alexander, 15, 230
Dudleston, Barry, 175
Duldig, Richard, 87
Dunne, Steve, 184, 186, 192–202
Durham, 120

e-mail barracking, 18
Ealham, Mark, 205–7
earnings, 7–8, 23, 194

Ebrahim, Fakruddin, 113–14
ECB *see* England and Wales Cricket Board
Eden Park, Auckland, 97, 101
Edrich, Bill, 241
Edrich, John, 172
Egar, Colin, 115
Eland, David, 28
Elizabeth II, 13, 234–5
Elliott, Matthew, 121, 156–9, 219
Emerald City (Williamson), 222
Emerson, Ross, 208–10
England Management Committee, 249–50
England and Wales Cricket Board (ECB), 3, 4, 9, 156–7, 190, 240–3, 247–8, 249–50
EU *see* European Union
euro, 236
European Union (EU), 236
Evans, Godfrey, 241
Everage, 'Dame' Edna, 234
excellence, pursuit, 239–53

facilities, 19; public decline, 244–7
Fairbrother, Neil, 205–8, 211
Federation, Australian colonies, 13
Fernando, Ranjit, 209
fielding, 189, 190–1; Fifth Test, 188; Third Test, 125, 131, 149
Fifth Test, 178–91
fighting, 49, 214–15, 252
film industry, 233
financial investments, 36
Fingleton, Jack, 147
First Test, 32–69
FitzSimons, Peter, 17, 151
Fleming, Damien, 34, 89, 163, 165–8
Fleming, Stephen, 188
Flintoff, Andrew, 190
Flood, Philip, 16
floodlights, 71, 133, 244
fluid consumption, 122, 134–5, 136, 138, 142, 194; *see also* alcohol consumption
four T's concept, 130
Fourth Test, 153–69, 170–7
Fouvy, David, 21, 22–23, 25
Francois, Andrea, 140
Fraser, Angus, 33, 108, 111–12, 135, 156, 159, 161–5, 168, 177
Fraser, Malcolm, 150
Fredericks, Roy, 95
'Fremantle Doctor' breeze, 95
Frindall, Bill, 73

Gabba ground, 71, 75; First Test, 52, 56, 59, 66, 68; lightning strikes, 77
gambling, 6, 42, 84, 86, 113–19
Gatting, Mike, 22, 56, 205

Gayleard, John, 74–75, 76, 79
Gibbs, Harry, 234
Gilbert, Ashley, 108, 112
Gilchrist, Adam, 190, 207
Giles, Ashley, 179, 205
Gillespie, Jason, 34, 45–6, 62, 91–2, 93–94
Gillette Cup, 244
'Go Aussie Go' campaign, 22, 56
Gooch, Graham, 33, 76, 156, 158, 177, 201–2, 205; Crawley incident, 49–50; management style, 38; work ethic, 104
Gough, Darren, 141, 156, 190, 204; Fifth Test, 179–81, 202–3; First Test, 33, 51, 59, 60, 66; Fourth Test, 162–8, 176; hat-trick, 180–1; one-day series, 208, 210; Second Test, 85; sociability, 175–6; Third Test, 122–6, 135
government spending, 24, 246–7
Gower, David, 40
Grace, W. G., 151
Graveney, David, 205
Graveney, Tom, 46
Greig, Tony, 29, 72, 78, 217–18
Griffiths, Lord, 252
grounds: building plans, 31; recreational cricket, 244–7
groundsmen, 95–102

Hair, Darrell, 106, 128, 192–203, 209, 216
Ham, Paul, 233–4
Hanson, Pauline, 14, 16
Harrity, Mark, 43
Harvey River soil, 95, 102
Hawke, Bob, 16, 143–5, 147, 148–51; description, 149; republican views, 235
Haygarth, Arthur, 174
Headingley, 203, 241
Headley, Dean, 47, 106, 111, 122–3, 141, 153, 165–8, 176–7, 190; Fifth Test, 178–80, 184–5, 198–9; 'Hanging Baskets of Babylon', 47; influence, 213, 215
Healy, Ian, 5, 168, 181, 213, 215, 219, 240; First Test, 33, 58, 60, 70, 75; Second Test, 90–91, 94
Hearne, J. T., 181
heatwave, Third Test, 120–31, 132–6
Hegg, Warren, 105, 160–8, 173–4, 183
Hewson, John, 145
Hick, Graeme, 47, 50; Fifth Test, 183; Fourth Test, 164–8, 177; Hobart, 156; injuries, 105; one-day series, 208, 211–12; Second Test, 86, 90, 99; Third Test, 124, 129–30
Higgs, Jim, 81, 187
Higgs, Ken, 89–90
Hilditch, Andrew, 80

Hill, the, Adelaide Oval, 133–8
Hobart, 153–60
Hodge, Brad, 108
Hohns, Trevor, 80, 189
Hollioake, Adam, 205, 208
Hollioake, Ben, 132, 157–8, 206; First Test, 36, 38, 40–41, 43; injury, 40–41; sweepstakes, 43
homosexuality, 220, 228–9
Hooper, Carl, 6–7
Horne, Donald, 17
Howard, John, 14, 132, 143–52, 234–6
Hughes, Merv, 171–3
Hughes, Peter, 193, 195
Hunt, Barrie, 232
Hunt, Nick, 175
Hurd, Douglas, 15
Hussain, Nasser, 154, 190; Fifth Test, 182–3, 186–7; First Test, 34, 42, 55, 58–60, 62–63, 67, 68; Fourth Test, 163, 165–8; one-day series, 208, 212; Third Test, 124–6
Hussein, Saddam, 148
Hyams, Jack, 140

ICC see International Cricket Council
Illingworth, Ray, 37–38, 76
immigrant players, 22, 25–6
income, 7–8, 23, 194
Independent, 47
India, 205, 213
inducements see bribery
Inside Sport, 115
Inspector Wardrobe, 50
International Cricket Council (ICC), 6, 192, 196, 201, 205, 209–11, 241, 250–1
International Olympic Committee, bribery, 9
Internet, 18, 77
Inverarity, John, 96, 100
investment, 23–24, 36
Iraq, 147–8
Ireland, 26, 230–1
Iron Mike see Atherton, Mike

Jameson, John, 170–1, 252
Jayasuriya, Sanath, 10, 209
Jayawardene, Mahela, 209
Jones, Dean, 74, 77–8, 117, 213–15, 229
journalists, relationships, 155, 160, 241
Julian, Brendon, 26, 40, 212

'Kanga' cricket, 144
'Kangaroo Route', 16
Kasprowicz, Michael, 26, 34, 48, 49, 62, 66, 81
Katich, Simon, 40, 42

Keating, Paul, 16, 145–6, 150, 233
Kelly, Paul, 237
Kent, 249
Killmier, Bronwyn, 139
King Edward VI Community College, Devon, 247
Knight, Michael, 227
Knight, Nick, 205, 212
Knott, Alan, 59
Knox, Malcolm, 151
Koos, Graeme, 78
Kwik Cricket, 247

Lamb, Allan, 109
Lamb, Tim, 241
Lambeth, 246
Lancashire, 248–9
Lane, Tim, 73, 77
Langer, Justin, 190; assessment, 123; Fifth Test, 179–80, 198, 202; First Test, 42, 58–59, 66; Fourth Test, 163–8; Third Test, 120–5, 136
Lara, Brian, 5, 6–7, 53–54, 67
Lawford, Simon, 92
Lawry, Bill, 72, 78
laws of conduct, 208–11, 251–3
Lawson, Geoff, 27
lawyers, 253; ICC hearings, 210–11, 251; recent changes, 224
Lehmann, Darren, 157, 165, 168
Lewinsky, Monica, 106
lightning strikes, 77, 79
Lilac Hill, West Australia, 39, 40
Lillee, Dennis, 20, 29, 41, 95, 96, 99–100, 114
Lloyd, Clive, 7
Lloyd, David, 2, 33, 37, 38, 47, 107, 156–7, 173–4, 240
Loader, Peter, 40
London, 223, 246–7
Lord's, 3, 128, 145, 170, 199, 203, 211, 244
Los Angeles, 226
'lost ball' law, 252
Lucky Country title, 17

McAllion, Mark, 28, 29, 30
McDermott, Craig, 85
MacGill, Stuart, 22; assessment, 190; Fifth Test, 182–3, 187–8, 200; First Test, 34–35; Fourth Test, 162–4, 168; magazine interview, 220; Second Test, 80–81; Third Test, 125–6, 129
McGrath, Glenn, 5; assessment, 190, 192, 207, 219; Fifth Test, 182–3, 185–8, 197–8, 201; First Test, 35, 54–55, 60–61, 62, 64, 65–66, 67–68, 79; Fourth Test,

163–4, 167; Hawke's view, 150; one-day series, 204, 207, 211; origins, 219; Third Test, 125–6, 129, 137–8
McGregor, Adrian, 31
McGregor, Campbell, 57
McGregor, Craig, 31, 219
McKenzie, Graham, 151
McLachlan, Ian, 145
MacLaurin, Lord, 140–1, 240, 243
McQuillan, Tony, 209
Macpherson, Elle, 99–100
Mahanama, Roshan, 210–11
Maher, Jimmy, 47, 48
Major, John, 15, 144, 146
Malcolm, Devon, 51, 82, 85
Maley, John, 96
Malik, Salim, 6, 113–119
Mallett, Ashley, 11
manager-selection criteria, 241–2
Mandelson, Peter, 15
Manuka Oval, Canberra, 96, 143, 147
marketing, 56; ACB, 22; importance, 189, 240; television, 217, 243
Marks, Alan, 77
Marks, Vic, 73, 87, 89
Marsh, Daniel, 148
Marsh, Geoff, 75, 80, 120, 189, 201, 215
Marsh, Rod, 20, 114, 172
Martin, Ray, 71
Martyn, Damien, 207
Marylebone Cricket Club (MCC), 34, 103, 147, 170, 171, 172, 252–3
Massie, Bob, 74
'mateship', 214
Matthews, Rohan, 97
Maxwell, Jim, First Test, 72, 73–74, 77
May, P. B. H., 246
May, Tim, 7, 113–17
media: relationships, 155, 160, 241; see also television
Melbourne, 160–9, 170–7, 207, 208
mentors, 213–14
Menzies, Robert, 144–5, 147, 150
Midland Guildford Cricket Club, 39
Millard, Tony, 249
Miller, Colin, 35, 81, 172; Fifth Test, 181, 183, 185–6; Second Test, 100; Third Test, 135–7
Miller, Keith, 241
Minogue, Kylie, 225
Moody, John, 92
Moody, Tom, 40, 92
Moody, Tony, 246
moral fibre, 131, 135, 241, 252–3
Morris, Arthur, 68
Morris, Hugh, 248

Morton, Wayne, 110, 205
Mullally, Alan, 126, 129, 166–8, 198, 206–7; First Test, 49, 55, 57–62, 66
Muralitharan, Muttiah, 10, 192, 204–5, 208–10
Murdoch, Rupert, 94
Murgatroyd, Brian, 49
Murphy, Florence Rose, 8

National Lottery, 246–7
Neighbours, 225
Net see Internet
New Images, 15
New South Wales, 28, 41, 57, 228
New Zealand, 97–98, 241, 250
Newman, Stephen, 171, 176
Nicholas, Mark, 72, 74, 75–6, 122
Nicholson, Matthew, 41, 42, 162–4, 167–8, 220
'no change no option' phrase, 3
non-British migrants, 22, 25–6
Norman, Greg, 23
Nottinghamshire, 245–6

Oliver, Neville, 77
Olympic Athlete Program, 24
Olympic Games: 1984, 226; 1996, 227; 2000, 9, 13, 24, 221, 223, 225–6, 229–31
one-day series, 204–12, 239, 250–1
O'Donnell, Simon, 72
O'Regan, Rob, 118–9
origins, Ashes, 8
Outlook, 114
Oval, The, 8, 246
ovals see playing fields

Pack, Simon, 35–36
Packer, Kerry, 1, 4, 7, 42, 56, 70
'paddock cricket', 21
Pakistan, 6, 32, 113–119, 121, 205, 250
Parker Bowles, Camilla, 235
Parks, Jim, 246
Pascoe, Lennie: origins, 26, 27
Passmore, John, 247
Patterson, 'Sir' Les, 15
Peacock, Ceri, 139–40
Peacock, Dave, 135, 138–9, 141–2
Perth, 211; Second Test, 80–94; pitch, 67, 95–102
Pervez, Salim, 117
Peshawar Test, 33, 53
Philpott, Peter, 33, 36, 71, 127, 162
Piano, Renzo, 223
pitch condition, 96, 99; cracks, 95; Fourth Test, 162, 164, 166; Hobart, 157; Perth,

67, 95; Second Test, 81, 86, 93, 95–102;
    Third Test, 120, 126–7, 132–3
plans: ACB, 27–28; new grounds, 31
playing fields, 19, 244–7
Pocock, Pat, 172
politicians, cricket support, 144–52, 187
Pollock, Shaun, 34, 55
Ponting, Ricky, 214–15, 220
popularity concerns, cricket, 23–4, 244–6
Potts, Jim, 232–3
practical jokes, 109, 111
preparations, 32–50
Prescott, John, 17
Prime Minister's XI, 143–52
Pringle, Derek, 47
private schools, Australia, 220
psychological advantages, 94
public decline, sporting facilities, 244–7
public schools, Britain, 220
pursuit of excellence, 239–53
Pyne, Tom, 49–50

Qadir, Abdul, 106
Qayyum, Mohammed Malik, 113–14, 116
Quee, Richard Chee, 26, 28

Rackemann, Carl, 26
rain: First Test, 67, 68; see also lightning
    strikes
Ramprakash, Mark, 111–112, 125–6,
    128–9, 156, 162–4, 166–8, 176–7; Fifth
    Test, 183, 200; First Test, 34, 44, 45–46,
    55, 66; Second Test, 85, 91, 92, 93, 99
Ranatunga, Arjuna, 10, 208–11, 251
recreational cricket, popularity concerns,
    23–4, 244–6
Rees-Mogg, William, 113
referees: Fifth Test, 192–203; see also
    umpires
regulations, 208–11, 251–3
Reid, John, 192–203
Reynolds, Luke, 30
Reynolds, Nadia, 30
Rhodes, Wilfred, 46
Rich, Donald, 122
Richards, Barry, 172
Richards, Corey, 158–9
Richards, David, 115, 117
Richards, Viv, 73
Richardson, Victor, 45
Riddle, Dean, 181
Roach, Peter, 107
Robertson, Gavin, 57
Roebuck, Peter, 73
Rogers, Chris, 40
Ronaldo, 229

Rousseau, Pat, 7
Royal National Coaching Scheme, 248
Russell, A. C. ('Jack'), 46

SACA see South Australian Cricket Associa-
    tion
Sawle, Lawrie, 149, 189
scandal, 113–119; see also corruption allega-
    tions
school playing fields, decline, 244–7
Second Test, 80–94
selectors, 120, 187, 189, 217
Selvey, Mike, 73; Second Test, 87
sermons, 91–92
Sheehan, Paul, 16
Sheffield Shield cricket, 41, 55, 81, 106
Simpson, Bobby, 4, 27, 50, 80, 115, 189,
    216–17, 252
singing, 56, 142
Slater, Keith, First Test, 39, 58
Slater, Michael, 70, 159, 164, 168, 190, 219;
    Fifth Test, 179–80, 184–5, 196,
    199–201; First Test, 51, 58, 64–5, 66;
    origins, 26; photograph, 30; Second Test,
    83, 85–86, 93; Third Test, 121–3, 128,
    137
'sledging', 150, 173, 192, 196, 198, 201,
    216
Smith, Chris, 96
smoking restrictions, 218
Snow, John, 175, 249
Sobers, Garfield, 65
society, 19–31, 213–20, 226–7, 230–8
Sohail, Aamir, 54
Solkar, Eknath, 188
South Africa, 5, 8, 199, 204, 216, 241, 244,
    247, 250; British Lions, 37; golf, 88;
    West Indies, 6–7
South Australia team, 43, 44, 46
South Australian Cricket Association
    (SACA), 136–7
Speed, Malcolm, 116, 189
sponsorship, 3, 23–24, 243–4, 247–9; see
    also television
sporting facilities, 19; public decline, 244–7
Sporting Times, 8
Sports Council, 246–7
Sri Lanka, 10, 50, 64, 106, 113, 204–11,
    250–1
Stackpole, Keith, 214
Statham, Brian, 147
statistics, 19–20, 23–24, 243–7
Steele, Jane, 61
Stewart, Alec, 1, 10, 146, 153–4, 174;
    'Barmy Army', 141, 170; Fifth Test, 182,
    185–6, 196–7, 200–1; First Test, 33, 42,

54, 60, 62, 67, 70; Fourth Test, 160–7;
one-day series, 208, 210, 211–12, 239;
Second Test, 86; Third Test, 125–6,
129–31, 139
'street cricket', 21
Such, Peter, 108, 122, 156, 184–5, 199
suicides, 241
supporters: current scene, 218, 244–5;
Fourth Test, 170–7; one-day series,
207–8; player relationships, 175–6;
politicians, 144–52, 187; singing, 142;
smoking restrictions, 218; Third Test,
124, 127, 132–42
surveys see statistics
Sussex, 241–2, 249
Sutherland, Joan, 234
Swan River, 39, 40, 43, 86
Swann, Graeme, 190
sweepstakes see gambling
Sydney, 169, 178–203, 207, 208, 211,
221–31; activities, 221–2, 228; arts, 228;
background, 221; changes, 223–4, 231;
climbing, 222; construction works, 223;
crime rates, 223; fireworks, 225–6; harbour attractions, 221, 225; Olympic
Games 2000, 9, 13, 24, 221, 223, 225,
229–31; 'party city', 227–8; traffic con-
gestion, 222–3; yacht disaster, 155, 229
Sydney Morning Herald, 132, 146, 151, 218
'symbolic' relationship, Britain, 14
Symonds, Andrew, 26

Tabois, Helen, 173
Tannock, Luke, 214–15
Tasmania, 153–5
Taufel, Simon, 184, 193–202
Taylor, Bob, 172
Taylor, Gary, 140
Taylor, Judi, 21, 51
Taylor, Mark, 2, 5, 21, 206, 219, 235;
accent, 219; assessment, 130–1, 188,
216, 219, 240, 253; Australian of the
Year award, 145; catches, 188; corruption allegations, 114–19, 141, 214; earnings, 23; Fifth Test, 179, 182, 188, 196,
198; First Test, 51–54, 58, 59, 68, 70;
Fourth Test, 163–4, 166–8; Howard relationship, 151–2; Prime Minister's XI,
146, 148; retirement, 143, 151, 188,
218; Second Test, 83, 90, 94; Third Test,
120–31, 133; This Is Your Life, 79; Time
magazine cover, 23
teamwork, 213–16
Tebbit, Norman, 30
television, 3, 9–10, 70, 71–72, 74–5, 242–3,
252; accent preferences, 233; marketing,

217, 243; political perspectives, 143;
Taylor, Mark, 53; umpires, 127–8, 184,
195–202; see also media
Tendulkar, Sachin, 73, 83
Test cricket, 36; limited games, 250–1; viability, 2
Test Match Special, 72, 77, 87, 162, 173
Thatcher, Margaret, 149, 236
Third Test: eve, 113–119; heatwave,
120–31, 132–6; supporters, 124, 127,
132–42
This Is Your Life, 79
Thomson, Jeff, 41, 73, 79, 95
Thorpe, Graham, 207; First Test, 43, 44–45,
61, 68; injuries, 110; Second Test, 85, 92;
surgery, 34
Thorpe, Nicola, 110
ticket prices, 218
Times, The, 113
toss, significance, 130, 178–9, 189
tourism, 12–13, 170–7
training, talent, 27–8, 30–1, 189–90,
213–14, 240–2, 247–9
triangular tournament, 8
Trueman, Fred, 76, 180–1
Tudor, Alex, 156, 161–2, 171, 174, 179–80,
183; First Test, 44, 45, 68, 76; Second
Test, 81–83, 90, 99
Turnbull, Malcolm, 232, 236
Twain, Mark, 221
two-day cricket, 249

umpires, 146, 176, 252; bladder control,
198; Fifth Test, 184–6, 192–203; income,
194; one-day series, 208–10; Prime Minister's XI, 147; social life, 200–1; television, 127–8, 184, 195–202; Third Test,
126–8

van der Merwe, Peter, 210–11, 251
varieties, cricket, 21
VCA see Victorian Cricket Association
Veletta, Mike, 26
Venuto, Michael Di, 26
Verma, Anurag, 30
Victoria, 28, 29, 30, 105–112
Victorian Cricket Association (VCA), 28, 29,
30
Vines, The, 87
violence, 49, 214–15, 252

WACA see Western Australian Cricket Asso-
ciation
Walcott, Clyde, 115, 251
Walmsley, Keith, 188
Walsh, Courtney, 7

Walters, Doug, 218

Warne, Shane, 5, 6, 29, 70, 130, 132–3, 168–9, 182–3, 214, 219; assessment, 190; corruption allegations, 114–19, 132; earnings, 23; emergence, 189; Fifth Test, 187, 202; First Test, 56, 72, 78; one-day series, 206–8, 211–12; origins, 26, 27, 220

Warwickshire, 249

Waugh, Mark, 5, 73, 142, 159, 190; corruption allegations, 114–19, 132–6, 214; Fifth Test, 178–80, 182–3, 185–6, 199; Fourth Test, 164–8; one-day series, 207; Second Test, 90, 92, 99, 100; Third Test, 121–4, 129–30, 133–6

Waugh, Steve, 5, 6, 7, 21, 25, 70, 152, 190, 213; assessment, 189, 240; 'baggy green cap', 216; earnings, 23; Fifth Test, 178–80, 182–3, 185; First Test, 54, 58, 59, 59–60, 60; Fourth Test, 164–8; one-day series, 206–7; Second Test, 90, 93; Third Test, 122–4

Web see Internet

Weekend Australian, 215, 237

Wells, Vince, 205–6, 212

Wesley, Charles, 120

Wessels, Kepler, 216

West Australian, 84, 99

West Indies, 95, 131, 197, 248; Cricket Board, 6–7; South Africa tour, 6–7; victory over England (1998), 5

Western Australia, 96

Western Australian Cricket Association (WACA), 38, 81, 86, 93, 95–102

'White Australia' policy, 9, 26

White, Patrick, 234

Whitlam, Gough, 150

Whittingdale, Patrick, 36–37

Williams, Lloyd, 42

Williamson, David, 222

Willis, Bob, 72, 75–6, 121

Winter, Richard, 95–102

Winter, Ron, 96

Winter, Sharon, 102

Wisden Cricket Monthly, 140–1

Woolmer, Bob, 241

Worcestershire, 249

World Championship of Test cricket, 52

World Cup: 1995–6, 205; 1999, 20, 204, 211, 239

World Test Championship, 250–1

Wright, Peter, 236

Wynne-Thomas, Peter, 244–5

yachting disaster, 155, 229

Yardley, Bruce, 35

Young, Bryan, 188

Zimbabwe, 37, 241, 250